SQL Server: Common Problems, Tested Solutions

NEIL PIKE

Apress™

SQL Server: Common Problems, Tested Solutions

Copyright ©2000 by Neil Pike

All rights reserved. No part of this work may be reproduced or transmitted in any form or by any means, electronic or mechanical, including photocopying, recording, or by any information storage or retrieval system, without the prior written permission of the copyright owner and the publisher.

ISBN (pbk): 1-893115-81-X

Printed and bound in the United States of America 12345678910

Trademarked names may appear in this book. Rather than use a trademark symbol with every occurrence of a trademarked name, we use the names only in an editorial fashion and to the benefit of the trademark owner, with no intention of infringement of the trademark.

Editorial Directors: Dan Appleman, Gary Cornell, Karen Watterson

Technical Editors: Darren Green, Paul Munkenbeck

Editor: Martin Minner

Projects Manager: Grace Wong

Production Editor: Janet Vail

Page Composition, Interior Design, and Accounting Procrastination: Bookmakers

Indexer: Julie Kawabata

Cover: Derek Yee Design

Distributed to the book trade in the United States by Springer-Verlag New York, Inc.,175 Fifth Avenue, New York, NY, 10010

and outside the United States by Springer-Verlag GmbH & Co. KG, Tiergartenstr. 17, 69112 Heidelberg, Germany

In the United States, phone 1-800-SPRINGER; orders@springer-ny.com; http://www.springer-ny.com

Outside the United States, contact orders@springer.de; http://www.springer.de; fax +49 6221 345229

For information on translations, please contact Apress directly at 901 Grayson Street, Suite 204, Berkeley, CA, 94710

Phone: 510-549-5931; Fax: 510-549-5939; info@apress.com; http://www.apress.com

The information in this book is distributed on an “as is” basis, without warranty. Although every precaution has been taken in the preparation of this work, neither the author nor Apress shall have any liability to any person or entity with respect to any loss or damage caused or alleged to be caused directly or indirectly by the information contained in this work.

Dedication

For Grace

About the Technical Editors

Darren Green is a relative newcomer to SQL Server. He started in healthcare information and then moved to Internet services while working for a leading independent financial advisor portal in the U.K.. He is a Microsoft SQL Server MVP, specializing in data transformation services. Darren is a regular presence on the SQL Server news groups and maintains a DTS-related section on `http://www.swynk.com`.

Paul Munkenbeck has been a DBA for fifteen years. He has worked on all types of databases, from desktop to mainframe. He was first exposed to Microsoft SQL Server 4.2 as a DBA, on a project early in 1995, and loved it so much he chose to specialize in it. Having worked for some major U.K. companies, Paul is now a database consultant with a global market research company that builds and run a variety of database applications for clients. He has shared his experiences by publishing several articles that have found their way into *SQL Server Professional*, *Xephon SQL Update*, and *MSDN*.

Contents at a Glance

Contents

Installation and Upgrades 241

Foreword

MY PUBLISHERS TOLD ME a foreword should cover "why I wrote the book." Well that's simple—because they asked me! (Well actually, Karen Watterson asked me, for which I thank her.) I had been asked to write books, or chapters of books, many times before, but always politely declined—I'm a full-time husband, father, and consultant, which leaves little spare time. The last time I had anything published was back in 1991 when I did some mainframe systems programming articles for technical journals. (My parents were around today visiting their granddaughter, and when I told them about the imminent book publishing event, my mother told me she still has the copy of "Xephon CICS Update" I had given her back in 1991 in her drawer! No doubt when this book with my name on it is out, she will be taking copies down to the gym to show her friends....)

What was different about this request was that it was to turn something I had already "written" into a book. I figured this wouldn't take too long, and I was partly right. It was more work than I had hoped, but less than I had feared. This was helped along by all the folks at Apress, especially Grace Wong and Marty Minner, who have been a pleasure to work with.

Apress asked for a book version of the unofficial "SQL Server FAQ" which is something I have been writing and maintaining since 1998 or so. I have been an active member of the online peer-support community for SQL Server since 1996, starting with Compuserve, and now also with the Microsoft public newsgroups. This involves answering lots of people's questions—often, the same question over and over again. For doing this work I was given the "MVP" status (explained in the FAQ) by Microsoft.

Being an essentially lazy person, I started the FAQ purely as a set of files on my laptop hard drive to save myself time writing answers to the most common questions. It turned into something a bit more formal when I was asked by a friend, John Savill, who runs the ntfaq Web site (`http://www.ntfaq.com`), for some SQL Server entries. I formalized the FAQ layout into what it is now, and the book version is laid out the same way. I still keep one FAQ article per file, and this is the reason for the sometimes slightly cryptic names the entries have. I also started adding FAQ articles written (or partly written) by other people.

It should be noted that:

- The FAQ articles are as accurate as possible, but mistakes do occur, and no legal liability is given or implied in the use of them.

- If third-party products or companies are listed in a FAQ article, it should not be taken as an exhaustive list—other products and companies no doubt exist and are not deliberately excluded (send me details and they will be added).

- The ordering of any listing of products or companies does not imply any preference for one product over another.

- You should always check the Microsoft-supplied documentation and online resources as well as the FAQ before attempting any problem resolution.

A foreword wouldn't be complete without a list of thank yous—but don't worry, I'll keep mine short. I would like to thank all the authors and co-authors of articles for providing them. I would like to thank the other SQL Server MVPs for being a great bunch of people from whom I continue to learn a lot. And finally thanks go to Darren Green and Paul Munkenbeck who, as the technical editors, have gone way above and beyond what technical editors normally are expected to do. The book is much improved due to their extensive efforts and may well never have reached the shelves without them—my biggest thanks must go to them (take a bow, guys).

I hope you find this book useful and accurate. Any corrections, additions or comments are gratefully accepted—just send them to `neilpike@compuserve.com`. And if you don't already use the Microsoft newsgroups, then please do, as this peer-to-peer forum is definitely the single best place to get your questions answered. I hope to "see" you there.

Application Design and Programming

This section covers the areas of interest to analysts and programmers using SQL Server.

16tables

Q: What is the limit on the number of tables in a query in SQL Server?

A: With SQL 6.5 and earlier the limit is 16—regardless of which version of SQL you are running. For example, Enterprise Edition allows no more than Standard. With SQL 7.0 the limit is 256. These figures are hard-coded into the SQL kernel and are arbitrarily chosen by the Microsoft developers—but with good reason. The more tables there are, the longer it takes to optimize a query properly. There has to be a trade-off between the speed of running a query and the speed of optimizing it.

It *is* possible to increase the limit of 16 in SQL 6.5 by setting trace flag -T105. This is an undocumented and unsupported trace flag, so Microsoft may not support you with any problems on a system that is running this. However, it was allegedly put into the product to allow some of the more complex Peoplesoft queries to run, and so it must have had some testing or QA done on it. It increases the limit to 32.

Normally, if a query needs more than 16 tables, you have a very bad query and/or database design. The best practice would be to break the query down into smaller parts and use temporary tables to hold interim result sets. This will also make the query more understandable and may even speed it up as the optimizer has more of a chance to choose correct access plans and indices.

Finally the table limit only applies to a single query, so you could always use a `UNION` statement to join the results of two separate queries.

Reference

v1.04 2000.03.09

Applies to SQL Server versions:	All
FAQ category:	Application Design and Programming
Related FAQ articles:	n/a
Related Microsoft Knowledge Base articles:	n/a
Other related information:	n/a
Author:	Neil Pike

256charstotextisnull

Q: In SQL 6.5 why does passing a 256-byte character string to a stored procedure expecting a TEXT field produce a NULL when checked?

A: The answer is that even though your stored procedure takes a TEXT parameter, SQL has no concept of a TEXT variable or constant. It treats your constant as a char and because chars can only be 255 characters, the 256 becomes 0.

Following is a sample query:

```
if ('914468 919215 1013036 1067140 1106909 1119345 591395
591426 591477 591491 591501 591528 591534 594829 594958
595032 595052 595065 595107 595191 595248 595343 609320
609482 611572 635771 639586 649072 653820 678868 702034
716129 797340 810128 859268 1013036' is null) print 'data
is null!'

  create proc myproc
  @stream text
  as

  if (@stream is null) print 'data is null'

  go

exec myproc <place a 256 character string here>
```

Reference

v1.01 2000.09.16	
Applies to SQL Server version:	6.5
FAQ categories:	Troubleshooting
Related FAQ articles:	n/a
Related Microsoft Knowledge Base articles:	n/a
Other related information:	n/a
Authors:	Neil Pike

416

Q: I am getting a SQL Server error 416. What can I do?

A: The full message is

```
Msg 416, Level 16, State 1
Create of work table failed because the row size would be <xxxxx>. This exceeds
the maximum allowable size of a row in a table, 2014.
```

This is because SQL Server needs to create a temporary table to resolve your query, and all the keys and fields it needs for this query would take the size over the maximum allowable (one page).

Reduce the number of fields in the query, or the number of group by's and order by's. Split the query into multiple ones with your own temporary tables if necessary. Or go to SQL 7 which has an 8KB page size.

Reference

v1.00 1999.02.18	
Applies to SQL Server versions:	4.x, 6.x
FAQ categories:	Application Design and Programming, Troubleshooting
Related FAQ articles:	n/a
Related Microsoft Knowledge Base articles:	n/a
Other related information:	n/a
Author:	Neil Pike

accessupsize

Q: How can I migrate from Access to SQL Server?

A: The best place to start is the free Access upsizing wizard on Microsoft's Web site. It works from Access 97 to SQL 6.5 or 7.0. It is available at `http://www.microsoft.com/AccessDev/ProdInfo/AUT97dat.htm`.

If you are using Access 2000, the Access Upsizing tool that ships as part of Office 2000 only supports SQL 7.0. This tool does not work with earlier versions or with

SQL 2000—no doubt an Office 2000 service release will ship a version that supports SQL 2000.

The supplied upsizing tools are by no means perfect and you should check and test the resulting database—check that the SQL Server datatypes it has used are sensible and look at the indexes it has created. Microsoft provides a lot more information on this in Knowledge Base articles and white papers.

There are also some third-party-products that you can try:

- `http://www.weirperf.com`
- `http://www.ssw.com.au`: SSW Upsize PRO! (works with Access 97 and 2000)

Reference

v1.07 2000.05.25

Applies to SQL Server versions:	All
FAQ categories:	Application Design and Programming, Installation and Upgrades
Related FAQ articles:	n/a
Related Microsoft Knowledge Base article:	Q237980 “INF: How to Convert an Access Database to SQL Server”
Other related information:	n/a
Author:	Neil Pike

adospreturn

Q: How can I get a return value or output parameter from a stored procedure in VB or VBScript?

A: You must use the ADO Command object and create parameters for the procedure. The following sample is written for ASP (VBScript) and writes the parameter values to the page, but can easily be used in VB.

Sample Stored Procedure Code

```
CREATE PROC spGetDate @DateOut char(10) OUTPUT AS
  SET @DateOut = CONVERT(char(10), GetDate(), 103)
  RETURN Year(GetDate())
```

Sample ASP VBScript Code

```
Const adInteger = 3
Const adChar = 129
Const adParamOutput = 2
Const adParamReturnValue = 4
Const adCmdStoredProc = 4

Dim sServer, sDatabase, sConnection
sServer = "."
sDatabase = "master"
sConnection = "Provider=SQLOLEDB;Data Source=" & sServer & _
  ";Initial Catalog=" & sDatabase & ";Integrated Security=SSPI;"

Dim oConn, oCmd
Set oConn = CreateObject("ADODB.Connection")
oConn.Open sConnection

Set oCmd = CreateObject("ADODB.Command")
oCmd.ActiveConnection = oConn
oCmd.CommandText = "spGetDate"
oCmd.CommandType = adCmdStoredProc

oCmd.Parameters.Append _
  oCmd.CreateParameter(, adInteger, adParamReturnValue)
oCmd.Parameters.Append _
  oCmd.CreateParameter("DateOut", adChar, adParamOutput, 10, "")

oCmd.Execute

Response.Write "<p>" & oCmd.Parameters(0).Value
Response.Write "<p>" & oCmd.Parameters(1).Value

Set oCmd = Nothing
oConn.Close
Set oConn = Nothing
```

Reference

v1.02 2000.04.15	
Applies to SQL Server versions:	7.0, 2000
FAQ category:	Application Design and Programming
Related FAQ articles:	n/a
Related Microsoft Knowledge Base articles:	n/a
Other related information:	"Using Return Code and Output Parameters for Stored Procedures" in Books Online 7
Author:	Darren Green

age

Q: How can I calculate someone's age in SQL Server?

A: Use the following:

```
SELECT CASE
        WHEN dateadd(year, datediff (year, d1, d2), d1) > d2
          THEN datediff (year, d1, d2) - 1
          ELSE datediff (year, d1, d2)
       END as Age
```

Reference

v1.01 2000.03.26	
Applies to SQL Server versions:	6.x, 7.0
FAQ category:	Application Design and Programming
Related FAQ articles:	n/a
Related Microsoft Knowledge Base articles:	n/a
Other related information:	n/a
Author:	Neil Pike

ansifips

Q: How can I tell if my code is ANSI-92 compliant?

A: You need to use the `SET FIPS_FLAGGER` T-SQL command. Search for "FIPS_FLAGGER" in the Books Online for more details. One item worth mentioning, which isn't documented, is that you need to put quotes around any value other than `OFF`.

Reference

v1.02 2000.09.16

Applies to SQL Server versions:	6.5, 7.0, 2000
FAQ category:	Application Design and Programming
Related FAQ articles:	n/a
Related Microsoft Knowledge Base articles:	n/a
Other related information:	n/a
Author:	Neil Pike

arraytosp

Q: How can I pass an array of values to a SQL Server stored procedure?

A: Basically you can't. SQL Server has no array type, and ANSI SQL 92 does not specify array support. But there are various ways around it:

- You could simulate an array by passing one or more varchar(255) fields with comma-separated values and then use a `WHILE` loop with `PATINDEX` and `SUBSTR` to extract the values.
- The more usual way to do this would be to populate a temporary table with the values you need and then use the contents of that table from within the stored procedure. An example of this follows:

```
create procedure mytest @MyParmTempTable varchar(30)
as
begin
    -- @MyParmTempTable contains my parameter list...
```

```
    -- For simplicity use dynamic sql to copy into a normal temp table...

    create table #MyInternalList (
        list_itemvarchar( 2 ) not null
    )

    set nocount on

    insert #MyInternalList
        exec ( "select * from " + @MyParmTempTable )

    set nocount off

    -- It is now easier to join..
    select *
    from sysobjects
    where type in ( select list_item from #MyInternalList )

end
go

To call..

create table #MyList (
    list_item varchar( 2 ) not null
)
insert #MyList values ( 'S' )
insert #MyList values ( 'U' )
insert #MyList values ( 'P' )
go

exec mytest "#MyList"
go
```

- If all you wanted to do was use the array/list as input to an IN clause in a WHERE statement you could use:

```
CREATE PROCEDURE sp_MyProcedure (@MyCommaDelimitedString Varchar(255))
AS
BEGIN
  EXEC ('SELECT * FROM MYTABLE
         WHERE MYFIELD IN (' + @MyCommaDelimitedString + ')')
END
GO
```

Reference

v1.02 2000.03.28

Applies to SQL Server versions:	All
FAQ category:	Application Design and Programming
Related FAQ articles:	n/a
Related Microsoft Knowledge Base articles:	n/a
Other related information:	n/a
Author:	Neil Pike

cascadedelete

Q: Where are the cascade update and delete functions in SQL Server?

A: These are not introduced until SQL 2000.

In earlier versions, you need to implement your own cascade functionality with triggers. See Q142480 in the Microsoft Knowledge Base for more information on this and the ways to work with foreign keys that cause problems because of the way triggers work and fire.

You can get some code samples for various triggers that implement this functionality from

- `http://www.mcse.org.il/isql/8/triggers.ppt`
- `http://www.mcse.org.il/isql/Maintaining%20Referential%20Integrity.ppt`

Reference

v1.05 2000.04.02

Applies to SQL Server versions:	4.x, 6.x, 7.0
FAQ category:	Application Design and Programming
Related FAQ articles:	n/a
Related Microsoft Knowledge Base article:	Q142480 "INF: Cascading Deletes and Updates of Primary Keys" (also available in Back Office Resources Kit/MSDN)
Other related information:	"Using Triggers to Define Business Processes" from Books Online 6 is informative
Author:	Neil Pike

casesensitivecompare

Q: How can I do a case-sensitive comparison on a SQL Server installed with a case-insensitive sort-order?

A: You can do this by converting the values to binary.

Assuming that you want to check a four-character field to see if it has "teST" in it (and you don't want to return values of "test" or "TEST".), use this syntax:

```
SELECT * FROM <tbl>
WHERE convert(varbinary(4), <col>) = convert (varbinary(4), 'teST')
```

Note that if the `<col>` to be tested is a Unicode datatype (such as nchar) then you have to double its length when converting to varbinary, and `CAST` the literal as a Unicode datatype as well:

```
SELECT * FROM <tbl>
WHERE convert(varbinary(8), <col>) = convert (varbinary(8), CAST('teST' AS
nchar(4)))
```

To compare between tables, use this syntax:

```
SELECT * FROM <tbl1>, <tbl2>
WHERE  <tbl1.col> = <tbl2.col>
and convert(varbinary(4), <tbl1.col>) = convert (varbinary(4), <tbl2.col>)
```

The reason for having the two comparisons here is that any indices will still be used. They won't be used just with a comparison that uses `convert`.

Reference

v1.01 2000.04.04

Applies to SQL Server versions:	All
FAQ category:	Application Design and Programming
Related FAQ articles:	n/a
Related Microsoft Knowledge Base articles:	n/a
Other related information:	n/a
Author:	Neil Pike

charvsvarchar

Q: Should I use char or varchar? What are the differences?

A: There's no "right" answer because the choice depends on your data and the access profile:

- If your field is fixed length or is almost fixed—for example, it is either eight or nine characters—then stick to char.

- If the field is heavily updated, then you will get the best update performance with a char field.

- If your data is *very* variable in length or may often be blank, then varchar may be the better choice. Smaller average row sizes give more rows per page and therefore faster performance when retrieving or scanning multiple consecutive rows. It also reduces the disk space required.

Many people still think that updating a varchar column causes a slower deferred update than one in place, and therefore don't advise their use for updateable columns. This has not been true since SQL 4.x. With 6.0 and above, for a single-row update, as long as the updated column will still fit on the same page, the update is done directly and therefore the performance overhead is not massive. With SQL 7.0 and above, all updates are direct.

The "Inside SQL Server" books from Microsoft Press cover the update strategies for the relevant version of SQL Server in great detail.

Reference

v1.03 2000.05.25

Applies to SQL Server versions:	All
FAQ category:	Application Design and Programming
Related FAQ articles:	n/a
Related Microsoft Knowledge Base articles:	n/a
Other related information:	SQL Server Resource Guide topic "Using Update in SQL Server 6.5" on MSDN
Author:	Neil Pike

checktableisthere

Q: How can I check in SQL whether a table already exists or not?

A: Use either of two methods, depending on which release of SQL you are using:

1. If object_id('<Table Name>') is not null:

```
<command>
```

2. In releases prior to SQL 7.0:

```
if exists (SELECT * FROM sysobjects WHERE id = object_id('<Table Name>') and
sysstat & 0xf = 4)
<command>
```

2b.In SQL 7.0 and above it is preferable to use OBJECTPROPERTY instead:

```
if exists (SELECT * FROM sysobjects WHERE id = object_id('<Table Name>') and
OBJECTPROPERTY(id, N'IsUserTable') = 1 )
<command>
```

Reference

v1.02 2000.05.25

Applies to SQL Server versions:	All
FAQ category:	Application Design and Programming
Related FAQ articles:	n/a
Related Microsoft Knowledge Base articles:	n/a
Other related information:	n/a
Author:	Neil Pike

Application Design and Programming

concatnulls

Q: Why do I get `NULL` when adding or concatenating a NULL value with SQL 7? I didn't with 6.5.

A: Look up the `SET concat_null_yields_null ON/OFF` command/option in Books Online. To meet ANSI standards the default for this is **on**.

When it is on, `SELECT 'abc' + NULL` will be `NULL`. With it off you will get `'abc'`.

Even if you set this off at the database level, be warned that it could be turned on again at the application level either through the ODBC DSN setting or the application configuration. For example, Query Analyzer turns this on by default and you have to turn it off via the file/configure menu (**New Connections ➤ Use Ansi Nulls, Paddings, and Warnings**), otherwise it will override your database setting!

Reference

v1.02 2000.04.15

Applies to SQL Server version:	7.0
FAQ category:	Application Design and Programming
Related FAQ articles:	n/a
Related Microsoft Knowledge Base articles:	n/a
Other related information:	n/a
Author:	Neil Pike

createdsnprogrammatically

Q: How can I programmatically create a DSN?

A: Use the `SQLConfigDataSource` command. This command is documented in the ODBC documents. (For SQL 7.0 this is in Books Online.)

Reference

v1.00 1999.11.14	
Applies to SQL Server versions:	All
FAQ category:	Application Design and Programming
Related FAQ articles:	n/a
Related Microsoft Knowledge Base articles:	n/a
Other related information:	n/a
Author:	Neil Pike

crlfremove

Q: How can I remove unwanted carriage returns and line feeds from a SQL table?

A: Here is a sample script. In 6.x it will get rid of only one CRLF per column, so you may want to stick the update in a loop and keep doing it until you get a zero rowcount. In SQL 7 there is a new REPLACE function that will find and update multiple occurrences in one string.

```
--example on pubs database
--insert a row with a carriage return
--CHAR(10) and line feed CHAR(13) in it
INSERT authors (au_id, au_lname, au_fname, phone, contract)
VALUES ( '111-34-3420', CHAR(10) + CHAR(13), 'john', '222 333-8899', 1)

--find the row with the cr/lf in it
SELECT
    *
FROM
    authors
WHERE
    PATINDEX('%'+ CHAR(10) + CHAR(13)+ '%', au_lname) > 0
--update the column with the cr/lf with an empty string
UPDATE
    authors
SET
    au_lname =
        STUFF(au_lname, PATINDEX(CHAR(10)+ CHAR(13), au_lname), 2, '')
-- or in 7.0   = REPLACE(au_lname, CHAR(10)+ CHAR(13), '')
```

```
WHERE
    PATINDEX('%'+ CHAR(10) + CHAR(13)+ '%', au_lname) > 0
--look for the row with the cr/lf in it (should be gone)
SELECT
    *
FROM
    authors
```

Reference

v1.01 2000.04.15

Applies to SQL Server versions:	All
FAQ category:	Application Design and Programming
Related FAQ articles:	n/a
Related Microsoft Knowledge Base articles:	n/a
Other related information:	n/a
Authors:	Neil Pike, Bob Pfeiff

crossdatabase

Q: How can I access data across two separate databases in SQL Server? What about different servers?

A: With SQL 6.5 and below, this is easy as long as the databases are on the same server. Just use the fully qualified names of the tables concerned:

```
SELECT * FROM database_name.[owner_name].table_name
```

for example:

```
SELECT * FROM db1..table1, db2..table2 WHERE ..........................
```

If the databases are on separate servers, 6.5 and below offer remote stored procedures (look them up in the Books Online) but that is your only server-side choice—there is no way to directly access the tables involved. The following example will extract data from a remote table into a local one:

```
INSERT INTO table_name EXEC server_name.master.dbo.sp_sqlexec 'SELECT * FROM
database_name.[owner_name].table_name '
```

If you need direct access, you will need to make two separate client connections to each server and process the data at the client end. Something like the JET engine can be used to make this easier and make the two servers look like one.

With SQL 7.0 and above you can access tables across servers with a single client connection because the fully qualified object name now allows the **server_name** to be passed, so you can do the following:

```
SELECT * FROM server1.db1..tab1, server2.db1..tab1 WHERE ..
```

This requires the remote server to be set up as a linked server—see Books Online for details on how to do this using either SQL Enterprise Manager or by using the **sp_addlinkedserver** stored procedure.

SQL 7.0 and above permits this to be any server accessible by an ODBC/OLE-DB datasource—therefore, you can join tables between SQL Server and Sybase, Oracle, AS400, or DB2.

Reference

v1.05 2000.04.15

Applies to SQL Server versions:	All
FAQ category:	Application Design and Programming
Related FAQ article:	"Are there any examples of heterogeneous data queries from SQL 7 to other sources?" (hdqexamples, see page 44)
Related Microsoft Knowledge Base articles:	n/a
Other related information:	n/a
Author:	Neil Pike

crosstab

Q: How can I do a cross-tab function using standard T-SQL in SQL Server?

A: It's obviously easier to use a product that has this sort of functionality built in, such as Excel, but it's possible to do it in standard SQL, though there the query has to be hard-coded to the number of columns and values required.

Take the following table:

```
Product_Code Criteria_Code Value
------------ ------------- -------
100011       ABC           112.2
100011       DEF           19.0
100011       GHI           32.4
100011       JKL           77.7
100012       ABC           16.7
100012       DEF           5.1
100012       GHI           11.2
100012       JKL           23.1
```

You want to view the table as follows:

```
Product_Code ABC     DEF     GHI     JKL
------------ ------- ------- ------- -------
100011       112.2   19.0    32.4    77.7
100012       16.7    5.1     11.2    23.1
```

With 6.0 and above, you have the CASE statement, which can be used as follows:

```
SELECT Product_Code,
    ABC = MAX(CASE WHEN Criteria_Code='ABC' THEN Value ELSE null END),
    DEF = MAX(CASE WHEN Criteria_Code='DEF' THEN Value ELSE null END),
    GHI = MAX(CASE WHEN Criteria_Code='GHI' THEN Value ELSE null END),
    JKL = MAX(CASE WHEN Criteria_Code='JKL' THEN Value ELSE null END)
FROM table_name
GROUP BY Product_Code
```

The use of MAX and GROUP BY compresses the four rows for each product group into a single row in the result set. The assumption is that there is only one set of values for each product code, but this approach works regardless as to whether Criteria_Code and Value are numeric or character data types. If there can be multiple sets of values for a product group and Value is numeric, then you probably want the cross-tab to aggregate the values. Simply use SUM, AVG, or COUNT in place of MAX, and the use of the null in the CASE statement will ensure that the calculation will be correct.

If you don't have a CASE statement (for example, in releases before SQL 6.0) then you have to find another way to perform a test on the Criteria_Code in such a way that a "true" result returns the Value if true or null if not.

If the Criteria_Code is a character datatype, then you can use CHARINDEX to return a 1 if it is true, zero otherwise, for example: CHARINDEX('ABC',Criteria_Code).

If Criteria_Code is numeric, then subtract it from the cross-tab column heading and check the sign of the result. The following expression again returns a 1 if the Criteria_Code equals the column heading (in this case 4), and zero otherwise: `(1 -ABS(SIGN(Criteria_Code - 4)))`.

How then do you return the Value if the Criteria_Code matches, and null otherwise? The answer is to base the expression on `SUBSTRING`, which returns null if the length parameter is zero. If Value is a numeric data type, the following expression does what we want:

```
Value * CONVERT(tinyint,substring('1',1, Criteria_Code_expression  ))
```

Alternatively, if Value is a character data type, then use the following:

```
SUBSTRING(Value, 1, DATALENGTH(Value) * Criteria_Code_expression)
```

So, the code for the example just shown (numeric Value, character Criteria_Code) would be:

```
SELECT Product_Code,
ABC = MAX(Value * CONVERT(tinyint,
        SUBSTRING('1',1,CHARINDEX('ABC',Criteria_Code))) ),
DEF = MAX(Value * CONVERT(tinyint,
        SUBSTRING('1',1,CHARINDEX('DEF',Criteria_Code))) ),
GHI = MAX(Value * CONVERT(tinyint,
        SUBSTRING('1',1,CHARINDEX('GHI',Criteria_Code))) ),
JKL = MAX(Value * CONVERT(tinyint,
        SUBSTRING('1',1,CHARINDEX('JKL',Criteria_Code))) )
FROM table_name
GROUP BY Product_Code
```

Reference

v1.01 2000.04.15	
Applies to SQL Server versions:	All
FAQ category:	Application Design and Programming
Related FAQ articles:	n/a
Related Microsoft Knowledge Base articles:	n/a
Other related information:	n/a
Authors:	Neil Pike, Paul Munkenbeck

currentdatabasename

Q: How can I get the current database name?

A: The DB_Name function, when used without parameters, will return the current database name:

```
SELECT DB_NAME()
```

Reference

v1.00 2000.06.13

Applies to SQL Server versions:	All
FAQ category:	Application Design and Programming
Related FAQ articles:	n/a
Related Microsoft Knowledge Base articles:	n/a
Other related information:	n/a
Author:	Neil Pike

date

Q: Is there a date function for SQL Server? I don't want to hold the time.

A: No, the SQL Server datetime format always holds both a date and a time. If you wish, you can strip out the time by setting it to 00:00:00.000 with the following:

```
SELECT CONVERT(DATETIME,CONVERT(CHAR(10),GETDATE(),101))
```

Reference

v1.01 2000.04.18

Applies to SQL Server versions:	All
FAQ category:	Application Design and Programming
Related FAQ articles:	n/a
Related Microsoft Knowledge Base articles:	n/a
Other related information:	"Date and Time Functions" in Books Online
Author:	Neil Pike

datetimerepresentation

Q: How can I change SQL Server's representation of datetime? Or, why do I get the error message, "The conversion of CHAR to DATETIME resulted in a DATE-TIME value out of range"?

A: SQL Server stores datetime internally as a pair of integers (2 or 4 bytes for small-datetime and datetime respectively). This is not how you input datetime data or how SQL Server outputs datetime data, however.

Input

SQL Server accepts three ways of expressing the date part of a datetime literal. The string is always enclosed in quotes.

- **Alphabetic**: As in "Apr 15, 1998".You can express the parts in any order, since SQL Server parses the string and converts it into its internal format.
- **Numeric**: As in "04/15/1998". Valid separators are slash (/), dot (.) and dash (-). How the parts are interpreted depends on the dateformat setting. This is determined with increasing priority by:
  - **sp_configure** default language (a language has a default dateformat setting)
  - Default language for the login id
  - SET LANGUAGE
  - SET DATEFORMAT
- Most languages (us_english is one exception) has the day before the month, and this can lead to problems if you express the date as per the ANSI SQL 92 standard (yyyy-mm-dd). If, for instance, you set the language to French or German and specify the date as "1998-05-03" (as per the ANSI standard), SQL Server will interpret it as the fifth of March instead of the third of May. And "1998-05-28" gives a conversion error (there is no 28th month). Make sure you operate with an appropriate dateformat (ymd for ANSI SQL 92) when using numeric formatted datetime literals.

- **Unseparated**: As in "19980528". This format uses no separators and is always interpreted as yyyymmdd. This can be a good choice because the interpretation doesn't depend on any language setting, but you can have problems with cross-platform portability.

- The time portion is expressed as "4:30:25 PM" or "16:30:25".

- If you exclude the date portion, you get 1900-01-01. If you exclude the time portion, you get 00:00:00. If you specify the year with two digits, SQL Server will convert 49 and less to 2000 and 50 and higher to 1900. This can be changed with **sp_configure**'s two digit year cutoff in version 7 and higher.

Output

The output is determined by several factors:

- The API used. DB-Library uses the format "Jun 11 2000 10:24". ODBC and OLEDB use "2000-06-11 10:23:53.630" (as per ANSI SQL 92). Try SELECT GETDATE() from OSQL.EXE and ISQL.EXE respectively.

- The client might also honor the regional setting in Windows (there is a configuration setting for that in Query Analyzer, for example).

- The client application can have further customization options.

- You can also use one of the available formatting codes with the CONVERT function (third parameter) to define which format the datetime data should be when converted to a string.

Reference

v1.02 2000.06.13

Applies to SQL Server versions:	6.5, 7.0, 2000
FAQ categories:	Application Design and Programming, Programming
Related FAQ articles:	n/a
Related Microsoft Knowledge Base articles:	n/a
Other related information:	n/a
Author:	Tibor Karaszi

deadlocks

Q: What can I do about handling blocking and deadlocks in SQL Server?

A: Several good Microsoft Knowledge Base articles cover this subject in depth:

- Q162361 "INF: Understanding and Resolving SQL Server Blocking Problems"
- Q169960 "INF: Analyzing and Avoiding Deadlocks in SQL Server"
- Q43199 "INF: Concurrency and Consistency and SQL Server Alternatives"

For details of a SQL 7.0 undetected deadlock, see Q239753 "BUG: 1205—Deadlock Situation Not Detected by SQL Server"

(Microsoft Knowledge Base articles are on Technet and `http://support.microsoft.com`.)

Reference

v1.01 2000.04.21

Applies to SQL Server versions:	All
FAQ categories:	Application Design and Programming, Troubleshooting
Related FAQ articles:	n/a
Related Microsoft Knowledge Base articles:	see above
Other related information:	n/a
Author:	Neil Pike

debugsp

Q: How do I configure SQL Server to debug stored procedures?

A: Microsoft's Visual Basic and Visual C Enterprise Edition contain built-in stored-procedure debugging code for SQL 6.5 and 7.0. See `http://msdn.microsoft.com/library/techart/msdn_storedproceduredebugtech.htm` for details on how to configure it.

With SQL 2000 the debugger is also integrated into the query analyzer tool so that you do not need to use an external development tool.

There are also third-party products available, including:

- `http://www.embarcadero.com`: RapidSQL
- `http://www.castsoftware.com`: SQL-Builder
- `http://www.compuware.com`: Xpediter
- `http://www.sfi-software.com`: SQL Programmer

Reference

v1.03 2000.05.25

Applies to SQL Server versions:	All
FAQ category:	Application Design and Programming
Related FAQ articles: n/a	
Related Microsoft Knowledge Base article:	Q170496 "INF: Tips for Debugging Stored Procedures from Visual Basic"
Other related information:	n/a
Author:	Neil Pike

deleteduprows

Q: How can I delete duplicates from a SQL Server table?

A: The first thing to understand is that every SQL table should have a unique key. In fact, if two rows are identical in every column there is *no way* in SQL to refer to just one of them. You can't deal with just the "first" one, or the "last" one, as tables are unordered sets.

This is not to say that you will not come across dirty data that must be cleaned up so that a key can be defined. Having to clean up dirty data happens all too often, and that is what we will try to deal with here. The reason we have to jump through some hoops is that while SQL is great for working with clean data, it is a bit of a kluge for working with garbage. After seeing how complicated it gets I hope you will better appreciate why every table needs a unique key.

There are different ways that a table can contain duplicates, and there are different issues with each. No explanation will cover all situations, so consider this a collection of ideas to draw from rather than a set of formulas to follow exactly.

Removing Duplicate Rows

The first question is: do we have entire duplicate rows, or just duplicate keys? Let's tackle the problem of removing completely duplicate rows first.

Without a Candidate Key

Duplicate rows, alternative 1, is best limited to a situation where you really don't have a candidate key for the table.

1.First make a copy of the table without any duplicate rows. *Do not* use a #temp table, as dropping your connection or stopping the server in mid process will lose your data.

```
SELECT DISTINCT *
  INTO HoldWhatver
  FROM Whatever
```

2. Second, clear the table. `DELETE` will always work, but `TRUNCATE TABLE` will be more efficient if you have the rights:

```
DELETE FROM Whatever
```

3. Now put everything back:

```
INSERT INTO Whatever
SELECT *
  FROM HoldWhatever
```

With a Candidate Key

Duplicate rows, alternative 2, uses a variation on the approach used in most of these examples. It assumes that you have a candidate key that will be unique once the duplicate rows are resolved. This could be a single column key or a multi-column key. We will use a single column key in the examples.

1. First, isolate the keys with dups so you can work with them:

```
SELECT id_no, count(*) as rows
     INTO Whatever_dupkeys
     FROM Whatever
    GROUP BY id_no
   HAVING count(*) > 1
```

2. Then make a copy of all the rows that are part of the problem:

```
SELECT DISTINCT *
  into Whatever_dups
  FROM Whatever as W
 WHERE EXISTS(select * from Whatever_dupkeys as K
              where W.id_no = K.id_no)
```

Note that since we had duplicate rows, the `DISTINCT` removed all the duplication.

3. Now remove the rows from the source table and put back the unique rows:

```
DELETE FROM Whatever
 WHERE EXISTS(select * from Whatever_dupkeys as K
              where Whatever.id_no = K.id_no)

 INSERT Whatever
 SELECT *
   FROM Whatever_dups
```

Working with Multiple Rows

The next variation is that we know what the unique key should be, but there are multiple rows for some keys, and those multiple rows are different in some non-key columns.

In this situation we *must* find a way to choose which rows stays and which goes. There is no way to tell SQL Server to leave just any row; you must give it instructions to leave one specific row.

The simplest case is when a non-key column can be used to order the duplicates and tell them apart, and you want the row with either the smallest or the largest of that value. Let's assume there is some sort of date column that will tell us which one to keep, and we want to save the one with the latest date while removing the rest.

In that case, we have the simplest approach of all:

```
DELETE FROM Whatever
 WHERE EXISTS(select * from Whatever as W2
              where Whatever.id_no = W2.id_no
                and Whatever.somedate < W2.somedate)
```

If there is no date, maybe there is some other column that would do the job; it all depends on having a single column that lets you sort the row to keep from the rest.

Isolating the Keys and Copying Rows

Now let's look at the case where there is nothing like that date to let us choose the rows we want to keep from the rest. This begins with a familiar process:

1. First, isolate the keys with dups so you can work with them:

```
SELECT id_no, count(*) as rows
     INTO Whatever_dupkeys
     FROM Whatever
    GROUP BY id_no
   HAVING count(*) > 1
```

2. Then make a copy of all the rows that are part of the problem:

```
SELECT DISTINCT *
  into Whatever_dups
  FROM Whatever as W
 WHERE EXISTS(select * from Whatever_dupkeys as K
              where W.id_no = W.id_no)
```

Note that the DISTINCT may have done nothing. Sometimes there is a mix of rows that are complete duplicates, and others with only the key duplicated. The distinct takes care of the rows that are complete dups. It never hurts, so leave it in.

At this point you need to spend some time looking for ways to clean up the **Whatever_dups** table. Pick the good rows from the ones to discard. In the best case you will come up with a singe SELECT that picks out the rows that are to be kept. If that is possible, continue with step 3. Otherwise, skip to the next section "Dealing With Key Values Individually."

3. Delete the unwanted rows from the source table:

```
DELETE FROM Whatever
 WHERE EXISTS(select * from Whatever_dupkeys as K
              where Whatever.id_no = K.id_no)
```

Insert the good rows back into the source table:

```
INSERT Whatever
SELECT *
  FROM Whatever_dups
 WHERE <whatever it takes to just return the rows to be kept>
```

Dealing with Key Values Individually

Sometimes it is just not possible to boil it all down to one SELECT that identifies the good rows. Sometimes you have to deal with each key value individually. In that situation I usually start deleting rows from the Whatever_dups table, using as many SQL commands as required, until it comes down to what you want. It might look like the following:

```
DELETE FROM Whatever_dups
 WHERE id_no = 1234
   AND somecol <> 'green'

DELETE FROM Whatever_dups
 WHERE id_no = 2345
   AND someothercol <> 0


DELETE FROM Whatever_dups
 WHERE id_no = 1234
   AND yetanothercol <> 12
   AND stillanothercol = 'G'
```

and so forth. When the Whatever_dups table can pass the test with no rows returned, the dups are gone:

```
SELECT id_no, count(*) as rows
  FROM Whatever_Dups
 GROUP BY id_no
HAVING COUNT(*) > 1
```

Just to make sure that you didn't remove all the rows for any key, run the following query:

```
SELECT *
  FROM DupKeys as K
 WHERE NOT EXISTS (select * from Whatever_Dups as D
                    where K.id_no = D.id_no)
```

If this returns any rows, you have deleted all the rows for a key from Whatever_dups, and need to start over.

Assuming that these tests are passed, and Whatever_dups contains just the good rows to be kept:

1. Delete the unwanted rows from the source table:

```
DELETE FROM Whatever
   WHERE EXISTS(select * from Whatever_dupkeys as K
                  where Whatever.id_no = K.id_no)
```

2. Insert the good rows back into the source table:

```
INSERT Whatever
SELECT *
  FROM Whatever_dups
```

Reference

v2.00 2000.06.13	
Applies to SQL Server versions:	All
FAQ category:	Application Design and Programming
Related FAQ article:	"How can I find duplicate rows in SQL Server?" (findduperows, see page 163)
Related Microsoft Knowledge Base article:	Q139444 "INF: How to Remove Duplicate Rows From a Table"
Other related information:	n/a
Authors:	Roy Harvey, Neil Pike

dirlist

Q: How can I get a list of all files in a directory into SQL Server?

A: Try the following code as a starter. It puts a full directory listing into the table and then deletes the directory header entries and other invalid lines. The SQL Server service account needs access to the directory. Adjust the size of the varchar column depending on the limits in your version of SQL Server.

```
use tempdb
go

drop table dirlist
go

create table dirlist (filename varchar(8000))
go

insert into dirlist(filename) exec master..xp_cmdshell 'dir d:\winnt'
go

delete dirlist where
    substring(filename,1,2) < '00' or
    substring(filename,1,2) > '99' or
    filename is NULL
go

select * from dirlist
```

Alternatively, you could use a Visual Basic program, or an ActiveX Script (standalone or as a step in a DTS package) using the File System Object to get the directory information.

Reference

v1.01 2000.04.21

Applies to SQL Server versions:	All
FAQ category:	Application Design and Programming
Related FAQ articles:	n/a
Related Microsoft Knowledge Base articles:	n/a
Other related information:	n/a
Author:	Neil Pike

dynamicsqlstringformatting

Q: How can I format a string for dynamic execution without concatenating several string values?

A: The methods here are presented as alternatives to formatting a string for dynamic SQL execution. These eliminate to some extent the coding involved in concatenating string values and making sure to add single quotes appropriately between values. This gets cumbersome, especially in cases where a long `SELECT` statement with several parameter values needs to be formatted. The solutions discussed here use similar logic—they use parameter markers in the dynamic SQL string and replace them with the values using functions or SPs.

```
-- Method #1 for SQL 6.x/7.0/2000
-- This will work for strings less than or
-- equal to 255 characters only in SQL 7.0/2000.
DECLARE @cmd varchar(255)
SELECT @cmd = 'exec sp_name ''%s'', ''%s'', %s'
-- where %s represents values to replace
EXEC master..xp_sprintf @cmd OUT, @cmd,
   'string value#1',  'string value#2' , '1245'
SELECT @cmd AS Replaced_Cmd
GO

-- Method #2 for SQL 6.x/7.0/2000
DECLARE @cmd varchar(255)
SELECT @cmd = 'exec sp_name ''%s1'', ''%s2'', %n'
-- where s1, s2 represents string values, %n is number
SELECT @cmd = STUFF(@cmd,
    CHARINDEX('%s1', @cmd) , LEN('%s1') , 'string value#1')
SELECT @cmd = STUFF(@cmd,
    CHARINDEX('%s2', @cmd) , LEN('%s2') , 'string value#2')
SELECT @cmd = STUFF(@cmd,
    CHARINDEX('%n', @cmd) , LEN('%n') , CONVERT(varchar , 1245))
SELECT @cmd AS Replaced_Cmd
GO
```

```
-- Method #3 for SQL 7.0/2000
DECLARE @cmd nvarchar(4000)
SET @cmd = N'''{call sp_name(''%s1'', ''%s2'', %n )}'''
-- where s1, s2 represents string values, %n is number
SET @cmd = REPLACE(@cmd, N'%s1', N'string value#1')
SET @cmd = REPLACE(@cmd, N'%s2', N'string value#2')
SET @cmd = REPLACE(@cmd, N'%n', CAST(1245 as nvarchar))
SELECT @cmd AS Replaced_Cmd
```

Reference

v1.01 2000.03.29

Applies to SQL Server versions: 6.x, 7.0, 2000

FAQ category:	Application Design and Programming
Related FAQ article:	"How can I issue a SQL command that uses a variable for the tablename or columns? How can I return values from some dynamic SQL?" (exec, see page 35)
Related Microsoft Knowledge Base articles:	n/a
Other related information:	n/a
Author:	Umachandar Jayachandran

erdiag

Q: What tools are available to produce entity relationship diagrams for SQL Server?

A: Several are on the market, including the following:

- CASEwise (`http://www.casewise.com/`)
- ERwin (`http://www.cai.com/products/platinum`)
- PowerDesigner a.k.a. S-Designor (`http://www.sybase.com/products/powerdesigner/`)
- ER/Studio (`http://www.embarcadero.com`)
- Visio Professional (`http://www.microsoft.com/office/visio/`)

These third-party tools (with the exception of Visio) have a wide range of abilities including project lifecycle and reverse engineering.

Microsoft products also have some built-in tools that just do E-R diagrams:

- Visual Database Tools do E-R diagrams
- SQL 7.0 has built-in E-R diagrams
- MS-Access (you'll have to connect all the SQL tables first)
- MS English Query was not designed to do this, but it has some great E-R diagramming capability with the version that comes with SQL Server 2000

Reference

v1.05 2000.05.25

Applies to SQL Server versions:	All
FAQ categories:	Application Design and Programming, Database Administration
Related FAQ articles:	n/a
Related Microsoft Knowledge Base articles:	n/a
Other related information:	n/a
Author:	Neil Pike

esql

Q: Where can I get Embedded SQL for SQL Server?

A: **A.** Go to `http://support.microsoft.com/download/support/mslfiles/ESQLC.EXE`.

Note that this only supports SQL 6.5 and earlier. It will work against SQL 7.0 but you won't have access to any SQL 7.0 only features because it uses the DB-Lib interface.

Reference

v1.01 1999.05.04

Applies to SQL Server versions:	All
FAQ category:	Application Design and Programming
Related FAQ articles:	n/a
Related Microsoft Knowledge Base articles:	n/a
Other related information:	n/a
Author:	Neil Pike

Application Design and Programming

exec

Q: How can I issue a SQL command that uses a variable for the tablename or columns? How can I return values from some dynamic SQL?

A: Look up the `sp_executesql` command, or the `EXECUTE` statement for versions prior to SQL 7. Note that the user must have permissions to the underlying tables or views when running dynamic SQL like this—it does not inherit the permissions from a stored procedure like static SQL does.

```
sp_executesql examples that return values.

declare @str nvarchar(500), @count int
set @str  = N'select @count = count(*) from pubs..authors'
execute sp_executesql @str, N'@count int out', @count out
select @count

declare @str nvarchar(500), @au_lname nvarchar(500)
set @str  = N'select TOP 1 @au_lname = au_lname from pubs..authors'
execute sp_executesql @str, N'@au_lname nvarchar(500) out', @au_lname out
select @au_lname
```

Here is a short example of EXEC that selects a column from a table:

```
USE pubs
go

DECLARE @str varchar(255)
DECLARE @columnname varchar(30)

SELECT @columnname='au_lname'

SELECT @str = 'SELECT ' + @columnname + ' FROM authors'
EXEC (@str)
```

Here is an `EXEC` example from Books Online. This example shows how `EXECUTE` handles dynamically-built strings with variables. This example creates a cursor (tables_cursor) to hold a list of all user-defined tables (`type = 'U'`).

```
DECLARE tables_cursor CURSOR
    FOR
    SELECT name FROM sysobjects WHERE type = 'U'
OPEN tables_cursor
DECLARE @tablename varchar(30)
FETCH NEXT FROM tables_cursor INTO @tablename
WHILE (@@fetch_status <> -1)
BEGIN
    /*
        A @@fetch_status of -2 means that the row has been deleted.
        No need to test for this as the result of this loop is to
        drop all user-defined tables.
    */          EXEC ("DROP TABLE " + @tablename)
    FETCH NEXT FROM tables_cursor INTO @tablename
END
PRINT "All user-defined tables have been dropped from the database."
DEALLOCATE tables_cursor
```

Reference

v1.05 2000.04.24

Applies to SQL Server versions:	6.x, 7.0
FAQ category:	Application Design and Programming
Related FAQ article:	"How can I format a string for dynamic execution without concatenating several string values?" (dynamicsqlstringformatting, see page 32)
Related Microsoft Knowledge Base articles:	n/a
Other related information:	"Using sp_executesql" in Books Online 7, "EXECUTE Statement" in Books Online 6.
Author:	Neil Pike

execconcatstring

Q: Why doesn't an EXEC command with "+" concatenation signs work?

A: Because the SQL parser expects a fully evaluated string expression for its parameter assignments. Consider the following T-SQL code fragment:

```
EXEC master.dbo.xp_sendmail '<recipient>', @message = 'Hello there ' + @name
```

This will generate the syntax error: "Incorrect syntax near '+'."

One way to get it to work is to evaluate the string expression first, as follows:

```
DECLARE @str varchar(255)
SELECT @str = 'Hello there' + @name
exec master.dbo.xp_sendmail '<recipient>', @message = @str
```

Another way is to use the "EXECUTE a character string" syntax. See the FAQ article "exec."

Reference

v1.01 2000.04.24	
Applies to SQL Server versions :	6.x, 7.0
FAQ category:	Application Design and Programming
Related FAQ article:	"How can I issue a SQL command that uses a variable for the tablename or columns? How can I return values from some dynamic SQL?" (exec, see page 35)
Related Microsoft Knowledge Base articles:	n/a
Other related information:	n/a
Author:	Neil Pike

execvariablenotdeclared

Q: Why do I get a "variable is not declared" inside my `EXEC` or `sp_executesql` statement?

A: This is because a variable is local to a batch of SQL. Normally batches are split up with GO statements. However, an "executed" statement is a separate batch and cannot see any local variables already created.

You must put the variable declarations you need inside the "executed" statement.

Reference

v1.01 2000.04.24	
Applies to SQL Server versions:	All
FAQ category:	Application Design and Programming
Related FAQ article:	"How can I issue a SQL command that uses a variable for the tablename or columns? How can I return values from some dynamic SQL?" (exec, see page 35)
Related Microsoft Knowledge Base articles:	n/a
Other related information:	"Using sp_executesql" in Books Online 7
Author:	Neil Pike

externalprogram

Q: How can I run an external (non-SQL) program or DLL from within a T-SQL SQL Server script? What sort of function can I perform?

A: As far as functionality goes, you can do anything you like—for example, read or write files, send network messages, call OLE/COM functions, kick off other programs, or run ftps.

There is a choice of ways for implementing this functionality:

- Using the Open Data Services API, write your own extended stored procedure—essentially a DLL with some SQL call constructs in it. See Q190987 for more details. You can't code XPs in VB, so you will need C (or Delphi) programming knowledge.

- For SQL 6.5 download the Programmers Tool Kit from `http://support.microsoft.com/download/support/mslfiles/PTK_I386.EXE`.

- For SQL 7 look on the CD under \devtools.

- Use the SQL OLE Automation calls (sp_OAxyz) to call a COM object. See Q152801 and Books Online for details of sp_OACreate, sp_OAMethod, sp_OAGetProperty, and sp_OASetProperty.

- Run an external .EXE via the supplied xp_cmdshell extended stored procedure. See Books Online for details.

Reference

v1.02 1999.12.12	
Applies to SQL Server versions:	All
FAQ category:	Application Design and Programming
Related FAQ articles:	n/a
Related Microsoft Knowledge Base articles:	Q190987 "INF: Extended Stored Procedures: What Everyone Should Know," Q152801 " INF: Examples of Sp_OA Procedure Use and SQLOLE.Transfer Object"
Other related information:	n/a
Author:	Neil Pike

flatfile

Q: How can I read or write to a flat file from inside a SQL Server T-SQL script, stored procedure, or trigger?

A: SQL Server doesn't have a handy `SPOOL` command like Oracle does for writing to files, but there are a number of ways of doing what you want.

- Use `xp_cmdshell` and the `ECHO` command. Use the > or >> redirection symbols to either create or append to a file.

```
xp_cmdshell "@ECHO test message >> C:\file.fil"
```

- Put the information you want into a table (this can't be an ordinary temporary table, but it can be a global temporary table) and then bcp it out to a file via `xp_cmdshell`.

```
xp_cmdshell "bcp <dbname>..<tablename> out c:\file.fil -Usa -P<password> -c"
```

- `BCP` or `BULK INSERT` (SQL 7 only) can also be used to read a flat file into a table, from which it can be processed.

- Write your own extended stored procedure. As this is a C program, it can use standard file access commands to achieve whatever you want.

- Run the SELECT through ISQL via xp_cmdshell and use the -o parameter to output the results to a file. This example uses the -E parameter to specify a trusted connection and avoid hard-coding a userid, and the –w to specify a line width of 255 characters.

```
DECLARE @str varchar(255)
SELECT @str = 'isql -Q"select * from <tablename>" -E -w255 -oc:\file.fil'
EXEC master..xp_cmdshell @str
```

3. A free utility that does this—sp_dbm_query_to_file—is available at http://www.dbmaint.com.

Reference

v1.05 2000.04.24	
Applies to SQL Server versions:	All
FAQ category:	Application Design and Programming
Related FAQ articles:	n/a
Related Microsoft Knowledge Base articles:	n/a
Other related information:	n/a
Author:	Neil Pike

getfiledetails

Q: How can I get file information using SQL Server?

A: Use the undocumented xp_getfiledetails procedure:

```
create table #info (
    alt_name            varchar(255) null,
    size_in_bytes       int null,
    creation_date       int null,
    creation_time       int null,
    last_written_date   int null,
    last_written_time   int null,
    last_accessed_date  int null,
    last_accessed_time  int null,
    attributes          int null
)

insert #info exec master..xp_getfiledetails 'C:\Directory\File.nam'
```

Reference

v1.00 1999.05.04

Applies to SQL Server versions:	All
FAQ category:	Application Design and Programming
Related FAQ articles:	n/a
Related Microsoft Knowledge Base article:	n/a
Other related information:	n/a
Author:	Neil Pike

gmt

Q: How can I get the current time in Greenwich Mean Time (GMT) rather than local time?

A: Use this code (courtesy of Microsoft PSS):

```
DECLARE @deltaGMT int

EXEC master.dbo.xp_regread
    'HKEY_LOCAL_MACHINE',
    'SYSTEM\CurrentControlSet\Control\TimeZoneInformation',
    'ActiveTimeBias',
    @DeltaGMT OUT

SELECT getdate() as LocalTime, dateadd(minute, @deltaGMT, getdate() ) as GMT
```

In SQL 2000 there will be a `getutcdate()` function to make this even easier.

Reference

v1.00 1999.12.23

Applies to SQL Server versions:	All
FAQ category:	Application Design and Programming
Related FAQ articles:	n/a
Related Microsoft Knowledge Base articles:	n/a
Other related information:	n/a
Author:	Neil Pike

goinstoredproc

Q: Why can't I use a GO in a stored-procedure?

A: GO is not a T-SQL command. It is a batch delimiter but it is parsed and processed by the front end query tool, such as ISQL, OSQL or ISQL/W.

When the front-end sees a GO it sends the previous batch of SQL to SQL Server for processing. SQL Server never sees the GO command and wouldn't understand it if it did.

Reference

v1.01 2000.05.02	
Applies to SQL Server versions:	All
FAQ category:	Application Design and Programming
Related FAQ articles:	n/a
Related Microsoft Knowledge Base articles:	n/a
Other related information:	n/a
Author:	Neil Pike

HandlingTextImageUsingSPs

Q: How can I insert or update text and image data using stored procedures?

A: Text and Image data can be passed only as parameters to stored procedures or specified as values in `INSERT` and `UPDATE` statements. The `UPDATETEXT` and `WRITETEXT` statements are provided to manipulate a portion of the text or image data.

However, passing the text or image value to the SP depends on which development tool you are using. Following are some of the functions available in data access technologies and development tools:

- ADO uses GetChunk and AppendChunk methods to read and update the BLOB data respectively. (Image and text data is often referred to as a BLOB, or Binary Large Object.) This can be used in VB or Access.

- ODBC uses SQLGetData and SQLPutData functions.

- In VFP you can just read or send the BLOB data by reference from a local table or cursor
- From T-SQL, you can only use the BLOB data as a constant value. Variables cannot be declared as text or image datatypes. They can only be specified as parameters to stored procedures.

Here is a T-SQL example that shows some of the ways to manipulate text or image data:

```
Create Procedure #BlobEx
(
 @InsertText text, @InsertImage image,
 @UpdateText text, @UpdateImage image,
 @InsertChars varchar(30), @InsertBins varbinary(2)
)
As
Declare @TextPtr varbinary(16), @ImagePtr varbinary(16), @TextPos int, _
  @ImagePos int
Create Table #blob ( T text , I image)
```

To insert the text and image data:

```
Insert #blob Values ( @InsertText , @InsertImage )
```

To display inserted text and image data:

```
Select Convert ( varchar(50) , T ) as TextData, _
  Convert ( varbinary(10) , I ) AS Imagedata
From #blob
```

To replace the text and image data:

```
Update #blob Set T = @UpdateText , I = @UpdateImage
```

To display replaced text and image data:

```
Select Convert ( varchar(50) , T ) as TextData, _
  Convert ( varbinary(10) , I ) AS Imagedata
From #blob
```

To get pointers to the BLOB data and position of data to the replaced:

```
Select @TextPtr = TEXTPTR(T) , @TextPos = PATINDEX('%REPLACED%', T) - 1,
 @ImagePtr = TEXTPTR(I) , @ImagePos = 2
From #blob

Updatetext #blob.T @TextPtr @TextPos 0 @InsertChars
Updatetext #blob.I @ImagePtr @ImagePos 1 @InsertBins
```

To display the modified text and image data:

```
Select Convert ( varchar(50) , T ) as TextData, _
  Convert ( varbinary(10) , I ) AS Imagedata
From #blob
go

Exec #BlobEx 'This is the INSERTED text.', 0x02498765bcde3, -- Insert _
  the BLOB data
  'This is the REPLACED text.', 0xab86ec64f8, -- Update & replace _
  the BLOB data
  'MODIFIED & ', -- insert this before the "REPLACED" text
  0xcd -- replace 3rd byte in image data
```

For more details on the complete syntax of `UPDATETEXT` and `WRITETEXT`, see Books Online. In SQL70, a new BLOB data type called "ntext" can be used to store Unicode data.

Reference

v1.01 2000.06.13

Applies to SQL Server versions:	All
FAQ category:	Application Design and Programming
Related FAQ article:	"How do I store and retrieve text and image data in SQL Server?" (imagetext, see page 165)
Related Microsoft Knowledge Base articles: n/a	
Other related information:	n/a
Author:	Umachandar Jayachandran

hdqexamples

Q: Are there any examples of heterogeneous data queries from SQL 7 to other sources?

A: Here are examples for several different data sources. Note that you will have to change filenames, drives, and regions, as necessary for your environment:

- This is how you select from an Excel spreadsheet using OpenRowSet. Here, c:\ramsql7.xls is a spreadsheet (note we haven't specified the extension). sheet1 is a sheet within the spreadsheet—note the trailing $.

```
SELECT * FROM OpenRowSet
  ('MSDASQL', 'Driver=Microsoft Excel Driver (*.xls);DBQ=c:\ramsql7', _
    'SELECT * FROM [sheet1$]')
  as a
```

- This is how you select from an Access-linked server database via Jet. The Access database is at c:\msd\invent97.mdb.

```
print 'add Jet 4.0 Invent'
-- Clear up old entry
if exists(select * from sysservers where srvname = N'INV')
 exec sp_dropserver N'INV', N'droplogins'
go
-- create linked server
exec sp_addlinkedserver @server = N'INV', @srvproduct = '', @provider =
N'Microsoft.Jet.OLEDB.4.0', @datasrc = N'c:\msd\invent97.mdb'
go
-- setup default admin login for Access
exec sp_addlinkedsrvlogin @rmtsrvname = N'INV', @useself = N'FALSE',
@locallogin = NULL, @rmtuser = N'admin', @rmtpassword = N''
go
-- Lists all tables in the linked server
exec sp_tables_ex N'INV'
go
-- Now select from a table in the Access db called INVENT
select * from INV...INVENT
go
```

- This is how you select from DB/2 accessed via Star SQL Driver with SNA 4.0:

```
print 'add DB2 LinkedServer'
if exists(select * from sysservers where srvname = N'DB2')
    exec sp_dropserver N'DB2', N'droplogins'

exec sp_addlinkedserver @server = 'DB2', @provider = 'MSDASQL', @srvproduct
= 'StarSQL 32',
@location = 'DBT1', @datasrc = 'DB2IBM'
exec sp_addlinkedsrvlogin @rmtsrvname = 'DB2', @locallogin = 'sa', @useself
= 'false',
@rmtuser = 'HDRUSER' ,@rmtpassword = 'SQL7'
go
```

```
-- test to see is catalog is accessible
sp_tables_ex N'DB2'
go
-- create view to see if select works
create view V007MUNI as select * from DB2..T1ADM007.V007MUNI
go
select * from V007MUNI
go
```

- This is how you select from DBASE IV:

```
print 'add DBase IV LinkedServer'
if exists(select * from sysservers where srvname = N'DBFs')
    exec sp_dropserver N'DBFs', N'droplogins'

EXEC sp_addlinkedserver
    'DBFs',
    'Jet 4.0',
    'Microsoft.Jet.OLEDB.4.0',
    'F:\DBFs',
    NULL,
    'dBase IV'
GO

 exec sp_addlinkedsrvlogin
 @rmtsrvname = 'DBFs',
 @useself = false,
 @locallogin = NULL,
 @rmtuser = NULL,
 @rmtpassword = NULL
 go

SELECT * FROM DBFs...test
go
```

- This is how you select from Visual FoxPro, using a FoxPro DBC file to group the DBF files. A predefined ODBC DSN called FOX that uses the Microsoft Visual FoxPro Driver 6.01.8440.01 has already been set-up.

```
-- FOX using Visual FoxPro Database file .DBC
print 'add FOXSERVER'
if exists(select * from sysservers where srvname = N'FOXSERVER')
 exec sp_dropserver N'FOXSERVER', N'droplogins'
```

```
exec sp_addlinkedserver @server=N'FOXSERVER',
                        @srvproduct ='',
                        @provider = N'MSDASQL',
                        @datasrc=N'FOX'

exec sp_addlinkedsrvlogin @rmtsrvname=N'FOXSERVER',
                          @useself = N'FALSE',
                          @locallogin = NULL,
                          @rmtuser = N'',
                          @rmtpassword =N''


exec sp_tables_ex N'FOXSERVER'

select * from [FOXSERVER].[D:\SQL\FOX\TESTDATA.DBC]..[customer]
```

- This is how you select from FoxPro using plain DBF files in a directory. This method uses an ODBC system DSN (called DBF) that uses the Microsoft Visual FoxPro Driver 6.01.8440.01.

```
-- DBF using plain .DBF files
print 'add DBFSERVER'
if exists(select * from sysservers where srvname = N'DBFSERVER')
 exec sp_dropserver N'DBFSERVER', N'droplogins'

exec sp_addlinkedserver @server=N'DBFSERVER',
                        @srvproduct ='',
                        @provider = N'MSDASQL',
                        @datasrc=N'DBF'

exec sp_addlinkedsrvlogin @rmtsrvname=N'DBFSERVER',
                          @useself = N'FALSE',
                          @locallogin = NULL,
                          @rmtuser = N'',
                          @rmtpassword =N''

exec sp_tables_ex N'DBFSERVER'

select * from [DBFSERVER].[D:\SQL\DBF]..[country]
```

• This is how you select from FoxPro using installable Jet 3.51 ISAM drivers:

```
print 'add FOXDBC using Jet 3.51'
if exists(select * from sysservers where srvname = N'FOXDBC')
    exec sp_dropserver N'FOXDBC', N'droplogins'
exec sp_addlinkedserver 'FOXDBC', 'Jet 3.51', 'Microsoft.Jet.OLEDB.3.51',
'c:\sql\fox', NULL, 'FoxPro 3.0'
exec sp_addlinkedsrvlogin @rmtsrvname = N'FOXDBC', @useself = N'FALSE',
@locallogin = NULL, @rmtuser = NULL, @rmtpassword = NULL
exec sp_helplinkedsrvlogin N'FOXDBC'
exec sp_tables_ex N'FOXDBC'
```

Reference

v1.05 2000.05.02	
Applies to SQL Server versions:	7.0, 2000
FAQ category:	Application Design and Programming
Related FAQ articles:	n/a
Related Microsoft Knowledge Base articles:	For more examples, search for "openrowset" or "openquery", e.g., Q207595 "HOWTO: Do SQL Server 7.0 Distributed Queries With Fox-Pro .dbf Files"
Other related information:	n/a
Author:	Neil Pike

identifyidentify

Q: How can I tell what columns in my SQL Server database are identity columns? How can I tell the seed and increment?

A: The following script works on SQL 6.5 and 7.0. To show all identity columns in current database:

```
SELECT o.name, c.name FROM syscolumns c, sysobjects o
WHERE c.id = o.id AND (c.status & 128) = 128

To tell the identity seed : SELECT IDENT_SEED('table_name')

To tell the identity increment : SELECT IDENT_INCR('table_name')
```

Reference

v1.01 2000.05.02

Applies to SQL Server versions:	6.5, 7.0
FAQ category:	Application Design and Programming
Related FAQ articles:	n/a
Related Microsoft Knowledge Base articles:	n/a
Other related information:	n/a
Author:	Neil Pike

identitymax

Q: What happens when a SQL Server identity field exceeds its maximum value?

A: You will get an arithmetic overflow error.

Reference

v1.01 2000.05.02

Applies to SQL Server versions:	6.x, 7.x
FAQ category:	Application Design and Programming
Related FAQ articles:	n/a
Related Microsoft Knowledge Base articles:	n/a
Other related information:	n/a
Author:	Neil Pike

iif

Q: What is the equivalent of the IIF command in SQL Server?

A: In Microsoft Access you would use:

```
SELECT iif(field>10,"large", "small") as Size from Table
```

```
With SQL Server, use the CASE command :-
```

```
SELECT Size =
  CASE
  WHEN field > 10 THEN "large"
  ELSE "small"
  END
from Table
```

Here is another example just using local variables:

```
DECLARE @V1 CHAR(10)
DECLARE @V2 INT
SET @V2 = 1

SET @V1 =
  CASE @V2
    WHEN 1 THEN 'Green(1)'
    WHEN 2 THEN 'Orange(2)'
    ELSE 'Unknown(3)'
  END

SELECT @V1
```

Reference

v1.03 2000.05.02	
Applies to SQL Server versions:	All
FAQ category:	Application Design and Programming
Related FAQ articles:	n/a
Related Microsoft Knowledge Base articles:	n/a
Other related information:	n/a
Author:	Neil Pike

instr

Q: What is the equivalent of the `INSTR` command in SQL Server?

A: `CHARINDEX ('pattern', expression)` where `'pattern'` is the string you want to find. There is a similar function called `PATINDEX` that accepts wildcards in the search string pattern.

Reference

v1.01 2000.05.06

Applies to SQL Server versions:	All
FAQ categories:	Application Design and Programming
Related FAQ articles: n/a	
Related Microsoft Knowledge Base articles:	n/a
Other related information:	Search Books Online for CHARINDEX for exact syntax and usage
Author:	Neil Pike

ipaddresschartoint

Q: How can I turn an IP address held as a string into the four separate integers?

A: Assuming that it is held as a char/varchar column called "ip" in a table called "IpAddress", then the following code fragment will work:

```
SELECT
CAST(SUBSTRING(ip, 1, CHARINDEX('.', ip) - 1) AS int) AS Octet1,

CAST(SUBSTRING(ip, CHARINDEX('.', ip) + 1,CHARINDEX('.', ip, CHARINDEX('.', ip)
+ 1) - CHARINDEX('.', ip) - 1) AS int) AS Octet2,

CAST(REVERSE(SUBSTRING(REVERSE(ip), CHARINDEX('.', REVERSE(ip)) + 1, CHARIN-
DEX('.', REVERSE(ip), CHARINDEX('.', REVERSE(ip)) + 1) - CHARINDEX('.',
REVERSE(ip)) - 1)) AS int) AS Octet3,

CAST(REVERSE(SUBSTRING(REVERSE(ip), 1, CHARINDEX('.', REVERSE(ip)) - 1)) AS int)
AS Octet4

FROM IpAddress
```

This code works only for versions that support the `CAST` function and the "start from" optional third parameter for `CHARINDEX`.

Reference

v1.01 2000.05.06	
Applies to SQL Server version:	7.0
FAQ category:	Application Design and Programming
Related FAQ articles:	n/a
Related Microsoft Knowledge Base articles:	n/a
Other related information:	n/a
Authors:	Neil Pike, Umachandar Jayachandran

isnull

Q: Why does a `SELECT ... WHERE col=NULL` not work in SQL Server?

A: According to the ANSI SQL standard, it is not possible for anything to be equal to NULL or not equal to NULL. Only non-null values can even be tested for equality. This leads to "three-valued logic" and a lot of headaches for developers who do not understand it.

However certain products (notably Sybase) defaulted to letting you evaluate NULLs in comparisons. Microsoft also allowed this when they started developing SQL Server from its Sybase roots through SQL versions including 1.1, 4.x, and 6.x.

You can change the default using the SET ANSI_NULLS option—there is plenty of information in this in the 6.x and 7.x Books Online.

The new ODBC and OLE DB drivers set the ANSI_NULLS option to ON. So with 6.5 you could get different results with ISQL/W (which used DB-Lib) and an Access/ODBC application. With SQL 7 all the tools (with the exception of ISQL.EXE) use ODBC or OLE DB and set this option by default at connect time.

Rather than using `WHERE col = NULL`, use `WHERE col IS NULL` to get the required result regardless of the setting.

Reference

v1.02 2000.05.15	
Applies to SQL Server versions:	6.5, 7.0, 2000
FAQ category:	Application Design and Programming
Related FAQ articles:	n/a
Related Microsoft Knowledge Base articles:	n/a
Other related information:	"ANSI-standard Null Handling" in Books Online 6, "ANSI Nulls" in Books Online 7
Authors:	Neil Pike, Roy Harvey

isnumericde

Q: Why does the ISNUMERIC function recognize values like "13d21" and "13e21" as numeric when they contain characters?

A: Because for floating point numbers, a **D** or **E** can be entered to specify the exponent value, and therefore, SQL Server thinks this is a valid floating point number. Similarly, a dollar sign prefix is also accepted as this is valid for a money datatype value.

See "The ISDATE and ISNUMERIC Functions (version 6.5)" in Books Online 6 for examples of string values that will pass the ISNUMERIC test.

Reference

v1.02 2000.05.25	
Applies to SQL Server versions:	All
FAQ category:	Application Design and Programming
Related FAQ articles:	n/a
Related Microsoft Knowledge Base articles:	n/a
Other related information:	n/a
Author:	Neil Pike

isqldoserrorlevels

Q: How can I get ISQL.EXE to return a DOS error level for me to test?

A: With isql, there are three ways of setting ERRORLEVEL:

- The first method is to use the special EXIT(*query*) command, and it works only if you're using isql with the /i switch or < redirection symbol to read an input file containing a T-SQL script. Think of both of these techniques as mimicking the GO command and executing the current batch including the query expression inside the brackets. However, this approach then quits isql and sets ERRORLEVEL based on the results of the final query expression. It takes the first column of the first result row and converts it into an integer—for instance, `EXIT(SELECT returncode = @@ERROR)` will set the return code to the last error value. Unfortunately, since the output from the EXIT query appears in the isql output, this can look quite untidy. For other versions of the EXIT statement, see Books Online.

- The second method is available only since SQL Server 6.5 and again works only with the /i switch or < redirection symbol. It uses the /b option. When this is specified, isql will exit when an error occurs and set ERRORLEVEL according to the severity of the error. The value returned to the DOS ERRORLEVEL variable is 1 when the SQL Server error message has a severity of 11 or greater; otherwise, the value returned is 0.

- The third method of setting ERRORLEVEL from isql is to use the RAISERROR statement with the state parameter set to the special value 127. The return code is set to the error message number, or 50000 if an ad hoc message string is used. So, `RAISERROR(50001,11,127)` generates an error message of severity 11 and sets ERRORLEVEL to 50001. If you're using isql with the /Q switch to execute a stored procedure, then this is the only practical way to get the ERRORLEVEL value set.

Note that you need to be running the SQL 6.5 SP5a version (or higher) of ISQL.EXE. Microsoft broke the returning of error information under certain circumstances and didn't make the fix public until this release (see Q214415). Also note that the documentation for isql /b is inaccurate (see related FAQ "isqlbatchreturncodenot10".)

Reference

v1.02 2000.05.06	
Applies to SQL Server versions:	All
FAQ category:	Application Design and Programming
Related FAQ article:	"With SQL 6.5 and the ISQL /b option, a DOS error level code is supposed to be set when errors with a severity of 10 or greater are returned. This doesn't work for me with a severity of 10, but it does for 11 and higher. What is wrong?" (isqlbatchreturncodenot10, see page 413)
Related Microsoft Knowledge Base article:	Q214415 "FIX: ISQL Does Not Return Errors in Last Batch When Using -b Switch"
Other related information:	n/a
Authors:	Neil Pike, Paul Munkenbeck

julian

Q: Does SQL Server have any built-in functions to work with Julian dates?

A: There are no functions to interpret a Julian date—you have to code your own stored procedure or query. You can generate a Julian date from a datetime column, or a character string in date format, by using the DATEPART function. This has separate options for extracting the year and day of year.

Here is some sample code.

1. Assuming the Julian date is held as a char, use this syntax:

```
DECLARE @julian char(8)
SELECT @julian = '1996.031'
DECLARE @dt datetime

SELECT @dt = DATEADD(dd,convert(int,right(@julian,3)) -1, CONVERT
(datetime,substring(@julian,1,4)+'0101',212))

SELECT @dt
```

2. To generate a Julian date in decimal format (e.g., 99123 is 123rd day of 1999) held in variable SDDRQJ, use this syntax:

```
SELECT DATEADD(day,CONVERT(int,SDDRQJ)-((1000*(CONVERT(int,SDDRQJ)/1000)))-1,
          DATEADD(year,CONVERT(int,SDDRQJ/1000),'1 Jan 1900'))
```

3. You can extract year and Julian date parts from a date. This produces integer values that you can then convert to characters and combine as you wish.

```
SELECT DATEPART(yy, '29 feb 1996'), CONVERT(DATEPART(dy, '29 feb 1996')
```

Reference

v1.02 2000.05.07

Applies to SQL Server versions:	All
FAQ category:	Application Design and Programming
Related FAQ articles:	n/a
Related Microsoft Knowledge Base articles:	n/a
Other related information:	n/a
Authors:	Neil Pike, Roy Harvey

milliseconds

Q: Why can't I get a time accurate to the nearest millisecond in SQL Server?

A: This is because SQL Server only holds times to the nearest 3.333 milliseconds. SQL Server's internal storage for time doesn't actually store milliseconds—it stores in a unit called clock-ticks, and there are 300 ticks to a second.

All the SQL functions like DATEADD will appear to take parameters of 1 or 2 milliseconds, but the functions are only accurate to 3.333 milliseconds and so the value is rounded to the nearest 3.333 milliseconds.

Reference

v1.00 2000.06.13

Applies to SQL Server versions:	All
FAQ category:	Application Design and Programming
Related FAQ articles:	n/a
Related Microsoft Knowledge Base articles:	n/a
Other related information:	n/a
Authors:	Neil Pike, Kalen Delaney

multilevelranking

Q: How can I update multiple different values with an UPDATE statement to create a ranking table?

A: Try the following code:

```
CREATE TABLE RankEg (
    DocId        int      not null,
    CreateDate   datetime not null,
    Revision     int      null
)
go

INSERT RankEg values ( 10, '1/1/99', null )
INSERT RankEg values ( 10, '2/1/99', null )
INSERT RankEg values ( 10, '3/1/99', null )
INSERT RankEg values ( 20, '1/1/99', null )
INSERT RankEg values ( 20, '2/1/99', null )
INSERT RankEg values ( 30, '1/1/99', null )
INSERT RankEg values ( 30, '2/1/99', null )
go

DECLARE @Start int
DECLARE @DocId int
SELECT @Start = 0

SELECT distinct DocId
into #docid
from rankeg

UPDATE r
    set @Start = Revision = case
                                when r.docid = @docid then @Start + 1
                                else 1
                            end,
        @DocId = d.docid
FROM rankeg r,
     #docid d
WHERE r.docid = d.docid
```

```
SELECT * FROM rankeg

DocId       CreateDate                Revision
----------- ------------------------- -----------
10          1999-01-01 00:00:00.000   1
10          1999-02-01 00:00:00.000   2
10          1999-03-01 00:00:00.000   3
20          1999-01-01 00:00:00.000   1
20          1999-02-01 00:00:00.000   2
30          1999-01-01 00:00:00.000   1
30          1999-02-01 00:00:00.000   2
```

Reference

v1.00 2000.06.13

Applies to SQL Server versions:	All
FAQ category:	Application Design and Programming
Related FAQ article:	n/a
Related Microsoft Knowledge Base article:	n/a
Other related information:	n/a
Author:	Tony Rogerson

multistatementtriggerdmltype

Q: How do I determine the type of DML operation in a multi-statement trigger—a single trigger for INSERT, UPDATE, and DELETE statements?

A: The "inserted" and "deleted" virtual tables contain the data modifications made by the INSERT, UPDATE or DELETE statement. These tables can be used to determine the type of DML statement that caused the multi-statement trigger to fire. The code sample below shows one way to determine the type of DML statement using these tables.

```
SET NOCOUNT ON
GO
CREATE TABLE Tr_Tbl(i int DEFAULT (0))
GO
CREATE TRIGGER Multi_Trigger_Test ON Tr_Tbl
FOR INSERT, UPDATE, DELETE
AS
```

```
IF EXISTS(SELECT * FROM Inserted) AND EXISTS(SELECT * FROM Deleted)
 PRINT 'Update...'
ELSE
 IF EXISTS(SELECT * FROM Inserted)
 PRINT 'Insert...'
 ELSE
 PRINT 'Delete...'
GO

INSERT Tr_Tbl DEFAULT VALUES
UPDATE Tr_Tbl SET i = i + 1
DELETE Tr_Tbl
GO
DROP TABLE Tr_Tbl
GO
```

Reference

v1.01 2000.06.13

Applies to SQL Server versions:	All
FAQ category:	Application Design and Programming
Related FAQ articles:	n/a
Related Microsoft Knowledge Base articles:	n/a
Other related information:	See "CREATE TRIGGER" topic in SQL Server Books Online
Author:	Umachandar Jayachandran

odbcthreadsafe

Q: Is ODBC thread-safe and therefore OK for a multi-threaded application?

A: ODBC itself is thread safe, however not all ODBC drivers are. You need to check this with your driver provider.

Reference

v1.01 2000.03.25	
Applies to SQL Server versions:	All
FAQ category:	Application Design and Programming
Related FAQ articles:	n/a
Related Microsoft Knowledge Base articles:	n/a
Other related information:	"Multithreaded Applications"
Author:	Neil Pike

onerrorresume

Q: Does SQL Server have an "ON ERROR RESUME"-type function in T-SQL to match the VB facility?

A: No. All you can do is check @@ERROR after a statement has been run and do something based on that—you could do a GOTO to an error routine if it is in the same batch of T-SQL.

Reference

v1.01 1999.04.08	
Applies to SQL Server versions:	All
FAQ category:	Application Design and Programming
Related FAQ articles:	n/a
Related Microsoft Knowledge Base articles:	n/a
Other related information:	"Using @@ERROR"
Author:	Neil Pike

oracleplsqltotsql

Q: Are there any resources or tools to aid in an Oracle PL/SQL-to-SQL Server T-SQL conversion?

A: A few resources exist:

- *Microsoft SQL Server 6.5 Programming Unleashed* (SAMS) has a chapter that discusses Oracle-to-Microsoft SQL migration.

- There is a paper on MSDN called "Migrating Oracle Databases to Microsoft SQL Server 7.0" (`http://msdn.microsoft.com/library/techart/oracle2sql.htm`).
- There is a third-party application called "TopLink" (`http://www.objectpeople.com/toplink/`).
- SQL Server Books Online carries these topics: "Oracle and SQL Server Terminology" and "Migrating *xyz objects* from Oracle to SQL Server."

Reference

v1.01 2000.04.09

Applies to SQL Server versions:	All
FAQ category:	Application Design and Programming
Related FAQ articles:	n/a
Related Microsoft Knowledge Base article:	n/a
Other related information:	`http://msdn.microsoft.com/library/techart/oracle2sql.htm`, `http://www.objectpeople.com/toplink/`
Author:	Neil Pike

orderbyvariable

Q: How can I code a dynamic varying ORDER BY statement in SQL Server?

A: First, let's illustrate the concept.

Using the "pubs" database that ships with SQL Server, let's say that we want to create a stored procedure that will allow the user to select the entire "authors" table sorted by "au_id", the author name, or ZIP code. To make it a bit more interesting, let's also support the option of sorting the author's name either first name first, or last name first.

Example: Four Possible Result Sets

In essence, we want to program a stored procedure that, via the value of a single input parameter, will enable any of the following four result sets to be generated. In short, we want to be able to execute:

```
EXEC spAuthors 1
```

or

```
EXEC spAuthors 2
```

or

```
EXEC spAuthors 3
```

or

```
EXEC spAuthors 4
```

and get the result sets presented next.

By Identification Code

Result set #1 is sorted by author identification code ("au_id").

The code we want to execute is

```
SELECT au_id, au_fname, au_lname
FROM authors
ORDER BY au_id
```

and this will create the following output:

```
au_id       au_fname  au_lname
----------- --------  --------
172-32-1176 Johnson   White
213-46-8915 Marjorie  Green
238-95-7766 Cheryl    Carson

. . .

893-72-1158 Heather   McBadden
899-46-2035 Anne      Ringer
998-72-3567 Albert    Ringer
```

By Name, First Name First

Result set #2 is sorted by author's name, first name first.

The code should be

```
SELECT au_id, au_fname, au_lname
FROM authors
ORDER BY au_fname, au_lname
```

which will produce

```
au_id       au_fname    au_lname
----------- --------    --------
409-56-7008 Abraham     Bennet
672-71-3249 Akiko       Yokomoto
998-72-3567 Albert      Ringer

. . .

846-92-7186 Sheryl      Hunter
724-80-9391 Stearns     MacFeather
807-91-6654 Sylvia      Panteley
```

By Name, Last Name First

Result set #3 is sorted by author's name, last name first.

The code will be

```
SELECT au_id, au_fname, au_lname
FROM authors
ORDER BY au_lname, au_fname
```

This code generates

```
au_id       au_fname    au_lname
----------- --------    --------
409-56-7008 Abraham     Bennet
648-92-1872 Reginald    Blotchet-Halls
238-95-7766 Cheryl      Carson

. . .
```

```
724-08-9931 Dirk        Stringer
172-32-1176 Johnson     White
672-71-3249 Akiko       Yokomoto
```

By ZIP Code

And finally, result set #4 is sorted by ZIP code.

The code will be

```
SELECT au_id, au_fname, au_lname
FROM authors
ORDER BY zip
```

With a result set of

```
au_id       au_fname    au_lname
----------- --------    --------
807-91-6654 Sylvia      Panteley
527-72-3246 Morningstar Greene
722-51-5454 Michel      DeFrance

. . .

472-27-2349 Burt        Gringlesby
893-72-1158 Heather     McBadden
648-92-1872 Reginald    Blotchet-Halls
```

Creating the Stored Procedure

Now that we have a firm idea of what we're looking for, let's see how we can go about creating a stored procedure with the flexibility we want.

Our coding options include:

1. Using IF ... THEN ... ELSE to execute one of four preprogrammed queries.
2. Constructing the SQL statements dynamically, and using either the EXECUTE() function or sp_executesql system stored procedure to execute it.
3. Using a CASE statement to choose the sequencing.

4. Using ANSI SQL-92 standard code suggested by renowned SQL Guru Joe Celko.
5. Using ANSI SQL-99 (SQL-3) code originated by the very gifted Richard Romley.

Using IF ... THEN ... ELSE

Option 1 is what probably first comes to mind to most individuals. The stored procedure would probably look something like this:

```
USE pubs
GO

CREATE PROCEDURE dbo.spAuthors
    @OrdSeq tinyint
AS

IF @OrdSeq = 1
   BEGIN
    SELECT au_id, au_fname, au_lname
    FROM authors
    ORDER BY au_id
   END

ELSE IF @OrdSeq = 2
   BEGIN
    SELECT au_id, au_fname, au_lname
    FROM authors
    ORDER BY au_fname, au_lname
  END

ELSE IF @OrdSeq = 3
   BEGIN
    SELECT au_id, au_fname, au_lname
    FROM authors
    ORDER BY au_lname, au_fname
   END

ELSE IF @OrdSeq = 4
   BEGIN
    SELECT au_id, au_fname, au_lname
    FROM authors
    ORDER BY zip
   END

GO
```

Each option has its advantages and disadvantages, so let's begin by critiquing this one.

The advantages include:

- The code is straightforward and easy to understand.
- The SQL Server query optimizer is able to create an optimized query plan for each SELECT query, thus ensuring maximal performance.

The primary disadvantage is that four separate SELECT queries have to be maintained should the reporting requirements change.

Constructing the SQL Statements Dynamically

Option 2 is an alternative that will also be frequently suggested, particularly by those with experience with using dynamic queries in SQL Server.

```
USE pubs
GO

CREATE PROCEDURE dbo.spAuthors
    @OrdSeq tinyint

AS
DECLARE @SQLstmt varchar (255)

SELECT @SQLstmt = 'SELECT au_id, '
SELECT @SQLstmt = @SQLstmt + 'au_fname, '
SELECT @SQLstmt = @SQLstmt + 'au_lname '
SELECT @SQLstmt = @SQLstmt + 'FROM authors '

SELECT @SQLstmt = @SQLstmt +
CASE @OrdSeq
   WHEN 1 THEN 'ORDER BY au_id'
   WHEN 2 THEN 'ORDER BY au_fname, au_lname'
   WHEN 3 THEN 'ORDER BY au_lname, au_fname'
   WHEN 4 THEN 'ORDER BY zip'
END

EXEC (@SQLstmt)
GO
```

Note that in SQL Server 7.0, you can use the system stored procedure sp_executesql in place of the EXEC() function. Please refer to the SQL Server Books Online for the advantages of sp_executesql over the EXEC() function.

While this is a perfectly good option, it has two significant disadvantages. Perhaps the more important of the two is that the user of the stored procedure must have appropriate permissions on any database objects referred to inside EXEC() or sp_executesql, in addition to an EXECUTE privilege on the stored procedure itself.

Also, another possible disadvantage of this coding is that the SELECT statement, when placed inside the EXEC() function, is not cached. Thus every invocation of the spAuthor stored procedure, when coded with a call to the EXEC() function, will result in SQL Server re-parsing the SELECT code, and generating a query plan anew. This is probably not a concern in most production environments, but it might be of importance in a high-performance OLTP shop. (Note that sp_executesql will cache the query plans.)

Using a CASE Statement

Option 3 has garnered some support on the Microsoft SQL Server newsgroups since it was first offered, although I believe that in practice it is perhaps the least flexibility of the five options presented here. Nevertheless, it does lead us away from the EXEC() function and sp_executesql.

```
USE pubs
GO

CREATE PROCEDURE dbo.spAuthors
    @OrdSeq tinyint

AS
SELECT au_id, au_fname, au_lname
FROM authors
ORDER BY CASE @OrdSeq
        WHEN 1 THEN au_id
        WHEN 2 THEN au_fname + ' ' + au_lname
        WHEN 3 THEN au_lname + ' ' + au_fname
        WHEN 4 THEN zip
        ELSE NULL
END

GO
```

It is easy to see why this is a very popular solution. At first glance, it seems to be the ideal solution, but it suffers from one very serious flaw. The CASE construction evaluates to value of a specific data type. In this case, all four columns—au_id, au_fname, au_lname, and zip—are character strings, and SQL Server will, when parsing the statement, look at the expressions after the THEN clause and construct a data type that can hold, without loss of precision, any of the individual expressions. In fact, the data type returned by the CASE construction in the preceding code will be varchar (61).

However, this technique just won't stand up to the demands of sequencing by columns of significantly different data types.

To see how fragile the code actually is, add the following before the WHEN 1 clause:

```
WHEN 0 THEN 6.44
```

and use the following to call the stored procedure:

```
EXEC dbo.spAuthors 1
```

Using ANSI SQL-92 Standard Code

The technique offered in Option 4 was first posted by well-known SQL guru Joe Celko in response to the technique in Option 3. Joe participated in the creation of the ANSI SQL-92 standard, and thus is a strong supporter of ANSI SQL-92 compliant code. Joe frequently makes the point that code written to the SQL-92 standard is portable to any database that supports the standard.

```
USE pubs
GO

CREATE PROCEDURE dbo.spAuthors
    @OrdSeq tinyint
AS

SELECT au_id, au_fname, au_lname,
CASE @OrdSeq
   WHEN 1 THEN au_id
   WHEN 2 THEN au_fname + ' ' + au_lname
   WHEN 3 THEN au_lname + ' ' + au_fname
   WHEN 4 THEN zip
```

```
   ELSE NULL
END AS OrdSeq
FROM authors
ORDER BY OrdSeq

GO
```

Note that this code requires an additional column (OrdSeq) in the result set so that the ORDER BY clause has something to "work" on. When Joe Celko posted the technique, there was criticism concerning the additional column. I'd offer as a thought that stored procedures should be invoked not by end users, but by applications. The application can ignore the "extraneous" column. Nevertheless, additional bytes are being pushed across a network, and that can be a performance consideration. It can also be argued that we have changed the definition of the problem to accommodate this solution. Nevertheless, I agree with Joe Celko that if portability of code is important, this solution is definitely worth considering.

The careful reader might notice that the columns au_id, au_fname, au_lname, and zip are all character strings, and might therefore conclude that the technique works only when with columns of similar data types. As Joe Celko pointed out, however, the ANSI SQL-92 standard also supports the CAST function to transform one data type into another. Since all of the common data types are ultimately human readable, they can be converted into an alphanumeric format, and thus columns of the various numeric data types can also be used along with character string data types. (The CAST function was introduced into SQL Server beginning with version 7.0. A SQL Server 6.5 solution would have to use the well-known CONVERT function.)

The authors table in pubs does not contain a column with a strictly numeric data type, so it is a bit difficult to illustrate. Let us assume however that the zip column in authors is actually defined as an integer data type rather than as char(5). In that case, the SELECT could be programmed.

```
SELECT au_id, au_fname, au_lname,
 CASE @OrdSeq
   WHEN 1 THEN au_id
   WHEN 2 THEN au_fname + ' ' + au_lname
   WHEN 3 THEN au_lname + ' ' + au_fname
   WHEN 4 THEN RIGHT ('00000' + CAST (zip as char(5)), 5)
   ELSE NULL
 END  AS OrderingSequence
FROM authors
ORDER BY OrderingSequence
```

In order for the sorting to work properly, we do have to be aware of, and take into account, the format of the output from the CAST function. In SQL Server, you can experiment and see for yourself that integer values cast to character format will result in left-aligned output. This will sort incorrectly, so we have to force a right-alignment. Because the ANSI SQL-92 standard is weak on string manipulation functions, we are forced to rely upon the SQL Server-specific RIGHT function to achieve this, thus breaking the portability of the code.

Using ANSI SQL-99 (SQL-3) Code

The last piece of code, Option 5, was originally posted by the very gifted Richard Romley. It is not ANSI SQL-92 compliant, but just might be with the SQL-99 (aka SQL-3) standard. It is my personal favorite.

```
USE pubs
GO

CREATE PROCEDURE dbo.spAuthors
    @OrdSeq tinyint

AS
SELECT au_id, au_fname, au_lname
FROM authors
ORDER BY
CASE @OrdSeq WHEN 1 THEN au_id ELSE NULL END,
CASE @OrdSeq WHEN 2 THEN au_fname + ' ' + au_lname ELSE NULL END,
CASE @OrdSeq WHEN 3 THEN au_lname + ' ' + au_fname ELSE NULL END,
CASE @OrdSeq WHEN 4 THEN zip ELSE NULL END

GO
```

There are many similarities between this code and the code presented in Options 3 and 4. However, Richard Romley has avoided the problems inherent with the fact that CASE can only return a value of one specific data type by breaking the ORDER BY into four separate CASE expressions. Using this construction, SQL Server can return an appropriate data type for each CASE expression, without ever getting tangled up trying to transform data types.

By the way, the reason this solution is not SQL-92 compliant is because the SQL-92 standard only permits ORDER BYs using a column, and not an expression. SQL Server has long supported ORDER BYs using an expression, and the SQL-99 appears to be ready to accept that extension.

Reference

v2.02 2000.06.03	
Applies to SQL Server versions:	6.5, 7.0, 2000
FAQ category:	Application Design and Programming
Related FAQ article:	"How can I issue a SQL command that uses a variable for the tablename or columns? How can I return values from some dynamic SQL?" (exec, see page 35)
Related Microsoft Knowledge Base articles:	n/a
Other related information:	n/a
Authors:	B.P. Margolin, Neil Pike

orderbyview

Q: Can I use an ORDER BY in a view in SQL Server?

A: With SQL 6.5 and below, the answer is a categoric no. Put the ORDER BY on the SELECT statement that is selecting from the view.

With SQL 7.0 you can put an ORDER BY in a view as long as that view uses the TOP statement. To use the TOP statement the database needs to be in 70 compatibility mode; check this with sp_dbcmptlevel.

Reference

v1.00 1999.03.02	
Applies to SQL Server versions:	All
FAQ category:	Application Design and Programming
Related FAQ articles:	n/a
Related Microsoft Knowledge Base articles:	n/a
Other related information:	n/a
Author:	Neil Pike

outerjoin

Q: Why am I getting different results between old-style outer joins (=*, *=) and the ANSI standard outer joins?

A: Let's start with an understanding of how the old-style outer joins work. Since examples are easier to follow than explanations, let's define some very simple tables and data:

```
CREATE TABLE t1
(
    PK_t1 INT   PRIMARY KEY,
    c1    VARCHAR (7)
)

CREATE TABLE t2
(
    PK_t2 INT   PRIMARY KEY,
    c2    VARCHAR (7)
)

INSERT INTO t1 VALUES (1, 'Mary')
INSERT INTO t1 VALUES (2, 'Karen')
INSERT INTO t1 VALUES (3, 'Dolly')

INSERT INTO t2 VALUES (2, 'Steven')
INSERT INTO t2 VALUES (3, 'Joseph')
```

Executing the following query:

```
-- Query #1

SELECT *
FROM t1, t2
WHERE t1.PK_t1 *= t2.PK_t2
```

produces the result set:

```
PK_t1       c1      PK_t2       c2
----------- ------- ----------- -------
1           Mary    NULL        NULL
2           Karen   2           Steven
3           Dolly   3           Joseph
```

If you are familiar with outer joins, this is exactly what is expected. However, let's say that you are really looking to determine which rows in table t1 lack matching rows in table t2. You might think that the following query would identify that row #1 in t1 lacks a corresponding row in t2:

```
-- Query #2

SELECT *
FROM t1, t2
WHERE t1.PK_t1 *= t2.PK_t2
AND   t2.PK_t2  IS NULL
```

However, executing this query produces:

```
PK_t1       c1      PK_t2       c2
----------- ------- ----------- -------
1           Mary    NULL        NULL
2           Karen   NULL        NULL
3           Dolly   NULL        NULL
```

Not only does it appear that SQL Server is ignoring the additional filtering criteria we added (t2.PK_t2 IS NULL), but it has also "messed up" the other rows as well.

The "problem" is that the old-style joins place both the join logic and the filtering conditions in the WHERE clause. Since both appear in the WHERE clause, SQL Server has no way of knowing whether the developer meant the join logic to be applied before or after the filtering condition.

In this case we know, via the description of the problem, that we wanted the join to occur first and then the filtering criterion to be applied. However, the old-style join syntax does not allow us to specify the sequence in which the join logic and filtering conditions are applied.

With old-style joins, SQL Server, in the desire to maximize performance, will apply filtering conditions before the join logic. By filtering first, SQL Server can reduce the number of rows participating in the subsequent join.

So the "problem" is not that SQL Server processed the query incorrectly, but that our expectation of how SQL Server should process the query was faulty. We were "misled" by our statement of the requested output.

In other words, there is an inherent ambiguity in SQL (the language) when the join logic and filtering conditions of outer joins are combined in the WHERE clause. Output can differ depending on whether the join logic is applied before or after the filtering criteria.

(It is left to you to verify, with the knowledge that when dealing with old-style joins, filtering occurs prior to joining, that SQL Server is indeed generating the correct output from Query #2.)

The individuals who sit on the ANSI SQL committee were aware of this ambiguity, and that is why syntax to explicitly support outer joins was not introduced until the adoption of the ANSI SQL-92 standard.

So let's code an outer join using ANSI SQL-92-compliant syntax to answer the question posed earlier: how to identify rows in table t1 missing a matching row in table t2:

```
-- Query #3

SELECT *
FROM t1
LEFT OUTER JOIN t2
  ON (t1.PK_t1 = t2.PK_t2)
WHERE t2.c2 IS NULL
```

Executing this gives the result set we want:

```
PK_t1       c1      PK_t2       c2
----------- ------- ----------- -------
1           Mary    NULL        NULL
```

While the coding appears very similar to the old-style join that "didn't work" (Query #2), there are important differences.

The join syntax introduced in ANSI SQL-92 explicitly separates the join conditions from the filtering conditions. The join conditions appear within the ON clause of the JOIN, while filtering conditions remain in the WHERE clause. More importantly, because the join logic is separated from the filtering criteria, the logical sequence of execution can be unambiguously defined. By fiat, the join conditions (that is the logic in the ON clause of the JOIN) occur before the filtering. This is in line with normal expectations since within an ANSI SQL-92 compliant query, the JOIN clauses precede the WHERE clause.

But it is critical to understand that this is exactly the opposite of how SQL Server handled the logic using the pre-ANSI SQL-92 syntax. In other words, porting from the old-style join to ANSI SQL-92 compliant joins is not a mere mechanical exercise. It requires that the developer understand the purpose and intent of the original query, and possibly recode it.

Taking a slightly different approach, if the output from Query #2 was indeed what we wanted, then "straight porting" of the Query #2 code would resemble Query #3, which would be incorrect. To reproduce the output from Query #2, one should code as follows:

```
-- Query #4

SELECT *
FROM t1
LEFT OUTER JOIN t2
  ON (t1.PK_t1 = t2.PK_t2  AND
      t2.c2 IS NULL)
```

By the way, while outer joins were not explicitly supported until ANSI SQL-92, the older standard (ANSI SQL-89) was able to produce the same results as explicit outer joins via WHERE EXISTS and WHERE NOT EXISTS sub queries. However, many SQL developers are not comfortable with this technique and wanted a "simpler and cleaner" syntax supporting outer joins. To accommodate the SQL developers, many RDBMS vendors introduced proprietary extensions to SQL (the Sybase/Microsoft *=, =* construct being the obvious example).

Reference

v2.00 2000.07.07

Applies to SQL Server versions:	All
FAQ category:	Application Design and Programming
Related FAQ articles:	n/a
Related Microsoft Knowledge Base articles:	n/a
Other related information:	"Transact-SQL Joins"
Author:	B.P. Margolin

padintegerswithzeroes

Q: How can I pad an integer value in SQL Server with zeroes?

A: Integer values in SQL Server are always displayed without leading zeroes. If you require leading zeroes, then the integer must be converted to a character value and padded with 0 characters. Here is an example from pubs:

```
SELECT RIGHT(REPLICATE('0',10)+ CONVERT(varchar(10),ytd_sales),10) FROM titles
```

Reference

v1.01 2000.04.09	
Applies to SQL Server versions:	All
FAQ category:	Application Design and Programming
Related FAQ articles:	n/a
Related Microsoft Knowledge Base articles:	n/a
Other related information:	n/a
Author:	Neil Pike

perl

Q: How do I connect to SQL Server from PERL?

A: You have several choices:

- Sybperl: This is the Sybase OpenClient extensions to Perl. Note that as SybPerl is designed for Sybase, you may have the same compatibility problems as with CT-Lib. See `http://www.mbay.net/~mpeppler/`.
- MSSQL::Dblib: This is a SQL Server port of Sybperl. See `http://www.algonet.se/~sommar/mssqlperl/`.
- The Perl Win32::ODBC extension; see `http://www.roth.net/perl/odbc/`
- If the version of Perl has COM extensions, then you can use ADO.
- Search `http://www.perl.com` for any other code available on the standard CPAN (Comprehensive Perl Archive Network) sites, such as DBD::ODBC. See also `http://www.symbolstone.org/technology/perl/DBI/index.html`.

Reference

v1.04 2000.06.03	
Applies to SQL Server versions:	All
FAQ categories:	Application Design and Programming, Connectivity
Related FAQ article:	"How do I connect to SQL Server from a non-Microsoft machine such as Unix or OS/2?" (odbcunix, see page 132)
Related Microsoft Knowledge Base articles:	n/a
Other related information:	n/a
Author:	Neil Pike

proper

Q: How can I convert a string to "proper" case in SQL Server (for example, turn "andrew" into "Andrew")?

A: SQL Server has no built-in function for this and does now support user-defined functions. Therefore your two choices are:

1. Write an extended stored procedure.

2. Write a T-SQL stored procedure.

An extended stored procedure is faster and lets you have the full range of C programming tools and techniques, but it is possible to implement a simple example in T-SQL.

If you only have a surname to update in a single field, then it is possible to do it in a single update statement. An example follows:

```
UPDATE MyTable
SET surname = SUBSTRING(surname,1,1) + LOWER(SUBSTRING(surname,2,(DATAL-
ENGTH(surname)-1)))
```

Following is an example of a stored procedure. It only handles simple cases and won't handle situations like the name "D'Arcy" properly. If you want full function stuff I recommend that you write your own generic C routine and then call it from an extended stored procedure.

```
CREATE PROCEDURE sp_proper
 @in varchar(255) output
AS
BEGIN
DECLARE @in_pos  tinyint,
  @inter  varchar(255),
  @inter_pos tinyint

SELECT @in_pos = 0,
  @in = LOWER(@in)
SELECT @inter = @in
SELECT @inter_pos = PATINDEX('%[0-9A-Za-z]%', @inter)
```

```
WHILE @inter_pos > 0
BEGIN
 SELECT @in_pos = @in_pos + @inter_pos
 SELECT @in = STUFF(@in, @in_pos, 1, UPPER(SUBSTRING(@in, @in_pos, 1))),
   @inter = SUBSTRING(@inter, @inter_pos + 1, DATALENGTH(@inter) - @inter_pos)
 SELECT @inter_pos = PATINDEX('%[^0-9A-Za-z]%', @inter)
 IF @inter_pos > 0
 BEGIN
  SELECT @in_pos = @in_pos + @inter_pos
  SELECT @inter = SUBSTRING(@inter, @inter_pos + 1, DATALENGTH(@inter) -
@inter_pos)
  SELECT @inter_pos = PATINDEX('%[0-9A-Za-z]%', @inter)
 END
END
END
GO
```

Reference

v1.03 2000.03.13

Applies to SQL Server versions:	All
FAQ category:	Application Design and Programming
Related FAQ article:	"How can I create a user-defined function in SQL Server?" (udf, see page 94)
Related Microsoft Knowledge Base articles:	n/a
Other related information:	n/a
Author:	Neil Pike

ptk

Q: Where can I get the SQL Server Programmers Toolkit?

A: For SQL 6.5, visit `http://support.microsoft.com/download/support/mslfiles/PTK_I386.EXE`. This contains everything you need for DB-Library (DB-Lib), ODBC, SQL Distributed Management Objects (SQL-DMO), Open Data Services (ODS) and Extended Stored Procedures-type programming against SQL Server.

For SQL 7, look on the CD under `\mssql7\devtools\`. This also includes samples for Data Transformation Services (DTS).

Reference

v1.02 1999.04.13

Applies to SQL Server versions:	All
FAQ category:	Application Design and Programming
Related FAQ articles:	n/a
Related Microsoft Knowledge Base articles:	n/a
Other related information:	Look up "Samples" in SQL Server 7 Books Online
Author:	Neil Pike

quotes

Q: How can I embed single quotes in a string and get SQL Server to store it correctly?

A: Double them up. Use two single quotes and not a double quote (shift-2). For example:

```
SELECT @str = 'Neil''s test string containing single quotes.  i.e.'''

@str contains : Neil's test string containing single quotes.  i.e.'
```

Reference

v1.01 2000.04.13

Applies to SQL Server versions:	All
FAQ category:	Application Design and Programming
Related FAQ articles:	n/a
Related Microsoft Knowledge Base articles:	n/a
Other related information:	n/a
Author:	Neil Pike

randomnumber

Q: How can I get random numbers from SQL Server? I always get the same sequence when I use `RAND()`.

A: This is because you need to start the RAND function off with a random number. Use something like:

```
SELECT RAND( (DATEPART(mm, GETDATE()) * 100000 )
         + (DATEPART(ss, GETDATE()) * 1000 )
         + DATEPART(ms, GETDATE()) )
```

Note that `GETDATE()` is only evaluated once in a query, so don't use this for multiple inserts for a single query if you're expecting different values per row.

Reference

v1.02 2000.04.13

Applies to SQL Server versions:	All
FAQ category:	Application Design and Programming
Related FAQ articles:	n/a
Related Microsoft Knowledge Base articles:	n/a
Other related information:	"Using RAND"
Author:	Neil Pike

randomrows

Q: How can I select random rows from a SQL Server table?

A: First you need to generate a random number. This assumes that you have some sort of numeric primary key on the table in the first place. Use something like:

```
SELECT @NUM = RAND( (DATEPART(mm, GETDATE()) * 100000 )
         + (DATEPART(ss, GETDATE()) * 1000 )
         + DATEPART(ms, GETDATE()) )
```

(You could also use another variable like @@IDLE or @@CPU_BUSY to generate "random" numbers.)

```
SELECT @PK = min (col1) + (max (col1) - min (col1)) * @NUM

SELECT * FROM <tbl> where col1 = @PK

Another way (courtesy of Joe Celko/Itzik Ben-Gan :-

USE pubs
SELECT T1.au_id
FROM authors AS T1, authors AS T2
WHERE T1.au_id <= T2.au_id
GROUP BY T1.au_id
HAVING COUNT(T2.au_id) =
  (SELECT COUNT(*) FROM authors AS S3) * RAND() + 1
```

Reference

v1.02 2000.04.15	
Applies to SQL Server versions:	All
FAQ category:	Application Design and Programming
Related FAQ article:	n/a
Related Microsoft Knowledge Base article:	randomnumber
Other related information:	n/a
Author:	Neil Pike

replacetext

Q: How can I replace, change, or delete characters in a SQL Server column?

A: SQL has a reasonably full set of string manipulation tools, all documented in Books Online. Some are detailed here:

- RTRIM or LTRIM: For leading or trailing spaces.
- SUBSTRING: Standard substring function.
- RIGHT: Returns *x* number of characters from right of string (SQL 7.0 and above also has LEFT).
- CHARINDEX or PATINDEX: Finds a particular character or pattern in string.

- STUFF: Replaces text at given offsets.
- REPLACE: Replaces all occurrences of specified string within the string supplied (SQL 7.0 and above only).

Reference

v1.01 2000.04.16

Applies to SQL Server versions:	All
FAQ category:	Application Design and Programming
Related FAQ articles:	n/a
Related Microsoft Knowledge Base articles:	n/a

Other related information: "String Functions"

Author: Neil Pike

rowcount

Q: How can I restrict the number of rows returned or affected by my query?

A: With SQL 6.5 and below, use the `SET ROWCOUNT <n>` option; for example:

```
SET ROWCOUNT 10
SELECT * FROM <tbl>
```

This option is still available in SQL 7.0 and above, but the new TOP function has better performance:

```
SELECT TOP 10 * FROM <tbl>
```

Note that the database concerned *must* be in SQL 7.0 compatibility mode; run `sp_dbcmptlevel <dbname>` to check whether it is.

Reference

v1.02 2000.04.16

Applies to SQL Server versions:	All
FAQ category:	Application Design and Programming
Related FAQ articles:	n/a
Related Microsoft Knowledge Base articles:	n/a

Other related information: "SET Statement," "Limiting Result Sets Using TOP and PERCENT"

Author:	Neil Pike

rownum

Q: Does SQL Server support row numbers asOracle does?

A: No. Row numbering is contrary to relational sets (which is what RDBMSs running SQL is all about). It is not an ANSI standard, and Microsoft has not implemented such a feature.

If you need to use row numbers, you should look at your application and see if it is really appropriate to a SQL database.

Reference

v1.01 2000.04.16

Applies to SQL Server versions:	All
FAQ category:	Application Design and Programming
Related FAQ articles:	n/a
Related Microsoft Knowledge Base articles:	n/a
Other related information:	n/a
Author:	Neil Pike

rowsize

Q: How many bytes can I fit on a row or page in SQL Server and why? Are there any workarounds?

A: Rows can never cross page boundaries. The page size in SQL 6.5 and earlier is 2KB, and in SQL 7.0 it is 8KB.

For SQL 6.5 and Earlier

Each 2048-byte page has a 32-byte header leaving 2016 bytes for data. You can have two rows of 1008 bytes or 10 rows of 201 bytes. The row size includes a few bytes of overhead in addition to the data itself; there is more overhead if there are variable length columns.

One row cannot be 2016 bytes—this is because when you insert, update or delete a row, the entire row must be written to the transaction log in a log record. Log pages also have 2016 available bytes per page, and need 50 bytes for transaction log specific information, so this gives a maximum size for a single row of 1962 bytes.

For SQL 7.0

Each 8192-byte page has a 32-byte header leaving 8060 bytes for data.

For All Versions

You *can* define a table with a rowsize greater than this as long as it contains variable or NULL columns. However, if you try at any point to insert or update a row that has data that actually exceeds this limit, then the operation will fail.

There are no workarounds for this. You will have to split the table into multiple tables if you need more data than a row can take.

For more details on page layouts see *Inside SQL Server 6.5* by Ron Soukup or *Inside SQL Server 7.0* by Kalen Delaney (both by Microsoft Press). Both are highly recommended.

Reference

v1.03 2000.04.16

Applies to SQL Server versions:	All
FAQ categories:	Application Design and Programming, Database Administration
Related FAQ articles:	n/a
Related Microsoft Knowledge Base articles:	n/a
Other related information:	See “Maximum Capacity Specifications” in SQL Server Books Online
Author:	Neil Pike

rulesvscheck

Q: What is the difference between a CHECK constraint and a RULE?

A: Functionally they are very similar in allowing you to control the actual data values that can be put into specific columns, but there are some differences:

A CHECK constraint is part of the actual table definition and is ANSI standard. It is only available in SQL 6.0 and above. A CHECK can apply to multiple columns; for example, `CHECK (col1 > col2)`. One column can have multiple check constraints.

A RULE is a separate database object that is bound to a particular column. It is specific to Sybase and SQL Server. A rule can only look at data in a single column. Only one rule can be defined per column. The one additional feature that rules have over check constraints is that you can bind rules to user-defined data types, so the rule can be defined once, bound to a data type once, and then used over and over in lots of different tables.

It is recommended that you always use CHECK constraints for compatibility. The only reason to use rules is if you rely on user-defined data types a lot.

Reference

v1.01 2000.04.16

Applies to SQL Server versions:	All
FAQ category:	Application Design and Programming
Related FAQ articles:	n/a
Related Microsoft Knowledge Base articles:	n/a
Other related information:	See "CREATE RULE (T-SQL)," "CHECK Constraints" in SQL Server Books Online
Author:	Neil Pike

sdi

Q: I'm getting an error message,"Cannot Load DLL 'SDI' Reason 126 (The specified Module Cannot be found)," when doing a stored procedure debug on SQL Server. (Or, the breakpoints just don't fire.) What should I do?

A: With SQL 6.5, VC5. or VB5, copy the sdi.dll file from your VB, VC or VS enterprise CD into the <sql>\binn directory.

For SQL 7.0, get the files from the SQL Server 7.0 CD \x86\other\sdi.

- VB 6.0: Copy SDI60.DLL into the <sql>\BINN directory.
- VC 6.0: Copy SDI.DLL into the <sql>\BINN directory.
- VI 6.0: Copy MSSDI98.DLL into the <sql>\BINN directory.

You can't debug SQL 7 with VB5/VC5.

Reference

v1.01 1999.11.03	
Applies to SQL Server versions:	All
FAQ categories:	Application Design and Programming, Troubleshooting
Related FAQ articles:	n/a
Related Microsoft Knowledge Base articles:	n/a
Other related information:	n/a
Author:	Neil Pike

selectrownumber

Q: How can I select a row, by row number, in SQL Server?

A: SQL Server does not support row numbering as it is not part of the ANSI SQL standard. There are various ways of achieving the goal, however.

- Select the rows into a cursor and then use the FETCH ABSOLUTE command to get the row you want.
- Select all rows into a temporary table using the IDENTITY function to give them a row number—then pick out the one you want from there. Following is some example code:

```
USE pubs
Go
IF OBJECT_ID('tempdb.dbo.#newtab') IS NOT NULL
    DROP TABLE #newtab
Go

SELECT IDENTITY(int,1,1) AS ID, *
 INTO #newtab
 FROM authors

SELECT * FROM #newtab
```

- As long as there is a unique column that you can use to find the row concerned, then you can use the following code sample (against "pubs" again). Note that it will perform extremely poorly against large tables.

```
USE pubs
Go

DECLARE @rownum int
SELECT @rownum = 13

SELECT *
FROM authors AS T1A
WHERE (SELECT COUNT(*) FROM authors AS T1B WHERE T1B.au_id <= T1A.au_id) = @rownum
ORDER BY au_id
```

Reference

v1.03 2000.04.16

Applies to SQL Server versions:	All
FAQ category:	Application Design and Programming
Related FAQ article:	"Does SQL Server support row numbers as Oracle does?" (rownum, see page 83)
Related Microsoft Knowledge Base articles:	n/a
Other related information:	See Joe Celko's *SQL for Smarties* book (Morgan Kaufmann)
Authors:	Neil Pike, Tibor Karaszi, Itzik Ben-Gan

sp_oaproceduresonly255chars

Q: Why do the sp_OA stored procedures not support more than 255 characters in SQL 7.0?

A: This is a known limitation—they also don't support Unicode data. Expect both of these issues to be resolved in SQL 2000.

Reference

v1.01 2000.05.25	
Applies to SQL Server versions:	7.0
FAQ category:	Application Design and Programming
Related FAQ articles:	n/a
Related Microsoft Knowledge Base articles:	n/a
Other related information:	n/a
Author:	Neil Pike

sql7preservecursors

Q: What has happened to SQL_PRESERVE_CURSORS in SQL 7.0?

A: The behavior of this statement was changed with SQL 7.0.

- SQL 6.5: SQL_PRESERVE_CURSORS apply to both COMMIT_BEHAVIOR and ROLLBACK_BEHAVIOR.
- SQL 7.0: SQL_PRESERVE_CURSORS only apply to COMMIT_BEHAVIOR.
- SQL 7.0 SP1/SP2: As 6.5.
- SQL 7.0 SP1/SP2 with -T7525 traceflag: As per 7.0.

Reference

v1.02 2000.06.04

Applies to SQL Server versions:	7.0
FAQ categories:	Application Design and Programming, Troubleshooting
Related FAQ article:	"Should I upgrade to SQL 7.0? Why or why not? What are the known bugs? What other differences are there between 6.5 and 7.0?" (sql7differences, see page 304)
Related Microsoft Knowledge Base article:	Q199294 "INF: Server Side Cursors Remain Open when CURSOR_CLOSE_ON_COMMIT Set OFF"
Other related information:	n/a
Author:	Neil Pike

storedprocreturnsbeforecomplete

Q: I'm running a stored procedure from Visual Basic. Why does it return control before the stored procedure has finished?

A: Either because the SP is returning multiple resultsets or because it has been invoked asynchronously.

Put `SET NOCOUNT ON` at the start of the procedure to suppress the `(x row(s) affected)` as seen in Query Analyzer, assuming you don't need them. Each of these messages behaves like a resultset.

Check the call parameters you making from DB-Library, ODBC, or ADO. Make sure it is a synchronous call and not an asynchronous one.

Reference

v1.01 2000.05.14

Applies to SQL Server versions:	All
FAQ category:	Application Design and Programming
Related FAQ articles:	n/a
Related Microsoft Knowledge Base articles:	n/a
Other related information:	n/a
Author:	Neil Pike

storingvariantdata

Q: How can I store different data types in a column and extract them?

A: SQL Server 2000 introduces the new sql_variant datatype that can hold int, decimal, char, binary, and nchar values. For earlier versions, the solution presented here shows how to store different data types in a column of a table and retrieve them. This simulates the variant data type in T-SQL using existing data types. The values for each data type are stored in a varbinary column and converted back to their original data type while reading.

```
create table #variant (data varbinary(8), data_type char(1))
insert #variant values(-291, 'i')
insert #variant values(1, 'i')
insert #variant values(convert(varbinary(8), 'czx'), 'c')
insert #variant values(convert(varbinary(8), 35.25), 'f')
insert #variant values(convert(varbinary(8), 35.3333), 'f')

select case when data_type = 'i' then convert(int, data) end as int_data,
 case when data_type = 'c' then convert(varchar, data) end as char_data,
 case when data_type = 'f' then convert(decimal(6, 4), data) end as
decimal_data,
 data_type
from #variant
```

Reference

v1.01 2000.03.29

Applies to SQL Server versions:	All
FAQ categories:	Application Design and Programming, Miscellaneous
Related FAQ articles:	n/a
Related Microsoft Knowledge Base articles:	n/a
Other related information:	See "Using sql_variant Data" in SQL Server 2000 Books Online
Author:	Umachandar Jayachandran

surrogatekey

Q: When might I want to use a surrogate key?

A: A surrogate key is a key that has no meaning other then uniquely identifying a row in the table. It contains no meaningful business information.

Reasons you might use one:

- There is no "good" primary key.
- The obvious primary keys are awkward to use.
- The obvious primary key is used in foreign key relationships and will require updating

Reference

v1.01 2000.05.14

Applies to SQL Server versions:	All
FAQ category:	Application Design and Programming
Related FAQ articles:	n/a
Related Microsoft Knowledge Base articles:	n/a
Other related information:	n/a
Author:	Neil Pike

synonym

Q: What is the equivalent of an Oracle synonym in SQL Server?

A: Create a view.

```
CREATE VIEW TitlesSynonym AS SELECT * FROM titles
```

Reference

v1.01 2000.05.14	
Applies to SQL Server versions:	All
FAQ category:	Application Design and Programming
Related FAQ articles:	n/a
Related Microsoft Knowledge Base articles:	n/a
Other related information:	n/a
Author:	Neil Pike

textsize

Q: Why can't I access more than 4KB of data in a TEXT field in SQL Server?

A: Probably because you haven't set the TEXTSIZE parameter, `SET TEXTSIZE <n>`.

This parameter specifies the size, in bytes, of text data to be returned with a SELECT statement. If you specify a TEXTSIZE of 0, the size is reset to the default (4KB). Setting TEXTSIZE affects the global variable @@TEXTSIZE.

The DB-Library variable DBTEXTLIMIT also limits the size of text data returned with a SELECT statement. If DBTEXTLIMIT is set to a smaller size than TEXTSIZE, only the amount specified by DBTEXTLIMIT is returned. For more information, see Microsoft SQL Server Programming DB-Library for C, which comes with the SQL Server Programmers Toolkit (PTK).

Reference

v1.01 2000.05.27	
Applies to SQL Server versions:	All
FAQ category:	Application Design and Programming
Related FAQ article:	"Where can I get the SQL Server Programmers Toolkit?" (ptk, see page 78)
Related Microsoft Knowledge Base articles:	n/a
Other related information:	"Retrieving ntext, text, or image Values" in Books Online 7.0, "Selecting text and image Values" in Books Online 6.5
Author:	Neil Pike

timestampview

Q: How do I view the contents of a TIMESTAMP field in SQL Server?

A: You don't. Timestamp columns, contrary to what the name implies, are *not* dates and times. They are just hex values that are guaranteed by SQL Server to be unique within the database. In normal circumstances the values are monotonically increasing.

Reference

v1.02 2000.05.27

Applies to SQL Server versions:	All
FAQ category:	Application Design and Programming
Related FAQ article:	n/a
Related Microsoft Knowledge Base article:	n/a
Other related information:	Q44415 "INF: Timestamps and Their Uses"
Author	Neil Pike

triggertypes

Q: Does SQL Server support before and after (pre and post) triggers? What about row vs. set triggers?

A: SQL Server 7.0 and below only supports "after" triggers, but you can see what the "before" data was by using the logical tables **inserted** and **deleted**, within the trigger.

SQL Server 2000 introduces INSTEAD OF triggers as well as the default "after" trigger. This trigger will be executed instead of the triggering statement, which makes it a very flexible alternative.

SQL Server triggers only fire once per query, so they are set triggers rather than row triggers.

SQL Server does not support SELECT triggers.

Reference

v1.02 2000.05.27	
Applies to SQL Server versions:	All
FAQ category:	Application Design and Programming
Related FAQ articles:	n/a
Related Microsoft Knowledge Base articles:	n/a
Other related information:	n/a
Author:	Neil Pike

udf

Q: How can I create a user-defined function in SQL Server?

A: This functionality is not available until SQL Server 2000, which introduces the CREATE FUNCTION statement. Prior versions had no equivalent and only limited workaround options, such as the following:

- You can write your own stored procedure (SP) or extended stored procedure (XP). However, you can only pass an SP or XP a set of parameters, so to "apply" it to a rowset you would have to cursor round the rows yourself and call the SP or XP "n" times. An example of using a stored procedure and cursor follows:

```
SET NOCOUNT ON
GO

/* Create the Sample Table and "Function" Stored Procedure */
IF EXISTS(SELECT * FROM sysobjects WHERE name = 'SumTable' AND Type = 'U')
   DROP TABLE SumTable
GO

CREATE TABLE SumTable (Num1 int, Num2 int, Result int)
GO

INSERT SumTable (Num1, Num2) VALUES(1,2)
INSERT SumTable (Num1, Num2) VALUES(2,3)
INSERT SumTable (Num1, Num2) VALUES(3,4)
GO
```

```
IF EXISTS(SELECT * FROM sysobjects WHERE name = 'spAdd' AND Type = 'P')
    DROP PROCEDURE spAdd
GO

CREATE PROCEDURE spAdd
(@num1 int, @num2 int, @Result int OUTPUT)
AS
    SELECT @Result = @num1 + @num2
GO

/* Process Table using "Function" Stored Procedure via a CURSOR */
DECLARE @Num1 int, @Num2 int, @Result int

DECLARE curSumTable CURSOR FOR SELECT Num1, Num2 FROM SumTable FOR UPDATE OF
Result
OPEN curSumTable

FETCH NEXT FROM curSumTable
INTO @Num1, @Num2

WHILE @@FETCH_STATUS = 0
BEGIN
    EXEC spAdd @Num1, @Num2, @Result OUTPUT
    UPDATE SumTable SET Result = @result WHERE CURRENT OF curSumTable
    FETCH NEXT FROM curSumTable
    INTO @Num1, @Num2
END

CLOSE curSumTable
DEALLOCATE curSumTable
GO

/* Display Results */
SELECT * FROM SumTable
GO

SET NOCOUNT OFF
GO
```

- As long as you can write the function in a simple one-line T-SQL statement, then you can simulate the function with a CASE statement. See Books Online for the full syntax.

```
SELECT FinalValue = CASE
                        WHEN <exp>
                             THEN <exp>
                        WHEN <exp>
                             THEN <exp>
                        ELSE <exp>
                    END
```

Reference

v1.05 2000.05.27	
Applies to SQL Server versions:	All
FAQ category:	Application Design and Programming
Related FAQ articles:	n/a
Related Microsoft Knowledge Base articles:	n/a
Other related information:	n/a
Author:	Neil Pike

unicode

Q: Does SQL Server support Unicode?

A: SQL Server 7.0/2000 has full UCS-2 Unicode support. There is no Unicode support in 6.5 and below, although DBCS (Double-Byte Character Set) is an alternative.

UCS-2 is the official Unicode two-byte definition for all characters. Some DBMS manufacturers have only implemented a space-conserving, pseudo-form of Unicode, UTF-8, which has mixed one-byte and two-byte encoding.

Reference

v1.03 2000.05.27	
Applies to SQL Server version:	7.0
FAQ category:	Application Design and Programming
Related FAQ articles: n/a	
Related Microsoft Knowledge Base article:	Q232580 "INF: Storing UTF-8 Data in SQL Server"
Other related information:	n/a
Author:	Neil Pike

unicodehyphens

Q: Why do I get invalid rows returned containing hyphens when my where clause doesn't specify them?

A: This only happens with Unicode columns because Unicode sorts and compares are based on the Windows standard, which effectively ignores the hyphen character.

To illustrate this use the following sample:

```
CREATE TABLE HyphenTest (cocode nvarchar(3))
GO

INSERT INTO HyphenTest VALUES ('AXB')
INSERT INTO HyphenTest VALUES ('AXC')
INSERT INTO HyphenTest VALUES ('A-Y')
GO

SELECT * FROM HyphenTest
WHERE (cocode > 'A-X') AND (cocode < 'A-Z')
```

The following results will be obtained:

```
cocode
------
AXB
AXC
A-Y

(3 row(s) affected)
```

If the cocode column is changed from nvarchar to varchar then the following result will be obtained:

```
cocode
------
A-Y

(1 row(s) affected)
```

Reference

v1.00 1999.10.27	
Applies to SQL Server versions:	7.0, 2000
FAQ category:	Application Design and Programming
Related FAQ articles:	n/a
Related Microsoft Knowledge Base articles:	n/a
Other related information:	n/a
Author:	Neil Pike

userdefinedcounters

Q: How can I set user-defined counters from a T-SQL batch or stored procedure and view them?

A: SQL Server provides 10 user-settable counters that can be set from T-SQL batches or stored procedures. These values of these counters can then be viewed using the NT Performance Monitor or queried like any other perfmon counter. The example below shows how to write a simple stored procedure that will set the user-defined counters value and view them. In SQL 6.x, the SPs sp_user_counter1 through sp_user_counter10 are just stubs. These stored procedures can be replaced with your own logic that does the same. The following example is specific to SQL 7.0 and can be used in a similar way in SQL 6.x.

```
-- Run this batch from the one ISQL/W window
DECLARE @Percent int, @TotalRows int, @Skipped int, @CurrentRow int
SELECT @CurrentRow = 0, @Skipped = 0, @TotalRows = 45
WHILE(@CurrentRow < @TotalRows)
BEGIN
 SET @CurrentRow = @CurrentRow + 1
 -- report logic
 SELECT @Percent = (@CurrentRow*100)/@TotalRows
 EXEC sp_user_counter1 @Percent

 WAITFOR DELAY '00:00:01'

 IF (@CurrentRow%2) = 0 SET @Skipped = @Skipped + 1
 EXEC sp_user_counter2 @Skipped
END
GO

-- Run the SELECT statement from another ISQL/W window
-- The counters can also be viewed using the NT Performance Monitor
select * from master..sysperfinfo
where object_name = 'SQLServer:User Settable' and
 patindex('User counter [12]', cast(instance_name as varchar)) > 0
```

Reference

v1.01 2000.03.29

Applies to SQL Server versions:	6.x, 7.x, 2000
FAQ categories:	Application Design and Programming, Miscellaneous
Related FAQ articles:	n/a
Related Microsoft Knowledge Base articles:	n/a
Other related information:	n/a
Author:	Umachandar Jayachandran

validateguidcounters

Q: How can I validate the format of GUID values in character variables or columns?

A: The form of the string constant for GUID values is "xxxxxxxx-xxxx-xxxx-xxxx-xxxxxxxxxxxx" where x represents a hexadecimal digit. The following solution uses a LIKE check to compare each digit with the valid values: numeric digits and characters a-f or A-F.

```
create table #guid_values ( guid_str varchar(36) )
insert #guid_values values ( 'BC1EAAAF-1B5A-4695-9797-3ED6C99B7FC5' )
insert #guid_values values ( 'BCXXAAAF-1B5A-4695-9797-3EDXXXXXXFC5' )
insert #guid_values values ( '-jk1029347 lka llur 193241 lk;qed' )
go
select guid_str,
 case when guid_str
  like replicate('[0-9a-fA-F]', 8) + '-' +
   replicate('[0-9a-fA-F]', 4) + '-' +
   replicate('[0-9a-fA-F]', 4) + '-' +
   replicate('[0-9a-fA-F]', 4) + '-' +
   replicate('[0-9a-fA-F]', 12)
  then 'Yes'
  else 'No'
 end AS ISGUID
from #guid_values
```

Reference

v1.01 2000.03.29

Applies to SQL Server versions:	7.0, 2000
FAQ category:	Application Design and Programming
Related FAQ articles:	n/a
Related Microsoft Knowledge Base articles:	n/a
Other related information:	n/a
Author:	Umachandar Jayachandran

weeknumber

Q: Why does SQL Server return the wrong week number? For example, `SELECT DATEPART(wk,'19990323')` returns 13, not the expected 12.

A: This is because SQL Server starts counting weeks from Jan. 1, and Week 1 is always the week with Jan. 1 in it.

The ISO standard is that Week 1 is the first week with four days in it.

In order to calculate the ISO Week, you can use T-SQL. SQL 2000 provides for user-defined functions. Following is a UDF to calculate the ISO Week:

```
CREATE FUNCTION ISOweek  (@DATE datetime)
RETURNS int
AS
BEGIN
   DECLARE @ISOweek int
   SET @ISOweek= DATEPART(wk,@DATE)+1
      -DATEPART(wk,CAST(DATEPART(yy,@DATE) as CHAR(4))+'0104')

--Special case: Jan. 1-3 may belong to the previous year.

   IF (@ISOweek=0)
      SET @ISOweek=dbo.ISOweek(CAST(DATEPART(yy,@DATE)-1
         AS CHAR(4))+'12'+ CAST(24+DATEPART(DAY,@DATE) AS CHAR(2)))+1

--Special case: Dec. 29-31 may belong to the next year.

   IF ((DATEPART(mm,@DATE)=12) AND
      ((DATEPART(dd,@DATE)-DATEPART(dw,@DATE))>= 28))
      SET @ISOweek=1
   RETURN(@ISOweek)
END
```

Reference

v1.03 2000.06.13

Applies to SQL Server versions:	All
FAQ category:	Application Design and Programming
Related FAQ articles:	n/a
Related Microsoft Knowledge Base articles:	n/a
Other related information:	n/a
Author:	Neil Pike

xml

Q: Does SQL Server support XML?

A: A SQL Server XML Technology Preview is available for download from Microsoft's Web site. It has been tested with SQL 6.5 (SP5)/SQL 7.0 and IIS 4.0 (NT4)/IIS 5.0 (Windows 2000).

SQL 2000 offers full XML support built-in.

Reference

v1.02 2000.04.28	
Applies to SQL Server versions :	6.5, 7.0, 2000
FAQ category:	Application Design and Programming
Related FAQ articles:	n/a
Related Microsoft Knowledge Base articles:	n/a
Other related information:	`http://msdn.microsoft.com/workshop/xml/articles/xmlsql/sqlxml_prev.asp`
Author:	Neil Pike

xpexamples

Q: Where can I get examples of XP code for SQL Server?

A: For SQL 6.5, download the Programmer's Tool Kit from `http://support.microsoft.com/download/support/mslfiles/PTK_I386.EXE`.

For SQL 7, look on the CD under \devtools\ or on your installation path if you chose to install the samples.

Reference

v1.02 2000.04.28	
Applies to SQL Server versions:	All
FAQ category:	Application Design and Programming
Related FAQ articles:	n/a
Related Microsoft Knowledge Base article:	Q186893 "INF: How to Obtain SQL Server 6.5 Programmer's Toolkit and Vbsql.ocx"
Other related information:	n/a
Author:	Neil Pike

xpproglanguages

Q: What programming languages can I use to write an extended stored procedure?

A: The official Microsoft answer is that you can only write them in C or C++. Certainly VB doesn't work.

However, Delphi 4 and 5 will also work. See an article on this subject in *The Delphi Magazine*, Issue 31. The source code is available on their site under Back Issues; see `http://www.itecuk.com` or `http://www.thedelphimagazine.com`.

Reference

v1.03 2000.04.28

Applies to SQL Server versions:	All
FAQ category:	Application Design and Programming
Related FAQ article:	xpexamples
Related Microsoft Knowledge Base articles:	n/a
Other related information:	See "Creating Extended Stored Procedures" in SQL Server Books Online
Author:	Neil Pike

Connectivity

This section covers all aspects of network connectivity, including Internet and firewalls.

16bitconnections

Q: I'm having problems getting more than <x> connections from a 16-bit client to SQL Server. I get "out of memory" or "unable to connect" errors.

A: This is because 16-bit clients, whether they use ODBC or DB-Lib, use a 64K buffer for all their control blocks and network buffers. You have to keep everything within this one area—there are no workarounds for this.

The main thing that uses up the memory is the space used for "network" buffers—actually these are buffers for the TDS packets. The actual network buffers may be bigger or smaller than these and the TDS packets may have to be fragmented by the network driver to get them on the network—but that is transparent to SQL.

The "network packet size" (TDS) can be specified by the client connection. If it is not, it uses the setting on the server that is set by sp_configure.

If you need more connections, the easiest thing to do is reduce the "network packet size" via sp_configure or the client connection until you get enough. The lower it is set, the more round-trips that SQL client-to-server has to take, which potentially can degrade performance.

Reference

v1.01 2000.03.09

Applies to SQL Server versions:	All
FAQ categories:	Connectivity, Troubleshooting
Related FAQ articles:	n/a
Related Microsoft Knowledge Base articles:	n/a
Other related information:	Search Books Online on "packet size"
Author:	Neil Pike

adsi

Q: How can I use SQL 7s HDQ (heterogeneous distributed query) facilities to get at NT domain or Exchange information?

A: This information is supposed to get ADSI working from SQL Server, but your mileage may vary.

In order to get an ADSI linked server to SQL Server 7.0, you will need to install the following prerequisites. ADSI 2.0 doesn't work with MDAC 2.1 (installed with SQL Server 7.0). For more information on ADSI 2.0 and MDAC 2.1, see `http://support.microsoft.com/support/kb/articles/q216/7/09.asp`.

Requirements

- You must install SQL Server 7.0. For more information about SQL Server, visit `http://www.microsoft.com/sql`.
- You must install ADSI 2.5 Runtime on the machine on which SQL Server is installed. This is built into Windows 2000—for earlier clients get the download from `http://www.microsoft.com/adsi`.
- You must either use Active Directory (Windows 2000), an NT 4.0 SAM database or Exchange Server as a basis for directory information.

Step-by-Step Instructions

In to add a linked server, do the following:

1. Run the Query Analyzer.
2. Logon the SQL Server machine.
3. Execute the following line:

```
sp_addlinkedserver 'ADSI', 'Active Directory Services 2.5',
'ADSDSOObject','adsdatasource'
go
```

This tells SQL Server to associate the word "ADSI" with the ADSI OLE DB provider—"ADSDSOObject."

Following is an example scenario of common operations:

```
SELECT * FROM OpenQuery(
ADSI,'<LDAP://DC=Microsoft,DC=com>;(&(objectCategory=Person)(objectClass=use
r));name, adspath;subtree')
```

Note: You should change the DC=.., DC=.. accordingly. This query asks for all users in the "Microsoft.com" domain.

You may also use the ADSI SQL Dialect, for example:

```
SELECT * FROM OpenQuery( ADSI, 'SELECT name, adsPath FROM
''LDAP://DC=Microsoft,DC=com'' WHERE objectCategory = ''Person'' AND
objectClass= ''user''')
```


Creating, Executing a View

You may create a view for data obtained from Active Directory. Note that only the view definition is stored in SQL Server, not the actual result set. Hence, you may get a different result when you execute a view later.

To create a view, type and execute:

```
CREATE VIEW viewADUsers AS
SELECT * FROM OpenQuery(
ADSI,'<LDAP://DC=Microsoft,DC=com>;(&(objectCategory=Person)(objectClass=use
r));name, adspath;subtree')
```

To execute a view, type:

```
SELECT * from viewADUsers
```

Heteregenous Join between SQL Server and Active Directory

Create an employee performance review table as a SQL table:

```
CREATE TABLE EMP_REVIEW
(
userName varChar(40),
reviewDate datetime,
rating decimal
)
```

Insert a few records:

```
INSERT EMP_REVIEW VALUES('Administrator', '2/15/1998', 4.5 )
INSERT EMP_REVIEW VALUES('Administrator', '7/15/1998', 4.0 )
```

Note: You can insert other user names.

Now join the two:

```
SELECT ADsPath, userName, ReviewDate, Rating
FROM EMP_REVIEW, viewADUsers
WHERE userName = Name
```

Now, you can even create another view for this join:

```
CREATE VIEW reviewReport AS
SELECT ADsPath, userName, ReviewDate, Rating
FROM EMP_REVIEW, viewADUsers
WHERE userName = Name
Advanced Operations
```

You may log on as different user when connecting to the Active Directory. To specify the alternate credential, do the following:

```
sp_addlinkedsrvlogin ADSI, false, 'MICROSOFT\Administrator',
'CN=Administrator,CN=Users,DC=Microsoft,DC=com', 'passwordHere'
```

This line tells Distributed Query that if someone logs on in SQL Server as "Microsoft\Administrator", the Distributed Query will pass the "CN=Administrator, CN=Users, DC=Microsoft, DC=com" and "passwordHere" to ADSI as the credentials.

To stop connecting as an alternate credential, type:

```
sp_droplinkedsrvlogin ADSI,'MICROSOFT\Administrator'
```

Reference

v1.03 2000.05.25	
Applies to SQL Server version:	7.0
FAQ Category:	Connectivity
Related FAQ articles:	"How can I access Exchange stores from SQL Server?" (exchangedrivers, see page 114)
Related Microsoft Knowledge Base article:	Q216709 "ADSI 2.0, 2.5, and MDAC 2.1 Compatibility Issues"
Other related information:	n/a
Author:	Neil Pike

connectiondrop

Q: How does SQL Server clear up orphaned connections?

A: It doesn't. It never terminates a connection unless told to by a user, a KILL command is issued, or the operating system tells it that the network connection it is using has been disconnected.

How long the operating system takes to kill a network connection, or whether it is done at all, depends on the net-lib and network protocol used. For parameters on keep-alive frames and session time-outs for the relevant network protocol, the best guide is the NT Server resource kit, which describes how NT's various network layers work. See Q137983 for some details pertinent to SQL Server.

Typically, named-pipe connections over NetBEUI will be timed out quite quickly, followed by named-pipes over IP. If you're using TCP-IP sockets then these sessions aren't timed-out at all by default.

Reference

v1.02 2000.04.15	
Applies to SQL Server versions:	All
FAQ category:	Connectivity
Related FAQ articles:	n/a
Related Microsoft Knowledge Base article:	Q137983 "INF: How to Troubleshoot Orphaned Connections in SQL Server"
Other related information:	See "Orphaned Sessions" in Books Online 7
Author:	Neil Pike

delphi

Q: How can I connect from Delphi to SQL 7?

A: You need to at least be on BDE (Borland Database Engine) version 5.01. This knows about SQL 7.0 systems tables and related topics. However, SQLLinks is still DB-Lib based and therefore will never support Unicode, varchars greater than 255 bytes, and any other SQL 7.0-only feature.

Inprise (Borland) has released ADO components with Delphi 5 and recommends using these to connect to SQL Server 7. Check their Web sites at `http://www.borland.com/devsupport/` or `http://community.borland.com/` for details.

Here are some additional sources:

- Download of current BDE: `http://www.borland.com/devsupport/bde/`
- BDE info: `http://www.borland.com/bde/`
- Delphi info: `http://www.borland.com/delphi/`
- SQLLinks info: `http://www.borland.com/sqllinks/`
- For non-Inprise solutions check out `http://www.kylecordes.com/bag/index.html`

Reference

v1.01 2000.04.21	
Applies to SQL Server version:	7.0
FAQ categories:	Connectivity, Application Design and Programming
Related FAQ articles:	n/a
Related Microsoft Knowledge Base articles:	n/a
Other related information:	n/a
Author:	Neil Pike

directhosting

Q: Why do I get slow or no connections to SQL Server using IPX from my Win3x and Win9x clients? From Windows NT they work fine.

A: This is because of a network feature called "direct hosting." To resolve the problem, either use another protocol completely or turn off the feature. On the NT Server this can be done by disabling the NWLink IPX/SPX binding in Windows NT Server service. After this is done, enable NWLink with NetBIOS on the client computer.

Alternatively, you can turn it off at the client end. For Windows 3.x machines, this can be done by editing the system.ini file and amending or adding the following entry.

```
[network]
DirectHost=off
```

For Windows 95, use regedit.exe to navigate to the following registry key:

```
HKEY_LOCAL_MACHINE\System\CurrentControlSet\Services\VxD\VNETSUP
```

Add a string value named DirectHost and set the string value to 0 (zero). Also, ensure that NetBIOS support is enabled for NWLink, if NWLink is the only transport protocol loaded on the client computer running Windows 95.

Reference

v1.01 2000.04.21

Applies to SQL Server versions:	All
FAQ categories:	Connectivity, Troubleshooting
Related FAQ articles:	n/a
Related Microsoft Knowledge Base article:	Search on "DirectHost"
Other related information:	n/a
Author:	Neil Pike

enterpriseconnect

Q: Why can't I connect Enterprise Manager to my local copy of SQL Server? It connects OK to other machines.

A: This has to do with the way that SQL interfaces with the NT networking code. The easiest way around this problem is to register the local server with a name of "." or "(local)"—ignore the double quotes in either case. Both of these names should force SQL to use a local-named pipe to connect which should work no matter what the default SQL connection parameters are set to.

Reference

v1.00 1998.10.02	
Applies to SQL Server version:	6.x
FAQ categories:	Connectivity, Server Administration and Tools
Related FAQ articles:	n/a
Related Microsoft Knowledge Base articles:	n/a
Other related information:	n/a
Author:	Neil Pike

exchangedrivers

Q: How can I access Exchange stores from SQL Server?

A: Several methods:

- Purchase an ODBC/OLE-DB driver from Intersolv/Merant (Merant is the new company name).

- Set up a connection to the *.?DB files from Access 2000. Then make this Access 2000 database a linked server from SQL Server. (Access 2000's JET drivers are capable of reading the Exchange files.)

- Exchange 2000 has an OLE-DB driver that can be used directly from SQL Server.

- Use ADSI as a linked server. You must have ADSI 2.5 installed.

```
sp_addlinkedserver 'ADSI', 'Active Directory Service Interfaces', 'ADSDSOObject',
'adsdatasource'
go
select * from openquery(ADSI, 'select * from ''LDAP://
<<ExchangeServerName>>''')
go
```

Reference

v1.02 2000.04.01	
Applies to SQL Server versions:	All
FAQ category:	Connectivity
Related FAQ articles:	n/a
Related Microsoft Knowledge Base articles:	n/a
Other related information:	n/a
Author:	Neil Pike

fastestnetlib

Q: Which SQL network library is the fastest?

A: In order, with the fastest first:

- TCP/IP sockets
- NWLINK IPX/SPX
- Named Pipes
- Multiprotocol without encryption
- Multiprotocol with encryption

One exception is when running the SQL Server client locally on the same computer as the server; for example, from IIS. In this case, Named Pipes will be the fastest.

However, on LAN and fast WAN links you are unlikely to see a real-world difference in response times between any of the network libraries. This is because network response/number of packets is not significant in these environments compared to application/database/server responses.

However, on slow network connections (anything 64 Kbits per second and below can be considered slow) then you will see a performance improvement if you use the TCP/IP sockets network library.

Reference

v1.02 2000.04.24	
Applies to SQL Server versions:	All
FAQ category:	Connectivity
Related FAQ articles:	n/a
Related Microsoft Knowledge Base articles:	n/a
Other related information:	n/a
Author:	Neil Pike

internet

Q: Can I replicate or connect to SQL Server over the Internet?

A: The Internet is nothing more or less than a large TCP/IP WAN (wide-area network). And a wide-area network works the same as a LAN (local-area network) just slower. So yes, anything you can do with SQL Server on the network in your office you can do over the Internet, assuming you *have connectivity* to the Internet. All issues are networking-related, not SQL-related. The servers at either end must be able to connect to the Internet either directly or via RAS. In the case of RAS you can use RASDIAL.EXE to automate connections as necessary.

The issues are:

- The Internet is TCP/IP only, so you must run TCP/IP on your clients and the servers.

- Physical connectivity. Do you have a routed or dial-up connection to the Internet? Are these routes being passed transparently into your internal network? You need to be able to PING <remote IP address> and PING <remote servername> from your local client/server and vice-versa.

- Security. You should really use a firewall for any Internet connection. Is this configured to allow your SQL traffic through? See the "firewall" FAQ entry for more information on port numbers for the various network libraries.

- Name-resolution. You can address the remote servers by IP address directly, but the better method is to put an entry in your local HOSTS file (<WINNT>\SYSTEM32\DRIVERS\ETC) or DNS/WINS server. Then put this name in your connection string.

Reference

v1.03 2000.05.06	
Applies to SQL Server versions:	All
FAQ category:	Connectivity
	Related FAQ article: "How do I connect to SQL Server through a firewall?" (firewall, see page 382)
Related Microsoft Knowledge Base articles:	n/a
Other related information:	See "Connecting to SQL Server Over the Internet" and "How to enable a publication for the Internet" in SQL Server Books Online
Author:	Neil Pike

jdbc

Q: Where can I get a JDBC driver for SQL Server? Does Microsoft write one? Which is the best one?

A: Microsoft doesn't supply a native JDBC driver for SQL Server, but it offers a JDBC-to-ODBC bridge that allows Java programmers to access back-end data sources using available ODBC drivers. The Microsoft JDBC-ODBC bridge is part of the core set of classes that come with the Microsoft Virtual Machine (Microsoft VM) for Java. For more information, see `http://www.microsoft.com/java/`.

You can get third-party drivers, servers, and bridges from a variety of vendors and some free open-source ones as well.

Which is the best one? As I don't use any of them I can't comment from personal experience. The two most commonly used seem to be WebLogic and OpenLink—and feedback on them seems good.

Some of the sites listed next maintain up-to-date lists of all vendors. The full list that I know of is:

- WebLogic: `http://weblogic.beasys.com` and `http://www.weblogic.com`: Type 2, 3 or 4; SQL 6.5 and 7.0; download a Type 4 driver direct from `http://www.weblogic.com/download/downloadkona.html`.
- `http://www.inetsoftware.de`: JDBC Type 4 drivers for Microsoft SQL Server 6.5, 7.0, and 2000; JDBC 1.22 driver to use with JDK 1.1x; and a JDBC 2.0 driver (i-net Sprinta) to use with Java 2 (JKD 1.2x).
- `http://www.inetsoftware.de/English/produkte/jdbctreiber/Default.htm`: JDBC 1.22.
- `http://www.inetsoftware.de/English/produkte/jdbc2/Default.htm`: JDBC 2.0.
- `http://www.openlinksw.com` (`http://www.openlinksw.co.uk`)
- `http://www.easysoft.com` and `http://beta.easysoft.com`: JDBC/ODBC bridge.
- `ftp://freetds.internetcds.com/pub/freetds_jdbc`: Type 4 open-source driver that is designed to work with SQL Server 6.5 and Sybase 11.x.
- `http://java.sun.com/products/jdbc`: From this page you may search or browse the database of JDBC technology drivers that support the JDBC 2.x and JDBC 1.x APIs.
- `http://lpv.home.texas.net`: LpVodbc is a multi-threaded JDBC-ODBC database server that runs on Windows 95, 98, and NT platforms.
- `http://www.avenir.net/products/jdbcdrivers.htm`
- `http://www.jturbo.com`
- `http://ourworld.compuserve.com/homepages/Ken_North/jdbcvend.htm`: Another list of JDBC drivers, servers, and vendors compiled by Ken North.
- `http://www.sco.com/java/`
- Merant. `http://www.merant.com/datadirect/products/jdbc/sl50/overview.asp`

Reference

v1.19 2000.06.13

Applies to SQL Server versions:	All
FAQ category:	Connectivity
Related FAQ article:	"How do I connect to SQL Server from a non-Microsoft machine such as Unix or OS/2?" (odbcunix, see page 132)
Related Microsoft Knowledge Base articles:	n/a
Other related information:	n/a
Author:	Neil Pike

mac

Q: How can I connect to SQL Server from a Macintosh?

A: It appears that the Microsoft-provided driver with Office for the Macintosh no longer works with SQL 7.0. It works fine with SQL 6.5 and below. Your options are:

- `http://www.snap.de` produces a DAL/ODBC DBMS called PrimeBase that can be used to front-end other ODBC applications.

- There are 32-bit 680x0 ODBC drivers on the Visual FoxPro for Power Macintosh CD version 3.0. The 32-bit drivers (v2.11 from Visigenic, v6.0b3 of the SQL Server driver) work with 16-bit FoxPro 2.6a as well. One issue is that on MacOS 8.5.1, you get Type 1, Type 3 or Type 10 errors when you quit the FoxPro 2.6, *but* if you compile a 680x0 executable it works OK.

- You can also get Mac drivers from `http://www.openlinksw.co.uk/`.

- `http://www.iodbc.org/` has an SDK.

- `http://www.meta-comm.com/odbcpatch` has a downloadable ODBC Incompatibility Fix for Microsoft Office 98 (Macintosh) and Microsoft SQL Server 7.0 to run on the server to make old clients connect OK.

- `http://odbc.net/router`

Reference

v1.10 2000.05.12	
Applies to SQL Server versions:	All
FAQ category:	Connectivity
Related FAQ article:	"How do I connect to SQL Server from a non-Microsoft machine such as Unix or OS/2?" (odbcunix, see page 132)
Related Microsoft Knowledge Base articles:	n/a
Other related information:	n/a
Author:	Neil Pike

mdacversion

Q: How do I know which version of MDAC I am running?

A: For a complete analysis of all data access components installed on your system, download and run the Component Checker tool from `http://www.microsoft.com/data`.

For a quick analysis of the core components, check the following table:

MDAC VERSION	MSDADC.DLL	OLEDB32.DLL
MDAC 1.5c	1.50.3506.0	N/A
MDAC 2.0 3.002.30 (GA)	2.0.3002.4	2.0.1706.0
MDAC 2.0 SP1 2.0.3002.23 (NT4 SP4)	2.0.3002.23	2.0.1706.0
MDAC 2.0 SP2 2.0.3002.28 (GA)	2.0.3002.23	2.0.1706.0
MDAC 2.1.0.3513.2 (SQL 7 / 6.5 SP5a)	2.10.3513.0	2.10.3513.0
MDAC 2.1.1.3711.6 (Internet Explorer 5)	2.10.3711.2	2.10.3711.9
MDAC 2.1.1.3711.11 (GA)	2.10.3711.2	2.10.3711.9
MDAC 2.1 SP2 2.1.2.4203 (GA)	2.10.4202.0	2.10.4202.0
MDAC 2.5 2.50.4403.12 (RTM/GA)	2.50.4403.0	2.50.4403.3

Reference

v1.04 2000.05.15	
Applies to SQL Server versions:	All
FAQ category:	Connectivity
Related FAQ articles:	n/a
Related Microsoft Knowledge Base articles:	n/a
Other related information:	n/a
Author:	Neil Pike

multiprotocolencryption

Q: How do I configure the Multiprotocol Net-Library to force encryption of packets in SQL Server?

A: To set up encryption for a specific user, follow these steps:

1. Create an account on the machine running SQL Server that matches the account (same username and password) on the client machine.

2. Turn on encryption for the Multiprotocol Net-Lib. This can be done for a specific client or through the server for all clients. For more information, see "Configuring Clients" in the Microsoft SQL Server Administrator's Companion.

To set up encryption for all users:

- On the machine running SQL Server:

1. In the Administrative Tools program group, in the User Manager utility, choose New User from the User menu. The New User dialog box appears.

2. In the dialog box, establish a user account with token1 as username and token2 as password.

3. Enable the Multiprotocol encryption option by following the instructions described in "Configuring Clients" in the Microsoft SQL Server Administrator's Companion.

4. Start SQL Server.

• On the machine running the client application:

5. In the Microsoft SQL Server 6.5 program group, double-click the SQL Client Configuration Utility. The SQL Server Client Configuration Utility dialog box appears.

6. Click the Advanced tab.

7. For the machine on which you set up the user account, specify a logical name in the Server box for SQL Server.

8. In the DLL Name list box, select Multiprotocol.

9. In the Connection String box, type the following:

   ncacn_ip_tcp: servername, token1, token2

   where

   servername specifies the DNS name for the server machine.

   token1 specifies the username of the user account on the server machine.

   token2 specifies the password for the user account on the server machine.

The username and password will be used by the client to establish an encrypted connection to SQL Server. Note that this user account is a valid Windows NT account and must be subject to Standard Security. The user account established on the server machine is not a SQL Server account. The client application must specify a valid SQL Server username and password to successfully connect to SQL Server. If the connection is unsuccessful because of an invalid username or password, the Multiprotocol Net-Lib will return error 5 (access denied).

You can also force using the Multiprotocol Net-Lib from the client by putting a `network=dbmsrpcn;` in your connect string.

Reference

v1.00 1999.04.26

Applies to SQL Server versions:	6.x, 7.0
FAQ categories:	Connectivity, Security
Related FAQ articles:	n/a
Related Microsoft Knowledge Base articles:	n/a
Other related information:	n/a
Author:	Neil Pike

multiprotocolencryptionworking

Q: How can I tell if Multiprotocol encryption is actually working?

A: The easiest way is to use a Network Sniffer between the client and the server to look at the network packets to see if any plain text is visible. Network Monitor is supplied free with NT 4.0 and above for this task.

For SQL 7.0, if encryption is set or forced at both the client and server then it doesn't encrypt. If it is set at only one end then it works fine. It is expected that this bug will be fixed in Service Pack 3 for 7.0.

Reference

v1.01 2000.03.25	
Applies to SQL Server versions:	6.x, 7.0
FAQ categories:	Connectivity, Security
Related FAQ articles:	"How do I configure the Multiprotocol Net-Library to force encryption of packets in SQL Server?" (multiprotocolencryption, page 121)
Related Microsoft Knowledge Base articles:	n/a
Other related information:	n/a
Author:	Neil Pike

netlibconnect

Q: Why can I connect to SQL Server with the TCP-IP Sockets Net-Library and not Named Pipes over IP/Multiprotocol?

A: Both these Net-Libs do indeed run over TCP-IP, so there are three reasons why IP Sockets may work and NamedPipes doesn't:

- Trusted connection: TCP-IP Sockets Net-Lib with SQL 6.5 and below does not require NT authentication whereas the other two do. For trusted connections you must be connecting from an NT domain or userid that the SQL Server machine can authenticate via its domain controller—usually this means a trust is needed if different NT domains are used for client and server.

- To prove whether this works or not, you can do a NET VIEW \\servername from the client. If this returns "invalid logon," "no domain controller exists" or "access denied," then the appropriate trust and credentials are not in place.

- Name resolution: You have probably done a PING <servername> and it has returned OK. This is fine for TCP-IP sockets as the name resolution methods are the same for PING as for sockets. However, for Named Pipes a different set of name-resolution methods is used (see NT Resource Kit/Technet for full details). Try a NET VIEW \\servername from the client to see if this connects OK—if it gets "error 53" then name resolution is probably the problem.

- Firewall sockets: Each of the Net-Libs uses different TCP-IP port numbers, so if there is a firewall involved maybe the correct ports are not being opened:

  - For TCP-IP sockets the default port for SQL Server is 1433.

  - For Multiprotocol (rpc) the ports are normally variable, but you can fix them. See Q164667 "Replication Setup Over a Firewall" in the Microsoft Knowledge Base for details.

  - For named pipes over IP, 137, 138 and 139 are used. As these are the same ones used for file/print, it is not recommended you allow these through the firewall.

Reference

v1.03 2000.04.08

Applies to SQL Server versions:	All
FAQ categories:	Connectivity, Troubleshooting
Related FAQ articles:	n/a
Related Microsoft Knowledge Base article:	Q164667 "Replication Setup Over a Firewall"
Other related information:	See "Connecting to SQL Server Over the Internet" in SQL Server Books Online
Author:	Neil Pike

netlibinfo

Q: How does a client talk to SQL Server? What is a Net-Lib? What network protocols are used? What Net-Libs support NT authentication or encryption?

A: There are good descriptions in the SQL Server portion of the Back-Office resource kits about how this all hangs together. This FAQ article will attempt to bring all the salient points together. It covers SQL 7.0 and earlier.

Client-to-server communication works in a layered fashion. Each layer "talks" to its neighboring layers in a standard fashion. I have given these layers arbitrary numbers—these numbers in no way correspond to the layer numbers in the OSI model. The only time layers can be bypassed are

- If a client application directly accesses the layer 3 low-level API interface, it can bypass layer 2.
- If shared-memory or a local named-pipe (".\pipe\sql\query") is used, layers 5 and 6 are bypassed.
- BCP and DTC do their own TDS formatting so bypass layer 3.

At the transport protocol layer this conversation goes between the client machine and the server machine (and back again). For all other layers the conversation is done locally, "in-memory" between the various DLLs involved.

Following is a list of the layers:

1. Client App: Written in VB, C or Delphi.
2. Client "High-Level" Data Access API: This level is optional—it is possible for the application to directly call the layer 3 interfaces. However, these interfaces generally need a lot of lines of client code or API calls to achieve the business requirement. Hence there are higher-level API's that call these lower level ones—higher-level API's need less client code or API calls to achieve the same result. Examples of these APIs are ADO, RDO, DAO, Embedded SQL and VBSQL.
3. Client DB Interface (OLE-DB, ODBC, DB-Library): Note that not all client languages can call this layer directly; for instance, VB cannot call OLE-DB directly, as VB lacks the necessary memory address pointer support.
4. Client TDS formatter: All communication to SQL Server has to be in TDS (Tabular Data Stream) format. See the "tds" FAQ article for more information.

5. Client Net-Lib: Shared Memory(local 95/98 only), Multi-Protocol, Named Pipes, TCP/IP Sockets, Novell IPX/SPX, AppleTalk(NT only), Banyan VINES.

6. Client Transport Protocol: NW Link IPX/SPX, NetBEUI, TCP/IP, AppleTalk, Banyan VINES.

Between layers 6 and 7 is where the actual network packets flow over Ethernet/ Token-Ring or FDDI.

7. Server Transport Protocol: NW Link IPX/SPX, NetBEUI, TCP/IP, AppleTalk, Banyan VINES.

8. Server Net-Lib: Shared Memory (local 95/98 only), Multi Protocol, Named Pipes(NT only), TCP/IP Sockets, Novell IPX/SPX, AppleTalk(NT only), Banyan VINES(NT only).

9. Server DB Interface (Open Data Services[ODS])

10. SQL Server

If you want to see some of the details described after this actually happens, you can do a network trace with Microsoft Network Monitor (or another network data-capture tool) and see the packets SQL sends and receives. If you use the version of NM that comes with Microsoft SMS 2.0 this contains a built-in TDS parser that will show detailed information.

If you want to see what Net-Lib a client has connected with, do a select from master..sysprocesses which shows the Net-Lib used.

The client and server *must* have at least one matching Transport Protocol. So if a client only runs TCP-IP, the server must have TCP-IP as one of its network protocols. To check what protocols are configured, look at Control Panel/Networks/ Protocols or run the command **NET CONFIG WORKSTATION** at a command prompt. The order in which these protocols are tried is determined by their binding order which you can see in the network applet in Control Panel under the Bindings tab. NT works will try all the protocols relevant to a Net-Lib "simultaneously"—it doesn't wait for one to fail to connect before trying the others. However, as only one network packet can be sent at a time, the various connection attempt packets must be sent in an order—which the bindings dictate. The first protocol used is usually the one to succeed (assuming the server is listening on that protocol).

The client and server *must* have at least one matching network library. For example, if the client connection is configured to use the Multi-Protocol Net-Lib, the server must be listening on that Net-Lib. A client is configured to have a default network library. If a connection needs to be set up to a server with a different Net-Lib, this can be configured with the advanced option of the SQL Client configuration utility. If you need to connect to the same server with different Net-Libs, this can be achieved by setting up multiple aliases via the advanced option.

The Multiprotocol Net-Lib is badly named. It should really be called the RPC Net-Lib. It uses the Remote Procedure Call API's that NT supports over netbeui, ip and ipx. It requires the Multiprotocol Net-Lib at both ends *and* the same network protocol. For example, netbeui rpc cannot talk to ip rpc.

To see what client Net-Libs are configured, run the SQL Client configuration utility, which is in the SQL program group.

To see what server Net-Libs are configured for SQL 6.5 and below, run SQL Setup and choose Configure Server and then the Network option. For SQL 7.0 you can run SQL Server Network Utility in the SQL program group.

Net-Libs and the Network Transport Protocol(s) They Support

NET-LIB	NETWORK TRANSPORT PROTOCOL SUPPORTED
Multi-Protocol	NW Link IPX/SPX, NetBEUI and TCP/IP
Named Pipes	NW Link IPX/SPX, NetBEUI and TCP/IP
TCP/IP Sockets	TCP/IP
IPX/SPX	NW Link IPX/SPX
AppleTalk	Appletalk
Banyan Vines	Vines IP
Shared-memory	Uses internal rpc calls; does not support a network transport protocol
DECNet	DECNet (this Net-Lib only existed in 6.5 and earlier)

Net-Libs and the DLLs They Use

NET-LIB	32-BIT DLL	16-BIT DLL
Multi-Protocol	dbmsrpcn.dll	dbmsrpc3.dll
Named Pipes	dbnmpntw.dll	dbnmp3.dll
TCP/IP Sockets	dbmssocn.dll	dbmssoc3.dll
IPX/SPX	dbmsspxn.dll	dbmsspx3.dll
AppleTalk	dbmsadsn.dll	n/a
Banyan Vines	dbmsvinn.dll	dbmsvin3.dll
Shared-memory	dbmsshrn.dll	n/a
DECNet	dbmsdecn.dll	n/a

Multi-Protocol and Named Pipes both support and enforce NT authentication for SQL 6.5 and below, but your client must be connected with a set of NT credentials that the server can validate. The easiest way to check this is to do a **NET USE \\<servername>\IPC$** command from the client. If this works then you can NT-authenticate with the server.

All Net-Libs support NT authentication for SQL 7.0 and above. SQL Server calls the NT SSPI interface to check credentials rather than the old NTLANMAN interface. However only Named Pipes and Multi-Protocol "enforce" this authentication—this is because the way these Net-Libs connect to the server they go through NT networking layers that demand authentication implicitly. If you use one of the other Net-Libs and do not make a trusted connection—you pass in SQL Server a standard userid and password—then you don't have to be NT authenticated. If you want to use these other Net-Libs with integrated security/NT authentication, you need to put `Trusted_Connection=yes` in your ODBC connection string, or `Integrated Security=SSPI` in your OLE-DB connection string.

Multiprotocol is the only Net-Lib that supports encryption in SQL 7.0 and below. (SQL 2000 supports encryption on other libraries via the operating system SSL support). All packets sent using Multiprotocol are encrypted—that includes all data, userid and password. Encryption (on/off) can be configured at the client and server end. At the server end you can enforce encryption—if you do this then any clients not configured for encryption won't be able to connect with the Multiprotocol Net-Lib. The encryption used is the built-in NT encryption libraries—therefore, the strength of encryption depends on NT. By default this is 40-bit—if you are able to apply the NT "high-encryption option" version then you will get 128-bit strength encryption.

If the clients are true NetWare clients they probably run IPX/SPX as their transport protocol (in Microsoft systems it may be NWLink, which is Microsoft's compatible protocol for IPX/SPX). In newer systems, you will find TCP/IP as the transport protocol because Netware is in a transition to TCP/IP as well. Keep in mind that even if we are talking about "true" Netware clients, they are still running a Microsoft operating system; there are no Netware clients that run a NW operating system.

The Client DB Interface APIs (OLE-DB, ODBC, DB-Library, Embedded SQL) do not call each other. ODBC does not run "over" DB-Lib or call it in any way. This is true for all current versions of these API's—in the past there was an early version of OLE-DB that used to work with an interface called Kagera that used to call ODBC, but this is an obsolete driver/version now.

Named Pipes requires "netbios" to be there to work. Therefore the relevant NT service has to be installed and working; for example, netbios over IP (NBT), or netbios over IPX.

It is possible to trace Net-Lib packets—at least with 6.5 and earlier anyway—without a network trace. This uses a tracing DLL/utility called NLSPY. This can be found with the BackOffice Resource Kit Part II.

SQL Server uses standard NT name resolution methods to turn a server name into a network level address.

Reference

v1.08 2000.06.13

Applies to SQL Server versions:	All
FAQ categories:	Connectivity
Related FAQ article:	"Where can I get details on the layout of the TDS protocol that SQL Server uses to talk to clients?" (tds, see page 138)
Related Microsoft Knowledge Base articles:	n/a
Other related information:	`http://msdn.microsoft.com/library/backgrnd/html/sqlquerproc.htm`, "Communication Components" in SQL Server Books Online
Author:	Neil Pike

netlibsetup

Q: How can I configure SQL Server to listen on other Net-Libraries? How can I tell what Net-Libraries are being used?

A: For SQL 6.5 and earlier, run SQL setup and choose Configure Server and then Network Support. This will tell you what Net-Libraries are installed and allows you to configure new ones.

For SQL 7.0 and above, the "Server Network Utility" installed in the SQL Server program group performs the same function.

For all versions of SQL Server you can check the SQL errorlog for "listening on" lines that tell you what Net-Libraries are being used.

Reference

v1.01 2000.03.25

Applies to SQL Server versions:	All
FAQ categories:	Connectivity, Server Administration and Tools
Related FAQ articles:	n/a
Related Microsoft Knowledge Base articles:	n/a
Other related information:	n/a
Author:	Neil Pike

odbcoledbjdbc

Q: Where can I get an OLE-DB/ODBC/JDBC driver to connect SQL Server to a particular product?

A: The best overall lists of ODBC/JDBC/OLEDB vendors I know are run by Ken North:

- `http://ourworld.compuserve.com/homepages/Ken_North/dataacce.htm`
- `http://ourworld.compuserve.com/homepages/Ken_North/odbcvend.htm`
- `http://ourworld.compuserve.com/homepages/Ken_North/jdbcvend.htm`
- `http://ourworld.compuserve.com/homepages/Ken_North/oledbven.htm`

Other links to try include:

- `http://www.unixodbc.org`
- `http://www.algonet.se/~sommar/mssqlperl/unix.html`

Reference

v1.03 2000.06.12

Applies to SQL Server versions:	All
FAQ category:	Connectivity
Related FAQ articles:	"How do I connect to SQL Server from a non-Microsoft machine such as Unix or OS/2?" (odbcunix, see page 132); "How can I connect to SQL Server from a Macintosh?" (mac, see page 119); "Where can I get a JDBC driver for SQL Server? Does Microsoft write one? Which is the best one?" (jdbc, see page 117)
Related Microsoft Knowledge Base articles:	n/a
Other related information:	n/a
Author:	Neil Pike

odbcstoredprocversion

Q: I get the following error connecting to SQL Server: "The ODBC catalog stored procedures installed on server <xxx> are version x.xx.xxx, version yy.yyy.yyyy or later is required to ensure proper operation." What should I do?

A: This is caused when the ODBC client code is upgraded and the server stored procedures are not. You can usually find a file called "INSTCAT.SQL" in your <nt>\system32 directory. Or you can download the latest drivers including this file from `www.microsoft.com/data`–they are part of the MDAC "product" which includes all odbc, rdo, ado and ole-db database access drivers.

Run the INSTCAT.SQL file against the relevant SQL servers using ISQL/ISQLW or any other query tool.

Reference

v1.01 2000.04.08

Applies to SQL Server versions:	All
FAQ categories:	Connectivity, Troubleshooting
Related FAQ articles:	n/a
Related Microsoft Knowledge Base articles:	Q137636 "INF: Relationship of the ODBC Driver to INSTCAT.SQL"

Other related information: "How to upgrade the catalog stored procedures"

Author: Neil Pike

odbcunix

Q: How do I connect to SQL Server from a non-Microsoft machine such as Unix or OS/2?

A: Microsoft doesn't supply its own drivers for non-Windows based clients any longer, so you have to use a third-party product. Your choices are:

- You can try acquiring, licensing or using a Sybase Open CT-Lib/Db-lib client if one exists for your operating system. Sybase supplies drivers for many non-Microsoft operating systems. The downside is that Sybase's and Microsoft's usage of the base TDS protocol has been diverging ever since the 4.x versions of SQL Server they both released. Since then 6.0, 6.5 and especially 7.0 of Microsoft's code, and versions 10, 11 and above of Sybase's code, mean that Sybase's CT-Libs may not give you full functionality and certainly won't give access to any SQL 7 or above specific features.

- To access SQL 7.0 you must use TDS 4.0 protocol versions of Sybase's CT-Lib libraries. With SQL 7.0, SP2 Microsoft has modified its server-side DB-Lib drivers to allow TDS 5.0 clients to connect. Further details are available in the Microsoft Knowledge Base Q239883 "FIX: SYBASE CT-Library Clients Cannot Connect to Microsoft SQL Server 7.0."

- You could reverse engineer the undocumented TDS protocol yourself. This could and does change between versions of SQL Server, so only attempt this if you want an ongoing maintenance challenge. Several people have done such reverse engineering for the portions of TDS they needed and have reported it's not that difficult. On such attempt is the FreeTDS project that is reverse engineering the TDS specification and is currently implementing CTLIB, DBLIB and JDBC interfaces for TDS. ODBC and Perl DBD drivers are planned.

- The FreeTDS JDBC driver is a type 4 driver and should work on any JVM. The CTLIB and DBLIB interfaces are known to compile under AIX, Linux and FreeBSD without any problems. You can obtain more information from `http://www.freetds.org`.

- If you are using a PERL script, see FAQ entry "perl," as some of the Perl options will work from non-Microsoft platforms.

- If you can use Java/JDBC, see the FAQ entry "jdbc" for details of those options.

- If you are connecting via Rexx, try `http://www.angelfire.com/wa/djawa`.

- The recommended option is that you acquire an ODBC/OLE-DB driver from a driver vendor that will offer ongoing support. However, many ODBC vendors have either moved from pure client drivers to "three-tier" driver systems which many people don't want, or they have moved from ODBC into OLE-DB. Therefore you may have trouble finding just what you want. (Success and failure stories are welcome—but be persistent with whichever vendors you talk to. They may not be actively advertising what you want, but that doesn't mean they don't still have old but working copies of it buried in a cupboard somewhere).

- Vendors to try are (in no particular order):

  - OpenLink—`http://www.openlinksw.com`

  - Merant—`http://www.merant.com/datadirect/products/odbc/Connect/overview.asp`

  - Easysoft—`http://www.easysoft.com`

  - If you need to connect from a Macintosh, see the "mac" FAQ entry.

  - For OpenVMS try Trifox Inc. They provide Perl, Java, JDBC, C, COBOL and C++ access from OpenVMS to Microsoft SQL server as well as 10 other DBMSs on various platforms. See their site at: `http://www.trifox.com`.

  - For other pointers to ODBC/JDBC/OLEDB vendors see the "odbcoledbjdbc" FAQ entry.

Connectivity

Reference

v1.39 2000.06.12	
Applies to SQL Server versions:	All
FAQ category:	Connectivity
Related FAQ articles:	perl, jdbc, mac, odbcoledbjdbc, tds
Related Microsoft Knowledge Base articles:	Q239883 "FIX: SYBASE CT-Library Clients Cannot Connect to Microsoft SQL Server 7.0"
Other related information:	n/a
Author:	Neil Pike

rcmd

Q: Why can't I use RCMD.EXE via xp_cmdshell from SQL Server?

A: To access any "network resources" you need to run SQL Server under a user account and not the default LocalSystem account. The LocalSystem account's permissions are restricted to the local machine, and cannot be authenticated by any other resource. You can check what account the MSSQLServer service is running under, by looking at Control Panel/Services, highlight MSSQLServer and choosing the Startup option. This should be changed as necessary.

Without this change you will get an "error 5 - Access denied."

However, RCMD.EXE doesn't seem to work even with this change. This is because of the way RCMD in the NT resource kit is coded—it probably expects there to be a keyboard/mouse defined in the user context, which there isn't.

So the short answer is that unless you use a version of rcmd.exe without this restriction, it won't work.

Reference

v1.01 2000.04.15	
Applies to SQL Server versions:	All
FAQ categories:	Connectivity, Troubleshooting
Related FAQ articles:	n/a
Related Microsoft Knowledge Base article:	n/a
Other related information:	n/a
Author:	Neil Pike

slowlink

Q: How can I speed up SQL Server applications running over slow links?

A: First we need to define what a "slow" link is. Typically this is anything from 64 Kbits per second down. On links of this speed the size of a resultset and the number of network packets that are exchanged can make a significant difference to overall response times.

First, either do a network trace, or use SQL Trace/Profiler to see what exactly is being transferred during a typical client session. Then try the following:

1. If large intermediate resultsets are being returned, see if you can write the logic into a stored procedure so that only the end results are returned. Try to reduce the number of sent and received pieces of SQL by using stored procedures as much as possible.

2. If the connection uses ODBC, and the overhead it creates running **sp_serverinfo**, **sp_cursor** or temporary stored procedures is causing the problem, then use passthrough queries if possible and turn off the temporary stored procedure creation in the ODBC dsn properties.

3. Configure the DB-Lib/ODBC connection to use the TCP-IP sockets Net-Lib. This performs best over slow network connections and can make a significant difference.

4. Is the application using client-side cursors? Try version 3 or above of ODBC, which should give you transparent server-side cursors.

5. Don't return 1000 rows to the client if all they need to see on the screen is the first 20.

6. If there are large amounts of static data that need to be retrieved, then consider replication to a client copy of Access, SQL 6.5 Workstation or, with SQL 7.0, a local copy of SQL Server. Over slow links this should only be used for mainly static data.

7. Don't send any SQL across the link at all. Use Citrix or NT Terminal Edition to run the application centrally and install ICA/RDP clients on the remote machines. The applications then all run locally on a server next to the SQL server (the same box isn't recommended). The only things that go across the slow link are screen updates, which are optimized and compressed and so will often work satisfactorily on a 14.4 Kbit per second modem link. This also has the advantage that there is no longer any client code to maintain at the remote sites either. Citrix, Microsoft and Compaq's sites provide white papers about sizing the servers you will need to run in this mode.

Reference

v1.01 2000.01.19

Applies to SQL Server versions:	All
FAQ categories:	Connectivity, Troubleshooting
Related FAQ articles:	n/a
Related Microsoft Knowledge Base articles:	n/a
Other related information:	n/a
Author:	Neil Pike

sockets

Q: How do I configure a connection to use TCP/IP sockets with SQL Server?

A: For SQL 6.x and below, follow these steps:

1. Run the SQL Client Configuration Utility on the client in question.

2. Select the Advanced tab.

3. In the Server box, type the name your application will use to reference the server.

4. For DLL Name, select TCP/IP Sockets.

5. For a server name that will be resolved to a numeric IP address, just enter the name into the Connection string. (This should work if you can PING that server by name.) For a numeric IP address, just type the IP address into the Connection String. If you want to use a different port from the default (1433 is the default) follow the IP name or address with a comma and the alternate port. For example: 123.123.123.123,1434.

6. Click the Add/Modify button.

For SQL 7.0 and above, follow these steps:

1. Run the SQL Server Client Network Utility.

2. One the General tab, click Add.

3. In the Server alias box, type the name your application will use to reference the server.

4. Select TCP/IP for the Network library.

5. For a server name that will be resolved to a numeric IP address, just enter the name into the Computer name box. (This should work if you can PING that server by name.) For a numeric IP address, just type the IP address into the Computer name box. If you want to use a different port from the default you can change it here—otherwise leave the default as 1433.

6. Click OK.

Reference

v1.01 2000.04.22

Applies to SQL Server versions:	All
FAQ category:	Connectivity
Related FAQ articles:	n/a
Related Microsoft Knowledge Base articles:	n/a
Other related information:	n/a
Author:	Neil Pike

sql7dblibsupport

Q: Does SQL 7.0/2000 support DB-Library? What about 16-bit clients such as DOS?

A: Yes it does, but DB-Library is functionally stabilized at the 6.5 level. Therefore, if a DB-Library client on whatever platform worked against a 6.5 database it should work against the same database migrated to SQL 7.0/2000.

None of the SQL 7.0 features, such as unicode or character columns greater than 255 characters, are in DB-Library though. So if you utilize any SQL 7.0 features, then these can only be accessed by ODBC 3.7 or OLE DB clients. This is also true for 16-bit clients. These clients are supported, but only with the 6.5 levels of ODBC/DB-Library code. 16-bit clients cannot access new SQL 7.0 features either.

The 16-bit client code is not supplied with 7.0/2000. You will have to get the code and DOS and Win 3.x drivers from the 6.5 CD-ROM.

Reference

v1.03 2000.04.28	
Applies to SQL Server versions:	7.0, 2000
FAQ category:	Connectivity
Related FAQ articles:	n/a
Related Microsoft Knowledge Base articles:	n/a
Other related information:	n/a
Author:	Neil Pike

tds

Q: Where can I get details on the layout of the TDS protocol that SQL Server uses to talk to clients?

A: Microsoft doesn't publish any information on the TDS protocol unfortunately, so your choices are:

1. Network trace and parse/reverse engineer the packets yourself. The Network Monitor 2.0 tool that comes with Microsoft SMS 2.0 has a TDS parser with it, so this formats packets in the trace for you.

2. Several people have done such reverse engineering for the portions of TDS

they needed and reported it's not that difficult. FreeTDS is a project that is reverse engineering the TDS specification and is currently implementing CTLIB, DBLIB and JDBC interfaces for TDS. ODBC and Perl DBD drivers are planned. The FreeTDS JDBC driver is a type 4 driver and should work on any JVM. The CTLIB and DBLIB interfaces are known to compile under AIX, Linux and FreeBSD without any problems.

More information is available from `http://www.freeTDS.org`.

For a mailing list archive, see `http://franklin.oit.unc.edu/cgi-bin/lyris.pl?enter=freetds`.

You can obtain source code from `ftp://freetds.internetcds.com/pub/freetds_dbd/` or `http://www.freetds.org/download.html`.

Reference

v1.04 2000.05.14

Applies to SQL Server versions:	All
FAQ category:	Connectivity
Related FAQ article:	"How does a client talk to SQL Server? What is a Net-Lib? What network protocols are used? What Net-Libs support NT authentication or encryption?" (netlibinfo, see page 125)
Related Microsoft Knowledge Base articles:	n/a
Other related information:	n/a
Author:	Neil Pike

Database Administration

This section covers database-specific administration topics including backups and performance. Programming topics that are specific to DBAs are also covered here.

amendcolumns

Q: How can I add, amend or delete columns in SQL Server? For example, how can I change Int to Char, char(5) to char(15) or NULL to NOT NULL?

A: Under SQL 7.0 all the above are easily done with the standard ANSI ALTER TABLE DDL command. Changes also can be made using the SQL Enterprise Manager GUI.

With SQL 6.5 and below, it is only possible to *add* a nullable column—or an IDENTITY column, which seems to work even if it's not NULLable. For *any* other change a new table must be created, the data copied across, and the tables renamed.

Certain third-party tools provide a GUI interface to do this—that makes it look transparent—however they are really doing all the work described above, so if you make the change to a large table it will take a long time to do the work.

Examples of tools include:

- Microsoft's Visual Database Tools (part of Visual Interdev Enterprise Edition)
- SQL Programmer: `http://www.sfi-software.com`
- Xcase: `http://www.xcase.com`
- Desktop DB: `http://www.cai.com/products/platinum`
- Speed Ferret

Database Administration

Reference

v1.10 2000.06.02

Applies to SQL Server versions:	All
FAQ category:	Database Administration
Related FAQ articles:	n/a
Related Microsoft Knowledge Base articles:	n/a
Other related information:	"Modifying Column Properties" in Books Online 7
Author:	Neil Pike

ansinullsinsp

Q: How can I tell if a stored procedure, trigger or view was created with the ANSI NULLS setting on?

A: You can use the OBJECTPROPERTY function:

```
SELECT OBJECTPROPERTY(OBJECT_ID('stored_procedure_name'),'ExecIsAnsiNullsOn')
```

This returns 1 for yes, 0 for no, and null if the parameters are invalid.

With SQL 6.5 this option is resolved at query execution time so this option is not relevant during object creates. With SQL 7.0, it is resolved at creation time and so the property has to be stored with the object.

This setting is important because it dictates how NULLs are compared and the default NULLability for created tables. With this option set OFF, NULL = NULL. With it ON, NULL does not equal anything. Much more information on this can be found in Books Online.

Reference

v1.03 2000.05.25	
Applies to SQL Server versions:	7.0, 2000
FAQ category:	Database Administration
Related FAQ articles:	n/a
Related Microsoft Knowledge Base articles:	n/a
Other related information:	"Ansi Nulls" in Books Online 7
Author:	Neil Pike

backupbuffersize

Q: Should I amend the SQL Server Backup Buffer Size? Why am I getting an error about it in SQL 7.0 with a third-party backup tool?

A: This parameter only applies to SQL 6.x. Under most circumstances it doesn't need to be changed and even then you would need to test in your own environment to see whether it made any difference in your particular disk or tape subsystem. There are too many variables such as disk speed, RAID controller buffers, tape speed and tape block size to say whether increasing this area of memory that SQL uses will make any difference.

The example figures below are taken from a large system doing a dump to three striped DLT 7000 drives from a very fast disk subsystem with 40 spindles and varying the "backup buffer size" parameter. The figures don't change that much, but in general lower numbers of buffers were better.

1	01:12:00.687
2	01:11:28.860
3	01:11:50.969
4	01:13:18.859
5	01:15:01.750
6	01:17:15.594
7	01:16:41.516
8	01:16:11.469

If you get an error saying "Configured value of backup buffer size is invalid," you are on SQL 7 and using a third-party backup agent. SQL 7 does not have this parameter any longer. Any third-party agent that produces this error needs to be upgraded to a SQL 7-aware version.

Reference

v1.02 2000.03.28

Applies to SQL Server versions:	6.x, 7.0
FAQ categories:	Database Administration, Troubleshooting
Related FAQ articles:	n/a
Related Microsoft Knowledge Base article:	Q143294 "INF: Implementing DUMP and LOAD to PIPE Devices"
Other related information:	n/a
Author:	Neil Pike

backupexpiredisk

Q: How can I overwrite expired backups on a disk device to save on space and still keep a rolling <x> days there?

A: You can't. Without searching the entire file, SQL has no way of knowing how much space each backup takes. To delete one part it would have to read the current backup file and write out all the unexpired dumps to a new file and then delete and rename. Only then could it write the new one to the end. All this would take far too long and too much disk space.

The expiration date is there to prevent accidental overwrites and nothing else.

If you want to keep a rolling number of dumps, write them out with different names each day using the DISK= option of the dump command. Then have a regular task check these dumps and delete old ones.

Reference

v1.00 1999.01.28

Applies to SQL Server versions:	All
FAQ category:	Database Administration
Related FAQ articles:	n/a
Related Microsoft Knowledge Base articles:	n/a
Other related information:	n/a
Author:	Neil Pike

backupstatsprogrammatically

Q: How can I programmatically kick off a SQL dump and dynamically get back statistics on how far it has proceeded?

A: You can do it with DMO. Here is some sample code supplied by Gert Drapers. You will need to wrap your own program and form around it.

```
Option Explicit

Dim mSQLServer As SQLDMO.SQLServer
Dim WithEvents mBackupEvents As SQLDMO.Backup

Private Sub cmdBackupWithEvents_Click()
    Dim mDatabase As SQLDMO.Database
    Dim mBackup As New SQLDMO.Backup
    Set mBackupEvents = mBackup

    For Each mDatabase In mSQLServer.Databases
        If (mDatabase.Name <> "model" And mDatabase.Name <> "tempdb") Then
            mBackup.Database = mDatabase.Name
            mBackup.Files = "c:\dump\" & mDatabase.Name & Format(Date,
"yyyy-mm-dd") & ".bak"
            mBackup.SQLBackup mSQLServer
        End If
    Next

    Set mBackupEvents = Nothing
    Set mBackup = Nothing

End Sub

Private Sub cmdConnect_Click()
    Set mSQLServer = New SQLDMO.SQLServer
    Call mSQLServer.Connect("(local)", "sa", "")
    Msg "Connected " & Now()
End Sub

Private Sub cmdDisconnect_Click()
    If (Not mSQLServer Is Nothing) Then
        mSQLServer.DisConnect
        Set mSQLServer = Nothing
    End If
    Msg "Disconnected " & Now()
End Sub

Private Sub mBackupEvents_Complete(ByVal Message As String)
    txtOut = txtOut & Message & vbCrLf
End Sub
```

```
Private Sub mBackupEvents_NextMedia(ByVal Message As String)
    txtOut = txtOut & Message & vbCrLf
End Sub

Private Sub mBackupEvents_PercentComplete(ByVal Message As String, ByVal
Percent As Long)
    txtOut = txtOut & Message & "Percent " & Percent & vbCrLf
End Sub
```

Reference

v1.02 2000.05.25

Applies to SQL Server versions:	6.5, 7.0, 2000
FAQ category:	Database Administration
Related FAQ articles:	n/a
Related Microsoft Knowledge Base articles:	n/a
Other related information:	"Handling SQL-DMO Events" in Books Online 7
Authors:	Neil Pike, Gert Drapers

backupzipdrive

Q: Why can't I backup and restore my SQL Server database to a Jaz or Zip drive from SQL Enterprise Manager?

A: The reason is that the SQL Enterprise Manager lists only those drives that NT tells it are permanently attached. Jaz drives, Zip drives and writeable CD-ROMS are all removable media and so they aren't listed.

However, as long as there is formatted media in the drive, all the MSSQLSERVER service does is issue standard NT I/O calls, so it is happy to write to it. You just need to use the underlying T-SQL commands—issued from ISQLW, for example—to do the job:

```
BACKUP DATABASE <xyz> TO DISK = 'J:\.....'
```

Alternatively, for Jaz or Zip drives you can use the IoMega tools to mark the drive as non-removable. After a restart of NT it should then see the drives.

Reference

v1.02 2000.03.28

Applies to SQL Server versions:	All
FAQ Category:	Database Administration
Related FAQ articles:	n/a
Related Microsoft Knowledge Base articles:	n/a
Other related information:	n/a
Author:	Neil Pike

bcptriggers

Q: Are triggers fired or constraints checked with BCP on SQL Server?

A: With SQL 6.5 and below, rules, triggers and constraints are ignored, even with BCP run in "slow" mode. Column defaults are used for fields with null values.

With SQL 7.0 there is an option to check constraints (not triggers), but this is not the default. If you want this, specify the "CHECK_CONSTRAINTS" hint. See Books Online for more details.

With SQL 2000 it is possible for triggers to fire as well.

Reference

v1.03 2000.05.25

Applies to SQL Server versions:	All
FAQ Categories:	Database Administration, Server Administration and Tools
Related FAQ articles:	n/a
Related Microsoft Knowledge Base articles:	n/a
Other related information:	"bcp Utility" in Books Online 7, "Copying Tables with Defaults, Rules, and/or Triggers" in Books Online 6
Author:	Neil Pike

changeowner

Q: How can I change the owner of an object?

A: With SQL 7.0 and above there is a stored procedure (sp_changeobjectowner) to do this, but it works only for tables, views, stored procedures, rules and defaults — not user-defined types or dependent objects such as triggers or constraints. Under SQL 6.5 and earlier the only supported method is to drop and recreate the object under the new owner (you must also drop any objects that depend on it and save and reload any data in any tables involved).

Alternatively, it can be achieved by using the unsupported approach of directly addressing and updating the appropriate system table, as follows.

1. Get the uid number for the current owner and the new owner from sysusers.
2. Configure your server to allow updates to system tables.
3. Begin a transaction.
4. Update the appropriate system table, changing the uid column value for the object concerned to the uid you want.
5. Check that the right number of rows have been affected.
6. Commit or rollback the transaction, depending on the result.
7. Configure your server to *not* allow updates to system tables.
8. Stop and start your SQL Server.

The last step is necessary as portions of system tables are kept in memory by SQL Server, and the only way to force these to update is to recycle SQL Server.

As an example:

```
select * from sysobjects where uid = user_id('user1')

exec sp_configure 'allow updates', '1'

reconfigure WITH OVERRIDE
```

```
go

BEGIN TRANSACTION

update sysobjects set uid = user_id('dbo') where uid = user_id('user1')

COMMIT TRANSACTION

exec sp_configure 'allow updates', '0'

reconfigure WITH OVERRIDE

go
```

Reference

v1.05 2000.05.25	
Applies to SQL Server versions:	All
FAQ category:	Database Administration
Related FAQ articles:	n/a
Related Microsoft Knowledge Base articles:	n/a
Other related information:	n/a
Author:	Neil Pike

checkident

Q: Why do my SQL Server identity values get out of sync causing gaps or duplicates? Is there anything I can do about it?

A: Why? Because of inherent problems with the way identity values were implemented. For performance reasons the current identity value isn't updated and committed in the system tables every time a row is inserted. This would lead to unacceptably bad performance, especially with SQL 6.x's page-level locking architecture—it could even lead to deadlocks. Therefore the value is stored in memory and only committed to disk when a clean shutdown of SQL occurs.

So, if SQL doesn't shut down cleanly, or there is some memory problem caused by an exception violation, the value will not be correct next time SQL starts. There are also some other bugs that would cause the value not to be updated, but Microsoft has fixed most of these with service packs.

The only thing you can do about this problem is to put dbcc checkident (<tablename>) statements in a startup stored-procedure (for details see Books Online) so that the values get fixed every time SQL starts. For very large tables this may take a few minutes.

MS's own code and stored procedures are not immune to this. One very common case is where you get duplicate key messages on sysbackuphistory (in MSDB) when you do a database dump. This is because the table uses an identity column.

This error should not occur with SQL 7.0 and above as Microsoft has reworked how the identity columns function internally.

Reference

v1.01 2000.01.22	
Applies to SQL Server versions:	All
FAQ categories:	Database Administration, Troubleshooting
Related FAQ articles:	n/a
Related Microsoft Knowledge Base article:	Q198572 "BUG: IDENTITY Out of Sync If Server Is Shut Down w/o Checkpoint"
Other related information:	"DBCC CHECKIDENT" in Books Online 6 and 7
Author:	Neil Pike

columnexists

Q: How can I tell if a column for a table already exists?

A: There are two ways (with SQL 7):

```
IF EXISTS(SELECT * FROM INFORMATION_SCHEMA.COLUMNS WHERE TABLE_NAME = '<tbl>'
AND COLUMN_NAME = '<col>')
```

or

```
if columnproperty (object_id('<tbl>'), '<col>', 'AllowsNull') IS NOT NULL
```

Reference

v1.00 1999.11.25	
Applies to SQL Server versions:	7.0
FAQ category:	Database Administration
Related FAQ articles:	n/a
Related Microsoft Knowledge Base articles:	n/a
Other related information:	n/a
Author:	Neil Pike

commentschema

Q: Can I add comments to SQL Server's schema as I can with Access?

A: No—SQL Server does not currently support this. You can, of course, store comments in a user table if you wish. If this table were created in the model database, it would be created automatically for all new databases.

Reference

v1.01 2000.02.28	
Applies to SQL Server versions:	All
FAQ category:	Database Administration
Related FAQ articles:	n/a
Related Microsoft Knowledge Base articles:	n/a
Other related information:	n/a
Author:	Neil Pike

comparetables

Q: How can I compare the contents of two tables to see whether they are identical?

A: You can use either of two methods:

- BCP them both out and use the NT COMP.EXE command to compare them. If you prefer a graphical utility to do the compare, try WINDIFF from the NT Resource Kit.

- If table A and table B have unique indexes on them, do:

```
select count(*) from tableA
select count(*) from tableB
```

- If they don't have unique indexes on them, then do:

```
select count(*) from (select distinct * from tableA) as a
select count(*) from (select distinct * from tableB) as b
```

- Check that the counts are the same. If they are not, then obviously the tables don't match. If the counts do match, then do:

```
select count(*)
from (select * from tableA
        UNION
        select * from tableB) as t
```

- If the count from this query is the same as the previous counts, then the two tables are identical. This is because a UNION does a DISTINCT merge of the two result sets. Therefore the two tables will "collapse" back into one if and only if they are identical.

Reference

v1.01 2000.04.15

Applies to SQL Server versions:	All
FAQ Category:	Database Administration
Related FAQ articles:	n/a
Related Microsoft Knowledge Base articles:	n/a
Other related information:	n/a
Authors:	Neil Pike, Roy Harvey

compress

Q: Can I compress a SQL Server .DAT device or file? Will it cause any problems? Can I compress data inside a table?

A: Yes you can as long as you stop SQL first—NT needs exclusive access to a file in order to compress it. With SQL 6.5 and below, in theory everything should be fine as SQL isn't interested in what is happening down at the file system level.

However, in practice, this is absolutely *not* recommended (even with 6.5) for the following reasons:

- With a compressed drive the NT writes are always done in a "lazy" asynchronous manner. For an application like SQL that *must* know when an I/O has completed to the disk and not to some unprotected memory area, this is unacceptable.

- It is not recommended or supported by Microsoft. Reason enough in itself! MS Product Support Services is unlikely to want to help you unless you can re-create your problem on an uncompressed database—so why bother?

- It can prevent the ability to recover due to SQL not really knowing how much disk space there is.

- Performance—especially if you compress an empty database or device and then start filling it up—there is then a lot of overhead in NTFS expanding the file as previously it had compressed very well due to the large number of binary zeroes used to pad empty pages. (I have seen systems halve in speed because the SQL devices or files were compressed.)

- SQL Server 7.0 depends on sector-aligned writes for the log file, which NT compressed files do not guarantee.

- Many people have reported problems with SQL 7 when doing disk-intensive updates like index creation. This may be due to the previous reason.

As for compressing data inside a table, SQL Server has no functionality to do this. You could do it yourself using code at the client end, or with an extended stored procedure, but that's it.

Reference

v1.08 2000.04.15	
Applies to SQL Server versions:	All
FAQ category:	Database Administration
Related FAQ articles:	n/a
Related Microsoft Knowledge Base article:	Q231347 "INF: SQL Server Databases Not Supported on Compressed Volumes"
Other related information:	n/a
Author:	Neil Pike

dbmaintwiz

Q: Why does the SQL Server Database Maintenance Wizard warn about using it on databases greater than 400MB in size?

A: The DMW sets up an "aggressive" set of DBCC and other health checks. On "large" databases this sort of housekeeping can take a long time, so you might not want to do everything every night. In this situation you might want to set up your own maintenance tasks, perhaps only running CHECKDB once per week, and NEWALLOC every night, with index rebuilds once a month or so.

Microsoft's definition of "large" is 400MB—probably a bit low given the speed of current CPU's and disks. The answer is, if you're happy with the time it takes to run the DMW generated tasks, then stick with it, regardless of your database size.

Reference

v1.01 2000.04.21	
Applies to SQL Server version:	6.x
FAQ category:	Database Administration
Related FAQ articles:	n/a
Related Microsoft Knowledge Base article:	Q170638 "INF: DB Maintenance Wizard Warns About Use on Large Databases"
Other related information:	n/a
Author:	Neil Pike

decryptsp

Q: How can I decrypt a SQL Server stored procedure?

A: Here is the code for SQL 6.5:

```
/**********************************************/
/* REVISED REC'D 5/21/98                      */
/* sp_decrypt_object       Tom Sager 01/26/98 */
/*                                            */
/* Decrypts objects (views, procedures & trigs) */
/* created with the WITH ENCRYPTION option.   */
/*                                            */
/* Uses the encrypt() built-in function to find */
/* a plaintext string that encrypts to the same */
/* value as stored in the text column of the  */
/* syscomments table.                         */
/*                                            */
/**********************************************/
create proc sp_decrypt_object
          (@objname varchar(30))
WITH ENCRYPTION
as

SET NOCOUNT ON

declare @errmsg    varchar(80)
declare @encrtext  varchar(255)
declare @decrtext  varchar(255)
declare @testtext  varchar(255)
declare @printline varchar(255)
declare @textlen   int
declare @lup       int
declare @match     char(1)
declare @testchar  smallint
declare @begblk    smallint
declare @endblk    smallint
```

Database Administration

```
if (select count(*)
      from sysobjects
      where name = @objname) = 0
  begin
    select @errmsg = 'Object '
                 +@objname
                 +' not found in database '
                 +DB_NAME()
    print @errmsg
    return 1
  end

if (select count(*) from sysobjects t1,
                         syscomments t2
                   where t1.name = @objname
                     and t1.id = t2.id
                     and t2.texttype & 4 != 0) = 0
  begin
    select @errmsg = 'Object '
                 +@objname
                 +' is not encrypted in database '
                 +DB_NAME()
    print @errmsg
    return 1
  end

DECLARE comments_cursor CURSOR for
        select t1.text
          from syscomments t1,
               sysobjects t2
         where t1.id = t2.id
           and t2.name = @objname
          order by t1.colid

OPEN comments_cursor

FETCH NEXT FROM comments_cursor
           INTO @encrtext
```

```
WHILE (@@fetch_status <> -1)
 BEGIN
  IF (@@fetch_status <> -2)
   BEGIN
    select @decrtext = REPLICATE(' ', 255)
    select @textlen = DATALENGTH(@encrtext)
    select @lup = 1
    select @match = 'n'
    while (@lup <= @textlen)
     begin
      select @testchar = 0
      select @match = 'n'
      while (@match = 'n')
       begin
        select @decrtext =
          STUFF(@decrtext,@lup,1,CHAR(@testchar))
        select @testtext = encrypt(@decrtext)
        if ASCII(SUBSTRING(@testtext,@lup,1)) =
           ASCII(SUBSTRING(@encrtext,@lup,1))
         begin
          select @match = 'y'
         end
         select @testchar = @testchar + 1
         if (@testchar > 255)
           begin
             print 'Error...no match found'
             return 1
           end
       end
       select @lup = @lup + 1
     end
     select @begblk = 1
     select @endblk = 1
     while (@endblk <= @textlen)
      begin
       if (substring(@decrtext,@endblk,1) = 0x0a)
        begin
         select @printline = @printline +
           SUBSTRING(@decrtext
                  ,@begblk
                  ,@endblk-@begblk+1)
         print @printline
```

Database Administration

```
          select @begblk = @endblk + 1
          select @endblk = @begblk
          select @printline = NULL
         end
        select @endblk = @endblk + 1
       end
      select @printline = @printline +
        SUBSTRING(@decrtext
                 ,@begblk
                 ,@endblk-@begblk+1)
    END
    FETCH NEXT FROM comments_cursor INTO @encrtext
  END
print @printline
CLOSE comments_cursor

DEALLOCATE comments_cursor
GO
```

Reference

v1.00 1999.12.14	
Applies to SQL Server version:	6.5
FAQ categories:	Database Administration, Security
Related FAQ articles:	n/a
Related Microsoft Knowledge Base articles:	n/a
Other related information:	n/a
Authors:	Neil Pike, Tom Sager

dropprimarykey

Q: How do I drop the index related to a primary key? DROP INDEX doesn't work.

A: Because the index is built as part of a constraint, the way to drop it is to drop the constraint:

First find the constraint_name by executing:

```
sp_helpconstraint table_name
```

Then drop the constraint with the following syntax:

```
ALTER TABLE [database.[owner].]table_name
  DROP CONSTRAINT constraint_name [, constraint_name2]...]
```

Reference

v1.01 2000.04.21

Applies to SQL Server versions:	All
FAQ category:	Database Administration
Related FAQ articles:	n/a
Related Microsoft Knowledge Base articles:	n/a
Other related information:	n/a
Author:	Neil Pike

fastestsortorder

Q: Which sort order should I choose for my SQL Server for the fastest performance?

A: Binary sort order is approximately 15 percent faster than others for key comparisons. However this is only one tiny part of the processing that SQL needs to do and with the massive increase in processor speed since SQL Server was first released this is no longer an issue.

For example, if you choose binary (or another case-sensitive sort order) then you may need to resort to queries with where clauses like "where UPPER(columnname) = UPPER(searchargument)". This prevents the query optimizer from selecting an index and forces a table scan—with disastrous performance consequences.

Therefore it is recommended that you only choose binary for other reasons—not performance.

Reference

v1.03 2000.04.24

Applies to SQL Server versions:	All
FAQ categories:	Database Administration, Installation and Upgrades
Related FAQ articles:	n/a
Related Microsoft Knowledge Base articles:	n/a
Other related information:	"Sort Order Performance" in Books Online 7, "Performance Comparisons" in Books Online 6
Author:	Neil Pike

filegroups-spreadtablesover

Q: Should I spread tables over multiple files or filegroups?

A: There's no straight answer to this question. It depends on the hardware your system is running on and the backup strategy and requirements you want to implement.

A common way to improve performance in the past was to spread tables and indexes across multiple files placed on different disks connected to multiple disk-controllers—this was achieved with the use of segments in SQL 6.5 and earlier. The idea behind this strategy is to have multiple parallel I/O channel in order to read in parallel as much data as possible.

As the price of hardware-based striping solutions (such as RAID level 0, 5 or 1+0) is much lower today, RAID is a fast and good implementation that guarantees good performance in most cases. Additionally it decreases the administrative work needed to create and maintain multiple files or filegroups.

You may still want to use filegroups to spread the data across multiple files under the following scenarios:

- If your system has multiple processors, SQL Server can perform multiple scans of the data if a table is placed on a filegroup that contains multiple files. Additionally, when a query joins tables on different filegroups, each table can be read in parallel.

- You want to be able to restore single tables of a database (SQL 7 and above don't support restoring single tables, but they do support restoring filegroups, so having just one table on a filegroup achieves this capability).

- Your system has multiple hardware stripe sets.

When planning the architecture of your system, keep in mind that SQL Server 7.0 sets the maximum number of concurrent asynchronous I/O operations (option "max async io") per file while previous versions used the option for the whole installation. This means that the more files you use, the more asynchronous I/O you can reach. With SQL 2000 and above, the max async io parameter no longer exists and is auto-tuned by SQL Server.

For example, if you set "max async io" to 32 with SQL Server 6.5 you can get a maximum of 32 outstanding asynchronous I/O operations, no matter how many devices you create or how smart your disk subsystem is. Setting the same value with SQL Server 7.0, which by the way is the default value, means that the maximum number of outstanding operations equals 32 multiplied by the number of files.

Please note that increasing the "max async io," or having multiple files, doesn't necessarily mean you will have an increase in performance. If your disk subsystem is not adequate you may well experience a loss in performance—if this happens then disk queues will occur which you can check for with NT Performance monitor. If a disk queue for a logical drive is regularly higher than the number of physical disks that make up the logical drive, you may have an overloaded disk subsystem.

For additional information about this topics see Books Online under:

- Optimizing Database Performance ➤ Database Design ➤ Physical Database Design ➤ Data Placement Using Filegroups
- SQL Server Architecture ➤ Server Architecture ➤ I/O Architecture
- Administering SQL Server ➤ Managing Servers ➤ Setting Configuration Options ➤ max async IO option

Reference

v1.02 2000.04.24	
Applies to SQL Server versions:	7.0, 2000
FAQ category:	Database Administration
Related FAQ articles:	n/a
Related Microsoft Knowledge Base articles:	n/a
Other related information:	Books Online
Authors:	Gianluca Hotz, Neil Pike

finddupe rows

Q: How can I find duplicate rows in SQL Server?

A: Issue the following query substituting table_name and column list for those columns that need checking for duplicates.

```
SELECT
     <list of all columns>
FROM
     table_name
GROUP BY
     <list of all columns>
HAVING
     count(*) > 1
```

Note that this code doesn't work if the table contains bit, text, or image datatypes as you cannot group by these.

The following example works if you have bit datatypes, by using SELECT DISTINCT to create a temporary holding table of distinct values:

```
SELECT DISTINCT *, 0 AS Counted
INTO #distincts
FROM table_name

UPDATE #distincts
SET Counted = (SELECT Count(*)
          FROM table_name
          WHERE #distincts.col1 = t1.col1
            AND #distincts.col2 = t1.col2
            AND #distincts.col3 = t1.col3, ... )

SELECT
     <list of all columns>
FROM #distincts
WHERE Counted > 1
```

Reference

v1.01 2000.04.24

Applies to SQL Server versions:	All
FAQ category:	Database Administration
Related FAQ articles:	"How can I delete duplicates from a SQL Server table?" (deleteduprows, see page 25)
Related Microsoft Knowledge Base article:	Q139444 "INF: How to Remove Duplicate Rows From a Table"
Other related information:	n/a
Authors:	Neil Pike, Paul Munkenbeck

imagetext

Q: How do I store and retrieve text and image data in SQL Server?

A: To store and retrieve this sort of data within T-SQL scripts you have to use the WRITETEXT and READTEXT commands rather than standard INSERT/SELECT statements. These are documented, with examples, in Books Online but are difficult to use. See the "HandlingTextImageUsingSPs" FAQ entry for more information on these commands.

More manageable commands are available from within the relevant programming languages—RDO and ADO from VB/C can use GetChunk and AppendChunk commands—but you still have to separate the image/text value into blocks (or chunks) and handle these one at a time. About the only upside of storing this sort of data within SQL Server is that it can be kept transactionally consistent with the other data. For sample code see Q194975—"Sample Functions Demonstrating GetChunk and AppendChunk."

For native ODBC access use the SQLPutData and SQLGetData commands.

If you just want to insert or retrieve an entire image or text then look at the TEXTCOPY program (textcopy /? for parameters) in the <sql>\BINN directory. It is a command-line program along the lines of BCP.

There is a very useful free DLL called DBImage.DLLavailable from `http://www.chriscrawford.com/DBImage/DBImage.DLL` (courtesy of Chris Crawford). It has three functions:

- GetImage: Used for getting an image from the database.
- StoreImage: Used to send an image to the database.
- GetWebImage: Used to send a DB image to a browser.

If transactional consistency doesn't matter, or can be achieved programmatically, then it is easier to store the data outside the database as an ordinary file. Within the database just hold a UNC pointer to where the file is held. This usually makes it much easier to display or edit the data as the name can simply be passed to whatever tool is doing the manipulation.

Reference

v1.05 2000.06.13	
Applies to SQL Server versions:	All
FAQ categories:	Database Administration, Application Design and Programming
Related FAQ articles:	HandlingTextImageUsingSPs (see page 42)
Related Microsoft Knowledge Base articles:	See Q194975 "HOWTO: Sample Functions Demonstrating GetChunk and AppendChunk" for other references
Other related information:	n/a
Author:	Neil Pike

insertdbcc

Q: How can I insert the output of a DBCC command into a SQL Server table?

A: Some DBCC commands support this directly via the "insert into exec" type format, and others don't. Examples of both follow.

A DBCC command that works "normally" is USEROPTIONS—this is an example from Books Online:

```
DROP TABLE #tb_setopts
go
CREATE TABLE #tb_setopts (SetOptName varchar(35) NOT NULL ,SetOptValue var-
char(35) null)
INSERT INTO #tb_setopts (SetOptName,SetOptValue) EXEC('DBCC USEROPTIONS')
select * from #tb_setopts
```

Another is DBCC SQLPERF:

```
DROP TABLE #TempForLogSpace
go
CREATE TABLE #TempForLogSpace
(
 DBName varchar(32),
 LogSize real,
 LogSpaceUsed real,
 Status int
)
```

```
DECLARE @sql_command varchar(255)
SELECT @sql_command = 'DBCC SQLPERF (LOGSPACE)'
INSERT INTO #TempForLogSpace EXEC (@sql_command)
SELECT * FROM #TempForLogSpace
```

Another is dbcc inputbuffer:

```
DROP TABLE #dbc
go
CREATE TABLE #dbc(c1 varchar(15), c2 int, c3 varchar(255))

INSERT #dbc EXEC('DBCC INPUTBUFFER(7)')
SELECT * FROM #dbc
```

One that doesn't work "normally" is DBCC CHECKDB. To make this work you'll need to use xp_cmdshell and ISQL as follows:

```
-- Note that all quotes are single quotes except the ones on the -Q option, which
are double quotes
DROP TABLE #maint
go
CREATE TABLE #maint (Results varchar(255) NOT NULL)
INSERT INTO #maint(Results) EXEC('master..xp_cmdshell ''ISQL -E -Q"DBCC
CHECKDB(master)"''')
select * from #maint
```

Reference

v1.03 2000.05.02

Applies to SQL Server versions:	All
FAQ category:	Database Administration
Related FAQ articles:	n/a
Related Microsoft Knowledge Base articles:	n/a
Other related information:	n/a
Author:	Neil Pike

internalvsexternalfragmentation

Q: What does Microsoft mean by "internal vs. external fragmentation" in SQL Server?

A: Internal fragmentation is having free space on a page. Due to deletes, updates, and inserts you might have more free space on a page than you "need."

External fragmentation is when pages are not nice and neat on contiguous extents. The ideal is to have one extent, fill it up, then get another, fill it up, get another, and so forth. When you have page splits, you have to link in a new page from another extent. So if you followed the page chain, you would be hopping around from extent to extent far more than you should. Ideally, you have one extent switch every eight pages; the degree to which you have more than this determines the external fragmentation.

Use the DBCC SHOWCONTIG command to show the level of fragmentation in a table.

Microsoft does not mean file system or disk fragmentation when they say "external." This sort of fragmentation occurs outside the knowledge of SQL Server (Though this is still a sensible definition of "external" and hence the confusion).

Reference

v1.02 2000.05.06

Applies to SQL Server versions:	All
FAQ category:	Database Administration
Related FAQ articles:	n/a
Related Microsoft Knowledge Base articles:	n/a
Other related information:	n/a
Authors:	Neil Pike, Kalen Delaney

listcolumns

Q: How can I list all the columns in a SQL Server table or view?

A: Three ways:

```
sp_columns table_name

sp_MShelpcolumns table_name

(SQL 7+ only) :
SELECT * FROM INFORMATION_SCHEMA.COLUMNS
WHERE TABLE_NAME = 'table_name'
```

Reference

v1.01 2000.05.07

Applies to SQL Server versions:	All
FAQ category:	Database Administration
Related FAQ articles:	"How can I list all databases on a SQL Server?" (listdatabases, see below); "How can I list all user tables on SQL Server?" (listtables, see page 170),
Related Microsoft Knowledge Base articles:	n/a
Other related information:	n/a
Author:	Neil Pike

listdatabases

Q: How can I list all databases on a SQL Server?

A: sp_helpdb lists databases and other information about them.

If you just want a list of database names, then the SQL Server specific way (all versions) is:

```
SELECT name FROM master..sysdatabases
```

The ANSI standard way (SQL 7 only) is:

```
SELECT CATALOG_NAME FROM INFORMATION_SCHEMA.SCHEMATA
```

Reference

v1.01 2000.05.07	
Applies to SQL Server versions:	All
FAQ category:	Database Administration
Related FAQ articles:	"How can I list all the columns in a SQL Server table or view?" (listcolumns , see page 169); "How can I list all user tables on SQL Server?" (listtables, see below)
Related Microsoft Knowledge Base articles:	n/a
Other related information:	n/a
Author:	Neil Pike

listtables

Q: How can I list all user tables on SQL Server?

A: The SQL Server-specific way (all versions) is:

```
SELECT name FROM sysobjects WHERE type = 'U'
```

The ANSI standard way (SQL 7 and above only) is:

```
SELECT TABLE_NAME FROM INFORMATION_SCHEMA.TABLES
```

Reference

v1.02 2000.06.06	
Applies to SQL Server versions:	All
FAQ category:	Database Administration
Related FAQ articles:	"How can I list all the columns in a SQL Server table or view?" (listcolumns , see page 169); "How can I list all databases on a SQL Server?" (listdatabases, see page 169)
Related Microsoft Knowledge Base articles:	n/a
Other related information:	n/a
Author:	Neil Pike

loading

Q: My SQL Server database has been marked "loading." What can I do?

A: In SQL 7 and above this could be either because a restore has failed or because the restore was using the NORECOVERY option. If the restore has failed, check the troubleshooting guide in SQL 7 Books Online and retry it from the beginning. If you decide to drop the database, DROP DATABASE should work. If the NORECOVERY option was used, identify any further transaction logs to be applied and restore them, using the RECOVERY option on the last one. If you have no more logs to apply, and just want to use the database as is, then run the following:

```
RESTORE DATABASE database_name WITH RECOVERY
```

In earlier versions of SQL Server, the loading status indicates that SQL thinks a restore is still in progress. Don't forget that a restore process may take a long time to complete all the recovery of transactions that were in-flight while the database was being backed up. If you are sure that the restore has failed and the database is no longer recovering, you can drop the database with sp_dbremove, re-create it and attempt the load again.

Reference

v1.02 2000.06.06

Applies to SQL Server versions:	All
FAQ categories:	Database Administration, Troubleshooting
Related FAQ articles:	n/a
Related Microsoft Knowledge Base articles:	n/a
Other related information:	"Troubleshooting Backup and Restore" in Books Online 7
Authors:	Neil Pike, Paul Munkenbeck

loggingoff

Q: Can I turn SQL Server logging off?

A: The short answer is no. It is an integral part of the SQL system and cannot be turned off.

Certain operations are "non-logged," such as fast-BCP and select into. This means they do not log record updates. However they *do* log extent allocations. They need to do this so that if the process is terminated unexpectedly (for example, the power goes out), SQL can recover the space. This greatly reduced logging can result in better performance—but as it makes the database non-recoverable from transaction logs it should be used with caution.

With SQL 7.0 and above, logging in tempdb is reduced because it doesn't bother recording the redo information needed for rolling forward. As tempdb is always re-created at start-up, this information is not needed. This can make inserts up to four times faster and so is sometimes a good reason to deliberately use a tempdb table.

Reference

v1.03 2000.06.06	
Applies to SQL Server versions:	All
FAQ category:	Database Administration
Related FAQ articles:	n/a
Related Microsoft Knowledge Base articles:	n/a
Other related information:	n/a
Author:	Neil Pike

logspace

Q: Why does my SQL Server log show that it's still full? I have truncated it.

A: If your log *really* is full—for example, you're getting an 1105 error on syslogs—then try a "DUMP TRANSACTION *database_name* WITH NO_LOG". If this doesn't fix it, then one of the following is occurring:

- You may have an open transaction. Check that with the following command:

```
USE database_name
go
DBCC OPENTRAN(database_name)
```

- You may be using transactional replication on this database and have transactions that have not yet been distributed. See Q184499 for information on this and how to clear it up.

- Your log may not really be full. The reason for this is that all the tools that interrogate log space—dbcc sqlperf, sp_spaceused and SQL Enterprise Manager—all just look at the system catalog information in sysindexes—the dpages column. In SQL 6.5 and earlier this information is *not* kept up to date, so it is often wrong. The reason it is not kept up to date is that it would cause a performance bottleneck.

The easiest way to correct the information is to run the following. Note that the database must be in single-user mode for this to have any effect:

```
DBCC CHECKTABLE(syslogs)
go
checkpoint
go
```

The information will then be correct until the next update, delete or insert transaction is issued.

Reference

v1.01 2000.05.12	
Applies to SQL Server versions:	4.x, 6.x
FAQ category:	Database Administration
Related FAQ articles:	n/a
Related Microsoft Knowledge Base articles:	Q110139 "INF: Causes of SQL Transaction Log Filling Up," Q184499 "INF: Transaction Log Still Full After DUMP TRAN WITH NO_LOG," Q183100 "PRB: Incorrect Log Size Reported in SEM or Performance Monitor"
Other related information:	n/a
Author:	Neil Pike

logview

Q: How can I view the SQL Server log? Can I recover individual transactions or data from it?

A: Most of the information in the SQL log (syslogs) is not accessible via standard SQL commands. There are ways of accessing this information from SQL 6.5 and below because in those versions syslogs is held (more or less) as a SQL table.

With SQL 7 this is no longer the case, and there is no API or file format published for it. Therefore log viewing tools for 7.0 are unlikely to ever appear.

Microsoft recognizes that this is a feature customers want to have and is working on ways to achieve this with the SQL 2000 product, but there is no fixed date for these tools to appear. They will not be shipped with the RTM SQL 2000 product. Whether they will be supplied afterwards with a resource kit, or with a service pack, or via a third party is unknown—but they will appear at some point.

For SQL 6.5 and below the options for getting log record information are:

- You can get transaction id and operation type only (no data) through a select * from syslogs. Or use the following code to make it a bit more readable.

```
SELECT
xactid AS TRAN_ID,
CASE op
   WHEN 0  THEN 'BEGINXACT    Start Transaction'
   WHEN 1  THEN 'Sysindexes Change'
   WHEN 2  THEN 'Not Used'
   WHEN 3  THEN 'Not Used'
   WHEN 4  THEN 'INSERT       Insert Row'
   WHEN 5  THEN 'DELETE       Delete Row'
   WHEN 6  THEN 'INSIND       Deferred Update step 2 insert record'
   WHEN 7  THEN 'IINSERT      NC Index Insert'
   WHEN 8  THEN 'IDELETE      NC Index Delete'
   WHEN 9  THEN 'MODIFY       Modify Row'
   WHEN 10 THEN 'NOOP'
   WHEN 11 THEN 'INOOP        Deferred Update step 1 insert record'
   WHEN 12 THEN 'DNOOP        Deferred Update step 1 delete record'
   WHEN 13 THEN 'ALLOC        Allocate Page'
   WHEN 14 THEN 'DBNEXTID     Allocate Next Object ID'
   WHEN 15 THEN 'EXTENT       Allocate Empty Extent'
   WHEN 16 THEN 'SPLIT        Page split'
   WHEN 17 THEN 'CHECKPOINT'
   WHEN 18 THEN 'SAVEXACT     Savepoint'
   WHEN 19 THEN 'CMD'
   WHEN 20 THEN 'DEXTENT      Deallocate extent'
   WHEN 21 THEN 'DEALLOC      Deallocate page'
   WHEN 22 THEN 'DROPEXTS     Delete all extents on alloc pg'
   WHEN 23 THEN 'AEXTENT      Alloc extent - mark all pgs used'
   WHEN 24 THEN 'SALLOC       Alloc new page for split'
   WHEN 25 THEN 'Change to Sysindexes'
   WHEN 26 THEN 'Not Used'
   WHEN 27 THEN 'SORT         Sort allocations'
```

```
    WHEN 28 THEN 'SODEALLOC    Related to sort allocations'
    WHEN 29 THEN 'ALTDB        Alter database record'
    WHEN 30 THEN 'ENDXACT      End Transaction'
    WHEN 31 THEN 'SORTTS       Related to sort allocations'
    WHEN 32 THEN 'TEXT         Log record of direct TEXT insert'
    WHEN 33 THEN 'INOOPTEXT    Log record for deferred TEXT insert'
    WHEN 34 THEN 'DNOOPTEXT    Log record for deferred TEXT delete'
    WHEN 35 THEN 'INSINDTEXT   Indirrect insert log record'
    WHEN 36 THEN 'TEXTDELETE   Delete text log record'
    WHEN 37 THEN 'SORTEDSPLIT  Used for sorted splits'
    WHEN 38 THEN 'CHGINDSTAT   Incremental sysindexes stat changes'
    WHEN 39 THEN 'CHGINDPG     Direct change to sysindexes'
    WHEN 40 THEN 'TXTPTR       Info log row    WHEN retrieving TEXTPTR'
    WHEN 41 THEN 'TEXTINFO     Info log for WRITETEXT/UPDATETEXT'
    WHEN 42 THEN 'RESETIDENT   Used WHEN a truncate table resets an identity
value'
   WHEN 43 THEN 'UNDO         Compensating log record for Insert Only Row Locking
(IORL)'
    WHEN 44 THEN 'INSERT_IORL  Insert with Row Locking record'
    WHEN 45 THEN 'INSIND_IORL  INSIND with IORL'
    WHEN 46 THEN 'IINSERT_IORL IINDEX with IORL'
    WHEN 47 THEN 'SPLIT_IORL   Page split with IORL'
    WHEN 48 THEN 'SALLOC_IORL  Alloc new page for split with IORL'
    WHEN 49 THEN 'ALLOC_IORL   Allocation with IORL'
    WHEN 50 THEN 'PREALLOCLOG  Pre-allocate log space for CLRs'
    ELSE 'Unknown Type' END  AS LOG_RECORD
FROM syslogs
```

- A third-party tool is Logview (available from `www.dbsg.com`).

- Another third-party tool is Image Analyzer (available from `http://www.cai.com/products/platinum/dba/im_an_ps.htm`). It doesn't access syslogs directly, but can report and recover historical data by generating data manipulation language (DML) statements from a backup enabling an audit report from archived files to maintain a record of data modifications.

- The DBCC LOG command. This command is not well documented, but some details are provided below for SQL 6.5. Note that as with most undocumented DBCC commands you need to do a DBCC TRACEON(3604) first to see the output.

```
DBCC LOG( [database_id][, OBJID=object_id] [,PAGE=page_number] [,ROW=row_id]
[,NRECORDS=number] [,TYPE={-1..36}], PRINTOPT={0|1} )

DBCC LOG (5, 0, 0, 0, -1, 0, 1)   -- Show the last begin transaction record in
the log
```

The meanings of the DBCC LOG parameters are as follows.

OBJID, PAGE and ROW:

- A negative value for OBJID indicates that PAGE and ROW represent a row in the log to use as a starting point in the scan of the log.
- A value of zero for OBJID indicates that log records for changes to PAGE will be included in the commands output.
- A positive value for OBJID followed by a non-zero value for PAGE indicates that PAGE and ROW represent a transaction ID. Log records for that transaction will be included in the output.
- A positive value for OBJID followed by zero values for PAGE and ROW indicates an object ID. Log records for changes to that object will be included in the output.

NRECORDS: The number of records to examine

TYPE: The value of the op column in syslogs. See CASE earlier.

PRINTOPT: The output option.

Reference

v1.02 2000.07.07

Applies to SQL Server versions:	All
FAQ categories:	Database Administration, Troubleshooting
Related FAQ articles:	n/a
Related Microsoft Knowledge Base articles:	n/a
Other related information:	n/a
Authors:	Neil Pike, Tibor Karaszi

maxrows

Q: What is the maximum number of rows in a SQL table? What other size limitations are there?

A: There is no maximum number. You can keep adding rows until the database runs out of space or reaches one of the following limits:

	SQL 6.5	SQL 7.0
Database size	1 TB	1,048,516 TB
Data file size	32 GB	32 TB
Files per database	32	32768

As far as other maximums go, there is an excellent comparison between SQL 6.5 and SQL 7.0 in Books Online 7.

Reference

v1.01 2000.05.12

Applies to SQL Server versions:	6.5, 7.0
FAQ category:	Database Administration
Related FAQ articles:	n/a
Related Microsoft Knowledge Base articles:	n/a
Other related information:	"Maximum Capacity Specifications" in Books Online 7
Author:	Neil Pike

Database Administration

networkbackup

Q: Why can't I backup or restore my SQL Server databases to a share on another server?

A: The reason is that the MSSQLSERVER service is running under a separate set of NT credentials—all services are related to an NT account. It doesn't matter who *you* are logged on as (after all SQL runs quite happily when nobody is logged on locally to the server). Therefore your logon account and any mapped drives are irrelevant. It is SQL Server doing the backup, not you. This is the same for backups done via SQL Executive/SQL Agent—they just pass the T-SQL to SQL Server to run, so it's still MSSQLSERVER doing the backup or restore.

For this reason the backup GUI does not show you mapped drives or allow a UNC path to be typed in. You have to use raw T-SQL commands to do the backup.

The default set of NT credentials used by MSSQLSERVER is the SYSTEM account. You can check what userid MSSQLSERVER is running under by looking at Control Panel ➤ Services, highlighting MSSQLSERVER and choosing the Start-up option.

The SYSTEM account has no access to shares on the network as it isn't an authenticated network account. Therefore SQL Server running under this account cannot backup to a normal network share.

So, if you want to backup to a network share you have two choices:

- Change the account the MSSQLSERVER service runs under to a user account with the relevant network rights.

- Amend the following registry value on the TARGET server and add the share name you want to dump to—the share does not then authenticate who is coming in and so a SYSTEM account will work. The server service on the target server must be re-started before the change takes effect. Note that this effectively removes *all* security on that share, so you're letting anyone or anything have access. This is probably not something you want to do with production business data.

```
HKEY_LOCAL_MACHINE\SYSTEM\CurrentControlSet\Services\LanmanServer\
Parameters\NullSessionShares
```

Whichever method you use, you *must* also use a UNC name to reference the file required and not a drive letter:

- In 6.5: DUMP DATABASE pubs to DISK='\\server01\share\backupdir\backup.dmp'
- In 7.0 and 2000: BACKUP DATABASE pubs to DISK='\\server01\share\backupdir\backup.dmp'

Reference

v1.04 2000.01.25	
Applies to SQL Server versions:	All
FAQ categories:	Database Administration, Connectivity
Related FAQ articles:	n/a
Related Microsoft Knowledge Base articles:	n/a
Other related information:	"Creating SQL Server Services User Accounts"
Author:	Neil Pike

networkdrivedatabases

Q: Can I create SQL Server databases on network drives?

A: First ask yourself what your reason is for doing this. Your performance will almost certainly be degraded and any network glitches (which are far more common than SCSI/fiber bus glitches) will cause database corruption. Putting I/Os across a network (even a fast, switched network) is typically slower than via SCSI/fiber and the latency is a lot longer. Network packet sizes are much smaller than SCSI packets giving less throughput and more CPU utilization by the device drivers on the host.

If you do use a network drive, make sure you have a dedicated cross-over or switched connection between the SQL Server box and the network drive machine, otherwise your performance will be further affected by contention with other network traffic.

SQL Server currently has no concept of sharing a database that is held on another server. Only one server can access the database file at any one time—the exception being that multiple SQL servers could probably open a read-only database on a shared-drive. Therefore there is no advantage to having it on a "network drive"—it can only be backed-up or accessed from the server running SQL Server anyway.

If the reason for wanting SQL databases on a network drive is to keep all your storage central, then you can't completely achieve that result this way because you can't boot NT from a network drive. You would still need disks in local servers for NT and pagefiles. These should be protected via hardware RAID as the loss of an NT disk will prevent users getting at your databases just as much as the loss of a disk containing the database itself.

Having said that, it *is* possible to store databases on network drives as long as SQL is fooled into thinking they are local drives. Under 6.5 you must map a drive letter to a network share—UNC paths will not work. With SQL 7.0, UNC paths will work as long as you use trace flag 1807.

More information on this is provided in Q196904. This describes the support being allowed in SQL 7.0 for use against Network Appliance networked RAID units only. Note that these will suffer the same performance penalties as if you were accessing a network share on an NT box, because effectively that is what they are. These boxes run a proprietary operating system on an embedded Alpha chip that talks the SMB protocol required to handle NT-style network file-I/O. They can be connected to almost any LAN/WAN infrastructure as they support all the standard network types.

If you want centralized storage, another method is to use a shared-SCSI/fiber disk array—these can be attached to servers via SCSI or fiber connectors and can achieve distances of up to 20 km (12.5 miles) using optical extenders. These arrays can support up to 64 or so separate servers and are sold by Digital (Compaq) Storageworks and EMC among others. Although it is a "single RAID unit," each server sees a physically separate set of "disks"—the partitioning logic in the RAID array can allow different servers to use the same physical disks but they are logically partitioned and the different servers cannot see this and see their storage as dedicated. There is no sharing of data at the partition/file/database level.

Another method is to use a SAN—storage area network. These are fiber or copper-based "networks" of storage and/or backup devices. The "network" is dedicated for data access. Each attached device is usually fiber-channel based, or is SCSI with an appropriate connector. Each device may be partitioned into sets of available resources (disk or tape), but each resource can currently only be allocated to a single server attached to the "network." Servers attach to a SAN with a SAN "NIC" card. As SAN technology matures it may be possible to share resources between multiple servers, but this requires changes to the NT kernel as well as the SAN/fiber drivers.

Reference

v1.07 2000.05.25

Applies to SQL Server versions:	All
FAQ category:	Database Administration
Related FAQ articles:	n/a
Related Microsoft Knowledge Base articles:	Q196904 "Support for Network Database Files"
Other related information:	n/a
Author:	Neil Pike

nextfreedevicenumber

Q: How can I programmatically get the next free device number (vdevno) in SQL Server?

A: A sample stored procedure is provided below. The requirement only applies to SQL 6.5 and below. In newer releases SQL Server does not require or use vdevnos, which are a holdover from Sybase days.

```
CREATE PROCEDURE sp_ms_NextDeviceNumber AS

/*
RETURNS THE NEXT AVAILABLE SEQUENTIAL DEVICE NUMBER
*/

/* Get a list of used device numbers > 0 and put in a temporary table */
SELECT
dev_num = CONVERT(tinyint, SUBSTRING(CONVERT(binary(4), d.low),v.low, 1))
INTO #TmpDevHoldTable
FROM master..sysdevices d, master.dbo.spt_values v
WHERE v.type = 'E'
AND v.number = 3
AND convert(tinyint, substring(convert(binary(4), d.low),v.low, 1)) > 0
ORDER BY dev_num

/* Now lets find the first available device from the temporary table */

SET ROWCOUNT 1 /* This gets only the first one available */
```

Database Administration

```
SELECT Next_Available_Device_# = t1.dev_num + 1
FROM #TmpDevHoldTable t1
WHERE NOT EXISTS /* When current dev number + 1 does not exist */
(SELECT t2.dev_num /* we are here and have our 1 row */
FROM #TmpDevHoldTable  t2
WHERE t1.dev_num + 1 = t2.dev_num)

SET ROWCOUNT 0
DROP TABLE #TmpDevHoldTable
GO
```

Reference

v1.00 1999.04.10

Applies to SQL Server versions:	4.x, 6.x
FAQ category:	Database Administration
Related FAQ articles:	n/a
Related Microsoft Knowledge Base articles:	n/a
Other related information:	n/a
Authors:	Mike Schellenberger, Neil Pike

permissionstable

Q: Where does SQL server store the permissions on tables?

A: For SQL 6.5 and below this is held in <dbname>..sysprotects.

For 7.0 and above, <dbname>..syspermissions.

Reference

v1.00 1999.07.12

Applies to SQL Server versions:	All
FAQ category:	Database Administration
Related FAQ articles:	n/a
Related Microsoft Knowledge Base articles:	n/a
Other related information:	n/a
Author:	Neil Pike

refreshview

Q: When I change a table definition it often invalidates any views on that table. How can I fix this without recreating the view?

A: Just as sp_recompile works for stored procedures, there is a way (in SQL 7.0 and SQL 2000 only) to do this for views:

```
sp_refreshview <viewname>
```

It is trivial to write a cursor around sysobjects and then run this automatically via EXEC (..) to refresh all views in a database.

Reference

v1.01 2000.04.15

Applies to SQL Server versions:	7.0, 2000
FAQ category:	Database Administration
Related FAQ articles:	n/a
Related Microsoft Knowledge Base articles:	n/a
Other related information:	"sp_refreshview (T-SQL)"
Author:	Neil Pike

Database Administration

resetidentity

Q: How can I clear a table and reset the identity back to 0?

A: If there are no foreign keys on the table, a simple TRUNCATE TABLE *tablename* will do the trick.

If there are foreign keys then first delete all rows—DELETE *tablename*.

Then reset the identity:

- Under 7.0: DBCC CHECKIDENT(*tablename*,RESEED,0)

- Under 6.5: DBCC CHECKIDENT(*tablename*)

Reference

v1.01 2000.04.16	
Applies to SQL Server versions:	6.5, 7.0, 2000
FAQ category:	Database Administration
Related FAQ articles:	n/a
Related Microsoft Knowledge Base articles:	n/a
Other related information:	"DBCC CHECKIDENT"
Author:	Neil Pike

restorespeed

Q: Why is a SQL Server full database restore so much slower than the original backup?

A: The answer is that SQL initializes all pages during a full database restore. So if you have 50MB of data in a 5GB database, the backup only processes the used 50MB. But when the restore occurs it loads the 50MB of data—which takes roughly the same time as the backup—and then initializes the rest of the 4.95GB of free space. This initialization is limited in speed by the performance of the disk subsystem.

Reference

v1.02 2000.05.15	
Applies to SQL Server versions:	All
FAQ category:	Database Administration
Related FAQ articles:	n/a
Related Microsoft Knowledge Base articles:	n/a
Other related information:	n/a
Authors:	Neil Pike

revokebug

Q: Why do I have problems revoking permissions on some tables with SQL Server? The command works, but the users still have permissions (as shown by sp_helprotect).

A: This is a known bug in SQL Server 6.5 with tables that have 8n-1 columns (7, 15, 22, and so on). To work around it, remove all entries from sysprotects and then re-grant permissions as necessary.

```
USE <dbname>
go
EXEC sp_configure 'allow updates',1
go
RECONFIGURE WITH OVERRIDE
go
DELETE sysprotects WHERE id = OBJECT_ID('<tblname>')
go
EXEC sp_configure 'allow updates',0
go
RECONFIGURE WITH OVERRIDE
go
```

Reference

v1.02 2000.04.16	
Applies to SQL Server version:	6.5
FAQ category:	Database Administration
Related FAQ articles:	n/a
Related Microsoft Knowledge Base articles:	n/a
Other related information:	n/a
Authors:	Neil Pike

Database Administration

rowcountforalltables

Q: How can I get row counts for all tables in a database?

A: You can use the undocumented stored procedure sp_Msforeachtable:

```
EXEC sp_MSforeachtable 'SELECT "?", COUNT (*) FROM ?'
```

Reference

v1.01 2000.04.16

Applies to SQL Server versions:	All
FAQ category:	Database Administration
Related FAQ articles:	n/a
Related Microsoft Knowledge Base articles:	n/a
Other related information:	n/a
Author:	Neil Pike

rowlevellocks

Q: How do I do row-level locking on SQL Server?

A: Only SQL 7.0 and above has full built-in row-level locking.

SQL 6.5 has limited row-level locking that only occurs for inserts to the end of the last page of a table. It can be set by running:

```
sp_tableoption 'tablename', 'Insert row lock', true
```

See Books Online for 6.5 for more information.

SQL 6.0 and previous have no row-level locking capabilities.

You can, however, effectively perform the equivalent of row-level locking with version 6.5 and earlier as long as each row takes up a whole page—thus locking one page is the same as one row. You can do this by padding a row with CHAR NOT NULL fields until the row length is forced to be greater than 1024 bytes (rows cannot span pages so this forces one row per page).

However, you should note that although the rows on this last data page are being row-level locked, any non-clustered index pages involved are not. These can be a source of contention and even deadlock—when two logically distinct transactions need to lock one or more index pages, and pessimistically in different orders.

Reference

v1.04 2000.04.16

Applies to SQL Server versions:	All
FAQ categories:	Database Administration, Application Design and Programming
Related FAQ articles:	n/a
Related Microsoft Knowledge Base articles:	n/a
Other related information:	"Insert Row-level Locking (IRL)", "Architecture Enhancements" in SQL Server Books Online
Author:	Neil Pike

scriptingem

Q: How can I script my database schema?

A: Follow these steps:

1. Fire up SQL Enterprise Manager.
2. Right-click the database you want to script.
3. Choose All Tasks.
4. Choose Generate SQL Scripts.
5. Select which objects (or all of them) you want to script, as well as setting any advanced options your require.

Reference

v1.01 2000.04.16	
Applies to SQL Server versions:	All
FAQ category:	Database Administration
Related FAQ article:	"How can I automate the scripting or transfer of a database or objects in SQL Server?" (automatescript, see page 392)
Related Microsoft Knowledge Base articles:	n/a
Other related information:	n/a
Author:	Neil Pike

settings

Q: What is the precedence of the SET commands, database options and session options in SQL Server?

A: Settings are defined on three levels:

1. server

2. database (on overlap, overrides the server level settings)

3. session (on overlap, overrides the server and database settings)

Considerations when using the SET statements:

- The SET FIPS_FLAGGER, SET OFFSETS, SET PARSEONLY and SET QUOTED_IDENTIFIER statements are set at parse time. All other statements are set at execute or run time. The parse time statements will take effect even if they are not executed directly. For example, if the statement is within an IF statement block that is never executed, the statement is still set as all code is parsed.

- If a SET statement is set in a stored procedure, the original value of the SET option is restored after control is returned from the stored procedure. Therefore, a SET statement specified in dynamic SQL does not affect the statements that follow the dynamic SQL statement.

- Stored procedures execute with the SET settings specified at execute time except for SET ANSI_NULLS and SET QUOTED_IDENTIFIER. Stored procedures specifying SET ANSI_NULLS or SET QUOTED_IDENTIFIER use the setting specified at stored procedure creation time. If used inside a stored procedure, these statements are ignored.

- The user options setting of sp_configure allows server-wide settings and works across multiple databases. This setting also behaves like an explicit SET statement, except that it occurs at login time.

- Database settings (set by using sp_dboption) are valid only at the database level and only take effect if not explicitly set. Database settings override server option settings (set using a SET statement) when an option appears at more than one level.

- With any of the SET statements with ON and OFF settings, it is possible to specify either an ON or OFF setting for multiple SET options. For example, SET QUOTED_IDENTIFIER, ANSI_NULLS ON sets both QUOTED_IDENTIFIER and ANSI_NULLS to ON.

- SET statement settings override database option settings (set by using sp_dboption). In addition, some connection settings are set ON automatically when a user connects to a database based on the values put into effect by the prior use of the sp_configure user options setting or the values that apply to all ODBC and OLE/DB connections.

- When a global or shortcut SET statement (for example, SET ANSI_DEFAULTS) sets a number of settings, issuing the shortcut SET statement resets the prior settings for all those options affected by the shortcut SET statement. If an individual SET option (affected by a shortcut SET statement) is explicitly set after the shortcut SET statement is issued, the individual SET statement overrides the corresponding shortcut setting.

- When batches are used, the database context is determined by the batch established with the USE statement. Ad hoc queries and all other statements that are executed outside of the stored procedure, and that are in batches, inherit the option settings of the database and connection established with the USE statement.

- When a stored procedure is executed either from a batch or from another stored procedure, it is executed under the option values that are currently set in the database that contains the stored procedure. For example, when stored procedure db1.dbo.sp1 calls stored procedure db2.dbo.sp2, stored procedure sp1 is executed under the current compatibility level setting of database db1, and stored procedure sp2 is executed under the current compatibility level setting of database db2.

- When a T-SQL statement refers to objects that reside in multiple databases, the current database context and the current connection context (the database defined by the USE statement if it is in a batch, or the database that contains the stored procedure if it is in a stored procedure) applies to that statement.

- With the exception of the SET QUOTED_IDENTIFIER and the SET ANSI_NULLS options, all SET options apply immediately after being set. Therefore, most T-SQL SET statements are interpreted during execution.

Reference

v1.01 2000.04.21	
Applies to SQL Server versions:	All
FAQ category:	Database Administration
Related FAQ articles:	n/a
Related Microsoft Knowledge Base articles:	n/a
Other related information:	n/a
Author:	Gert Drapers

shrinkdatabaseonlytolog

Q: Why can't I shrink my database any smaller than <xxx> MB?

A: The probable reason is that you're still on 6.5 or below. With this setup you can only shrink a database back to the last portion of log. So if you defined a database as 400MB data, 100MB log, you can never shrink it.

If you defined it as 400MB data, 100MB log, and then expanded by 500MB data, you could then shrink down any or all of this last 500MB—assuming it wasn't being used.

Reference

v1.00 1999.07.20	
Applies to SQL Server version:	6.5
FAQ category:	Database Administration
Related FAQ articles:	n/a
Related Microsoft Knowledge Base articles:	n/a
Other related information:	n/a
Author:	Neil Pike

sourcecontrol

Q: What packages are available to do source control on SQL Server stored procedures, triggers or other DDL code?

A: Microsoft has integrated its Repository into SQL 7 so there will probably be some function there with new versions of Visual SourceSafe, but assuming VSS doesn't meet your needs, then third-party DBMS tools offer these features:

- Cast Workbench: `http://www.castsoftware.com`
- SQL Programmer: `http://www.sfi-software.com`
- Rapid SQL: `http://www.embarcadero.com`

Reference

v1.03 2000.04.22	
Applies to SQL Server versions:	All
FAQ category:	Database Administration
Related FAQ articles:	n/a
Related Microsoft Knowledge Base articles:	n/a
Other related information:	n/a
Author:	Neil Pike

spt_values

Q: Where can I get more information on the spt_values table?

A: This is an internal look-up table used by lots of different bits of SQL Server. It is undocumented because it is for Microsoft internal use, but two good articles on it for SQL 6.5 and below have appeared in *SQL Server Professional* (`http://www.pinpub.com`):

- "SQL Server Internals: spt_values, Part 1" (April 1999)

- "SQL Server Internals: spt_values, Part 2" (June 1998)

If you subscribe you can get back issues and download articles, or pay to view individual articles on their site.

Part 1 is also available by subscription to MSDN (`msdn.microsoft.com`).

The table is used to look up the "names" for status bit information, like when you use sp_dboption. Each bit in sysdatabases.status means something, but to translate the bit into English, spt_values is used.

If you do sp_helptext on a few system stored procedures you will see how it is used — for example,. sp_helpdb, sp_lock and sp_helprotect.

Reference

v1.01 2000.03.04

Applies to SQL Server versions:	All
FAQ category:	Database Administration
Related FAQ articles:	"What are some good SQL Server books and other reference sources?" (sqlbooks, see page 355)
Related Microsoft Knowledge Base articles:	n/a
Other related information:	`http://www.pinpub.com`
Author:	Neil Pike

sql7loadtable

Q: How can I restore a single table in SQL 7 and above?

A: You can't directly—LOAD TABLE is no longer supported since SQL 6.5. You will have to restore the database backup to a different server or database and then use DTS, BCP or normal T-SQL to transfer the data.

You *can* restore a single file though, so if you place a table in a file on its own, you'll be able to restore it. For SAP systems with thousands of tables, however, the administration of separate files would be a nightmare!

Reference

v1.02 2000.04.29

Applies to SQL Server versions:	7.0, 2000
FAQ category:	Database Administration
Related FAQ articles:	n/a
Related Microsoft Knowledge Base articles:	n/a
Other related information:	n/a
Author:	Neil Pike

sql7scriptsuse65

Q: Can I generate SQL 7.0 scripts in 6.5 format so I can run them against old servers?

A: Unfortunately not, and the pervasive use of square brackets in scripts generated in SQL 7.0 causes these to fail in 6.5 and below. You can only post-process these scripts with some homegrown code. AWK, PERL or SED would be the best for doing things like this.

Reference

v1.00 1999.02.15

Applies to SQL Server versions:	7.0
FAQ category:	Database Administration
Related FAQ articles:	n/a
Related Microsoft Knowledge Base articles:	n/a
Other related information:	n/a
Author:	Neil Pike

sql7shrinklognowork

Q: Why won't my log shrink in SQL 7/2000?

A: This is because the log file is internally divided into smaller virtual logs and shrinking will only happen when the active part of the log is at the beginning of your log file. You can use the DBCC LOGINFO(*dbname*) command to see where the active part of the transaction log is—any logs marked with a Status of 2 are active.

The output below shows that the active virtual log file is the last in the physical file, and therefore no real shrinkage is possible.

```
FileId FileSize StartOffset FSeqNo Status Parity CreateTime
------ -------- ----------- ------ ------ ------ -----------------------
2      13041664 8192        0      0      0      1999-03-16 10:27:24.917
2      13041664 13049856    0      0      0      1999-03-16 10:25:56.730
2      13041664 26091520    0      0      0      1999-03-16 10:25:56.730
2      13041664 39133184    0      0      0      1999-03-16 10:25:56.730
2      13041664 52174848    0      0      0      1999-03-16 10:25:56.730
2      13041664 65216512    0      0      0      1999-03-16 10:25:56.730
2      13041664 78258176    0      0      0      1999-03-16 10:25:56.730
2      13557760 91299840    5      2      64     1999-04-06 12:32:27.833
```

In order to be able to shrink the log:

1. Backup or truncate the log to make sure earlier Virtual Log Files are reusable (check their status).

2. Execute dummy transactions (in a loop) against a test table until the active virtual log moves back to the start of the list.

3. Execute DBCC SHRINKDATABASE or DBCC SHRINKFILE to mark a shrink-point (the actual shrink is performed asynchronously normally).

4. Issue a backup or truncate log command to force the shrinkage to happen immediately.

If it is at the end of the log file, you could write a small while loop that does some inserts in a test table to move the active part to the beginning of the real file. Then the SHRINKFILE command should work OK—note that SHRINKFILE works asynchronously.

As a last resort you can always checkpoint the database, shut down SQL Server and delete the physical log file. When SQL restarts it will create a new 2Mb log device. Note that this is unsupported by Microsoft and while it has always worked for the author, others have reported problems doing this.

The following stored procedure was first published in the February 2000 issue of *Microsoft SQL Server Professional* (Pinnacle Publishing). It is reproduced here by the kind permission of Andrew Zanevsky.

```
create proc sp_force_shrink_log
---------------------------------------------------------------------------
-
-- Purpose: Shrink transaction log of the current database in SQL Server 7.0.
-- Author:  Andrew Zanevsky, AZ Databases, Inc., 12/25/1999, v2 - 02/16/2000
--          zanevsky@azdatabases.com
---------------------------------------------------------------------------
-
    @target_percent tinyint = 0,
    @target_size_MB int = 10,
    @max_iterations int = 1000,
    @backup_log_opt nvarchar(1000) = 'with truncate_only'
as
set nocount on

declare @db         sysname,
        @last_row   int,
        @log_size   decimal(15,2),
        @unused1    decimal(15,2),
        @unused     decimal(15,2),
        @shrinkable decimal(15,2),
        @iteration  int,
    @file_max   int,
    @file       int,
    @fileid     varchar(5)
```

Database Administration

```
select  @db = db_name(),
        @iteration = 0

create table #loginfo (
    id          int identity,
    FileId      int,
    FileSize    numeric(22,0),
    StartOffset numeric(22,0),
    FSeqNo      int,
    Status      int,
    Parity      smallint,
    CreateTime  datetime
)

create table #logfiles ( id int identity(1,1), fileid varchar(5) not null )
insert #logfiles ( fileid ) select convert( varchar, fileid ) from sysfiles
where status & 0x40 = 0x40
select @file_max = @@rowcount

if object_id( 'table_to_force_shrink_log' ) is null
    exec( 'create table table_to_force_shrink_log ( x nchar(3000) not null )' )

insert  #loginfo ( FileId, FileSize, StartOffset, FSeqNo, Status, Parity,
CreateTime ) exec ( 'dbcc loginfo' )
select  @last_row = @@rowcount

select  @log_size = sum( FileSize ) / 1048576.00,
        @unused = sum( case when Status = 0 then FileSize else 0 end ) /
1048576.00,
        @shrinkable = sum( case when id < @last_row - 1 and Status = 0 then
FileSize else 0 end ) / 1048576.00
from    #loginfo

select  @unused1 = @unused -- save for later

select  'iteration'           = @iteration,
        'log size, MB'        = @log_size,
        'unused log, MB'      = @unused,
        'shrinkable log, MB'  = @shrinkable,
        'shrinkable %'        = convert( decimal(6,2), @shrinkable * 100 /
@log_size )
```

```
while @shrinkable * 100 / @log_size > @target_percent
  and @shrinkable > @target_size_MB
  and @iteration < @max_iterations begin
    select  @iteration = @iteration + 1 -- this is just a precaution

    exec( 'insert table_to_force_shrink_log select name from sysobjects
           delete table_to_force_shrink_log')

    select @file = 0
    while @file < @file_max begin
        select @file = @file + 1
        select @fileid = fileid from #logfiles where id = @file
        exec( 'dbcc shrinkfile( ' + @fileid + ' )' )
    end

    exec( 'backup log ' + @db + ' ' + @backup_log_opt )

    truncate table #loginfo
    insert  #loginfo ( FileId, FileSize, StartOffset, FSeqNo, Status, Parity,
CreateTime ) exec ( 'dbcc loginfo' )
    select  @last_row = @@rowcount

    select  @log_size = sum( FileSize ) / 1048576.00,
            @unused = sum( case when Status = 0 then FileSize else 0 end ) /
1048576.00,
        @shrinkable = sum( case when id < @last_row - 1 and Status = 0 then
FileSize else 0 end ) / 1048576.00
    from    #loginfo

    select  'iteration'          = @iteration,
            'log size, MB'       = @log_size,
            'unused log, MB'     = @unused,
            'shrinkable log, MB' = @shrinkable,
            'shrinkable %'       = convert( decimal(6,2), @shrinkable * 100 /
@log_size )
end

if @unused1 < @unused
select  'After ' + convert( varchar, @iteration ) +
        ' iterations the unused portion of the log has grown from ' +
        convert( varchar, @unused1 ) + ' MB to ' +
        convert( varchar, @unused ) + ' MB.'
union all
```

```
select'Since the remaining unused portion is larger than 10 MB,' where @unused > 10
union all
select'you may try running this procedure again with a higher number of itera-
tions.' where @unused > 10
union all
select'Sometimes the log would not shrink to a size smaller than several Mega-
bytes.' where @unused <= 10

else
select  'It took ' + convert( varchar, @iteration ) +
        ' iterations to shrink the unused portion of the log from ' +
        convert( varchar, @unused1 ) + ' MB to ' +
        convert( varchar, @unused ) + ' MB'

exec( 'drop table table_to_force_shrink_log' )
go
```

Reference

v1.05 2000.06.13

Applies to SQL Server versions:	7.0/2000
FAQ category:	Database Administration
Related FAQ articles:	n/a
Related Microsoft Knowledge Base articles:	n/a
Other related information:	n/a
Authors:	Neil Pike, Andrew Zanevsky

sql7sysindexesentries

Q: Why am I seeing entries in sysindexes (or sp_helpindex) for indexes I have not created?

A: sysindexes contains rows per object as follows:

- Every table has a row with an indid value of either 0 (heap) or 1 (if it has a clustered index).
- Every non-clustered index has a row with indid > 1.
- If text/image columns are used, these use rows.

- (SQL 7 only.) There are rows for keeping track of non-index statistics on columns that SQL decides to capture statistics on even though there is no physical index on the column. Their names are _WA_Sys_<column>_<number>. These "indexes" cannot be dropped with a drop index command. They are there for the SQL optimizer to best choose query plans, but if you want to drop them they can be dropped with the drop statistics command.

- (SQL 7 only.) When the index tuning wizard runs, it creates "hypothetical" indexes with names like hind_<type>_<column>_<number>. These are removed when you create a "real" index on those columns using the script that the wizard produces for you.

You can spot the "hidden" indexes using the following query:

```
SELECT * FROM sysindexes WHERE status & 32 = 1
```

Reference

v1.03 2000.06.01	
Applies to SQL Server versions:	All
FAQ category:	Database Administration
Related FAQ articles:	n/a
Related Microsoft Knowledge Base articles:	n/a
Other related information:	n/a
Author:	Neil Pike

sql7systemtables

Q: How can I tell whether a table is a system (Microsoft) table in SQL 7/2000?

A:

```
SELECT * FROM sysobjects WHERE OBJECTPROPERTY(id, 'IsMSShipped') = 1
```

The OBJECTPROPERTY function is fully documented in SQL Server Books Online, and can be used on any object, not just tables.

Reference

v1.01 2000.04.29	
Applies to SQL Server versions:	7.0, 2000
FAQ category:	Database Administration
Related FAQ articles:	n/a
Related Microsoft Knowledge Base articles:	n/a
Other related information:	"OBJECTPROPERTY" in SQL Server Books Online
Author:	Neil Pike

sql7systemtablesdiagram

Q: Where can I get a diagram of the SQL 7 system tables?

A: A poster was shipped with the September 1999 MSDN pack.

There is also an image at `http://www.swynk.com/friends/hotek/articles/ss70_schema.asp`.

In addition, you can order a poster from `http://www.bmc.com/products/sqlserver/`.

Reference

v1.04 2000.04.29	
Applies to SQL Server version:	7.0
FAQ category:	Database Administration
Related FAQ articles:	n/a
Related Microsoft Knowledge Base articles:	n/a
Other related information:	n/a
Author:	Neil Pike

startupstoredproc

Q: How can I run some SQL code every time SQL Server starts?

A: With SQL 6.x use the sp_markstartup supplied stored procedure. This will run any stored procedure you write as soon as SQL Server finishes initializing.

With SQL 7.0 the same result is achieved using sp_procoption to mark the stored procedure for auto-start. Another way, assuming that you use SQL Agent, is to define a SQL Agent job with the "Start automatically when the SQLServerAgent starts" option. However, this will run the job every time SQL Agent is restarted (if it ever is).

Reference

v1.00 2000.01.17	
Applies to SQL Server versions:	6.x, 7.0
FAQ category:	Database Administration
Related FAQ articles:	n/a
Related Microsoft Knowledge Base articles:	n/a
Other related information:	n/a
Author:	Neil Pike

storedproccurrentline

Q: How can I see what line a stored procedure is on?

A: With SQL 6.5 you can use the following method:

```
DBCC TRACEON (3604)
DBCC PSS (suid, spid, 0)
```

Look in the output for a pline parameter — this shows the current line of the stored procedure.

Reference

v1.02 2000.15.05	
Applies to SQL Server version:	6.5
FAQ category:	Database Administration
Related FAQ articles:	n/a
Related Microsoft Knowledge Base articles:	n/a
Other related information:	n/a
Author:	Neil Pike

sysbackuphistory

Q: Is it safe to clear down the msdb..sysbackuphistory table in SQL Server as it is filling up the database?

A: Yes, it is safe. The easiest way to do this is install the stored procedure defined in the associated Microsoft Knowledge Base article. This clears down sysbackuphistory and the related sysrestorehistory as well.

In SQL 7.0 and above these tables have been replaced. The new system stored procedure sp_delete_backuphistory performs this function.

Reference

v1.03 2000.05.14	
Applies to SQL Server versions:	6.5
FAQ category:	Database Administration
Related FAQ articles:	n/a
Related Microsoft Knowledge Base article:	Q152354 "PRB: Database Dumps and Restore May Fill Up MSDB Database"
Other related information:	n/a
Author:	Neil Pike

systemtables

Q: How can I amend the system tables in SQL Server? Can I put a trigger on one?

A: First, it should be said that unless you are using code that Microsoft has published, any direct updates to the system tables are not supported. If you're not sure, either don't do it or take a backup first.

With the exception of "materialized" tables like syslocks and sysprocesses, you can pretty much use standard SQL commands to update the system tables.

As far as triggers go, you can define triggers on system tables, however SQL Server updates most system tables internally via its own APIs — only some get done via standard T-SQL. Only updates done via standard T-SQL result in a trigger firing, however there is no list of what tables this works with, and it certainly wouldn't be supported if you used it.

To update system tables first you have to set the "allow updates" flag as follows:

```
sp_configure 'allow updates',1
go
RECONFIGURE WITH OVERRIDE
go
```

Then you can make updates. Make sure you always do this within a transaction so that if you affect more rows than you meant to, it can be rolled back. Afterwards reset the "allow updates" flag.

```
sp_configure 'allow updates',0
go
RECONFIGURE WITH OVERRIDE
go
```

There are also a few occasions where Microsoft has put in extra protection to minimize the risk of users causing damage. One example is sysindexes, where you must specify the name, id and indid in the where clause otherwise the update will fail.

Reference

v1.02 2000.05.14	
Applies to SQL Server versions:	All
FAQ category:	Database Administration
Related FAQ articles:	n/a
Related Microsoft Knowledge Base articles:	n/a
Other related information:	n/a
Author:	Neil Pike

tempdbmaster

Q: How do I remove the tempdb database from a master or default device?

A: Do the following for SQL 6.5 and below:

1. Configure tempdb to be in RAM for 2MB. Use SQL Enterprise Manager or sp_configure.

2. Stop and restart SQL Server.

3. Add a new device for tempdb. Do not call it temp_db — any other name should be OK.

4. Make that new device a "default" device; make sure no other device is marked as default, especially master. You can check or change default status either using SQL Enterprise Manager, or the sp_diskdefault stored procedure. Both are fully described in Books Online.

5. Configure tempdb to *not* be in RAM (set value to 0).

6. Stop and restart SQL Server.

7. Re-mark whichever devices you want to be default.

For SQL 7.0 and above, tempdb is always in its own set of files anyway, but if you want to move them:

1. `ALTER DATABASE tempdb ALTER FILE logicalname FILENAME = newlocation ....`

2. Stop and restart SQL Server.

Reference

v1.02 2000.05.18

Applies to SQL Server versions:	6.5, 7.0, 2000
FAQ category:	Database Administration
Related FAQ articles:	n/a
Related Microsoft Knowledge Base articles:	Q187824 "INF: How to Move Tempdb to a Different Device"
Other related information:	n/a
Author:	Neil Pike

triggerorder

Q: How can I guarantee the order in which SQL Server fires triggers?

A: SQL Server 7.0 does not guarantee the firing order of multiple triggers for the same action. If you need things to happen in a particular order, you'll need to put all the code in a single trigger.

In SQL 7.0 triggers actually fire in object id order, but this is *not* documented or guaranteed and therefore could change without warning in a service pack or new version.

With SQL 2000 you can now define the first and last trigger to fire using sp_settriggerorder. This is only available for AFTER triggers. See the Books Online topic "First and Last Triggers" for a full explanation of this new feature.

Reference

v1.04 2000.05.27

Applies to SQL Server versions:	7.0, 2000
FAQ categories:	Database Administration, Application Design and Programming
Related FAQ articles:	n/a
Related Microsoft Knowledge Base articles:	n/a
Other related information:	n/a
Author:	Neil Pike

This section covers the DTS functions and tools built into SQL Server.

DTS

dtsactxdebug

Q: How can I debug ActiveX scripts in DTS packages?

A: You can use the Microsoft Script Debugger tool to debug ActiveX scripts in DTS packages, as follows:

1. Start Enterprise Manager.
2. Open the DTS package, and place a STOP statement in your ActiveX script.
3. Execute the package.

The Script Debugger will be invoked when the STOP statement is encountered. If no debugger is installed the STOP statement will be ignored.

Alternatively you can use a MsgBox statement to halt execution. From within the Script Debugger Running Documents window, select the document under "..\mmc.exe", then click Break On Next Statement. When you clear the message box you will be in debug mode.

Reference

v1.00 2000.03.25

Applies to SQL Server versions:	7.0, 2000
FAQ category:	DTS
Related FAQ articles:	n/a
Related Microsoft Knowledge Base articles:	n/a
Other related information:	`http://msdn.microsoft.com/scripting/`
Author:	Darren Green

dtsbackup

Q: How can I back up DTS packages?

A: Local server and repository (Meta Data) packages are both stored in the msdb database, so by backing this up you also back up your DTS packages.

Some people prefer to keep copies of their packages as file packages, which will obviously be covered by your normal file backup routine. Use the Save As option in the DTS Package Designer to save packages to file.

Reference

v1.00 2000.04.29	
Applies to SQL Server versions:	7.0, 2000
FAQ category:	DTS
Related FAQ articles:	n/a
Related Microsoft Knowledge Base articles:	n/a
Other related information:	`http://www.swynk.com/friends/green/dtsbackupvb.asp`
Author:	Darren Green

dtscocreateinstance

Q: Why do I get the error "DTS Wizard Error — CoCreateInstance Class not Registered"?

A: This is probably caused by the installation of newer Visual Studio code. Try installing or re-installing the latest service pack for SQL 7. If that doesn't work, manually reregister dtspkg.dll.

```
regsvr32 \<sql>\binn\dtspkg.dll
```

Reference

v1.01 2000.04.22	
Applies to SQL Server version:	7.0
FAQ categories:	DTS, Troubleshooting
Related FAQ articles:	n/a
Related Microsoft Knowledge Base articles:	n/a
Other related information:	n/a
Author:	Neil Pike

dtscolstorows

Q: How can I use DTS to transform columns into rows?

A: The simplest method is to use the DataPump task, and an ActiveX transformation script, as explained next:

Example Source Data File:

```
Role, Name_1, Name_2, Name_3
Authors, Neil, Tony, Umachandar
Publishers, Gary
Reviewers, Darren, Paul
```

Example Destination Table:

```
[Role] [varchar] (20)
[Name] [varchar] (20)
```

Results of "SELECT * FROM [dbo].[ColsToRows]":

```
RoleName
------------ ---------
Authors     Neil
Authors     Tony
Authors     Umachandar
Publishers  Gary
Reviewers   Darren
Reviewers   Paul
```

DTS

1. Add a SQL Server connection.

2. Add an Execute SQL task with the following code:

```
if exists (select * from sysobjects where id = object_id(N'[dbo].
  [ColsToRows]') and OBJECTPROPERTY(id, N'IsUserTable') = 1)
drop table [dbo].[ColsToRows]
GO
CREATE TABLE [dbo].[ColsToRows] (
    [Role] [varchar] (20) NOT NULL ,
    [Name] [varchar] (20) NOT NULL
) ON [PRIMARY]
GO
```

3. Execute the package to create the destination table.

4. Add an ActiveX script (VBScript) with the following code:

```
Function Main()
    DTSGlobalVariables("Counter") = 1
    Main = DTSTaskExecResult_Success
End Function
```

5. Add a text file (source) connection, pointing to the source file defined above, ensuring you define the file properties as Comma Delimited.

6. Add a Data Pump task between the text file connection and the SQL Server connection. Double-click the transformation to set the properties.

   Source: The file defined by the text file connection will already be set.

   Destination: Select your table created in Step 3.

   Transformations: Delete any existing transformations. Select all source and destination columns and add a new ActiveX transformation. Use the following code to define your transformation:

```
Function Main()
 Dim sSourceColumn

 DTSGlobalVariables("Counter") = DTSGlobalVariables("Counter") + 1

 If DTSGlobalVariables("Counter") <= 4 Then
     sSourceColumn = "Col00" & DTSGlobalVariables("Counter")
     If IsNull(DTSSource(sSourceColumn).Value) Then
         DTSGlobalVariables("Counter") = 1
         Main = DTSTransformStat_SkipInsert
     Else
         DTSDestination("Role") = DTSSource("Col001")
         DTSDestination("Name") = DTSSource(sSourceColumn)
         Main = DTSTransformStat_SkipFetch
     End If
 Else
     DTSGlobalVariables("Counter") = 1
     Main = DTSTransformStat_SkipInsert
 End If

End Function
```

7. Add an On Success Workflow constraint between the ActiveX script task and the Execute SQL task.

8. Add an On Success Workflow constraint between the Execute SQL task and the text file (source).

9. Execute the package.

This method works particularly well when you can have 1 to n occurrences of the same data item after your initial items, in this case multiple names after the role, because it uses the ColumnCounter to get the correct source column without having to code for each and every one. It also handles the uneven number of occurrences of name per row easily.

Another method is to use a Case statement on the counter and define the mapping for every column. Note that this example requires the Name column to accept nulls due to the uneven number of occurrences of name per row in my input file.

```
Function Main()

    DTSGlobalVariables("Counter") = DTSGlobalVariables("Counter") + 1

    If DTSGlobalVariables("Counter") <= 4 Then
        DTSDestination("Role") = DTSSource("Col001")
        Main = DTSTransformStat_SkipFetch
        Select Case DTSGlobalVariables("Counter")
            Case 2
                DTSDestination("Name") = DTSSource("Col002")
            Case 3
                DTSDestination("Name") = DTSSource("Col003")
            Case 4
                DTSDestination("Name") = DTSSource("Col004")
        End Select
    Else
        DTSGlobalVariables("Counter") = 1
        Main = DTSTransformStat_SkipInsert
    End If

End Function
```

Reference

v1.00 2000.04.24

Applies to SQL Server versions:	7.0, 2000
FAQ category:	DTS
Related FAQ articles:	n/a
Related Microsoft Knowledge Base articles:	n/a
Other related information:	n/a
Author:	Darren Green

dtscomponentcategories

Q: Why do I get the error "Could not create component categories manager" or "Could not create an instance of the DTS package"?

A: This can happen after you have installed additional software onto your SQL Server machine and certain DLLs have been overwritten with a different version.

The main culprit is Comcat.dll (winnt\system32). DTS requires version 4.71, however certain software such as Visual Studio Service Pack 3 will install version 5.

Replace the version 5 copy with version 4.71 from your SQL Server CD-ROM.

Reference

v1.00 2000.04.09	
Applies to SQL Server versions:	7.0, 2000
FAQ category:	DTS
Related FAQ articles:	n/a
Related Microsoft Knowledge Base articles:	n/a
Other related information:	n/a
Author:	Darren Green

dtsconnectionrefresh

Q: When I use the Step ExecutionStatus to re-execute a DataPump task, after dynamically changing the connection, the new source is not recognized. How can I fix this?

A: The new connection source is not recognized because the connection properties have not been reevaluated since the change. To force a refresh for the next loop:

1. Right-Click the DataPump task.
2. Select Workflow Properties, and move to the Options tab.
3. Check Close connection on completion.

Reference

v1.00 2000.04.09	
Applies to SQL Server versions:	7.0, 2000
FAQ category:	DTS
Related FAQ articles:	n/a
Related Microsoft Knowledge Base articles:	n/a
Other related information:	`http://www.swynk.com/friends/green/dtsdirloopstep.asp`
Author:	Darren Green

dtscustomtask

Q: How can I build a DTS custom task?

A: You can build a custom task in any COM-compliant language, such as Visual C++ or Visual Basic. For C++ you just implement the IDTSCustomTask interface, and for VB you must implement the CustomTask interface. There is a C++ sample on the SQL Server CD-ROM (`\Devtools\Samples\Dts\Dtstask\`).

To create a custom user interface you must also implement the DTSCustomTaskUI interface. All custom tasks require two properties, Name and Description, which must be handled correctly.

In Visual Basic you must create stubs to all of the required methods for both CustomTask and CustomTaskUI regardless of their usage. You can use the Object Browser to see the methods. Samples and more complete guidance are available at the URLs provided below, or in SQL Server 2000 Books Online which is far superior to SQL 7.0, in particular the topic "DTS Custom Task Examples."

Reference

v1.01 2000.04.29	
Applies to SQL Server versions:	7.0, 2000
FAQ category:	DTS
Related FAQ articles:	n/a
Related Microsoft Knowledge Base articles:	n/a
Other related information:	`http://www.swynk.com/friends/green/DTSCustomTaskUI1.asp`, `http://www.sqlmag.com/articles/Content/5911_01.html`, "DTS Custom Task Examples" in Books Online 2000
Author:	Darren Green

dtsdatabase

Q: How can I dynamically change a SQL Server connection's database property?

A: You can reference a connection from within an ActiveX script task and then change the database property, as follows:

```
Dim oPKG
Dim oConn
' Gain Reference to the Package Object
Set oPKG = DTSGlobalVariables.Parent
' Gain reference to the SQL Server Connection by Name
Set oConn = oPKG.Connections("SQL Connection Name")
' Set DataSource (Database) property to Global Variable
oConn.DataSource = DTSGlobalVariables("Global_Variable_Name").Value
```

For SQL Server 2000 this can be more easily accomplished by using the Dynamic Properties task.

Reference

v1.00 2000.03.18	
Applies to SQL Server versions:	7.0, 2000
FAQ category:	DTS
Related FAQ articles:	"How can I pass parameters to a DTS package?" (dtsparams, see page 231)
Related Microsoft Knowledge Base articles:	n/a
Other related information:	`http://www.swynk.com/friends/green/dtshowto3.asp`
Author:	Darren Green

dtsexecvb

Q: How can I execute a DTS package from Visual Basic?

A: The most common method is to execute the package using the DTS Package Object Library. The process follows the stages of loading a package, executing a package and checking for errors. To use the DTS Object library in Visual Basic you must check "Microsoft DTSPackage Object Library" under the project references.

To load the package, use one of these three methods—LoadFromSQLServer, LoadFromRepository or LoadFromStorageFile—depending on the storage location of the package.

Next, call the Package Object Execute method.

Finally you should check for any errors in the execution of your package. For this there are three options:

- Check the step ExecutionResult for each step in the package.
- Use the GetExecutionErrorInfo method for each step in the package. Note that this method cannot be used to get the full error description in VBScript, as the method has ByRef parameters of defined types. VBScript passes parameter ByVal (Q197956 "Passing Parameters By Reference to a VB COM Object").
- Declare the Package Object WithEvents (Dim WithEvents oPackage As DTS.Package) and use the package OnError (oPackage_OnError) event to capture all events as they happen.

A simple example using the ExecutionResult error checking method is given next:

```
'Load Package
Dim oPkg As DTS.Package
oPkg.LoadFromSQLServer ".", "", "", _
  DTSSQLStgFlag_UseTrustedConnection, "", "", "", "PackageName"

' Ensure ExecuteInMainThread in True
Dim oStep As DTS.Step
For Each oStep In oPkg.Steps
    oStep.ExecuteInMainThread = True
Next

' Execute Package
oPkg.Execute

' Check for Errors and display results
Dim sErrors As String, bSuccess As Boolean
bSuccess = True
```

```
For Each oStep In oPkg.Steps
    If oStep.ExecutionResult = DTSStepExecResult_Failure Then
        MsgBox sErrors = sErrors & "Step [" & oStep.Name & _
          "] Failed" & vbCrLf
        bSuccess = False
    Else
        MsgBox sErrors = sErrors & "Step [" & oStep.Name & _
          "] Succeeded" & vbCrLf
    End If
Next
If bSuccess Then
    sErrors = sErrors & vbCrLf & "Package Execution Succeeded"
Else
    sErrors = sErrors & vbCrLf & "Package Execution Failed"
End If

' Clean Up
oPkg.UnInitialize
Set oPkg = Nothing
```

All methods, enumerations and properties are fully documented in SQL Server Books Online.

Another method is to use the SQL Namespace interface. This calls the execution dialog from Enterprise Manager for use within you own application, with the benefit of the progress bar and complete error messages for each step. For an example of this in action check out the SQL-NS Browse sample project (`\mssql7\devtools\samples\sqlns\vb\browse\`) that comes with SQL Server.

Reference

v1.02 2000.03.26	
Applies to SQL Server versions:	7.0, 2000
FAQ categories:	DTS, Application Design and Programming
Related FAQ article:	"What is 'Run-Time Error—2177221499 (80040005) Provider generated code execution exception: EXCEPTION_ACCESS_VIOLATION' for DTS?" (dtsthread, see page 235)
Related Microsoft Knowledge Base articles:	Q221193 "How To Install DTS Event Handlers In Visual Basic," Q240221 "How To Handle Errors in DTS Package and Step Objects," and Q240406 "DTS Object Model Error Handling Doesn't Show Cause in VB"
Other related information:	n/a
Author:	Darren Green

dtsfilename

Q: How can I dynamically change the text file connection filename property?

A: You can reference a text file connection from within an ActiveX script task, and then change the filename property:

```
Dim oPKG
Dim oConn
' Gain Reference to the Package Object
Set oPKG = DTSGlobalVariables.Parent
' Gain reference to the Text Connection by Name
Set oConn = oPKG.Connections("Text File (Source)")
' Set DataSource (Filename) property to Global Variable
oConn.DataSource = DTSGlobalVariables("Global_Variable_Name").Value
```

For SQL Server 2000 this can be more easily accomplished by using the Dynamic Properties task.

Reference

v1.00 2000.03.18	
Applies to SQL Server versions:	7.0, 2000
FAQ category:	DTS
Related FAQ article:	"How can I pass parameters to a DTS package?" (dtsparams, see page 231)
Related Microsoft Knowledge Base articles:	n/a
Other related information:	`http://www.swynk.com/friends/green/dtshowto3.asp`
Author:	Darren Green

dtsfromsp

Q: How can I run a DTS package from within SQL Server—for example, a stored procedure?

A: You have a choice of four methods:

- Use DTSRUN.EXE utility from within a SQL Agent job step, from the xp_cmdshell stored procedure, or from a command prompt.

- If a SQL Agent job is set up to use DTSRUN.EXE, as above, you could invoke the job from the Job object in SQL-DMO. No example of this is provided.

- Use SQL_Namespace with the ExecuteCommandBy... methods. This supports a DTS package as the object.

- Use sp_OA sp's. An example of this follows (courtesy of Bill Hodghead):

```
IF EXISTS (SELECT * FROM sysobjects
  WHERE ID = OBJECT_ID(N'[dbo].[sp_displayoaerrorinfo]')
  AND OBJECTPROPERTY(id, N'IsProcedure') = 1)
    DROP PROCEDURE [dbo].[sp_displayoaerrorinfo]
GO

IF EXISTS (SELECT * FROM sysobjects
  WHERE ID = OBJECT_ID(N'[dbo].[sp_displaypkgerrors]')
  AND OBJECTPROPERTY(id, N'IsProcedure') = 1)
    DROP PROCEDURE [dbo].[sp_displaypkgerrors]
GO

IF EXISTS (SELECT * FROM sysobjects
  WHERE ID = OBJECT_ID(N'[dbo].[sp_executepackage]')
  AND OBJECTPROPERTY(id, N'IsProcedure') = 1)
    DROP PROCEDURE [dbo].[sp_executepackage]
GO

CREATE PROC sp_displayoaerrorinfo
    @object AS int
AS
DECLARE @hr int
DECLARE @output varchar(255)
DECLARE @source varchar(255)
DECLARE @desc varchar(255)

    PRINT 'OLE Automation Error Information'

    EXEC @hr = sp_OAGetErrorInfo @object, @source OUT, @desc OUT
    IF @hr = 0
    BEGIN
        SELECT @output = '  Source: ' + @source
        PRINT @output
        SELECT @output = '  Description: ' + @desc
        PRINT @output
    END

    ELSE
    BEGIN
        PRINT '  sp_OAGetErrorInfo failed.'
```

DTS

```
        RETURN
    END
GO


CREATE PROC sp_displaypkgerrors
    @pkg as int
AS
DECLARE @numsteps int
DECLARE @steps int
DECLARE @step int
DECLARE @stepresult int
DECLARE @pkgresult int
DECLARE @hr int

    SELECT @pkgresult = 0

    EXEC @hr = sp_OAGetProperty @pkg, 'Steps', @steps OUTPUT
    IF @hr <> 0
    BEGIN
        print 'Unable to get steps'
        EXEC sp_displayoaerrorinfo @pkg --, @hr
        RETURN
    END

    EXEC @hr = sp_OAGetProperty @steps, 'Count', @numsteps OUTPUT
    IF @hr <> 0
    BEGIN
        print 'Unable to get number of steps'
        EXEC sp_displayoaerrorinfo @steps --, @hr
        RETURN
    END

    WHILE @numsteps > 0
    BEGIN
        EXEC @hr = sp_OAGetProperty @steps, 'Item', @step OUTPUT,
          @numsteps
        IF @hr <> 0
        BEGIN
            print 'Unable to get step'
            EXEC sp_displayoaerrorinfo @steps --, @hr
            RETURN
        END

        EXEC @hr = sp_OAGetProperty @step, 'ExecutionResult',
          @stepresult OUTPUT
        IF @hr <> 0
```

```
        BEGIN
            print 'Unable to get ExecutionResult'
            EXEC sp_displayoaerrorinfo @step --, @hr
            RETURN
        END

        SELECT @numsteps = @numsteps - 1
        SELECT @pkgresult = @pkgresult + @stepresult
    END

    IF @pkgresult > 0
    BEGIN
        PRINT 'Package had ' + CAST(@pkgresult as varchar) +
          ' failed step(s)'
    END
    ELSE
        PRINT 'Packge Succeeded'

GO


CREATE PROC sp_executepackage
    -- Package name, gets most recent version
    @packagename varchar(255),
    -- Login pwd
    @userpwd varchar(255) = Null,
    -- Use non-zero to indicate integrated security
    @intsecurity bit = 0,
    -- Package password
    @pkgPwd varchar(255) = ''
AS
DECLARE @hr int
DECLARE @object int

    -- Create a package object
    EXEC @hr = sp_OACreate 'DTS.Package', @object OUTPUT
    IF @hr <> 0
    BEGIN
        EXEC sp_displayoaerrorinfo @object --, @hr
        RETURN
    END

    -- Load the package (ADD integrated security support)
    DECLARE @svr varchar(15)
    DECLARE @login varchar(15)
    SELECT @login = SUSER_NAME()
    SELECT @svr = HOST_NAME()
    DECLARE @flag int
    SELECT @flag = 0
```

DTS

```
IF @intsecurity = 0
BEGIN
    IF @userpwd = Null
    BEGIN
        -- ServerName As String, [ServerUserName As String],
        -- [ServerPassword As String],
        -- [Flags As DTSSQLServerStorageFlags],
        -- [PackagePassword As String], [PackageGuid As String],
        -- [PackageVersionGuid As String],
        -- [PackageName As String], [pVarPersistStgOfHost])
        EXEC @hr = sp_OAMethod @object, 'LoadFromSqlServer',
          NULL, @ServerName=@svr, @ServerUserName=@login,
          @PackageName=@packagename, @Flags=@flag,
          @PackagePassword = @pkgPwd
    END
    ELSE
    BEGIN
        EXEC @hr = sp_OAMethod @object, 'LoadFromSqlServer',
          NULL, @ServerName=@svr, @ServerUserName=@login,
          @PackageName=@packagename, @Flags=@flag,
          @PackagePassword = @pkgPwd, @ServerPassword = @userpwd
    END
END
ELSE
BEGIN
    SELECT @flag = 256
    EXEC @hr = sp_OAMethod @object, 'LoadFromSqlServer', NULL,
      @ServerName=@svr, @PackageName=@packagename, @Flags=@flag,
      @PackagePassword = @pkgPwd
END

IF @hr <> 0
BEGIN
    PRINT 'LoadFromSQLServer failed'
    EXEC sp_displayoaerrorinfo @object --, @hr
    RETURN
END

-- Execute it
EXEC @hr = sp_OAMethod @object, 'Execute'
IF @hr <> 0
BEGIN
    PRINT 'Execute failed'
    EXEC sp_displayoaerrorinfo @object --, @hr
    RETURN
END

-- Return the step errors as a recordset
EXEC sp_displaypkgerrors @object
```

```
        -- Unitialize the package
        EXEC @hr = sp_OAMethod @object, 'UnInitialize'
        IF @hr <> 0
        BEGIN
            print 'UnInitialize failed'
            EXEC sp_displayoaerrorinfo @object --, @hr
            RETURN
        END

        -- Release the package object
        EXEC @hr = sp_OADestroy @object
        IF @hr <> 0
        BEGIN
            EXEC sp_displayoaerrorinfo @object --, @hr
            RETURN
        END
GO
```

Reference

v1.02 2000.04.22	
Applies to SQL Server versions:	7.0, 2000
FAQ category:	DTS
Related FAQ articles:	n/a
Related Microsoft Knowledge Base articles:	n/a
Other related information:	`http://www.swynk.com/friends/green/dtsole.asp`
Author:	Neil Pike

dtsGetExecutionErrorInfo

Q: Why do I get a Type Mismatch error when I use the Step GetExecutionErrorInfo method in an ActiveX script?

A: This is because the GetExecutionErrorInfo method requires its parameters to be passed by reference, but VBScript passes arguments by value as the method's parameter data types are *not* variants. Put another way, it requires its arguments to be of the correct type, and VBScript can only handle the variant type so it is impossible to pass the error code as the required Long data type.

To work around this issue you can pass the step object to a COM object and let this call the GetExecutionErrorInfo method.

Reference

v1.00 2000.04.29

Applies to SQL Server versions:	7.0, 2000
FAQ category:	DTS
Related FAQ articles:	n/a
Related Microsoft Knowledge Base articles:	n/a
Other related information:	Q197956 "PRB: Passing Parameters By Reference to a VB COM Object"
Author:	Darren Green

dtshandlefile

Q: How can I delete or rename a file from DTS?

A: Two methods are available:

- Use Execute Process Task to execute a standard DOS command. This can be set dynamically by altering the ProcessCommandLine property.
- Use the Scripting FileSystemObject from within an ActiveX script task. The file system object is not installed as part of SQL Server but is available as part of other products including the Windows NT Option Pack or as part of Windows Scripting Host (`http://msdn.microsoft.com/scripting/`).

Reference

v1.00 2000.04.29

Applies to SQL Server versions:	7.0, 2000
FAQ category:	DTS
Related FAQ article:	"How can I dynamically change the text file connection filename property?" (dtsfilename, see page 220)
Related Microsoft Knowledge Base articles:	n/a
Other related information:	n/a
Author:	Darren Green

dtsinvalidclassstring

Q: I get the error "The parameter is incorrect," "Invalid class string" or "The system cannot find the file specified" when trying to open or execute a DTS package. What should I do?

A: This is caused by incompatibilities between the DTS package format of SQL Server 7 RTM or SQL Server 7 Service Pack 1 and SQL Server 7 Service Pack 2 or SQL Server 2000.

You cannot edit or run a package on a pre-SP2 machine once an SP2 or SQL 2000 machine has saved it, unless you use a package password. The standard format used to save packages has been changed after SP1. The encrypted package format, however, is the same, so using a package password will bypass the issue. Alternatively, open a version of the package prior to the SP2/2000 edit, and only save changes using RTM or SP1 tools.

The message "The system cannot find the file specified" is specific to SQL 2000, for which the standard format has changed again from that of SQL 7.0 SP2. The use of a package password will overcome this issue as well.

Further enhancements to ensure full compatibility are expected in SQL Server 7.0 Service Pack 3, including the ability to save packages in either SQL 7.0 SP2 or SQL 2000 format.

Reference

v1.03 2000.07.06

Applies to SQL Server versions:	7.0, 2000
FAQ categories:	DTS, Troubleshooting
Related FAQ articles:	n/a
Related Microsoft Knowledge Base articles:	n/a
Other related information:	n/a
Author:	Darren Green

dtslicenseerror

Q: I'm getting the following error with SQL 7 DTS: "The license for the installation of Microsoft SQL Server on your source and destinations connections does not permit the use of DTS to transform data. Refer to your license for more information." What should I do?

A: The small print on the license agreement says you can't do distributed operations (distributed query, replication, DTS) between SQL Server Desktop and Standard/Enterprise version if the Standard/Enterprise version is installed in "per server" mode.

Switch the SQL Server to "per seat" mode via the licensing applet in control panel, and ensure that you have a client access license for each computer on which you have installed the Desktop Edition.

Reference

v1.01 2000.04.22

Applies to SQL Server version:	7.0
FAQ categories:	DTS, Troubleshooting
Related FAQ articles:	n/a
Related Microsoft Knowledge Base article:	Q207809 "INF: DTS/Replication Licensing for Desktop SQL Server 7.0"
Other related information:	"SQL Server 7.0 Databases on the Desktop" in Books Online 7
Author:	Neil Pike

dtslistpkgs

Q: How can I list get a list of DTS packages?

A: The method depends on the location of the package:

- Local packages are stored in the sysdtspackages table. You can query this table directly:

```
SELECT DISTINCT name FROM sysdtspackages
```

As each version of a package is a row in sysdtspackages, use the DISTINCT clause to show unique names only.

The Microsoft approach is to use the stored procedure sp_enum_dtspackages

```
exec msdb..sp_enum_dtspackages
```

- Repository packages are a bit more difficult to get at because they are stored in the repository tables. Direct access to these tables is discouraged, but this query will work:

```
SELECT DISTINCT RTblNamedObj.Name, TFMPackage.PackageID FROM TfmPackage INNER
   JOIN RTblNamedObj ON TFMPackage.IntID = RTblNamedObj.IntID
```

- You can also use SQL Namespace (SQL-NS) to retrieve lists of both local and repository packages. For an example of this see the Browse.exe sample (\mssql7\devtools\ samples\sqlns\vb\browse\).

- Repository packages can also be enumerated through the Repository Object. See Q241249 for some sample code.

- SQL Server 2000 has the new DTS Application object. Using the GetPackageSQLServer or GetPackageRepository methods returns a PackageSQLServer object. From this you can use the EnumPackageInfos method to get the PackageInfos collection. The PackageInfo object has several useful properties including Name and PackageID. See "Retrieving DTS System, Package, and Log Data" in Books Online for more details.

Reference

v1.01 2000.07.10

Applies to SQL Server versions:	7.0, 2000
FAQ category:	DTS
Related FAQ articles:	n/a
Related Microsoft Knowledge Base article:	Q241249 "INF: How to Obtain a List of DTS Packages"
Other related information:	n/a
Author:	Darren Green

dtsoracle

Q: What issues are there with SQL 7's DTS functions and Oracle?

A: See the reference provided below.

Reference

v1.02 2000.04.22

Applies to SQL Server version:	7.0
FAQ categories:	DTS, Troubleshooting
Related FAQ articles:	n/a
Related Microsoft Knowledge Base articles:	n/a
Other related information:	"DTS Data Conversion and Transformation Considerations" in Books Online 7.
Author:	Neil Pike

dtsorjobdoesntworkwhenscheduled

Q: I can run some SQL code or a DTS package myself fine, but when I run it using the SQL Scheduler it doesn't work. Why not?

A: When run via SQL Executive/SQL Agent, the job runs with the NT credentials of the NT user account that the SQL Executive/SQL Agent service is running under. This account needs to have access to the network resources concerned—for example, shares, files, and printers.

Check which account is being used by going to Control Panel ➤ Services ➤ Startup and checking.

If it is using the LocalSystem account, this has no network access.

For any network resources you use, make sure they are referenced by UNC name and not a specific drive letter, for example, \\server1\bcps and not H:\.

See the FAQ article "bcpxpcmdshell" for additional suggestions about allowing access to SQL Server service accounts.

Reference

v1.01 2000.04.22	
Applies to SQL Server versions:	All
FAQ categories:	DTS, Troubleshooting
Related FAQ article:	"I am having problems with SQL Server running BCP from xp_cmdshell—why does it not run or see the files I want it to?" (bcpxpcmdshell, see page 489)
Related Microsoft Knowledge Base article:	Q269074 "INF: How to Run a DTS Package as a Scheduled Job"
Other related information:	n/a
Author:	Neil Pike

dtsparams

Q: How can I pass parameters to a DTS package?

A: You cannot do this directly in SQL Server 7.0, but several workarounds are available, depending on the execution method you choose.

Whichever method you choose, I recommend that you separate the passing of parameters and setting of properties. To do this I suggest you set any parameters as global variables within the package. You can then use an ActiveX script task or Dynamic Properties task (SQL 2000 only) to read the global variables and assign them to the relevant connection or task properties. This method makes it easy to change the execution method without redesigning the package.

When executing from a stored procedure, using the sp_OAxxx stored procedures, you can add some additional sp_OAxxx calls to set DTS GlobalVariables. Due to the cumbersome nature of the sp_OAxxx syntax and their associated error handling, it is far simpler to set global variables as opposed to properties.

Visual Basic can be used to load and execute packages, and once loaded you can easily set a global variable or property. You could even write a simple VB program that accepts command line parameters which are used to set task or connection properties prior to calling the Execute method.

The version of DTSRun.exe supplied with SQL Server 2000 now supports the passing of global variables as command line parameters.

Another variation is to use an ActiveX script task to read the parameters from a location of your choice, such as a file, SQL Server Table or the Windows registry. The script can then set the task or connection properties as required. The method is ideal for scheduled packages or packages executed via DTSRUN.

Reference

v1.00 2000.03.16	
Applies to SQL Server versions:	7.0, 2000
FAQ category:	DTS
Related FAQ articles:	"How can I run a DTS package from within SQL Server – for example, a stored procedure?" (dtsfromsp, see page 220), "How can I dynamically change the text file connection filename property?" (dtsfilename, see page 220), and "How can I dynamically change a SQL Server connection's Server Name property?" (dtsserver, see below)
Related Microsoft Knowledge Base articles:	n/a
Other related information:	n/a
Author:	Darren Green

dtsserver

Q: How can I dynamically change a SQL Server Connection, Server Name property?

A: You can reference a Connection from within an ActiveX Script Task, and then change the Server property, as follows:

```
Dim oPKG
Dim cn
' Gain Reference to the Package Object
Set oPKG = DTSGlobalVariables.Parent
' Gain reference to the SQL Server Connection by Name
Set cn = oPKG.Connections("SQL Connection Name")
' Set DataSource (Server) property to Global Variable
cn.DataSource = DTSGlobalVariables("Global_Variable_Name").Value
```

For SQL Server 2000 this can be more easily accomplished by using the Dynamic Properties Task.

Reference

v1.00 2000.03.18

Applies to SQL Server versions:	7.0, 2000
FAQ category:	DTS
Related FAQ article:	"How can I pass parameters to a DTS package?" (dtsparams, see page 231)
Related Microsoft Knowledge Base articles:	n/a
Other related information:	`http://www.swynk.com/friends/green/dtshowto3.asp`
Author:	Darren Green

dtssizes

Q: How can I set DataPump's Insert Commit size to a value greater than 9,999?

A: The DataPump (Transform Data task) GUI has a limit of 9,999 for the Insert Commit Size and Fetch Buffer properties. This is only a GUI limitation so you can set higher values via code. Use the following sample in an ActiveX script task to set a value of 10,000 for the Insert Commit Size:

```
Function Main()
   DTSGlobalVariables.Parent.Tasks("DTSTask_DTSDataPumpTask_1")._
        CustomTask.InsertCommitSize = 10000
    Main = DTSTaskExecResult_Success
End Function
```

The SQL 2000 GUI has an Insert Batch Size (Insert Commit Size) limit of 999999. In addition to the method above, you can use the Disconnected Edit feature or the Dynamic Properties task to increase the value although such a high value would almost certainly have a negative impact on performance.

Reference

v1.00 2000.05.27

Applies to SQL Server versions:	7.0, 2000
FAQ category:	DTS
Related FAQ articles:	n/a
Related Microsoft Knowledge Base articles:	n/a
Other related information:	n/a
Author:	Darren Green

dtsskiprows

Q: How can I skip certain rows during my DTS import?

A: If it is simply a case of skipping header rows, you can set the First Row property (see Advanced properties sheet) of the DataPump task. If your source is a text file, this has the Skip Rows property (see file properties of the connection) which you can also use.

If you want to be able to exclude rows that can occur anywhere in your source data, you can import into a staging table and delete them from there, before moving the data to its final location, or use an ActiveX transformation to avoid importing them at all:

```
Function Main()
    If DTSSource("Col001") = 2 Then
        Main  = DTSTransformStat_SkipRow
    Else
        DTSDestination("RowType") = DTSSource("Col001")
        DTSDestination("NameText") = DTSSource("Col002")
        Main = DTSTransformStat_OK
    End If
End Function
```

The key to this is the use of the DTSTransformStat_SkipRow constant to stop processing of the unwanted rows, in this case those with a RowType of 2.

Reference

v1.00 2000.04.24	
Applies to SQL Server versions:	7.0, 2000
FAQ category:	DTS
Related FAQ articles:	n/a
Related Microsoft Knowledge Base articles:	n/a
Other related information:	"DTSTransformStatus" in SQL Server Books Online
Author:	Darren Green

dtssqlns

Q: How can I use the Enterprise Manager Executing DTS Package dialog within my own application?

A: This dialog is available through SQL Namespace (SQL-NS). For an example of this see `mssql7\devtools\sqlns\vb\browse\` or `http://www.swynk.com/friends/green/dtsbrowseVB.asp`.

Reference

v1.00 2000.04.09	
Applies to SQL Server versions:	7.0, 2000
FAQ category:	DTS
Related FAQ articles:	n/a
Related Microsoft Knowledge Base articles:	n/a
Other related information:	`http://www.swynk.com/friends/green/dtsbrowseVB.asp`
Author:	Darren Green

dtsthread

Q: What is "Run-Time Error—2177221499 (80040005) Provider generated code execution exception: EXCEPTION_ACCESS_VIOLATION" for DTS?

A: Visual Basic is an apartment-threaded application but DTS is free-threaded. When executing a package from Visual Basic or a package that contains a custom task created in Visual Basic, conflicts may occur.

This can be overcome simply by setting the step's ExecuteInMainThread property to true. When executing from VB this must be done for every step. When you are not executing from VB but are using a VB custom task, this only needs to be set for the custom task's step.

To do this manually, right-click a task and select Workflow Properties, then select the Options sheet. In the Execution frame you will see the Execute on Main Package Thread option which needs to be checked. This can also be done programmatically—see dtsexecvb for an example of this.

Reference

v1.00 2000.03.19	
Applies to SQL Server versions:	7.0, 2000
FAQ category:	DTS
Related FAQ article:	"How can I execute a DTS package from Visual Basic? " (dtsexecvb, see page 217)
Related Microsoft Knowledge Base articles:	n/a
Other related information:	n/a
Author:	Darren Green

pkgwithinpkg

Q: How can I execute a package from within a package?

A: You can execute a package from within a package in the following ways:

- Use DTSRUN from with an Execute Process task:

```
dtsrun /Sserver_name /Uuser_nName /Ppassword /Npackage_name /Mpackage-password
```

- See Books Online topic "DTSRUN Utility" for the full syntax.
- Use the DTS Package Object Execute method from with an ActiveX script task, as follows:

```
Function Main()

    Const DTSSQLStgFlag_UseTrustedConnection = 256
    Main = DTSTaskExecResult_Success

    ' Load and Execute Local Package "PackageName", using integrated security
    Dim oPKG
    Set oPKG = CreateObject("DTS.Package")
  oPKG.LoadFromSQLServer "." , , , DTSSQLStgFlag_UseTrustedConnection,_
  , , , "PackageName"    oPKG.Execute
```

```
    Check for execution errors and set Task result flag to failure if appropriate
    Dim oStep
    For Each oStep In oPKG.Steps
        If oStep.ExecutionResult = DTSStepExecResult_Failure Then
            MsgBox oStep.Name & " Failed"
            Main = DTSTaskExecResult_Failure
        End If
    Next
    oPKG.Uninitialize()
    Set oPKG = Nothing


End Function
```

- SQL Server 2000 provides a new Execute Package task. Advantages of this include the ability to pass global variables to the child package, and executing the child package within the package transaction of the master package.

Reference

v1.01 2000.03.18

Applies to SQL Server versions:	7.0, 2000
FAQ category:	DTS
Related FAQ articles:	n/a
Related Microsoft Knowledge Base articles:	n/a
Other related information:	n/a
Author:	Darren Green

ScriptPkg

Q: What is ScriptPkg and where does it come from?

A: ScriptPkg is a small utility written in Visual Basic 6. It can be found on the SQL Server 7 CD-ROM or on your PC, if you selected to install the Development Tools. Run the self-extracting archive \mssql7\devtools\samples\dts\dtsdemo.exe, then look in the new folder Designer.

ScriptPkg loads a package and generates Visual Basic code to rebuild the specified package. It is very useful in understanding the DTS object model because you can compare properties set in the designer with the code produced. Using this knowledge you can then dynamically alter task and connection properties at runtime, making your packages more flexible.

The SQL Server 2000 DTS Designer has a new Location Visual Basic File from the Save As dialog which performs the same function as ScriptPkg, but produces neater code.

Reference

v1.00 2000.03.19

Applies to SQL Server versions:	7.0, 2000
FAQ category:	DTS
Related FAQ articles:	n/a
Related Microsoft Knowledge Base article:	Q239454 "INF: ScriptPkg Tool Generates DTS Object Model Code to Help Use DTS Programmatically"
Other related information:	n/a
Author:	Darren Green

transferdtspackages

Q: How can I transfer DTS packages from one SQL server to another?

A: You have four choices:

- For Local packages, you can use DTS to transfer the package data between the two servers directly, as local packages are stored in the system table msdb.dbo.sysdtspackages.

1. Create a new DTS package, with a two SQL Server connections, one each for the source and destination servers.

2. Add a DataPump task, setting the source and destination tables to [msdb].[dbo].[sysdtspackages]. You will need to manually enter the table name, as system tables are not available in the drop-down box. For SQL 2000, the ability to type in table names has been removed, but you can use Disconnected Edit. Once you have added the DataPump task, but before you open the properties sheet, use Disconnected Edit to set both the DestinationObjectName and SourceObjectName properties to [msdb].[dbo].[sysdtspackages]. Then open the properties sheet and select the Transformations sheet to auto-build the transformations correctly.

3. Accept the default transformations and execute the package.

You can enhance this process by using a query for the source to limit which packages or package versions are transferred:

Transfer only the most recent version of each package:

```
SELECT T1.* FROM dbo.sysdtspackages AS T1
INNER JOIN (
  SELECT [name], [id], MAX([createdate]) AS [createdate]
  FROM dbo.sysdtspackages GROUP BY [name], [id]) AS T2
ON T1.[id] = T2.[id] AND T1.[createdate] = T2.[createdate]
```

Transfer only the last five versions of each package:

```
SELECT T1.* FROM dbo.sysdtspackages AS T1
INNER JOIN (
  SELECT T2.[name] , T2.[id], T2.[createdate] FROM dbo.sysdtspackages T2
  GROUP BY T2.[name], T2.[id], T2.[createdate]
  HAVING T2.[createdate] IN (SELECT TOP 5 T3.[createdate]
    FROM dbo.sysdtspackages T3
    WHERE T2.[id] = T3.[id]
    ORDER BY T3.[createdate] DESC) ) AS T2
ON T1.[id] = T2.[id] AND T1.[createdate] = T2.[createdate]
```

- For repository packages, or to transfer packages between servers with no network connection, you can save each DTS package as a COM structured storage file. Open the package in EM and select Save As, changing the Location to Storage File. Copy the xxxx.dts files created to the target machine. From EM, right-click Data Transformation Packages and choose All Tasks, Open Package for each package. You can use Save As to save them to your new server or repository.

- A free utility available from `http://www.swynk.com/friends/green/dtsbackupvb.asp` has both GUI and command line modes that can be used to speed up or automate this process. It uses the load and save methods of the Package Object. Unfortunately these do not maintain package layout or annotations.

- Open them in the package designer. Choose Save As, and change the Server options to save them to the new server.

The first option is the quickest for lots of packages, but has limitations.

Reference

v1.05 2000.09.10	
Applies to SQL Server versions:	7.0, 2000
FAQ categories:	DTS, Server Administration and Tools
Related FAQ articles:	n/a
Related Microsoft Knowledge Base articles:	n/a
Other related information:	n/a
Authors:	Neil Pike, Darren Green

Installation and Upgrades

This section covers the installation and upgrade of SQL Server, tools, and client utilities.

421to7

Q: Can I upgrade SQL 4.x to 7.0 directly?

A: No. Follow these steps:

1. Upgrade to NT 3.51 if you're not already at that level.
2. Upgrade from SQL 4.x to SQL 6.5.
3. Install SQL 6.5 Service Pack 3 or above.
4. Upgrade to NT 4.0 if you're not already at that level.
5. Install NT 4.0 Service Pack 4 or above.
6. Install IE 4.0 SP1 or above.
7. Upgrade SQL 6.5 to SQL 7.
8. Install the latest SQL 7.0 Service Pack.

The procedure is easy, if a little manual.

Reference

v1.04 2000.05.25

Applies to SQL Server versions:	4.x, 7.0
FAQ category:	Installation and Upgrades
Related FAQ articles:	n/a
Related Microsoft Knowledge Base articles:	Q195444 "INF: Frequently Asked Questions—Conversion" and Q122352 "INF: Supported Windows Versions for SQL Server"
Other related information:	"Upgrading SQL Server" in Books Online 6.x, and "Upgrading from an Earlier Version of SQL Server" in Books Online 7
Author:	Neil Pike

betaprogram

Q: How can I get on a beta program for new versions of SQL, OLAP, orMSEQ?

A: For any beta of Microsoft software you can e-mail betareq@microsoft.com telling them why you want to be on the program.

If you have Microsoft sales or support contacts (such as a TAM for Premier Support), approach them.

You can subscribe to TechNet Plus which includes many of the betas—these CD's are shipped or refreshed monthly.

If you subscribe to MSDN Universal, some betas are shipped as part of your subscription.

Reference

v1.01 2000.04.01

Applies to SQL Server versions:	All
FAQ category:	Installation and Upgrades
Related FAQ articles:	n/a
Related Microsoft Knowledge Base articles:	n/a
Other related information:	n/a
Author:	Neil Pike

clientinstall32

Q: How can I install the 32-bit SQL Server client for NT or Windows 9x?

A: Under 6.5 and earlier, run setup from the \I386 directory as if you were installing the whole of SQL Server on the client. Then just check "Install client utilities only" when asked. This will just install the client utilities and Net-Libs.

For SQL 7.0 do the same thing—just choose the client connectivity component only. If you install from a "server" CD, Win9x and NT workstation clients will only be able to install the client drivers anyway.

This includes all the tools like SQL Enterprise Manager (which runs fine on Win9x).

If all you want are ODBC-type drivers and no utilities, then the latest version of these can be installed as part of the current Microsoft Data Access Components release, which can be downloaded from `http://www.microsoft.com/data/`.

Reference

v1.03 2000.04.15

Applies to SQL Server versions:	All
FAQ category:	Installation and Upgrades
Related FAQ articles:	n/a
Related Microsoft Knowledge Base articles:	n/a
Other related information:	n/a
Author:	Neil Pike

clientregistry

Q: What registry entries does SQL Server's client use?

A: For 16-bit Windows clients, WIN.INI is used. For all 32-bit clients the following are used:

```
HKEY_LOCAL_MACHINE\SOFTWARE\Microsoft\MSSQLServer\Client\ConnectTo
```

```
DSQUERY : REG_SZ : default protocol - defaults to named-pipes
```

Individual entries can appear for server aliases set up using the Client Network Utility, for example:

```
aliasname1 : REG_SZ : DBNMPNTW,\\SERVER\pipe\sql\query
aliasname2 : REG_SZ : DBMSSOCN,10.1.1.1
```

and so forth.

Reference

v1.02 2000.04.15

Applies to SQL Server versions:	All
FAQ categories:	Installation and Upgrades, Connectivity
Related FAQ articles:	n/a
Related Microsoft Knowledge Base articles:	n/a
Other related information:	"dbopen" in Books Online
Author:	Neil Pike

clientregistry

Q: What registry entries does SQL Server's client use?

A: For 16-bit Windows clients, WIN.INI is used. For all 32-bit clients the following are used:

```
HKEY_LOCAL_MACHINE\SOFTWARE\Microsoft\MSSQLServer\Client\ConnectTo

DSQUERY : REG_SZ : default protocol - defaults to named-pipes
```

Individual entries can appear for server aliases set up using the Client Network Utility, for example:

```
aliasname1 : REG_SZ : DBNMPNTW,\\SERVER\pipe\sql\query
aliasname2 : REG_SZ : DBMSSOCN,10.1.1.1
```

and so forth.

Reference

v1.02 2000.04.15

Applies to SQL Server versions:	All
FAQ categories:	Installation and Upgrades, Connectivity
Related FAQ articles:	n/a
Related Microsoft Knowledge Base articles:	n/a
Other related information:	"dbopen" in Books Online
Author:	Neil Pike

dedicatedserver

Q: Can I run SQL Server on the same machine as Oracle or Exchange? Can it be a PDC/BDC?

A: The technical answer is yes, as long as there are sufficient resources for all services and you don't mind putting several eggs in one basket. However, for performance, resilience, and ease of maintenance and upgrades, it is always better to have SQL Server running on its own dedicated server.

There are no known compatibility problems with running SQL alongside any other Microsoft or third party products—DBMS or otherwise.

The same holds true for the domain controller question—if you have a very large domain with lots of trusts and authentication requests, then co-hosting SQL on it probably isn't a good idea. You *will* see articles from Microsoft saying that putting SQL Server on a DC is a no-no, but these articles date from the time when an NT machine was a 486/33 with 16Mb of RAM, not the 4x800Mhz Xeon 4Gb RAM monsters currently available.

So give it a try and monitor the resources with NT Performance Monitor. Check CPU usage and waits, disk usage and waits, network usage and waits. The most important counter to check is memory pages/sec, which will tell you if the memory is over-committed and actually causing physical paging to disk. With SQL Server 6.5 and below, you may want to restrict the amount of memory allocated to SQL Server in order to release memory to other processes, and thus minimize paging. With SQL 7.0, this is unnecessary because SQL Server automatically tunes its own memory usage according to demand.

Reference

v1.04 2000.04.21	
Applies to SQL Server versions:	All
FAQ category:	Installation and Upgrades
Related FAQ article:	"Does SQL Server have memory leaks? How can I tell? Why is SQL Server using so much memory? What do I do about virtual memory errors?" (memoryleak, see page 512)
Related Microsoft Knowledge Base articles:	n/a
Other related information:	n/a
Author:	Neil Pike

desktopinstall

Q: How can I install the Desktop Edition of SQL 7.0? It doesn't appear as an option.

A: Run `setupsql k=Dk`. This tells the setup routine to install the Desktop Edition.

Reference

v1.00 2000.06.13

Applies to SQL Server versions:	All
FAQ category:	Installation and Upgrades
Related FAQ articles:	n/a
Related Microsoft Knowledge Base articles:	n/a
Other related information:	n/a
Author:	Neil Pike

download

Q: Where can I download SQL Server utilities and service packs?

A: Start at `http://www.microsoft.com/sql/`.

Alternatively there is an ftp location at `ftp://ftp.microsoft.com/bussys/sql`.

Reference

v1.02 2000.04.21

Applies to SQL Server versions:	All
FAQ category:	Installation and Upgrades
Related FAQ articles:	n/a
Related Microsoft Knowledge Base articles:	n/a
Other related information:	n/a
Author:	Neil Pike

evalnt

Q: Why does my copy of SQL Server say it is the 120-day evaluation edition when it is the full commercial copy?

A: This is because you have it installed on an evaluation copy of NT—SQL Server also checks the licensed state of the operating system. You will need to reinstall a retail version of NT.

Reference

v1.02 2000.06.01

Applies to SQL Server versions:	All
FAQ category:	Installation and Upgrades
Related FAQ articles:	n/a
Related Microsoft Knowledge Base articles:	n/a
Other related information:	n/a
Author:	Neil Pike

evalupgrade

Q: How can I upgrade the 120-day evaluation version to the full SQL version?

A: See Q237303 as well as the following.

For SQL 6.5

One method would be to backup the databases, uninstall SQL, reinstall SQL and then load the databases again.

A faster method is to:

1. Back up your databases first (just in case).
2. Copy over all the .DLLs and .EXEs from the full version, over the top of the evaluation version.

3. Then from the <sql>\binn directory run the following, making sure the case is correct:

```
setup /t RegistryRebuild = On
```

4. The setup routine will now run and ask you all the normal questions. Answer these as you did for the 120-day evaluation version (putting in the same paths) and it will just update the registry entries and icons. It will leave the databases alone.

For SQL 7.0

If you can connect to SQL then you can do the first two steps, otherwise it doesn't matter, but you'll have to create the logins again manually unless you do a Restore of master.

1. Detach your user databases (sp_detach_db).
2. Create a script file for all logins (or BCP out sysxlogins).
3. Stop SQL Server.
4. Back up all user database files—*.mdf/*.ndf/*.ldf.
5. Uninstall SQL Server eval.
6. Install a retail copy of SQL Server.
7. Run a script to create logins (or BCP in sysxlogins).
8. If user databases were deleted by the uninstall (they shouldn't have been) then restore from backup.
9. Attach user databases (sp_attach_db).

Reference

v1.07 2000.06.01	
Applies to SQL Server versions:	All
FAQ category:	Installation and Upgrades
Related FAQ articles:	n/a
Related Microsoft Knowledge Base articles:	Q237303 "INF: How to Upgrade From SQL Server 7.0 Evaluation Edition to Retail Version" and Q157805 "BUG: RegistryRebuild Option of Setup Is Not Documented"
Other related information:	n/a
Author:	Neil Pike

hardwareperformance

Q: What specification hardware do I need to run SQL Server for good performance?

A: 1) How long is a piece of string? 2) It depends.

These are the two most accurate answers that can be given, as complete information is needed regarding the size of the database, complexity, triggers, indices, DRI, the number of users, transactions per minute, update ratio, row length and key sizes before even a rough estimate can be provided. Moreover, hardware performance in terms of CPU power and disk performance is always increasing at phenomenal rates.

Some hardware manufacturers have hardware sizing tools that calculate the best models for a particular application's characteristics. For example, see Solution Sizers at

`http://www.compaq.com/activeanswers.`

However, here are some general pointers:

Memory is the most important resource until you get to a 95 percent cache-hit ratio. It then doesn't matter too much how much extra memory you add. Start with 128MB RAM (because RAM is cheap), but make sure you have spare SIMM or DIMM slots for expansion.

Next come disks and the disk subsystem—especially for updates. Battery-backed write-back cache is good—the more the better. The more RAID controllers you have the better—not because they are generally a bottleneck, but because you can have multiple sets of read and write-back cache assigned. Dedicating a controller to the transaction log is good because this provides some dedicated write-back cache.

Processors usually come last. SQL rarely gets processor-bound except on the biggest systems, but if you have the money then get two or more. The biggest benefit comes from the second, and the law of diminishing returns kicks in after that. SQL scales well to four processors, and scales reasonably well to eight (depending on the hardware implementation), but after that, results are generally not worth the investment. Remember that with 6.5 and below, a single query will only ever use a single processor, whereas in SQL 7.0 it will parallelize queries if it thinks that will make it run faster.

Don't forget network cards and network design. You won't get 500 concurrent users through a single 10MB Ethernet ISA card. If you have a significant workload in terms of users or large result sets, make sure you have multiple network cards of the PCI bus master variety. Have the cards on different rings or segments if your users are devolved that way, otherwise attach the cards directly to a switch for full-duplex throughput and consider the use of either software or hardware card aggregation (like RAID for disks, but for cards). Some cards have this facility built into the hardware, but some third party software drivers will make it work for any card.

Reference

v1.01 2000.05.02

Applies to SQL Server versions:	All
FAQ categories:	Installation and Upgrades
Related FAQ articles:	n/a
Related Microsoft Knowledge Base articles:	n/a
Other related information:	n/a
Author:	Neil Pike

hotfixes

Q: What are SQL Server hot fixes and where can I get them?

A: Hot fixes are builds of SQL Server just like service packs. However, they are not fully packaged or given the same level of testing as a service pack. They should be applied only to resolve a particular problem.

To get them, the official answer is that you must contact Microsoft Product Support Services by phone. You can get contact details from `http://support.microsoft.com/support/supportnet/default.asp`. The call screener answering the phone will charge your account or credit card for the call—in the U.S. this is currently $195. Then when the engineer you are put through to determines the call is about a Microsoft bug they will refund it. They will tell you where to get the hot fix, or will send it to you.

Unofficially, you can pick up hot fixes from `ftp.microsoft.com/bussys/sql/transfer` as long as you know the build number and PKZIP password you need. The files are called SQLbbbm.EXE where bbb is the build number and m is the machine type. So SQL324I.EXE is build 324 for Intel. The files are PKZIP password protected.

Wherever you get one, be aware that hot fixes are typically *not* regression tested and can cause a lot more damage than they can fix. You are strongly urged to discuss using any hot fix with a Microsoft PSS representative before applying it.

Reference

v1.03 1999.11.04

Applies to SQL Server versions:	All
FAQ categories:	Installation and Upgrades, Troubleshooting
Related FAQ articles:	n/a
Related Microsoft Knowledge Base articles:	n/a
Other related information:	n/a
Author:	Neil Pike

ie5

Q: Are there any known issues with IE5 and SQL Server 7.0?

A: Yes. See Q225084.

Installing Microsoft Internet Explorer 5.0 on Windows 95 or Windows 98 computers running the Microsoft SQL Server 7.0 client may cause exceptions and GPFs when using wizards and property sheets. It affects only the user of the client wizard tool. There is no effect on the server.

The problem is fixed in SQL 7.0 SP1.

Reference

v1.02 2000.05.02	
Applies to SQL Server version:	7.0
FAQ category:	Installation and Upgrades
Related FAQ articles:	n/a
Related Microsoft Knowledge Base article:	Q225084 "FIX: IE 5.0 Hinders SQL Server 7.0 Wizards and Tabbed Dialogs on Windows 95 or 98 Computers"
Other related information:	n/a
Author:	Neil Pike

install

Q: I'm having trouble installing SQL Server/MSDE. What could be going wrong?

A: Try the following checklist of things that could go wrong. Notes apply to all versions and types of SQL Server unless otherwise specified.

- On an NT box, make sure you have administrator level-permissions on the machine in question, because SQL needs to create registry entries and services.

- Make sure that the Server and Workstation services are running. If the server service is not running you may see an error, "Error 2114 occurred while attempting to perform operation 'NetServergetInfo'" Look in the NT event log to ascertain the chain of events that caused the services not to start.

- Make sure the machine is of the required spec to run the version of SQL you are installing. For example, if it is SQL EE, make sure you have NT EE. For SQL 7.0/MSDE you need a 100 percent Pentium-compatible chip or an Alpha—older Cyrix/IBM chips that do not support the full Pentium instruction set will not work. With SQL 7.0 the setup routine will tell you the chip is no good, but MSDE will seem to install OK, but will AV on start-up. There is more information in the "platform" FAQ article.

- If you have tried to install SQL before, it is a *very* good idea to manually clean up all the files and registry entries using the instructions in the "uninstall" FAQ article first.

- If SQL is complaining about not enough space being available, this could be due to a known bug when there is between <n> times 4,295,917 KB and <n> times 4,367,417 KB. To get around this, either create temporary files to use space up, or start the SQL setup program as follows. Spacing is important.

  ```
  <sqldir>\i386\setup /t SpaceChecking = Off
  ```

  See Q192139 "BUG: Setup Fails with Insufficient Space Message on Large Drives."

- SQL Server is dependent on network functionality—even for the setup routines. Specifically it needs to use named-pipe/mailslot functionality (on NT machines—see the next checklist item for Win9x). These usually require a network card to be present. If you don't have a network card, go to Control Panel/Networks, choose Add Adapter and then add the Microsoft Loopback Adapter—which is just a dummy driver, no hardware involved. This needs to have one or more working network protocols bound to it. Let whichever protocols you have use default parameters, *except* for TCP-IP. If you are using this, do *not* specify the dhcp-assigned address—use 192.168.1.1 as the IP address and 255.255.255.0 as the subnet mask. This is a standard RFC1918 nonrouted IP address so it shouldn't clash with any dial-up address you may be given by an ISP. If you are using the IPX/SPX protocol, accept the default frame type of 802.3.

  If the server service does not start after installing the Loopback Adapter and you get the message "The server service terminated with the following error: Not enough server storage is available to process this command" in the event log, then you need to reinstall your most recently applied service pack to synchronize your NT networking files.

  One way of testing that the named-pipes functionality works is to run the makepipe and readpipe utilities that come with SQL Server. Run makepipe in one command window. Then run readpipe in another. If these work (readpipe connects to makepipe and closes it down), then it is a good indication that networking functionality is OK.

  See also Q155697 "BUG: SQL Setup Fails If Non-NIC Hardware Profile Is Used."

- If you're installing SQL 7.0 on Windows 9x, you have to install Microsoft Client for Networks via the Network applet in Control Panel (note—this isn't the "Microsoft Family" network that will get installed by default). It must also be your primary network logon. Make sure this has a working protocol on it (see earlier checklist item). Once SQL 7.0 is installed, it doesn't need to be your Primary Network Logon, but it still needs to be installed.

- Because a named pipe, used by the setup routine, is effectively a file as far as the operating system is concerned, real-time virus scanners can cause problems. Most of these have been fixed so they don't interfere with SQL's named pipes, so make sure you're running the latest version of whichever virus package you use. But if in doubt, disable the virus software for the duration of the install as they are prime culprits for install errors and hangs.

- Other software packages and services can also interfere with SQL's install on NT systems—typically they interfere with named pipes/mailslot connectivity by intercepting requests. Setup will terminate with an error like "unable to write to mailslot....." Shut down any or all of these for the duration of the install. Packages that are known to interfere with SQL's setup routines include:

  - IIS (Internet Information Server): The Web parts, not FTP
  - PWS (Personal Web Server)
  - Exchange Server
  - SNA Server
  - Oracle
  - DBWeb
  - Backup software such as Arcserve/Backup Exec
  - Systems management tools: UniCentre or Compaq Insight Manager, for example
  - Microsoft SMTP
  - Microsoft NNTP
  - Disk Keeper
  - Protected Storage (part of Internet Explorer)
  - SNMP Services

- On Win9x systems you may also get problems if you are running Quicken Download Manager.

- If the dial-up networking icon or window appears and tries to make a network connection, stop and disable the "Remote Access Autodial Manager" service via Control Panel/Services. This is an NT issue rather than a SQL one, but disabling auto-dial is the easiest way around it. (See the "autodial" FAQ article for more information).

- If you are upgrading, make sure the default database for the "sa" login is master.

- If the error has to do with SQL Performance Monitor counters—SQLCTRxx.DLL—try removing the SNMP service and all third-party network/server monitoring tools such as HP NetServer Agents and Compaq Insight Manager.

- If you are getting a GPF or registry error installing on NT, this could be a known issue with SNMP caused when SNMP managers that come with some server management tools (especially with HP servers) register a lot of SNMP extensions—specifically when HKEY_LOCAL_MACHINE\System\CCS\Services\SNMP\Paramaters\ExtensionAgents gets to around 1K or more.

  Either remove the SNMP service before installing SQL Server, or try the following workaround:

  1. Stop SNMP service.
  2. Save the contents (all the values) of the mentioned subkey (use regedt32 for these operations).
  3. Delete all values except the one with the "largest" name (the names are composed of digits).
  4. Install SQL Server.
  5. Check the "extensionagents" subkey. Setup will have added a value entry for SQL Server—save the value name and value somewhere so you can manually add it again later.
  6. Restore all "extensionagents" values previously saved in step 2.
  7. Add the sqlserver entry in case it got nuked in the previous step.
  8. Restart SNMP.

- If the problem has to do with ODBC files not installing due to their being "in use"—typically a SQL 7.0 problem—check that nothing has the ODBC files open. This could be other SQL utilities, Exchange, IIS, SNMP Service, Compaq Insight Manager, Backup Exec, Microsoft Netshow Program server, Terminal Server License Server and many other services. Download NTHANDLE/X from `www.sysinternals.com` (free) if you can't figure out what has the files open—check the view DLLs, then go into the search function and look for odbc*.dll. It could also be that the ODBC files on your hard drive have been marked as read-only. Check with ATTRIB.EXE or Explorer to see if this is the case.

- If the error is "Critical Error, could not open the file named D:\MSSQL\BINN\SQLCTRxx.DLL," then first try just retrying because the way Performance Monitor works it could just have a temporary lock on the file. If that doesn't work, use NTHANDLE/X (see earlier checklist item).

- If it hangs on the "Setup is now installing the initial SQL Server configuration" screen, it could be a timing problem caused by a *very* fast hard disk subsystem. Check the instmsb.out file in the <sql>\install directory and look for the following messages:

  - 98/01/28 12:28:31.43 spid11 Database 'msdb' cannot be opened - it is currently being created. Wait and try query again.

  - 98/01/28 12:28:31.43 spid11 Unable to proceed with the recovery of dbid <5> because of previous errors. Continuing with the next database.

  If this is the error then copy the SQL Server installation files to the local hard disk drive. Edit the Instmsdb.sql file. Add a WAITFOR DELAY '0:00:01' statement to the very beginning of the script.

  See Q180649 "BUG: SQL Server Setup May Stop Responding When Installing on a Very Fast Drive.""

  - If the .OUT files indicate that ISQL cannot connect to the SQL Server to run scripts, you can try the following (note—this isn't supported, and the author has only used it to fix service pack installs so far, but it *may* work for full installs as well). After making the change run `setup /t Local = Yes.`

  Make a backup of the setup.inf first, then find the following line:

```
set !ServerName = $(!ComputerName)
```

Now add the following three lines after it:

```
ifstr(i) $(!Local) == "Yes"
set !ServerName = "."
endif
```

- If it still can't connect to the server during install, this could be a timing problem due to your choosing a nondefault codepage or sort order. Try installing using the default settings. If this works, rerun the setup program after install and rebuild master to the settings you want.

- For SQL 7.0, check the cnfgsvr.out file in <sql>\install. If you get "An error occurred while attempting to start the service (5)," this error means that the service has had an access denied. Check that the account you have asked SQL Server or SQL Agent to start under has the "logon as a service" permission.

- Make sure for upgrades that SQL Server has a name. Run `sp_helpserver` and check what name srvid of 0 has. If it is not there, run `sp_addserver '<servername>', 'LOCAL'`.

- If you're getting a 109 error starting SQL Executive, this is a permissions problem with the NT account you've supplied not having permissions to the relevant service or registry keys—HKEY_LOCAL_MACHINE\SOFTWARE\MICROSOFT\MSSQLSERVER. The easiest thing to do is install both MSSQLSERVER and SQLEXECUTIVE with the localsystem account and then go back and change it later.

- With SQL 7.0, if you get application errors after "Setup is registering ActiveX components..." message, it is a problem with SQL putting an older version of a DLL in on machines with Visual Studio installed.

  Search the hard drive for the ATL.DLL file—it will probably be in C:\WINDOWS\SYSTEM. Rename it to ATL.OLD and run the install of SQL 7.0 again. Once the install is complete, go back and rename SQL's version of ATL.DLL to ATL.SQL, and rename ATL.OLD back to ATL.DLL.

  If you have Quarterdeck's "remove-it" program that uses and locks atl.dll, then you'll need to stop that or go into safe-mode (Win9x) to delete or rename the file.

  REASON:

  - Visual Studio installed ATL.DLL as a 68 KB file, dated 6/17/98, version 3.00.8168, product version 6.00.8168.

- SQL Server 7.0 Desktop Edition installs a 21 KB file, dated 1/24/97, version 2.00.7024, product version 5.00.000.

- If you're upgrading from MSDE to full SQL Server and the MSDE came from the Office 2000 developer edition, you may get an error "You cannot install a version which is older (7.00.623) than the version on your machine (7.00.677). Uninstall the older version." This is due to an incorrect version number being put in the registry. To fix this problem and allow setup to work amend "HKEY_LOCAL_MACHINE/Software/Microsoft/MSSQLServer/MSSQLServer/CurrentVersion" to have a value of 7.00.623. For more details see Q234915 "FIX: Upgrade to SQL Server Fails When MSDE Installed from MOD."

- If you get a 432 error then check the file "uninst.exe" in the <WINNT> directory. Make sure that you have permissions to it—take ownership of it if necessary.

- With a 6.5 to 7.0 upgrade (or version switch) you can sometimes get a problem if registry permissions have been changed. Check that you have full permission on the following registry keys:

  - HKEY_LOCAL_MACHINE\Software\Microsoft\MSSQLServer

  - HKEY_LOCAL_MACHINE\Software\Microsoft\MSSQLServ65

  - HKEY_LOCAL_MACHINE\Software\Microsoft\MSSQLServ70

  Take control of the keys with regedt32.exe if necessary. Make sure that the account you are logged on as (presumably an admin account) has full permissions.

- If the message is "cannot connect to SQL Server," try starting the SQL Server service manually (NET START MSSQLSERVER). If it starts OK this way, rerun setup and see if it works this time.

- If you get the error "an internal error occurred during install (failed to update package id)" or "A service control operation failed for the MSSQLServer service: 267 The directory name is invalid," then you are probably running Windows 2000. Make sure that the "Remote Registry" service is started and these problems should not occur.

- One or more of the preceding 27 fixes should get the setup routine run through. If it still isn't installing, check the *.OUT files in the <sql>\install directory for clues as to what is going on. Look for the one with the newest date/time.

- If the setup seems to run OK but then SQL won't start, try the following for SQL 6.5 and below. From the <sql>\binn directory run the following, making sure that the spacing and case are correct:

```
setup /t RegistryRebuild = On
```

  The setup routine will now run and ask you all the normal questions. Answer these as if you were performing the install again (using the same paths) and it will just update all the registry entries and icons. It will leave the databases alone.

- Once installation is complete, if you have trouble registering your SQL Server by name in SQL Enterprise Manager, register it with a name of just a period—"." without the quotes. This again bypasses the network layer and ensures that a local named pipe is used.

Reference

v1.40 2000.06.13

Applies to SQL Server versions:	All
FAQ category:	Installation and Upgrades
Related FAQ articles:	"I am having problems installing a SQL Service Pack. What should I do?" (spinstall, see page 293); "What are the minimum hardware and software requirements for SQL Server? What operating systems will it run with?" (platform, see page 278); "How can I completely uninstall SQL Server?" (uninstall, see page 330)
Related Microsoft Knowledge Base articles:	see article
Other related information:	n/a
Author:	Neil Pike

installdesktopeditionfrom-backoffice

Q: How can I install SQL 7.0 Desktop Edition from the Back Office 4.5 CDs?

A: You can install SQL 7.0 Developer Edition on Small Business Server clients by using CD 2 of BackOffice Small Business Server version 4.5. Go into the SQL70 directory and run SETUPSQL.EXE. From here it will allow you to install the desktop edition.

Alternatively run `setupsql k=Dk`.

This should install the desktop edition.

Reference

v1.02 2000.05.02

Applies to SQL Server version:	7.0
FAQ category:	Installation and Upgrades
Related FAQ articles:	n/a
Related Microsoft Knowledge Base article:	Q240715 "How to Install SQL 7.0 Desktop Edition on SBS 4.5 Clients"
Other related information:	n/a
Author:	Neil Pike

installsql7eeonntserver

Q: When installing SQL 7.0, why am I getting the message, "The Enterprise Edition server component cannot be installed on Windows NT Server using this CD. Only client components will be available for installation"?

A: You are trying to install SQL 7.0 Enterprise Edition on an ordinary copy of NT Server. You can install SQL 7.0 Enterprise Edition only on NT Enterprise Edition.

You may get this error if Windows NT was upgraded to Enterprise Edition from NT Workstation. See Q234060. If you think you are trying to install SQL 7.0 Standard Edition, it may be due to you getting a mislabeled set of CD disks. See Q222106.

Reference

v1.01 2000.05.02

Applies to SQL Server versions:	7.0
FAQ category:	Installation and Upgrades
Related FAQ articles:	n/a
Related Microsoft Knowledge Base articles:	Q234060 "PRB: Cannot Install SQL Server 7.0 Enterprise Edition After Upgrade to Windows NT 4.0 Enterprise Edition"and Q222106 "PRB: Cannot Install Enterprise Edition on Windows NT Server"
Other related information:	n/a
Author:	Neil Pike

installwin9x

Q: I'm having trouble installing SQL Server on Windows 9x. What could be going wrong?

A: Try the following checklist of things that could go wrong—these are specific to Win9x and SQL 7. You may also want to look at the generic "install" FAQ article.

- Make sure the machine is of the required spec to run the version of SQL you are installing. For example, if it is SQL Enterprise Edition then make sure you have NT Enterprise Edition. For SQL 7.0 you need a 100 percent Intel Pentium-compatible chip or an Alpha. There is more information in the "platform" FAQ article.

- You have to install Microsoft Client for Networks via the Network applet in Control Panel. It must also be your primary network logon. Once SQL 7.0 is installed, it doesn't need to be your Primary Network Logon.

- If you are upgrading, make sure the default database for the "sa" login is master.

- If the problem has to do with ODBC files not installing, check that nothing has the ODBC files open. It could also be that the ODBC files on your hard drive have been marked as read-only. Check with ATTRIB.EXE or Explorer to see if this is the case.

- If you have Quicken Download Manager installed, disable it—this runs as a driver and interferes with the install process.

- If you get the error "Cannot start the setup program! (CreateProcess() returned error code 0x000000c1h)," you may have a previous partially installed SQL setup. Uninstall the previous version completely first and then try installing.

- If you get an error like "Invalid VxD dynamic link call from VWIN32(05)," deinstall Norton Crash Guard—this can prevent SQL from installing.

- Check the *.OUT files in the <sql>\install directory for clues as to what is going on.

Reference

v1.04 2000.05.19	
Applies to SQL Server versions:	7.0, 2000
FAQ categories:	Installation and Upgrades
Related FAQ articles:	"I'm having trouble installing SQL Server/ MSDE. What could be going wrong?" (install, see page 254); "What are the minimum hardware and software requirements for SQL Server? What operating systems will it run with?" (platform, see page 278)
Related Microsoft Knowledge Base articles:	n/a
Other related information:	n/a
Author:	Neil Pike

instmsdb

Q: I am missing the whole of MSDB, or just some tables. How do I create them?

A: In the <sql>\INSTALL directory are the scripts that SQL runs to create the MSDB database and its tables. Before running these make sure the devices and files for MSDB are there and create them if not.

The scripts you need to run are

- instmsdb.sql
- servrmsgs.sql
- web.sql

These are most easily run with ISQL/W or ISQL/OSQL.

After you do this, reapply your current SQL Server Service Pack.

Reference

v1.02 2000.05.02

Applies to SQL Server versions:	All
FAQ categories:	Installation and Upgrades, Troubleshooting
Related FAQ articles:	n/a
Related Microsoft Knowledge Base article:	Q141530 "INF: Rebuilding the MSDB Database in SQL Server 6.0 and 6.5"
Other related information:	n/a
Author:	Neil Pike

intelalpha

Q: How can I transfer SQL Server data between an Intel box and an Alpha?

A: With 6.5 and below you cannot use the DUMP and LOAD DATABASE commands—it does not do the necessary byte re-ordering to make this work. Therefore you must use BCP, DTS, the transfer tools supplied in SQL Enterprise Manager or write your own ODBC/DMO-based applet.

With SQL 7.0 the byte reordering is done for you, so dumps and loads across architectures are supported.

It is *not* possible to use the upgrade wizard installed with SQL 7.0 to convert between Intel and Alpha, however.

Reference

v1.02 2000.02.28

Applies to SQL Server versions:	All
FAQ category:	Installation and Upgrades
Related FAQ articles:	n/a
Related Microsoft Knowledge Base articles:	n/a
Other related information:	n/a
Author:	Neil Pike

internetconnectorinstall

Q: What does the SQL Server Internet Connector license cover? How do I install it?

A: You don't install it. This isn't software, just a piece of paper licensing you to use SQL Server in this manner. Just increase the number of SQL Server connections via sp_configure, and licenses via Control Panel/License Manager yourself.

It covers any number of Internet users connecting to a SQL 6.5 machine. See the license agreement for the exact definition of an "Internet User." For your users that connect via an intranet, the Internet connector license does not apply as each individual user requires a Client Access License (CAL).

For SQL 7.0 the same is true except that an Internet connector license is required *per CPU* on the server. So for a quad-SMP box you would require four licenses. (Intranet users with CAL's are not affected.)

For details on Microsoft's licensing policies, see

- `http://www.microsoft.com/SQL/productinfo/licensesummary.htm`
- `http://www.microsoft.com/SQL/productinfo/pricing.htm`

Reference

v1.02 2000.05.06	
Applies to SQL Server versions:	6.x, 7.0
FAQ category:	Installation and Upgrades
Related FAQ article:	"How do I know whether SQL Server is in per-seat or per-server mode? How can I change it? How can I add licenses? How does licensing work?" (licensing, see page 416)
Related Microsoft Knowledge Base articles:	n/a
Other related information:	n/a
Author:	Neil Pike

loadsql65dumpordatintosql7

Q: Can I load a SQL 6.5 dump or device file into SQL 7.0?

A: No and no.

If you have a SQL 6.5 dump file, you will have to load it into a SQL 6.5 server first.

If you have a device file, you will have to install SQL 6.5 and then DISK REINIT and DISK REFIT (details in Books Online) it into SQL 6.5.

The *only* ways to transfer SQL 6.x databases into SQL 7.0 are:

- Use the Upgrade Wizard. This is the best option. It requires a running SQL 6.5 system to extract from.

- Use the DTS object copy tools in SQL 7.0 to copy objects from SQL 6.5. Note that when DTS copies tables from a SQL Server 6.5 source to a SQL Server 7.0 destination, it does not copy identity attributes, indexes, primary keys, or other constraints. One workaround is to use the \Mssql7\Upgrade\Scptxfr.exe tool as described in Knowledge Base article Q220163.

- Script the SQL 6.5 database using SQL Enterprise Manager scripting. Recreate it using the script on SQL 7.0. Use BCP to copy the data.

Reference

v1.01 2000.05.12

Applies to SQL Server version:	7.0
FAQ category:	Installation and Upgrades
Related FAQ articles:	n/a
Related Microsoft Knowledge Base article:	Q220163 "PRB: DTS Does not Copy Identity, Indexes, Primary Key or Other Constraints"
Other related information:	n/a
Author:	Neil Pike

loopback

Q: What is the Microsoft Loopback Adapter and why do I need it for SQL Server?

A: SQL Server is dependent on network functionality—even for the setup routines. Specifically it needs to use named-pipe/mailslot functionality on NT machines. These usually require a network card to be present.

If you don't have a network card, adding the loopback adapter will simulate one. It is just a dummy driver—no physical hardware is involved.

With Windows NT you add it by going to Control Panel/Networks, choosing Add Adapter and then adding the MS Loopback Adapter.

With Windows 2000 you go to Device Manager, go to Network cards, right-click and choose Add Device. Don't detect the device—choose it from the drop down list (Microsoft is the vendor).

Once you've added the adapter, you need to have working network protocols bound to it. Let whichever protocols you have use default parameters, *except* for TCP/IP. If you are using this, do *not* specify DHCP assigned address. Use a standard RFC1918 nonrouted IP address that shouldn't clash with any dial-up address you may be given by an ISP—for example, 192.168.1.1 as the IP address and 255.255.255.0 as the subnet mask (this is just an example RFC1918 address—if in doubt, contact someone at your company who does network support).

If the server service does not start after installing the Loopback Adapter and you get the following message in the event log, then you need to reinstall your most recently applied NT service pack to synchronize your NT networking files. "The server service terminated with the following error: Not enough server storage is available to process this command."

One way of testing that the named-pipes functionality works is to run the makepipe and readpipe utilities that come with SQL Server. Run makepipe in one command window. Then run readpipe in another. If these work (i.e. readpipe connects to makepipe and closes it down) then it is a good indication that networking functionality is OK.

For Win9x machines you don't need a Loopback Adapter to install but you need to have the "MS Network Family Driver" installed as the default network client.

Reference

v1.03 2000.06.06

Applies to SQL Server versions:	All
FAQ categories:	Installation and Upgrades, Connectivity
Related FAQ article:	"I'm having trouble installing SQL Server/ MSDE. What could be going wrong?" (install, see page 254)
Related Microsoft Knowledge Base articles:	Q171225 "PRB: Unable to Connect to Stand-Alone SQL Server," Q229608 "BUG: SQL 7.0 Desktop Edition Install on Windows 98 Causes 'Assertion Failed File: ..\SRC\SQLSSPI.C Line: 119'"
Other related information:	"Testing network named pipes" in Books Online 6
Author:	Neil Pike

mdac21

Q: I am getting problems with ODBC apps since upgrading to SQL 6.5 SP5a or installing SQL 7.0. What should I do?

A: Microsoft introduced a lot of compatibility problems (especially with Jet) with the versions of MDAC released with SQL 6.5 SP5a and initial release of SQL 7.0.

Microsoft issued MDAC 2.1 SP2 to resolve the problems. This is distributed in SQL 7.0 Service Pack 2, but it is also generally available at `http://www.microsoft.com/data` and can be applied to clients using any earlier SQL Server release.

You could also try upgrading to MDAC 2.5 or later.

Reference

v1.03 2000.06.06

Applies to SQL Server versions:	6.5, 7.0
FAQ categories:	Installation and Upgrades, Troubleshooting
Related FAQ articles:	n/a
Related Microsoft Knowledge Base articles:	n/a
Other related information:	n/a
Author:	Neil Pike

mdacrunssqlsetup

Q: When I run the MDAC setup routine that comes with SQL Server SP5(a), why does it reinvoke the service pack setup?

A: Because you didn't expand the service pack file with the /d option. If you do, it will create an I386\Mdac or Alpha\Mdac folder with the mdac_typ.exe file in it. When run from this subdirectory it will invoke the right setup program.

Reference

v1.01 2000.05.15

Applies to SQL Server version:	6.5
FAQ category:	Installation and Upgrades
Related FAQ articles:	n/a
Related Microsoft Knowledge Base articles:	n/a
Other related information:	n/a
Author:	Neil Pike

mmcinstall

Q: How can I reinstall just the MMC for SQL Server?

A: On the SQL 7.0 CD, run `x86\other\instmmc.exe`.

Reference

v1.01 2000.05.15

Applies to SQL Server version:	7.0
FAQ category:	Installation and Upgrades
Related FAQ articles:	n/a
Related Microsoft Knowledge Base articles:	n/a
Other related information:	n/a
Author:	Neil Pike

movesqltonewserver

Installation and Upgrades

Q: I need to move SQL Server to a new NT server. What are my options?

A: There are several options. For SQL 7.0, using option 4 is by far the easiest.

With any of these options you are likely to run into problems with orphaned login or user accounts. Some of these problems can be fixed using the sp_change_users_login stored procedure—this is documented in Books Online.

Option 1: NT Copy

These instructions are for SQL 6.5.

1. Install SQL Server on the new server in the same install path and make sure the data location is also in the same directory as the Old Server. (If you can't make the path the same, you'll have to manually change device names—see the "movedevice" FAQ article.)

2. Stop the new and the old SQL servers.

3. Copy all the .dat files from old server to the new server into the same Data folder. This includes all the DAT files—master.dat, msdb_data.dat, msdb_log.dat, and all the DAT files for your user databases. The new server system databases will all be overwritten with the old server versions.

4. Start the new SQL server.

5. Connect using isql_w and login to the SQL Server as "sa".

6. Run the following:

```
sp_dropserver old_server_name
sp_addserver new_server_name, local
```

7. See the "changeservername" FAQ for more details and what to do with SQL 7.0.

8. This will move the databases, but you might have problems with your SQL Server logins. Standard logins will work, but NT integrated logins will need to be reconfigured.

9. Revoke the orphaned local/domain groups and local/domain users from the new SQL server using SQL Security Manager.

   Add all the local groups and local users using NT User Manager on the new SQL server machine.

10. Put any domain users and groups in these local groups using NT User manager.

11. Grant the local groups and local users you just created above on the new server using SQL Server Security Manager.

Option 2: Transfer Manager

1. Install SQL Server on the new server. Create all databases as needed.

2. Transfer from source to target server using Transfer Manager.

Option 3: Dump/Load

1. Install SQL Server on the new server. Create all databases as needed. They must have segments in the same order for SQL 6.5 and below, so use sp_help_revdatabase on the source server to create a script to be run on the target.

2. Dump and restore the databases across, either via the network or by using a tape.

Option 4: Detach/Attach

These instructions are for SQL 7.0 and above only.

As per option 3, but this time use sp_detach_db and sp_attach_db stored procedures. See Books Online for details.

Reference

v1.02 2000.06.06

Applies to SQL Server version:	All
FAQ category:	Installation and Upgrades
Related FAQ articles:	"How can I move a SQL Server device from one disk to another, or rename it?" (movedevice, see page 420); "How do I change the name of SQL Server?" (changeservername, see page 395)
Related Microsoft Knowledge Base article:	Q168001
Other related information:	n/a
Author:	Neil Pike

msdeinstallwithsql7

Q: Can I install SQL 7.0 and MSDE on the same machine?

A: No. MSDE *is* SQL Server. So you can't have both on the same machine.

Reference

v1.01 2000.05.15

Applies to SQL Server version:	7.0
FAQ category:	Installation and Upgrades
Related FAQ article:	"What versions or types of SQL 7 are there and what are the differences? How can I tell which one I am running?" (sql7versions, see page 323)
Related Microsoft Knowledge Base articles:	n/a
Other related information:	n/a
Author:	Neil Pike

msdeupgrade

Q: I am trying to upgrade MSDE to full SQL Server and getting an error: "You cannot install a version which is older (7.00.623) than the version on your machine (7.00.677). Uninstall the older version." What should I do?

A: This is due to an incorrect version number being put in the registry by the version of MSDE that came with the Office 2000 developer edition.

To fix this problem and allow setup to work, amend the CurrentVersion value under "HKEY_LOCAL_MACHINE/Software/Microsoft/MSSQLServer/MSSQLServer/CurrentVersion" to have a value of 7.00.623.

Reference

v1.01 2000.03.25	
Applies to SQL Server version:	7.0
FAQ category:	Installation and Upgrades
Related FAQ articles:	n/a
Related Microsoft Knowledge Base article:	Q234915 "FIX: Upgrade to SQL Server Fails When MSDE Installed from MOD"
Other related information:	n/a
Author:	Neil Pike

mtxcluerror

Q: Why am I getting an "MtxClu..." error after applying SQL 6.5 SP5a?

A: The full error is "SQLEW.exe - entry point not found. The procedure entry point MtxCluGetListOfDTCUsableSharedDisksA could not be located in the dynamic linked library MTXCLU.dll."

The error is fixed by reapplying the NT 4 Option Pack.

Reference

v1.00 1999.02.25	
Applies to SQL Server version:	6.5
FAQ categories:	Installation and Upgrades, Troubleshooting
Related FAQ articles:	n/a
Related Microsoft Knowledge Base articles:	n/a
Other related information:	n/a
Author:	Neil Pike

NT4SP4

Q: Should I apply NT 4.0 SP4 to my SQL Server system?

A: For SQL 7.0 you *have* to—it is a prerequisite.

NT Service Packs do not have any shared code that affects the SQL Server kernel, so application of NT Service Packs should be independent of SQL Server and should be applied based on the stability or instability of your NT system—plus its exposure to security infractions, denial-of-service and similar problems. Many of these have been fixed in NT4 SP4.

Always confirm with your hardware vendor and any suppliers of third-party device drivers, systems management software and virus checkers that they support SP4 and that application of it won't stop the server from booting! In particular there are issues with Adaptec and Compaq Array controllers (for Compaq Smart IIP controllers make sure your firmware as at least version 3.08). If you have some identical or similar hardware on less critical or test systems, apply the SP to these first. For Compaq servers as a whole you need to be on at least SSD 2.11.

However, SQL Server tends to stress the hardware/memory/pci bus/disk subsystem and could therefore expose a bug or compatibility problem between the NT kernel and the hardware or third-party hardware device drivers. Therefore it is technically possible for it to expose a bug in an NT driver that doesn't otherwise show itself.

Reference

v1.04 2000.04.08	
Applies to SQL Server versions:	All
FAQ category:	Installation and Upgrades
Related FAQ articles:	n/a
Related Microsoft Knowledge Base articles:	n/a
Other related information:	n/a
Author:	Neil Pike

NT4SP5

Q: Should I apply NT 4.0 SP5 to my SQL Server system?

A: NT Service Packs do not have any shared code that affects the SQL Server kernel, so application of NT Service Packs should be independent of SQL Server and should be applied based on the stability or instability of your NT system—plus its exposure to security infractions, denial-of-service and similar problems. Many of these have been fixed in NT4 SP4 and SP5.

Always confirm with your hardware vendor and any suppliers of third-party device drivers, systems management software and virus checkers that they support SP5 and that application of it won't stop the server from booting! In particular there are issues with Adaptec and Compaq Array controllers (for Compaq Smart IIP controllers make sure your firmware as at least version 3.08). If you have some identical or similar hardware on less critical or test systems, apply the SP to these first. For Compaq servers as a whole you need to be on at least SSD 2.11.

However, SQL Server tends to stress the hardware/memory/pci bus/disk subsystem and could therefore expose a bug or compatibility problem between the NT kernel and the hardware or third-party hardware device drivers. Therefore it is technically possible for it to expose a bug in an NT driver that doesn't otherwise show itself.

Reference

v1.01 2000.04.08	
Applies to SQL Server versions:	All
FAQ category:	Installation and Upgrades
Related FAQ articles:	n/a
Related Microsoft Knowledge Base articles:	n/a
Other related information:	n/a
Author:	Neil Pike

obdcinstall

Q: I'm installing SQL Server and am getting a problem with ODBC. The error is: "Setup has detected previous versions of ODBC files that need to be updated. The files are being used by other applications, you must shut down all the applications and reboot." What should I do?

A: Check to see what application or service has the ODBC files open.

1. Any SQL application, such as SQLMANGR.EXE or SQL Enterprise Manager, will hold them open.

2. Other applications and services like IIS, Backup Exec, SNMP service, Systems Management tools, Compaq Insight Manager, Microsoft Netshow Program server and Terminal Server License Server could have them open.

3. If you can't figure out what has them open, then download a free tool called NTHANDLE from `http://www.sysinternals.com`–this will show you what has the files open.

4. If nothing has the files open, it could be that the ODBC files on your hard drive have been marked as read-only. Check this with File Manager, Explorer or the attrib command. Take the read-only flag off and try again.

Reference

v1.03 2000.04.08

Applies to SQL Server versions:	All
FAQ categories:	Installation and Upgrades, Troubleshooting
Related FAQ articles:	n/a
Related Microsoft Knowledge Base articles:	n/a
Other related information:	n/a
Author:	Neil Pike

platform

Q: What are the minimum hardware and software requirements for SQL Server? What operating systems will it run with?

A: That depends on whether you mean SQL Server "server"—the database itself—or SQL Server client tools to set up and maintain the database. The below table lists the requirements for both.

To just access SQL Server itself as a client, the only requirement is to be able to run a DB-Lib/ODBC/OLE-DB driver. These are available for just about any platform—for non-Microsoft platforms you would need to get third-party drivers.

General notes on the table:

Where no hardware is mentioned, any hardware that runs the relevant version of the NT operating system will also run SQL Server.

Unless otherwise specified, SQL Server will run on any type of NT, such as a workstation, server, or EE, though there may be licensing implications that you should check first. With SQL 7.0 Microsoft is checking licensing restrictions in the SQL setup program for the first time—i.e. you are unable to install the Server edition onto NT workstation.

References to NT 5.0 are now replaced with Win2000.

For compatibility with "Terminal Server" see the "terminalserver" FAQ article.

Where a reference is made to a type of Windows NT/2000—such as NT Server—then that type of SQL Server will run on that type of Windows NT or higher. For example, if NT 4 Server is mentioned, then it will also run on NT 4 Enterprise Edition.

References to versions of operating system are specific—running on Windows 95 does not imply running on Windows 98 unless specified.

The operating systems listed are the *supported* ones. For example, SQL 4.21a will run on NT 4.0 (with only minor issues), but it is not a supported configuration.

If you run SQL Server on NT workstation, you are restricted by the maximum number of incoming connections that NT allows. If you run SQL Server on a connection-limited or evaluation copy of NT, SQL Server will suffer the same restrictions..

SYSTEMS SOFTWARE REQUIREMENTS

SQL 1.1 Server	OS/2 1.30
SQL 1.1 Client Tools	Dos, OS2, Win3x, Win9x, NT
SQL 4.20 Server	OS/2 1.30, NT 3.1/3.5/3.51
SQL 4.20 Client Tools	Dos/OS2/Win3x/Win9x/NT 3.1/3.5/3.51
SQL 4.21a Server	NT 3.5/3.51
SQL 4.21a Client Tools	Dos/OS2/Win3x/Win9x/NT 3.1/3.5/3.51
SQL 6.0 Server	NT 3.51
SQL 6.0 Client Tools	Win9x/NT 3.51
SQL 6.5 Server	NT 3.51/4.0/Win2000[2]
SQL 6.5 Client Tools	Win9x/NT 3.51/4.0/Win2000
MSDE (SQL 7)	Win9x/NT 4.0/Win2000[1,3]
SQL 7.0 Server "Desktop"	Win9x/NT 4.0/Win2000[1,3]
SQL 7.0 Server "Server"	NT 4.0 Server/Win2000 Advanced Server[1,3]
SQL 7.0 Server "Enterprise"	NT 4.0 EE/Win2000 DataCentre Server[1,3]
SQL 7.0 Client Tools	Win9x/NT 4.0/Win2000[4]
SSDE (SQL 2000)	Win98/Windows ME/NT 4.0/Win2000[1,5]
SQL 2000 Server "Desktop"	Win98/Windows ME/NT 4.0/Win2000[1,5]
SQL 2000 Server "Server"	NT 4.0 Server/Win2000 Advanced Server [1,5]
SQL 2000 Server "Enterprise"	NT 4.0 Server/Win2000 DataCentre Server[1,5]
SQL 2000 Client Tools	Win98/Windows ME/NT 4.0/Win2000[6]

SYSTEMS SOFTWARE REQUIREMENTS (CONTINUED)

1. Requires a Dec Alpha or 100 percent Intel Pentium compatible. It will not run on 486 machines or some AMD/Cyrix/IBM processors—it needs to support CMPXCHG8B (Compare and Exchange 8 bytes) and RDTSC (Read Time-Stamp counter) instructions. SQL 7.0 *will* run on Pentiums slower than 166Mhz, but Microsoft dos not "officially" support it. However, they are unlikely to refuse to take your fault call and fix the problem, unless it is directly performance related.

   The following quote is from Cyrix: "Recently an issue with SQL Server 7.0 has been discovered with the non-MMX Media GX and the 6x86 processors. A fix for this issue can be obtained from Cyrix technical support at: tech_support@cyrix.com" (however, I'm not aware that any such fix actually exists).

   If you do manage to get SQL 7.0/MSDE installed on a non-100 percent compatible Pentium then it will AV on start-up with the below messages. Because the MSDE setup routine does not do as much checking as the SQL Server setup routines, it is most likely that you will see this problem with MSDE.

   ```
   2000-03-16 11:28:49.81 spid0    Using 'sqlimage.dll' version '4.0.5'
   Stack Dump being sent to C:\msde\log\SQL00001.dmp
   Stack Dump being sent to C:\msde\log\SQL00002.dmp
   2000-03-16 11:28:53.84 spid0    Problem creating symptom dump file due to
   internal exceptionUnable to get thread context - no pss
   2000-03-16 11:28:53.86 spid0    Problem creating stack dump file due to
   internal exception
   ```

2. DUMP/LOAD DATABASE fails with SQL 6.5 under Win2000 unless you have applied at least 6.5 SP5.

3. SQL 7.0 requires NT4 SP4+ or Win2000 Beta2+. It also requires IE 4.01 SP1+.

4. SQL 7.0 tools require IE 4.01 SP1+.

5. SQL 2000 requires NT4 SP5+ or Win2000 RTM. It also needs IE 5.

6. SQL 2000 tools require IE 5.

Reference

v1.12 2000.06.13

Applies to SQL Server versions:	All
FAQ category:	Installation and Upgrades
Related FAQ articles:	n/a
Related Microsoft Knowledge Base articles:	Q156437 "Cyrix 5x86 or 6x86 CPU Reported as 486" and Q229453 "Unable to Install Office 2000 Server Extensions on Cyrix CPU"
Other related information:	"Hardware and Software Requirements for Installing SQL Server"
Author:	Neil Pike

redist

Q: What SQL Server EXEs, DLLs, Controls and other files can I redistribute with my application?

A: In the root of the SQL Server CD is a file called redist.txt that gives you this information.

Reference

v1.00 2000.03.03

Applies to SQL Server versions:	All
FAQ category:	Installation and Upgrade
Related FAQ articles	n/a
Related Microsoft Knowledge Base articles	n/a
Other related information:	n/a
Author:	Neil Pike

reinstallnt

Q: How can I reinstall SQL Server without losing any data under a new version of NT I have installed?

A: This is easy to recover from as long as the original SQL files are all still there.

For SQL 6.5 and below—from the <sql>\binn directory run the following, making sure the case is correct:

```
setup /t RegistryRebuild = On
```

The setup routine will now run and ask you all the normal questions. Answer these as if you were performing the install again (put in the same paths). It will appear like a normal install but it will run much more quickly and just insert or update all the registry entries and icons that are needed. None of the existing files will be touched. Once finished you should be able to start the SQL Server service again and access your data.

Microsoft made it even easier with SQL 7.0 and introduced the regrebld.exe command—regrebld.exe /? will give you the options as will the documentation.

Reference

v1.02 2000.04.15

Applies to SQL Server versions:	All
FAQ categories:	Installation and Upgrades, Troubleshooting
Related FAQ articles:	n/a
Related Microsoft Knowledge Base articles:	n/a
Other related information:	"regrebld Utility" in SQL Server Books Online
Author:	Neil Pike

sapassworddefault

Q: How can I connect to SQL Server? I've just installed it and when I type in my NT userid and password to connect it tells me the login failed.

A: This is because SQL standard logins are separate from NT ones. If your SQL Server box takes standard SQL logins—for example, it is on a Windows 9x/ME machine and that is all these operating systems will allow—then try the default "admin" password.

When SQL Server is first installed, the login it creates is called sa and has no password. This should get you in and allow you to create other logins with the tools provided.

Reference

v1.00 2000.06.13

Applies to SQL Server version:	All
FAQ category:	Installation and Upgrades
Related FAQ articles	n/a
Related Microsoft Knowledge Base articles	n/a
Other related information:	n/a
Author:	Neil Pike

snmp

Q: I am getting a GPF/registry error installing SQL Server. What is happening?

A: This could well be a known issue with SNMP caused when SNMP managers that come with some server management tools (especially with HP servers) register a lot of SNMP extensions. Specifically when the registry entry at HKLM\System\CCS\Services\SNMP\Paramaters\ExtensionAgents gets to around 1K or more. This problem only affects SQL 6.x—SQL 7.0 and above are unaffected.

You can either remove the SNMP service before installing SQL Server (and reinstall afterwards), or try the following workaround:

1. Stop SNMP service.
2. Save the contents (all the values) of the mentioned subkey (use regedt32 for these operations).
3. Delete all values except the one with the "largest" name (the names are composed of digits).
4. Install SQL Server.
5. Check the "extensionagents" subkey. Setup will have added a value entry for SQL Server. Save the key name and value somewhere so you can manually add it again later.

6. Restore all "extensionagents" values previously saved in step 2.

7. Add the sqlserver entry as it will have been deleted in the previous step.

8. Restart SNMP.

If you reinstall SNMP, remember to reapply your NT Service Pack to keep all the system DLLs in sync.

Reference

v1.02 2000.04.22	
Applies to SQL Server version:	6.x
FAQ categories:	Installation and Upgrades, Troubleshooting
Related FAQ articles	"I'm having trouble installing SQL Server/ MSDE. What could be going wrong?" (install, see page 254)
Related Microsoft Knowledge Base articles	n/a
Other related information:	n/a
Author:	Neil Pike

sp

Q: What SQL Server Service Pack am I running? How can I get new ones?

A: First get the version number in one of the following ways:

- Execute `select @@version`.
- Look at the top of the latest SQL errorlog file.
- Look at the file properties of the sqlservr.exe file.

All should return the same value, which can be compared with the table below.

For SQL Server OLAP Services, look on the About screen accessed from the Help menu in OLAP Manager. (Make sure you select the OLAP help menu, not that of Microsoft Management Console).

If it isn't listed here, then it is a "hot-fix" build that Microsoft PSS has given you to fix a specific problem. Hot-fix releases are *not* regression tested, so they should only be applied to production systems to fix a known problem and under the advice of Microsoft PSS. Hot-fixes (password protected) are available at `ftp://ftp.microsoft.com/bussys/sql/transfer`. Microsoft PSS will provide passwords as long as you prove you have the bug in question. The reason for restricting hot-fixes this way is so that PSS can track customers who run them and let them know when a regression-tested fix is available.

Service packs can be downloaded from the Microsoft Download Center at `http://www.microsoft.com/downloads/search.asp` or from the FTP site at `ftp://ftp.microsoft.com/bussys/sql/`.

Note that you can't apply 6.5 SP4 to either SBS or EE versions of SQL Server. SP5 and above are compliant with all these releases—it can be applied to any model of SQL Server, such as Workstation, Server, EE, or SBS.

8.00.047 SQL Server 8.0/2000 EAP4

8.00.078 SQL Server 8.0/2000 EAP5

8.00.100 SQL Server 8.0/2000 Beta 2

8.00.149 SQL Server 8.0/2000 "gold" release

7.50.198 SQL Server 7.5/2000 Beta 1

7.00.517 SQL Server 7.0 Beta 3

7.00.583 SQL Server 7.0 RC1

7.00.623 SQL Server 7.0 "gold" release

7.00.677 MSDE from Office 2000

7.00.689 SQL Server 7.0 SP1 Beta

7.00.699 SQL Server 7.0 SP1

7.00.835 SQL Server 7.0 SP2 Beta

7.00.842 SQL Server 7.0 SP2

7.0.1073 SQL 7.0 OLAP "gold" release

7.0.1245 SQL 7.0 OLAP SP1

7.0.1325 SQL 7.0 OLAP SP2 Beta

7.0.1458 SQL 7.0 OLAP SP2

6.50.201 SQL Server 6.5 "gold" release

6.50.213 SQL Server 6.5 with Service Pack 1

6.50.240 SQL Server 6.5 with Service Pack 2

6.50.252 SQL Server 6.5 with "bad" Service Pack 3—SP3 was pulled and re-issued. Do not use this version.

6.50.258 SQL Server 6.5 with Service Pack 3

6.50.259 SQL Server 6.5 on SBS only

6.50.281 SQL Server 6.5 with Service Pack 4

6.50.297 SQL Server 6.5 included in Site Server 3

6.50.339 SQL Server 6.5 "Y2K" Hot-fix

6.50.415 SQL Server 6.5 with Service Pack 5—SP5 was re-issued as SP5a. Do not use this version.

6.50.416 SQL Server 6.5 with Service Pack 5a

6.50.479 SQL Server 6.5 with Post Service Pack 5a Update

6.00.121 SQL Server 6.0 "gold" release

6.00.124 SQL Server 6.0 with Service Pack 1

6.00.139 SQL Server 6.0 with Service Pack 2

6.00.151 SQL Server 6.0 with Service Pack 3

Here's a stored procedure you can run (amended from an original by Jerry Spivey) to show the version:

```
drop PROC VERSION_INFO
go
CREATE PROC VERSION_INFO
AS
SET NOCOUNT ON
SELECT CONVERT(CHAR(25),@@SERVERNAME) AS 'SQL SERVER',
 SUBSTRING(@@VERSION,23,4) AS 'PRODUCT VERSION',
 SUBSTRING(@@VERSION,35,3) AS 'BUILD NUMBER',
 CASE SUBSTRING(@@VERSION,35, 3)
  WHEN '121' THEN 'NO SP'
  WHEN '124' THEN 'SP1'
  WHEN '139' THEN 'SP2'
  WHEN '151' THEN 'SP3'
  WHEN '201' THEN 'NO SP'
  WHEN '213' THEN 'SP1'
  WHEN '240' THEN 'SP2'
  WHEN '252' THEN 'SP3 ** BAD **'
  WHEN '258' THEN 'SP3'
  WHEN '259' THEN 'SP3 + SBS'
  WHEN '281' THEN 'SP4'
  WHEN '297' THEN 'SP4 + SBS'
  WHEN '339' THEN 'SP4 + Y2K'
  WHEN '415' THEN 'SP5 ** BAD **'
  WHEN '479' THEN 'Post SP5
  WHEN '416' THEN 'SP5a'
  WHEN '517' THEN 'Beta 3'
  WHEN '583' THEN 'RC1'
  WHEN '623' THEN 'NO SP'
  WHEN '677' THEN 'MSDE (Office 2000)'
  WHEN '689' THEN 'SP1 Beta'
  WHEN '699' THEN 'SP1'
  WHEN '835' THEN 'SP2 Beta'
  WHEN '842' THEN 'SP2'
  WHEN '198' THEN 'Beta 1'
  WHEN '047' THEN 'EAP4'
  WHEN '078' THEN 'EAP5'
  WHEN '100' THEN 'Beta2'
  WHEN '149' THEN 'NO SP'
ELSE 'Unknown - Must be a Hot-Fix version'
 END AS 'SERVICE PACK'
go
EXEC VERSION_INFO
```

Reference

v1.21 2000.06.08	
Applies to SQL Server versions:	All
FAQ category:	Installation and Upgrades
Related FAQ articles:	n/a
Related Microsoft Knowledge Base articles:	n/a
Other related information:	n/a
Author:	Neil Pike

sp4bugs

Q: Should I apply SQL Server 6.5 Service Pack 4? Are there any known issues?

A: All service packs come with problems, however in most cases they fix a lot more problems than they cause. Ninety-nine percent of the bugs you may find in Service Pack 4 will be present in the gold release and all subsequent service packs—they are unfixed or unknown bugs that are present in every release.

SP4, as SQL 6.5 Service Packs go, is a very stable one. For a list of bugs fixed in SP4, download it and check the fixlist.txt file.

Service Packs can be downloaded from the Microsoft Download Center at `http://www.microsoft.com/downloads/search.asp` or from the FTP site at `ftp://ftp.microsoft.com/bussys/sql/`.

There are a couple of known problems with SP4 that don't occur with other service packs:

- There is a regression of a numeric index bug. With SP4 if you say

```
WHERE <fieldname> = 1
```

then it will tablescan even if there is an index on the numeric fieldname. But if you specify

```
WHERE <fieldname> = 1.0 then it will work ok.
```

The Instdist.sql script that comes with SQL Server 6.5 Service Pack 3 can cause problems with replication if it is run more than once. This file is also distributed with Service Pack 4, so if you go from SP3 to SP4 then it is run a second time. This obviously only affects systems that use replication. Full information can be found in Microsoft KB article Q184882 "FIX: Intstdist.sql Updates MSjob_commands Incorrectly."

Reference

v1.03 2000.04.22	
Applies to SQL Server version:	6.5
FAQ category:	Installation and Upgrades
Related FAQ article:	"What SQL Server Service Pack am I running? How can I get new ones?" (sp, see page 284)
Related Microsoft Knowledge Base article:	Q184882 "FIX: Intstdist.sql Updates MSjob_commands Incorrectly"
Other related information:	n/a
Author:	Neil Pike

sp4win95

Q: Why can't I install SQL 6.5 SP4 for SQL Server to my Win9x machine as the Readme.txt says I can?

A: This is because when Microsoft released SP4 for SQL 6.5 they got the setup.inf file wrong and it wouldn't install to Win9x clients. They subsequently fixed it and rereleased the service pack but it didn't synchronize to the Web download properly.

Get SP4 from `ftp://ftp.microsoft.com/bussys/sql` and it should work.

Reference

v1.02 2000.04.22	
Applies to SQL Server version:	6.5
FAQ category:	Installation and Upgrades
Related FAQ articles:	n/a
Related Microsoft Knowledge Base articles:	n/a
Other related information:	n/a
Author:	Neil Pike

sp5BUGS

Q: Should I apply SQL Server 6.5 Service Pack 5? Are there any known issues?

A: Service Pack 5 was released on Dec. 24, 1998. It was reissued as SP5a on Jan. 26 to fix a problem with 603's on loading dumps. Make sure you apply SP5a (build 416) and not SP5 (build 415). If you are already on SP5 (415) then the only files you need to update are sqlservr.exe (and .dbg) and opends60.dll (and .dbg).

SP5a has undergone more testing and beta releases than any other service pack because it offers Y2K compliance. However, it contains many fixes and therefore new or regressed bugs are inevitable. Known regressions are listed at the bottom of the article.

Due to the number of fixes it has gone through many more build numbers than previous releases have—though in this case about 50 of the builds should be ignored because Microsoft jumped a load due to internal source release issues. The Fixlist is pointed to at the bottom of this article.

For any new release or service pack you are advised to apply and test on test systems first, and if at all possible do a stress test so that any problems with blocking or locks are found before rolling out to a production system.

All service packs come with problems, however in most cases they fix a lot more problems than they cause. Ninety-nine percent of bugs you may find in SP5a will be present in the gold release and all previous service packs as well—they simply aren't fixed in SP5a.

Should you apply it? As it gives Y2K compliance then the answer is probably yes. But see the list of known regressions below and also check the Microsoft Knowledge Base—`http://support.microsoft.com`. Search on SQL AND KBBUG AND SP5. If you don't want to apply SP5a because of one of these bugs, either wait for SP6 (date unknown) or contact Microsoft PSS about the availability and stability of hot-fixes (see the FAQ entries for "MSPSS" and "hotfixes").

Service packs can be downloaded from the Microsoft Download Center at `http://www.microsoft.com/downloads/search.asp` or from the FTP site at `ftp://ftp.microsoft.com/bussys/sql/`.

Service Pack 5: Known Bugs and Regressions

These are problems that occur in SP5a but do not occur in SP4 or below.

- Error 4409 when selecting on a view. Hot-fix build 422 available.

```
CREATE TABLE MyTable
(
 X int NOT NULL,
 ORDER_NUM numeric(15,4) NOT NULL
)
go

CREATE VIEW MyView AS
SELECT t1.ORDER_NUM from MyTable t1
UNION
SELECT t1.ORDER_NUM from MyTable t1
go

SELECT *
FROM MyTable T1 INNER JOIN MyView T2 ON T1.ORDER_NUM = T2.ORDER_NUM
go
```

- 605 errors in tempdb. Script below to reproduce, no fix at the moment.

```
CREATE VIEW View_Crash_Test AS
SELECT NUMBER = 1
UNION
SELECT NUMBER = CONVERT(numeric(19, 4), 0.0)
go

SELECT NUMBER
FROM View_Crash_Test
WHERE NUMBER <> 0.0
```

- SP5(a) treats all columns in an inserted row as updated for the purposes of checking in a trigger. See Q216700 "FIX: 'IF UPDATE' Functionality Does Not Work in SQL Server 6.5 Service Pack 5 and 5a" for more information. Fixed in hot-fix build 422.

- You may get access violations caused by high-stress tempdb deadlocking and attention signals. Errors 603 and 803 are symptomatic. See Q231323 "FIX: SP5a Regression: Access Violations with tempdb Deadlocking, Attentions" for more information. Fixed in hot-fix build 437.

- Under certain conditions dynamic cursors may go into an infinite loop with SP5a. Putting SP5 or below back on the machine, without changing the data, fixes the problem. Fixed post SP5a—this doesn't occur in build 440, for example. Or make the cursor INSENSITIVE, which fixes it.

- User doesn't have permission to call sp_b directly but calls it via sp_a. This used to work fine, but with SP5a if a user calls sp_b directly, and rightly fails, they then get access denied to sp_a on all subsequent calls. Fixed in build 446.

- If you're using a 4mm DAT tape device you may experience errors unless you have the 4mmdat.sys from NT 4.0 SP4 or above applied. SP5 makes a call to a function in the driver that isn't there in earlier versions.

- When GETDATE() is used in a cursor with WHERE CURRENT OF you will get "Jan 1 1900" as a date. This is fixed in a post-SP5 build—it works OK on build 452.

Service Pack 5: Possible Issues

These are issues that haven't been confirmed:

- **User Comment:** "I upgraded from SP4 to SP5(a) over the weekend and am running into fatal blocking problems all over the place in an app or database that's been running for years."

- **Reply:** Microsoft has applied several fixes in SP5(a) where table locks have been taken or kept where they weren't needed. These have been removed, which should improve concurrency and throughput. However, on systems that don't use best practices to reduce locking problems, the extra page-level contention could cause extra blocking or deadlocks.

- Reports of index corruptions.

- Incorrect results from count(*) as opposed to select * in view with multiple unions.

- Stored procedures returning incorrect results in low-memory situations.

Microsoft SQL Server 6.5 Service Pack 5a Fixlist

See Q197174 "FIX: SQL Server 6.5 Service Pack 5a Fixlist" for the official fixlist.

One that isn't documented in this release is the fact that SP5 offers Win2000 compliance—previous versions of SQL Server had problems with DUMP and LOAD DATABASE commands under NT5/Win2000 betas.

Another is that ADO had problems resulting in "invalid token" errors due to its use of an undocumented browsetable command. This has been fixed.

Reference

v1.23 2000.04.22

Applies to SQL Server version:	6.5
FAQ categories:	Installation and Upgrades, Troubleshooting
Related FAQ articles:	": I am getting an error 603 restoring a database ever since I applied SP5 to SQL 6.5 What's wrong?" (603sp5, see page 474); sp, mspss, hotfixes, 4409sp5
Related Microsoft Knowledge Base articles:	Q216700, Q216700, Q231323, Q197174
Other related information:	n/a
Author:	Neil Pike

sp5install

Q: Why am I getting a "cfgchar" problem installing SQL Server 6.5 SP5?

A: Check the following:

1. Make sure that there are no quotes in the path on the machine you are setting up. Check this in control panel/system or just type the "path" command at a command prompt.

2. Check that the full directory path you are installing FROM does not include any spaces; for instance, it doesn't have the sp install files in "C:\program files\x" or "c:\x".

3. Check that the registry entry [HKEY_LOCAL_MACHINE\SOFTWARE\Microsoft\MSSQLServer\Setup\SQLPath] ends in a "\" and add one if it doesn't.

4. Make sure that named-pipes is enabled and is the default net-lib on the server. Run the SQL Client Configuration Utility to check this.

5. Check that SQL Server isn't starting in single-user mode

6. Make sure that the "sa" password does not contain blanks or any other }special characters.

7. Make sure that the master database has at least 3MB of free space.

Also make sure you are installing SP5a (SP5 was pulled for other reasons). SP5a is build 416. The "bad" SP5 was 415.

Reference

v1.06 2000.04.22

Applies to SQL Server version:	6.5
FAQ category:	Installation and Upgrades
Related FAQ article:	"I am having problems installing a SQL service pack. What should I do?" (spinstall, see page 295)
Related Microsoft Knowledge Base article:	Q219063 "BUG: Service Pack 5 and 5a Setup May Fail Depending on SQLPath"
Other related information:	n/a
Author:	Neil Pike

spcumulative

Q: Do SQL Service Packs have to be applied in order or can I just apply the latest one?

A: You can just apply the latest one.

Reference

v1.00 1999.01.08

Applies to SQL Server versions:	All
FAQ category:	Installation and Upgrades
Related FAQ articles:	n/a
Related Microsoft Knowledge Base articles:	n/a
Other related information:	n/a
Author:	Neil Pike

spinstall

Q: I am having problems installing a SQL Service Pack. What should I do?

A: Try the following checklist:

- Make sure you have administrator-level permissions on the machine in question, as SQL needs to create registry entries and services.

- SQL Server is dependent on network functionality—even for the setup routines. Specifically it needs to use named-pipe/mailslot functionality. These usually require a network card to be present. If you don't have a network card, go to Control Panel/Networks, choose Add Adapter and then add the Microsoft Loopback Adapter—which is just a dummy driver, no hardware involved. This needs to have one or more working network protocols bound to it. Let whichever protocols you have use default parameters, *except* for TCP/IP. If you are using this then do *not* specify DHCP assigned address, use 192.168.1.1 as the IP address and 255.255.255.0 as the subnet mask. This is a standard RFC1918 nonrouted IP address so it shouldn't clash with any dial-up address you may be given by an ISP.

- Make sure that there are no quotes in the path on the machine you are setting up. Also check that the full directory path you are installing from does not include any spaces. Either of these will cause part of the setup to fail (usually the cfgchar.exe bit). Also make sure the registry entry [HKEY_LOCAL_MACHINE\SOFTWARE\Microsoft\MSSQLServer\Setup] ends in a "\" and add one if it doesn't.

- Because a named pipe, used by the setup routine, is effectively a file as far as the operating system is concerned, real-time virus scanners can cause problems. Most of these have been fixed so they don't interfere with SQL's named pipes, but make sure you're running the latest version of whichever virus package you use. If in doubt, disable the virus software for the duration of the install.

- Other software packages can also interfere with SQL's install—typically they interfere with namedpipe/mailslot connectivity and setup will terminate with an error like "unable to write to mailslot....." Shut down any of these for the duration of the install. Packages that are known to interfere with SQL's setup routines include:

  - IIS (Internet Information Server): The Web parts, not FTP

  - PWS (Personal Web Server)

- Exchange Server
- Any application that will have an OBDC or OLE-DB driver open
- The following are from the SQL 7.0 SP2 Readme.htm:
- Microsoft Search
- MSDTC
- MSSQLServer
- MSSQLServerOLAPService
- SQLServerAgent
- Microsoft Transaction Server
- Microsoft Message Queue Server
- Microsoft COMTI
- All applications, including Windows NT Control Panel

- If the dial-up networking icon or window appears and tries to make a network connection, stop and disable the "Remote Access Autodial Manager" service via Control Panel/Services. This is an NT issue rather than a SQL one, but disabling auto-dial is the easiest way around it.
- Make sure that NamedPipes is enabled and is the default Net-Lib on the server. Make sure SQL is listening on .\pipe\sql\query, which is the default.
- If your "sa" password had a space in it, change the password so it doesn't have a space before installing the service pack.
- Make sure that SQL Server has a name. Run `sp_helpserver` and check what name srvid of 0 has. If it is not there, run `sp_addserver '<servername>', 'LOCAL'`.
- Check whether the value at HKEY_LOCAL_MACHINE\SOFTWARE\Microsoft\MSSQLServer\Setup\SQLPath has a "\" at the end. If you have used a long directory name you may need to add this yourself.

- (6.5 and below.) Make sure you haven't deleted the probe account from the master database. If you have:

  ```
  use master
  go
  exec sp_addlogin probe, NULL, master
  exec sp_adduser probe
  go
  ```

  Then run <sql>\install\Procsyst.sql to grant relevant permissions back to the userid.

- Installing SP1 to SQL 7.0 on a cluster may say "updating system files" and then error and terminate. This happens if your CD-ROM is not shared out—share it out as F$ (or whatever) and that should resolve the problem.

- If setup is complaining that the master database does not have enough space, check how much space it has free. Note that just expanding the master device is not enough—you need to expand master db to use the space if necessary.

- If the error is "Critical Error, could not open the file named D:\MSSQL\BINN\SQLCTR60.DLL," then look for a service that has this file open. The easiest way to see which one is to get NTHANDLEX from `http://www.sysinternals.com` (free). You can retry the copy on this. If you get this error then check the version of the file at the end to see if it has indeed been updated (the version of the file for SP5a is 6.50.410).

  If you have deleted any of the sample databases (pubs, northwind), then try putting these back. Some service packs fail to install if they are not there—and there really isn't any good reason to remove them.

- If it still isn't installing, check the *.OUT files in the <sql>\install directory for clues as to what is going on.

- If the .OUT files indicate that ISQL cannot connect to the SQL Server to run scripts, you can try the following unsupported hack (it worked for me on SP4 and SP5) by modifying the service pack's setup.inf. After modifying the setup script run `setup /t Local = Yes`.

  Make a backup of the setup.inf first, then find the following line:

  ```
  set !ServerName = $(!ComputerName)
  ```

Now add the following three lines after it:

```
ifstr(i) $(!Local) == "Yes"
set !ServerName = "."
endif
```

Reference

v1.20 2000.06.02

Applies to SQL Server versions:	All
FAQ category:	Installation and Upgrades
Related FAQ articles:	"I'm having trouble installing SQL Server/ MSDE. What could be going wrong?" (install, see page 254); "Why am I getting a "cfgchar" problem installing SQL Server 6.5 SP5?" (sp5install, see page 295)
Related Microsoft Knowledge Base article:	Q171225 "PRB: Unable to Connect to Stand-Alone SQL Server"
Other related information:	n/a
Author:	Neil Pike

sql2000accessupsize

Q: Is there an Access upsizing wizard for SQL Server 2000?

A: At the time of writing there is not, and the Access 97/2000 upsizing wizards do not work with SQL 2000.

Microsoft will supply an upsizing wizard after the RTM of SQL 2000, but whether it will be delivered via Web download, an Office Service Release or Office 2001 is unknown.

Reference

v1.00 2000.06.13

Applies to SQL Server version:	7.0
FAQ category:	Installation and Upgrades
Related FAQ articles:	n/a
Related Microsoft Knowledge Base articles:	n/a
Other related information:	n/a
Author:	Neil Pike

sql2000enterpriseedtiondifferences

Q: What does the Enterprise Edition of SQL Server have that the Standard Edition does not?

A: The following are the features that are unique to the Enterprise Edition. Note that it will install OK on Windows NT 4 Server and Windows 2000 Server (unlike with SQL 7.0). If you install Server rather than the Enterprise Edition you may be limited by underlying o/s limits on memory.

The Developer Edition of SQL Server has the same functionality but is licensed only for testing and development.

Enterprise Edition's unique features are:

- More than four processors
- Four-node clustering
- More than 2GB of memory
- Partitioned OLAP cubes; for example, OLAP cubes running on multiple servers
- Index views
- Parallel index creation
- Parallel DBCC
- Log shipping
- Snapshot backup

Reference

v1.00 2000.06.13

Applies to SQL Server version:	2000
FAQ category:	Installation and Upgrades
Related FAQ article:	"What are the minimum hardware and software requirements for SQL Server? What operating systems will it run with?" (platform, see page 278)
Related Microsoft Knowledge Base articles:	n/a
Other related information:	n/a
Author:	Neil Pike

sql2000versions

Q: What versions or types of SQL 2000 are there and what are the differences? How can I tell which one I am running?

A: There are six true versions or types of SQL 2000, all built on the same code-base, so they are all SQL 2000. The same service packs can be applied to all of them.

- **Enterprise Edition**: Only runs on NT 4/Windows 2000 Server and higher. Supports > 4 processors. Supports four-node symmetrical clustering. Supports > 2Gb memory. Supports partitioned OLAP cubes—i.e. OLAP cubes running on multiple servers. Supports index views, parallel index creation, parallel DBCC, log shipping and snapshot backup. Note that with SQL 2000 you can install it on an "ordinary" Windows NT/2000 server if you wish.

- **Standard Edition**: Only runs on NT/Windows 2000 Server or higher. Supports up to four processors. Supports non-partitioned OLAP cubes. This is the version that will come with BackOffice 2000 when it ships.

- **Personal Edition**: Can run on Windows NT 4, Windows 2000, Windows 98 and Windows ME. Some feature and performance limitations—not all optimizations (like parallelism), only single-threaded recovery, not as much use of async io (Windows 9x doesn't support at all), databases only opened when needed, TCP-IP-only network support. Performance has generally been throttled back to make it unsuitable for a multiple-client environment—if you try to use more than five concurrent users you will find performance tapers off. Note: You can't buy the Personal Edition on its own. You have to buy the Standard or Enterprise edition, the installs for which allow a desktop installation to be done. The personal edition just needs a CAL per copy as a license. Full-text search engine, English Query and OLAP are not supported on Personal Edition.

- **Microsoft SQL Server Desktop Engine**: This is the run-time engine (equivalent to MSDE in SQL 7.0). Instead of being delivered with Office it is shipped on the SQL 2000 CD's—which makes more sense! Performance and other features are limited in the same way as the Personal Edition. It only ships with the OSQL.EXE command-line program as an "admin" tool. Does not include DTS design tools though you can run pre-developed DTS packages against it. The footprint in disk space is 38MB–48MB. As with Personal Edition, if you connect it to a Standard or Enterprise edition, it requires a CAL. Otherwise it is license-free and can be redistributed.

- **Developer Edition**: This is supplied with Visual Studio Enterprise Edition. This supports the same features as Enterprise Edition but comes with a develop/ test-only license.

- **Evaluation Edition**: In addition to the other versions there is an Evaluation Edition that is the same as Standard Edition, but is a 120-day time-limited version.

To detect which version you are running, parse the output from `SELECT @@VERSION`, which will have in it the following strings:

```
Personal Edition on .............
Desktop Engine on ................
Standard Edition on ................
Enterprise Edition on ...............
Developer Edition on ...............
Standard Edition Evaluation on ................
```

For example, `IF (CHARINDEX('Engine', @@version) > 0 ) .... <<<`, you have MSDE (Desktop Engine).

Reference

v1.00 2000.06.13

Applies to SQL Server version:	2000
FAQ category:	Installation and Upgrades
Related FAQ article:	"What are the minimum hardware and software requirements for SQL Server? What operating systems will it run with?" (platform, see page 278)
Related Microsoft Knowledge Base articles:	n/a
Other related information:	n/a
Author:	Neil Pike

sql65stillavailable

Q: I know SQL 6.5 is no longer the current release, but can I still buy it?

A: SQL Server 6.5 is still available from Microsoft fulfillment. You need to buy 7.0 and associated licenses and then call the Microsoft Fulfillment office with the serial numbers and details and they will ship you the 6.5 media.

Reference

v1.05 2000.09.06	
Applies to SQL Server versions:	6.5, 7.0
FAQ category:	Installation and Upgrades
Related FAQ article:	"How much longer will Microsoft support SQL 6.5?" (support65, see page 359)
Related Microsoft Knowledge Base articles:	n/a
Other related information:	n/a
Author:	Neil Pike

sql7166mhz

Q: Do I really need a 166MHz Pentium processor to run SQL Server 7.0?

A: No. But you *do* need a 100 percent Pentium-compatible chip, which rules out some Cyrix and IBM processors. The only way around this is for the chip vendor to offer a micro-code upgrade. (Some non-Intel chips say they are Pentiums, but in fact only implement the 486 chip-set).

The following quote is from Cyrix: "Recently an issue with SQL Server 7.0 has been discovered with the non-MMX Media GX and the 6x86 processors. A fix for this issue can be obtained from Cyrix technical support at: `tech_support@cyrix.com`."

The actual speed of the processor doesn't matter as long as it runs the full Pentium instruction set—it needs to support CMPXCHG8B (Compare and Exchange 8 bytes) and RDTSC (Read Time-Stamp counter) instructions. Microsoft has made this a requirement because it is the minimum spec machine that they have developed and tested with—which is OK if you get most of your equipment donated, lent, or replaced by hardware companies free of charge, but this isn't the case with most businesses!

As long as the server previously ran SQL 6.5 (and is 100 percent Pentium-compatible) you should find that it will run SQL 7.0 and will offer significant performance improvements, so don't upgrade hardware for the sake of it.

The following quote is from Microsoft Product Support Services:

"When using SQL Server v7.0, Microsoft recommends a processor speed of 166MHz or higher for server machines. Our extensive testing of the product has been done on machines of this calibre and we believe customers will get a better price performance with the product when used in this configuration. Microsoft will support SQL Server v7.0 when run on server machines with slower processors. However customers should recognize that if our findings are that major problems can be eliminated by using faster processors we will continue to recommend, and in some cases may require, compliance with this suggestion."

The reason for this caveat is that some of the decisions the optimizer makes on a 166MHz Pentium may not make so much sense on a 60Mhz Pentium—the extra CPU time a 60MHz part needs may mean that a nonoptimal plan had been chosen.

Reference

v1.04 2000.04.24

Applies to SQL Server version:	7.0
FAQ category:	Installation and Upgrades
Related FAQ article:	"What are the minimum hardware and software requirements for SQL Server? What operating systems will it run with?" (platform, see page 278)
Related Microsoft Knowledge Base articles:	n/a
Other related information:	n/a

Author: Neil Pike

sql7accessupsize

Q: Is there an Access upsizing wizard for SQL Server 7.0?

A: For Access 97 it is downloadable from `http://www.microsoft.com/accessdev/prodinfo/aut97dat.htm`.

Access 2000 comes with it built-in.

Reference

v1.02 2000.04.24	
Applies to SQL Server version:	7.0
FAQ category:	Installation and Upgrades
Related FAQ articles:	n/a
Related Microsoft Knowledge Base articles:	n/a
Other related information:	n/a
Author:	Neil Pike

sql7differences

Q: Should I upgrade to SQL 7.0? Why or why not? What are the known bugs? What other differences are there between 6.5 and 7.0?

A: Apologies for the length of this FAQ article, but there is a lot of material to cover.

General Issues

SQL 7.0 generally has a much more stable and better performing kernel than SQL 6.5 SP5. For every bug you find with the basic kernel of SQL 7.0 there will be 20 known bugs with SQL 6.5 SP5, and an order of magnitude more of unknown ones. However, having said that, there is going to be a small percentage of queries that will run slower or fail under SQL 7.0 than under 6.5. As these are reported they will be improved or fixed in future service-packs, but the rewrites to make 98 percent of queries run faster is going to have a detrimental effect somewhere. Some specific points are noted later.

SQL 7.0 shouldn't be treated as a version 1 release—even though most of the code has been rewritten, it has had far more testing (both internal and external to MS) than any previous version of SQL Server—though as always, some people like to wait for at least one service pack (we currently have two).

A concerted effort was made to test and fix all reported bugs with 6.5 on the 7.0 code-base. In addition an automated testing tool (RAGS) that generated and validated hundreds of complex SQL queries every minute was written and run against SQL 7.0 (see `http://research.microsoft.com/users/DSlutz/` for details).

Most of the original bugs and issues were with the new features such as text indexing, DTS GUI and the MMC tools, the majority of which have now been addressed in the service packs.

Where you get errors with the kernel, these could well have to do with SQL 7.0's stricter checking of SQL/ANSI rules. Though many of these are picked up and even simulated (yes, Microsoft deliberately reproduced broken code in some instances) under the 6.5 compatibility mode, you may find extra things "break" when you go to full SQL 7.0 mode (see sp_dbcmptlevel in Books Online). You need set your database compatibility level to 70 to take advantage of the new syntax, so it is recommended that you do this as soon as possible.

For any new release you are advised to apply and test on non-production systems first, and if at all possible do a stress test so that any problems that only occur under stress are found before rolling out to a production system.

Some known bugs and issues with SQL 7.0 are discussed in this article—for the official current list search the Microsoft Knowledge Base for "sql70" and "kbbug."

The rest of this article could be entitled "SQL 7.0—the Good, the Bad and the Ugly." In particular this articles deals with features that aren't covered in the documentation or are not immediately obvious in Books Online, as well as issues to think about and check out before and during a SQL 7.0 migration. It isn't meant to be all-encompassing, but read it in conjunction with the Microsoft-supplied documentation and Knowledge Base articles.

Install

Some things to check before a SQL 7.0 upgrade:

- All databases are checkdb'ed, newalloc'ed and checkcatalog'ed and have no errors.
- No databases are in suspect or loading status.
- Free space in master for new 6.5 system procs—5MB or so should do.
- At least 10MB tempdb.
- At least 6.0 SP3 or 6.5 SP3 is required on the source system.
- Syscomments source is available for all stored procedures and triggers.

Good

- Speed. Speed is overall much better than with 6.5—there are exceptions, noted in the Bad and Ugly sections where known. As an example, the speed of a large batch processing suite was improved by 300 percent by going to SQL 7.0 from 6.5—a 200 percent increase was achieved just by migrating with no changes and the extra improvements were made by optimizer fixes in SP1, plus changing BCP to BULK INSERT, using parallel indexes and some rewrites of queries that were manually optimized in the past for SQL 6.5. The batch run consists of about 30 separate jobs each with 5–10 steps, consisting of bcp in of data, index creation, many SELECT INTOs on criteria and many GROUP BYs and aggregations. Time taken has reduced from 10 hours to 3 hours, 20 minutes with no change in hardware or memory.

- The optimizer in SQL 7.0 is far more powerful than in 6.5, utilizing many more types of joins and multiple indexes. It is worth looking at old SQL that may have been split into multiple steps in SQL 6.5 or earlier because the optimizer couldn't handle things like greater-than-four-way joins or multiple aggregations. This SQL could be rewritten back into one large query for better performance. The downside to all these optimizer improvements is that it can take significantly longer to work out the best query plan compared with 6.5 and can result in increased CPU usage.

- Reliability. You should get far fewer AVs with SQL 7.0 than with 6.5. Also fewer database corruptions—as of writing, 18 months after the RTM of SQL Server 7.0, there has not been a single instance of database corruption with SQL 7.0 that was not caused by hardware failure (information provided by Microsoft PSS).

- Note: I've found SQL 6.5 SP4 and above to be pretty resilient to corruption. Make sure all 6.5 systems are on at least SP4—I've seen about a dozen systems needlessly fall victim to a pre-SP4 bug with LRU corruption when buffers get stressed on SMP systems.

- Create indexes concurrently. Under 6.5 this would cause locks on system tables and the indexes would build serially. Under 7.0 if you kick off creates of nonclustered indices on the same table at the same time, from separate connections, they will all create concurrently. The re-use of the read-ahead buffers from the main table gives near linear performance. Especially useful for data-warehouse/MI type systems with lots of NC indexes on large tables.

- Max Async IO. Under 6.5 if you allocated max async io "too high," performance would nose-dive. With 7.0 this doesn't seem to be the case—the law of diminishing returns still applies, but max async io can be set much higher—even to the maximum of 255—without worrying too much.

- DBCC performance. On complex or fragmented databases I have seen DBCC performance for a full CHECKDB/CHECKCATALOG of 60 times faster than the equivalent CHECKDB/NEWALLOC/CHECKCATALOG on a 6.5 system. For non-fragmented, simple databases where not so much disk head movement was needed anyway under 6.5 I still see DBCC times that are twice as fast.

- Query parallelism—it really does work. Tests have shown greatly increased performance when running on an otherwise identical four-way box compared to a two-way.

- Database size. Due to the new 8K page size and improvements in the storage of text/index data most databases will shrink in size when migrated to SQL 7.0. This isn't guaranteed and many factors are involved (see NC index material in the Ugly section), but reports of 50GB SAP systems shrinking to < 30GB are common.

- Under 6.5 the realistic maximum size systems that you could put on SQL Server was around the 300GB mark due to backups, healthchecks and recovery taking too long. With 7.0 this rises to around the TAB mark and quite possibly higher given appropriate hardware (SQL 7.0 has been backed up at 600GB per hour using a stripe of 24 AIT tape drives—and more importantly restored at 500GB/hour!).

Bad

- BCP slower. Under many circumstances a BCP into a file with few indices will be slower under SQL 7.0 than 6.5—this is probably due to the overhead of using OLE-DB internally, however it should mean an end to problems caused by using fast-BCP and its bypassing of certain SQL checks. With many NC indexes it is quicker than 6.5 though. Using the new BULK INSERT command returns it to as fast or faster than BCP due to the removal of context switches. Setting table-lock on really helps due to the extra overhead of row-locks. I've seen jobs reduce from 80 minutes to 50 minutes with this change.

- Microsoft Management Console (MMC) and Enterprise Manager. The MMC is dog-slow regardless of the power of the machine it is being run on. Service Pack 1 noticeably improves the speed and reliability of MMC.

- If you repeatedly open server-side cursors with small result sets, you will see significantly slower performance from SQL Server. This is because the query is being optimized each time and this takes time with SQL 7.0. This is fixed in SP1 (a trace flag was needed for the original hot-fix but the default behavior is changed in SP1). After applying SP1 the plans generated for cursors are kept as they are for stored procedures. See Q197800 " FIX: Cursor Overhead Higher on SQL Server 7.0 for Small Result Sets" for more details.

- Large queries monopolizing the system. This was an issue with SQL 6.5, but if anything it is "worse" with 7.0—the queries generally complete a lot quicker with 7.0 though. If you have a very large query running and it grabs all the processors to run it will make the system very slow or unresponsive to other users and queries. SQL dynamically decides how many processors to use for a query when it kicks off, and if there is no other activity at the time it will be given all the processors by default. This is not necessarily what you want. The maximum number of processors a query can use can be set per query (MAXDOP hint) or via sp_configure for a server wide setting—the default is all CPU's. Once a query has started and has grabbed all the CPU's, it can't give them back.

- Long stored procedures that create lots of temporary tables as they go can take a lot longer to run under SQL 7.0—this is due to SQL 7.0 re-evaluating the stored procedure every time a new temporary table is created. The idea behind this is that it can then choose the best access plan, but reevaluating is an overhead. Create all temp tables at the start of the stored procedure if possible.

- If you have two stored procedures, the first creating a temp table, calling a second stored procedure, and second stored procedure manipulating it, this will run fine as long as only one copy of each is running at a time. If more than one process runs concurrently, stored procedure #1 will recompile. Users have reported 10-20 times performance degradation in this scenario. To work-around it either bring the stored procedure #2 code in-line to stored procedure #1, or create temporary stored procedures uniquely named for every SPID and call them to prevent re-compilation.

- Nested RAISERRORs cause an AV. Repro script below (this error only occurs when a global variable is used):

```
CREATE PROCEDURE Proc2
AS
    RAISERROR('Test Error',16,-1)
GO

CREATE PROCEDURE Proc1
AS
    EXEC Proc2
    IF @@ERROR <> 0
    BEGIN
        RAISERROR(@@ERROR,16,-1)
        RETURB
    END
GO

EXEC Proc1
```

- If you have a trigger on a table with an identity field and the trigger inserts into another table without an identity, the value of @@identity is set to NULL when the trigger finishes. This is different from 6.5. Fixed in Service Pack 1.

Ugly (or Just Different)

- SQL 7.0 is much more "fussy" about things like invalid dates and times, lengths of data and numeric overflows. SQL 6.5 and below would often just convert something to NULL if it couldn't handle it or truncate a string if too long and not tell you. You can revert most of this back to the SQL 6.5 behavior if you `SET ANSI WARNINGS OFF`. Many of these changes only appear when you switch a database from 65 compatibility mode to 70. I prefer to fix the SQL/code/data concerned as the SQL 7.0 behavior is better.

- The MMC Enterprise Manager interface has no option to set column level permissions via the GUI. This won't be fixed until the SQL 2000 (Shiloh) release, so it's back to T-SQL until then.

- If a user or login doesn't have permissions to a database they can still see it in the database selection drop-down of Query Analyzer (ISQL/W) or in SQL Enterprise Manager. This is a different from 6.5. It is due to the overhead of scanning all the NT users and groups in the new integrated role security.

- Sixteen-bit ODBC applications may have problems with the new potential extended size of char data (even if the new size isn't used). You also may get GPF's in vbdb300.dll when accessing SQL Server. See FAQ article "sql7odbc2vbdb300."

- The new 3.70 ODBC drivers have a few compatibility issues. For example, I have seen ODBC calls fail with errors from complex Access 97 front ends and MDAC 2.1. This is fixed in the later versions of MADC (2.1 SP2 or 2.5). Also if you use PASSTHRU, then integer columns (datatype int4) are returned as decimal, when the ODBC Datasource is configured with "use regional settings."

- SQL 7.0 is supposed to grab and release memory as needed, to work with varying workloads. It does this quite well except in the case of Microsoft Exchange. These both dynamically allocate as much memory as possible and don't "play" too well together. If you do run Exchange and SQL Server on the same box then it is recommended to fix the amount of memory SQL Server 7 has.

- The enhanced optimizer, as well as improvements in disk throughput, mean that SQL 7.0 is more likely to be CPU-bound than 6.5 was. Most systems will still be i/o bound though. The new sp_datatype_info used extensively for ODBC connections is much more heavy on CPU due to the extra calculations, increased numbers of datatypes and attempt at backwards compatibility. If you constantly break and make connections this can add up—one user reported a system running at 92 percent CPU, largely because of this. When he amended the procedure to just return a fixed set of types stored in a permanent table for the purpose, the CPU for the system dropped from 92 percent to 72 percent.

- Some databases and tables may grow in size with SQL 7.0. One reason is because nonclustered indexes point to the clustering key if available rather than a page number. With long keys this can increase the size of the indexes significantly. Watch out for this if any key sizes are very large.

- Another reason for tables growing in size is that NULL columns used to take up no space at all, but that is no longer true. So a NULL CHAR(10) now uses 10 bytes rather than 1, a NULL MONEY now uses 8 instead of 1. A NULL varchar will take 0 as before.

- DECIMAL and NUMERIC data can take up a bit more space. Following are the tables for 6.5 and 7.0:

SQL 6.5

Precision	Storage Bytes
1 - 2	2
3 -4	3
5-7	4
8-9	5
10-12	6
13-14	7
15-16	8
17-19	9
20-21	10
22-24	11
25-26	12
27-28	13

SQL 6.5 (Continued)

29-31	14
32-33	15
34-36	16
37-38	17

SQL 7

Precision	Storage Bytes
1 - 9	5
10-19	9
20-28	13
29-38	17

- Watch out for 16-bit DB-Library applications and network packet size (sp_configure option). The default with SQL 6.0 and below was that the client dictated the network packet size, and would default to about 1500 bytes. With 6.5 and 7.0 the server option overrides this if no explicit dbsetlpacket is issued. The default server size is 4096 and so this significantly increases the client memory buffer space needed. With multiple 16-bit DB-Library applications, or a DB-Library application that makes multiple connections, this can easily overflow the fixed size allowed for all connections in the client buffers, and cause out of memory errors, GPF's or the system to hang. It doesn't matter whether it's on an NT client—the restriction is in the 16-bit DB-Library and it's use of "low dos" memory. To resolve either, change the application to specifically ask for a smaller packet size or reduce the server "network packet size" via sp_configure. (Note: This is a SQL Server TDS application packet size and in no way relates to actual physical network packet sizes that are configured per NIC.)

- When you do an outer join to a table with a bit data type on SQL Server 6.5 and there is no corresponding record, the bit column yields a 0 instead of a null. On SQL Server 7, the same query yields a null.

- Constants returned by a case statement are implicitly right-trimmed. This has been fixed in SP2.

- On an insert, if a trigger fires it thinks all columns have been updated even if some fields have not been explicitly inserted. Fixed in Service Pack 1.

- SQL Server 7 no longer guarantees that inserted records can be retrieved in the same order *unless* you use an ORDER BY clause or have a clustered index. In SQL 6.5 this would work without them. With 7 if you were using this facility to create a table just to BCP the contents out then you will need to insert some sort of ascending key to keep the rows in order.

- Changes in binary handling.

  The format for display of binary (hex) data in isql/w from version 6.x is in lower case, but in isql/w (Query Analyzer) from 7.0 is upper case.

  The @@MICROSOFTVERSION variable is documented in 6.x Books Online.

  @@MICROSOFTVERSION: This version is used internally to track the current version of the server. Note that in 7.0 the major version is now in the most significant byte.

  The order of the date and time components in CONVERT(binary(8), GETDATE()) has been reversed.

  See the following code for examples of this:

```
SELECT CONVERT( binary(4), @@MICROSOFTVERSION ), CONVERT( binary(8), GETDATE() )

<SQL Server 6.x (6.0 in this case)>
---------- ------------------
0x00060097 0x00e42af600008dcb

<SQL Server 7.0 build 623>
---------- ------------------
0x0700026F 0x00008DCB00E415AB
```

- With SQL 6.5, you could call stored procedures from ASP without prefixing them with the EXECUTE command. With SQL 7.0 you have to use EXECUTE.

- SQL Server 6.5 internally treated nullable chars not as fixed length, but as varchars. SQL 7.0 does not treat them this way when the compatibility mode of the db is set to 70. If you depend on the 6.5 behavior, you might get different SQL results; for example:

```
DECLARE @var1 char(50)
SELECT @var1 = 'option_cmt_des_txt_no'
SELECT @var1

DECLARE @var2 char(50)
SELECT @var2 = right(@var1, 6)
SELECT @var2
```

  With 6.5 this would return "txt_no".

  With 7.0 it would return blanks.

Miscellaneous

- Service packs. As of writing, Service Pack 2 for SQL 7.0 was the latest one out. Service Pack 1 was very well received with almost no regressions or new problems. Service Pack 2 has shown a few more of these issues, but is still a solid and recommended service pack. To see the known issues with these service packs see the "sql7sp1bugs" and "sql7sp2bugs" FAQ entries.

- IE5 and Win9x. A bug in SQL's use of a common Internet control causes crashes on Win9x machines with IE5 installed. SP1 fixes this.

- "SQL Server out of locks." You can still get this message even though SQL Server dynamically allocates locks. What the error really means is that SQL Server is out of memory—the lock manager has been denied its request for more memory. Either give the machine more memory or reduce the load SQL Server is under.

- DTS. This is a marvelous tool, but had quite a few glitches pre-SP1. One "feature" that is still there is that if you refer to columns in a transform by their column name, it can be significantly slower than by their column number – for example, DTSSource("EmployeeID") rather than DTSSource(13). One DTS job sped up from 2 hours and 45 minutes to 32 minutes just by hard-coding column numbers instead of names.

- Watch out for the default setting of SET CONCAT_NULL_YIELDS_NULL. This is ON which means that SELECT 'abc' + NULL yields NULL. This has been known to break some applications.

- Remember that when upgrading a 6.5 database it stays in 65 compatibility mode. In this mode, new commands like TOP will not work. You will need to change the compatibility level to 70 as mentioned above.

- Log files. These can get very big if set to autogrow. If you then try to shrink them with DBCC SHRINKFILE invariably it doesn't work too well. See FAQ article "sql7shrinklognowork" for more details on this.

- Putting the same column into a GROUP BY twice causes an AV. It's stupid and basically incorrect syntax to do this anyway, but SQL 6.5 let it go. Repro script based on Northwind. (This one has been fixed in SP2).

```
SELECT Employees.EmployeeID,ProductName,
    UnitPrice=AVG(ROUND(Od.UnitPrice, 2)),
    SUM(Quantity),
    Discount=SUM(CONVERT(int, Discount * 100)),
    ExtendedPrice=SUM(ROUND(CONVERT(money, Quantity * (1 - Discount) *
Od.UnitPrice), 2))
FROM Products P
inner join [Order Details] Od on (Od.ProductID = P.ProductID )
inner join Orders on (Od.OrderID = Orders.OrderID)
inner join Suppliers on (P.SupplierID = Suppliers.SupplierID)
Inner Join Customers on (Orders.CustomerID=Customers.CustomerID)
Inner join Shippers on (Orders.ShipVia=Shippers.ShipperID)
Inner join Employees on (Orders.EmployeeID = Employees.EmployeeID)
Group by Employees.EmployeeID,P.ProductID,
P.ProductName,Employees.EmployeeID
with cube
Order by Employees.EmployeeID
```

- "Msg 8623,Internal Query Processor Error: The query processor could not produce a query plan." This happens with some complex queries—especially on single-processor machines. Some queries that fail on one-processor machines work OK on multi-processor machines.

- tempdb performance may be affected by the auto-creation of statistics. You can experiment with turning off this feature just for tempdb and seeing if it helps.

- sysfiles virtual table does not behave as expected, when referenced from a stored procedure created in master with the sp_ name prefix. Repro script follows:

```
USE master
GO
DROP PROC sp_MyProc
GO
CREATE PROC sp_MyProc
AS
SELECT TOP 1 name FROM sysobjects WHERE type = 'U'
SELECT name FROM sysfiles
GO

USE pubs
GO
EXEC sp_MyProc

SELECT name FROM sysfiles
SELECT TOP 1 name FROM sysobjects WHERE type = 'U'
```

Both sysobjects calls will return authors as their one row. The stored procedure call to sysfiles, in sp_MyProc, will return the master database file names, but the other will return the expected pubs database file names

Reference

v2.14 2000.06.13

Applies to SQL Server versions:	All
FAQ category:	Installation and Upgrades
Related FAQ articles:	"If I lose my primary data file (MDF) in SQL 7, I can't back up the log to recover to a point in time. Why not?" (backuplognotruncatefails, see page 486); "Why does my ODBC v2 application not work with SQL 7? Why do I get a GPF in VBDB300.DLL?" (sql7odbc2vbdb300, see page 537); "Why won't my log shrink in SQL 7/2000?" (sql7shrinklognowork, see page 194); "Should I apply Service Pack 1 for SQL Server 7.0? Are there any known issues?" (sql7sp1bugs, see page 316); "Should I apply Service Pack 2 for SQL 7? Are there any known issues?" (sql7sp2bugs, see page 318)
Related Microsoft Knowledge Base article:	Q197800 "FIX: Cursor Overhead Higher on SQL Server 7.0 for Small Result Sets"
Other related information:	n/a
Author:	Neil Pike

sql7sp1

Q: Where can I get SQL Server/OLAP Services 7.0 Service Pack 1?

A: SQL Server 7.0 Service Pack 1 and SQL Server 7.0 OLAP Services Service Pack 1 are available from the Microsoft Download Center at either of the following sites:

- `http://www.microsoft.com/downloads/search.asp?`
- `ftp://ftp.microsoft.com/bussys/sql/public/fixes/usa/SQL70/Sp1`

The SQL Server and OLAP Services Service Packs are separate downloads with versions for both Intel and Alpha platforms. The SQL Server Service Pack also covers MSDE 1.0.

Reference

v1.02 2000.04.29	
Applies to SQL Server version:	7.0
FAQ category:	Installation and Upgrades
Related FAQ article:	"Where can I get SQL Server/OLAP Services 7.0 Service Pack 2?" (sql7sp2, see page 318)
Related Microsoft Knowledge Base article:	Q225019 "INF: SQL Server 7.0 Service Pack 1 Fixlist"
Other related information:	n/a
Author:	Neil Pike

sql7sp1bugs

Q: Should I apply Service Pack 1 for SQL Server 7.0? Are there any known issues?

A: Service Pack 1 (1) for SQL 7.0 underwent extensive beta testing prior to release and so should be pretty stable.

However, it contains many fixes and therefore new or regressed bugs are inevitable. When these are known they are listed at the bottom of the article.

For any new release or service pack you are advised to apply and test on test systems first, and if at all possible do a stress test so that any problems with blocking or locks are found before rolling out to a production system.

All service packs come with problems, however in most cases they fix many more problems than they cause. Ninety-nine percent of bugs you may find in SP1 will be present in the gold release and all previous service packs as well—they simply aren't fixed in SP1.

Should you apply it? Yes.

See FAQ article "sql7sp1" for details on how to obtain Service Pack 1.

Service Pack 1: Known New Bugs and Regressions

- A query that uses a like on an indexed Unicode column will behave correctly prior to SP1. After SP1 is applied the query will return no records. This is fixed in build 710.

- SP1 + ODBC driver (Build 690-820) cannot `SQLExtFetch() rows` with more than one TEXT or BINARY column, when a server cursor is used. MS bug number 56513. Workarounds are:

  - *Use SQLFetch instead of SQLExtendedFetch.

  - Don't use SQLSetStmtAttr to ask for a keyset cursor. Just take the default.

  - Use an older version of the driver (even 3.70.0623 and below work fine).

Reference

v1.05 2000.04.29

Applies to SQL Server version:	7.0
FAQ categories:	Installation and Upgrades, Troubleshooting
Related FAQ articles:	"Where can I get SQL Server/OLAP Services 7.0 Service Pack 1?" (sql7sp1, see page 316); "Should I upgrade to SQL 7.0? Why or why not? What are the known bugs? What other differences are there between 6.5 and 7.0?" (sql7differences, see page 304)
Related Microsoft Knowledge Base articles:	Q225019 "INF: SQL Server 7.0 Service Pack 1 Fixlist" and Q232574 "INF: Readme.txt for SQL Server 7.0 Service Pack 1"
Other related information:	n/a
Author:	Neil Pike

sql7sp2

Q: Where can I get SQL Server/OLAP Services 7.0 Service Pack 2?

A: SQL Server 7.0 Service Pack 2 and SQL Server 7.0 OLAP Services Service Pack 2 are available from the Microsoft Download Center at `http://www.microsoft.com/downloads/search.asp?`.

The SQL Server and OLAP Services Service Packs are separate downloads with versions for both Intel and Alpha platforms. The SQL Server Service Pack also covers MSDE 1.0.

Reference

v1.00 2000.04.29	
Applies to SQL Server version:	7.0
FAQ category:	Installation and Upgrades
Related FAQ article:	"Where can I get SQL Server/OLAP Services 7.0 Service Pack 1?: (sql7sp1, see page 316)
Related Microsoft Knowledge Base article:	Q254369 "INF: SQL Server 7.0 Service Pack 2 Fixlist"
Other related information:	n/a
Author:	Neil Pike

sql7sp2bugs

Q: Should I apply Service Pack 2 for SQL 7.0? Are there any known issues?

A: Service Pack 2 (SP2) for SQL 7.0 underwent extensive beta testing before release and so should be pretty stable.

However, it contains many fixes and therefore new or regressed bugs are inevitable. When these are known they are listed at the bottom of the article.

For any new release or service pack you are advised to apply and test on test systems first, and if at all possible do a stress test so that any problems with blocking or locks are found before rolling out to a production system.

All service packs come with problems, however in most cases they fix many more problems than they cause. Ninety-nine percent of bugs you may find in SP2 will be present in the gold release and all previous service packs as well—they simply aren't fixed in SP2.

Should you apply it? Yes, assuming you have tested your applications first, of course. For this service pack pay special attention to cursor performance.

See FAQ article "sql7sp2" for details on how to obtain Service Pack 2.

Service Pack 2: Confirmed New Bugs/Regressions

- An internal error on a trigger update where two indices cover the updated column. Fixed in hot-fix build 871.
- Repro script courtesy of Mike Kincaid (mkincaid@fm.ucsf.edu):

```
-- Remove the unnecessary index bbb1 below and the problem will go away.
USE tempdb
go

DROP TABLE aaa
go

DROP TABLE bbb
go

CREATE TABLE aaa  (
   idno  char(15) NOT NULL,
   description  varchar(70) NOT NULL)
go

CREATE TABLE bbb  (
   idno  char(15) NOT NULL,
   num  int NOT NULL,
   description  varchar(70) NOT NULL)
go

CREATE INDEX bbb1 ON bbb
  (idno)
go

CREATE UNIQUE INDEX bbb2 ON bbb
  (idno,description)
go
```

```
CREATE TRIGGER t_aaa ON aaa FOR INSERT,UPDATE AS
BEGIN
UPDATE bbb SET
   bbb.idno = inserted.idno
   FROM bbb,inserted,deleted
   WHERE deleted.idno = bbb.idno
END
go

/* Error occurs when running this UPDATE */
UPDATE aaa SET description=description
go
```

- The grid output of the tools has a bug whereby if you save the results of a large query not all the rows are saved to the text/csv file. For example, if you save 600 rows, only 128 may get saved. Use text output rather than grid output and the problem will not occur.

- If you use SQLMAINT.EXE to generate database maintenance plans and set the "Attempt to repair any minor problems" option (-CKDBrepair) then some databases may be left in single user mode. Before SP2, because single-user mode was not set it didn't actually do anything. The option is now set, but doesn't get unset if the dbmaint job can't get back into the database to unset it (because something else has grabbed the connection). More details in the Q259551 Knowledge Base article.

  I would recommend not using this option routinely as corruptions so rarely occur with SQL 7.0. The corruptions that have been found were all due to faulty hardware.

- Merge replication issue. If you have a large amount of filtered articles in your Merge publication then the Snapshot Agent may fail with 4408 and/or 50007 errors. Further details in Q261216 Knowledge Base article.

- When you put SP1 or SP2 on your machine with standard SQL Security it leaves the sa password in a file. See `http://www.microsoft.com/technet/security/bulletin/fq00-035.asp` for a fix.

- You may see 8623 errors with insert or select statements that use NOT EXIST or NOT IN sub-query clauses.

- If you use ADO to connect to a SQL Server that has embedded spaces in column or table names, applying SP2 will cause this connectivity to fail.

Service Pack 2: Potential New Bugs/Regressions

These are issues that haven't been encountered by enough people to say with certainty that they are bugs, or there is not enough detail on why or when they happen.

- Veritas Backup Exec SQL Agent (v7) may cease to work after SP2. Not all Veritas users report this.

- A single report of databases being left in single-user mode after an index optimization job. This may well have been the SQLMAINT issue above.

- Reports of SQL Server using 100 percent CPU. No details are available.

- Queries involving cursors may slow down—in some cases significantly. Several reports of this have been reported, but the exact scenarios causing the problem are unknown.

Service Pack 2: Changes (Not Bugs)

These are things that have changed in SP2 but they are not bugs.

- It appears that SP2 optimizations have resulted in more cases where rows from heap tables (no clustered index) are not returned in insert order. This has never been guaranteed and is documented as such, so it is not a bug. If you want rows back in order, you must use an ORDER BY clause.

- SP2 changes the format of DTS packages, and is documented as such in the Readme.txt file that accompanies SP2. A full description this can be found in the FAQ article "dtsinvalidclassstring."

Reference

v1.15 2000.07.01

Applies to SQL Server version:	7.0
FAQ categories:	Installation and Upgrades, Troubleshooting
Related FAQ articles:	"Where can I get SQL Server/OLAP Services 7.0 Service Pack 2?" (sql7sp2, see page 318); "Should I apply Service Pack 1 for SQL Server 7.0? Are there any known issues?" (sql7sp1bugs, see page 316); "Should I upgrade to SQL 7.0? Why or why not? What are the known bugs? What other differences are there between 6.5 and 7.0?" (sql7differences, see page 304); "I get the error "The parameter is incorrect," "Invalid class string" or "The system cannot find the file specified" when trying to open or execute a DTS package. What should I do?" (dtsinvalid-classstring, see page 227)
Related Microsoft Knowledge Base articles:	Q254369 "INF: SQL Server 7.0 Service Pack 2 Fixlist" and Q254555 "INF: Readme.txt for SQL Server 7.0 Service Pack 2"
Other related information:	n/a
Author:	Neil Pike

sql7sql65samebox

Q: Can I run SQL 6.5 and SQL 7.0 on the same machine?

A: You can have both installed at the same time and switch between them, but there is no supported way for both to be running at the same time.

Reference

v1.00 1999.01.22

Applies to SQL Server versions:	6.5, 7.0
FAQ category:	Installation and Upgrades
Related FAQ articles:	n/a
Related Microsoft Knowledge Base articles:	n/a
Other related information:	n/a
Author:	Neil Pike

sql7upgradentadmin

Q: When upgrading from SQL 6.5 to SQL 7.0 between two machines I get the error message "Unable to connect to export server. Please verify that you are an NT administrator on that machine."

A: This is one case where it does matter who *you* are logged on as. SQL Server isn't making the connection to the machine—the upgrade wizard (running in *your* user context) is. It is directly reading the necessary files by connecting to \\server\c$\mssql\data etc. and therefore *you* need to be an administrator.

Reference

v1.00 1999.02.29	
Applies to SQL Server version:	7.0
FAQ category:	Installation and Upgrades
Related FAQ articles:	n/a
Related Microsoft Knowledge Base articles:	n/a
Other related information:	n/a
Author:	Neil Pike

sql7versions

Q: What versions or types of SQL 7.0 are there and what are the differences? How can I tell which one I am running?

A: There are six true versions or types of SQL 7.0, all built on the same code base, so they are all SQL 7.0. The same service packs can be applied to all of them.

- **Enterprise Edition**: Only runs on NT Enterprise Edition and Windows 2000 Advanced Server or higher. Supports > 4 processors. Supports two-node symmetrical clustering. Supports > 2Gb memory. Supports partitioned OLAP cubes; for example, OLAP cubes running on multiple servers.

- **Standard Edition**: Only runs on NT/Windows 2000 Server or higher. Supports up to four processors. Supports non-partitioned OLAP cubes. This is the version that comes with BackOffice 4.5.

- **Desktop Edition**: Can run on any NT, Windows 2000 or Windows 9x machine. Some feature and performance limitations—no parallel queries, only single-threaded recovery, not as much use of async io (Windows 9x doesn't support at all), databases only opened when needed, TCP-IP-only network support, no fiber mode scheduling, no read-ahead scans and no merge or hash joins. Performance has generally been throttled back to make it unsuitable for a multiple-client environment—if you try to use more than five concurrent users you will find performance tapers off. Note: You can't buy the Desktop Edition on its own. You have to buy the Standard or Enterprise edition, the installs for which allow a desktop install to be done. The Desktop version just needs a CAL per copy as a license. Full-text search engine, English Query and OLAP are not supported on Desktop Edition.

- **Small Business Edition (part of SBS 4.5)**: Same as Standard Edition except limited to 100 users and 10Gb per database. This version can be updated to the Standard Edition if needed.

- **MSDE**: This is a run-time engine, delivered as part of Office 2000, and can act as a back end to Access 2000 instead of Jet—although Jet will still be supported. Performance and other features are limited in the same way as the Desktop Edition. It only ships with the OSQL.EXE command-line program as an "admin" tool. Does not include DTS design tools though you can run pre-developed DTS packages against it. Footprint in disk space is 35Mb, working set is 6-7Mb at startup, 2-5Mb for processing. Limited to 2Gb per database. MSDE is freely distributable as long as the application you package it with was developed using a licensed copy of the Microsoft Office 2000 Developer Edition. Note: MSDE is packaged as v1.0 but it's still really SQL 7.0.

- **Developer Edition**: This is supplied with Visual Studio Enterprise Edition. This is the same as Standard Edition but comes with a develop/test only license.

- **Evaluation Edition**: In addition to these other versions there is an Evaluation Edition that is the same as Standard Edition, but is a 120-day time-limited version.

To detect which one you are running you need to parse the output from `SELECT @@VERSION`, which will have the following strings in it:

```
MSDE on .............
Desktop Edition on ................
Standard Edition on ................
Enterprise Edition on ...............
Small Business Server Edition on ...............
Developer Edition on ...............
Standard Edition Evaluation on ................
```

For example, `IF (CHARINDEX('MSDE', @@version) > 0 ) ....` <<<, you have MSDE.

Reference

v2.01 2000.06.13

Applies to SQL Server version:	7.0
FAQ category:	Installation and Upgrades
Related FAQ articles:	n/a
Related Microsoft Knowledge Base articles:	n/a
Other related information:	n/a
Author:	Neil Pike

sqlservicepacks

Q: Where can I get SQL Server Service Packs? What is the latest one?

A: SQL 7.0 SP2 and SQL 6.5 SP5a are the latest released service packs.

They (and some previous service packs) can be downloaded from either of these sites:

- `http://www.microsoft.com/downloads/search.asp?`
- `ftp://ftp.microsoft.com/bussys/sql/public/fixes` (pre-SQL7 SP2 only)

Reference

v1.04 2000.05.09

Applies to SQL Server versions:	6.5, 7.0
FAQ category:	Installation and Upgrades
Related FAQ article:	"What SQL Server service pack am I running? How can I get new ones?" (sp, see page 284)
Related Microsoft Knowledge Base articles:	n/a
Other related information:	n/a
Author:	Neil Pike

sspiassertionwin9x

Q: Why do I get an error in sqlsspi.c ?

A: The full message is

```
Assertion Failed!
Program:C:\"Application Name"
File: ../src/sqlsspi.c
Line: 120
Expression: Count
```

The reason for this is that you are probably running a Win9x client/server that does not have the "Client for Microsoft Networks" installed. This is needed for (among other things) accessing network security information.

Reference

v1.00 1999.07.18	
Applies to SQL Server version:	7.0
FAQ category:	Installation and Upgrades
Related FAQ articles:	n/a
Related Microsoft Knowledge Base articles:	n/a
Other related information:	n/a
Author:	Neil Pike

sspicontext

Q: Why do I get an error "CANNOT GENERATE SSPI CONTEXT"?

A: This is an issue with a SQL 7.0 client not being able to check the NT credentials in use. It always calls the SSPI interface to check this.

Make sure that if you're running a Win9x client, Microsoft Client Network is installed. Without this, checking the NT credentials may not be possible.

If you're running NT Workstation then check that the netlogon service is started.

Reference

v1.02 2000.05.09

Applies to SQL Server version:	7.0
FAQ categories:	Installation and Upgrades, Troubleshooting
Related FAQ articles:	"I'm having trouble installing SQL Server/ MSDE. What could be going wrong?" (install, see page 254); "I'm having trouble installing SQL Server on Windows 9x. What could be going wrong?" (installwin9x, see page 263)
Related Microsoft Knowledge Base articles:	n/a
Other related information:	n/a
Author:	Neil Pike

tcpipnetlibdoesntappear

Q: Why do the TCP/IP Net-Libraries not appear as an option in SQL Setup?

A: Two possible reasons:

- With 6.5 and below you have integrated security defined. Integrated security requires NT authentication of Net-Libraries connections, and TCP/IP Sockets does not offer this.

- The server does not have TCP/IP loaded as a network protocol. Check this via Control Panel/Networks/Protocols.

Reference

v1.01 2000.05.14

Applies to SQL Server versions:	All
FAQ categories:	Installation and Upgrades, Connectivity
Related FAQ articles:	n/a
Related Microsoft Knowledge Base articles:	n/a
Other related information:	n/a
Author:	Neil Pike

terminalserver

Q: Can I install SQL on a Terminal Server machine?

A: Several points here:

- For the same reason that Microsoft doesn't "recommend" installing SQL Server on a PDC, you should avoid installing it on Terminal Server. SQL Server and Terminal Server are very memory hungry and could starve each other of resources.
- SQL 6.5 has not been tested on any form of Terminal Server, but should work.
- SQL 7.0 is supported on NT 4 Terminal Server (NTTE) as long as you install at least SP1 for SQL 7.0.
- SQL 7.0 is not supported on Windows 2000 Server with Terminal Services installed.
- SQL 2000 is supported on Windows 2000 with Terminal Services.
- SQL 2000 is not supported on NT 4 Terminal Server.

Reference

v1.05 2000.06.13

Applies to SQL Server versions:	6.5, 7.0, 2000
FAQ category:	Installation and Upgrades
Related FAQ article:	"Where can I get SQL Server/OLAP Services 7.0 Service Pack 1?" (sql7sp1, see page 316)
Related Microsoft Knowledge Base article:	Q232574 "INF: Readme.txt for SQL Server 7.0 Service Pack 1"
Other related information:	n/a
Author:	Neil Pike

unattendedclient

Q: How can I install SQL Server client tools in unattended mode?

A: The setup.inf file Microsoft provides with 6.5 and below doesn't allow for this, so your choices are:

- Amend the setup.inf to provide this support, or write a new one.

- Do a script to copy the relevant files across and update any registry parameters needed. You could use something like Sysdiff (in the NT Resource Kit) to help you do this. Other tools would be SMS Installer or WinInstall (now owned by Veritas).

For SQL 7.0 and above, the setup routine uses initialisation files, samples of which can be found on the CD-ROM. In addition you may record your own or amend the samples provided. Full details can be found in Books Online.

Reference

v1.02 2000.06.13

Applies to SQL Server versions:	All
FAQ category:	Installation and Upgrades
Related FAQ articles:	n/a
Related Microsoft Knowledge Base article:	Q233312 "INF: Customizing SQL/MSDE Unattended Installation Files"
Other related information:	n/a
Author:	Neil Pike

unattendedinstall

Q: I'm having trouble with SQL Server's unattended install. What could be going wrong?

A: Check the "install" FAQ article for generic install problems. Then check here for unattended-specific issues.

If you get an error "Configure SQLServer Agent / The server service is not started" while installing MSDE on NT with the standard unattend.iss response file, change AutoStart from 61455 to 255 in the unattend.iss file.

Reference

v1.03 2000.06.13

Applies to SQL Server version:	7.0
FAQ category:	Installation and Upgrades
Related FAQ articles:	"I'm having trouble installing SQL Server/MSDE. What could be going wrong?" (install, see page 254); "How can I install SQL Server client tools in unattended mode?" (unattendedclient, see page 329)
Related Microsoft Knowledge Base article:	Q233312 "INF: Customizing SQL/MSDE Unattended Installation Files"
Other related information:	n/a
Author:	Neil Pike

uninstall

Q: How can I completely uninstall SQL Server?

A: If the standard uninstall utility doesn't do the trick for some reason:

1. Remove the <sql> directory and everything under it.
2. Remove the <sql> dir from the path (use Control Panel/System for this).
3. Remove the SQL registry entries using regedt32/regedit. These are:

   - All versions:

   ```
   HKEY_LOCAL_MACHINE\SYSTEM\CurrentControlSet\Services\MSSQLServer
   HKEY_LOCAL_MACHINE\SOFTWARE\Microsoft\MSSQLServer
   ```

   - 6.0 and above:

   ```
   HKEY_LOCAL_MACHINE\System\CurrentControlSet\Services\MSDTC
   HKEY_LOCAL_MACHINE\SYSTEM\CurrentControlSet\Services\SQLExecutive
   ```

- 7.0 and above:

```
HKEY_LOCAL_MACHINE\SYSTEM\CurrentControlSet\Services\SQLServerAgent
HKEY_LOCAL_MACHINE\Software\Microsoft\Microsoft SQL Server 7
HKEY_LOCAL_MACHINE\Software\Microsoft\MSSQLServ65
HKEY_LOCAL_MACHINE\SYSTEM\CurrentControlSet\Services\MSSQLServerOLAPService
```

- 2000 and above:

```
HKEY_LOCAL_MACHINE\Software\Microsoft\Microsoft SQL Server
HKEY_LOCAL_MACHINE\SYSTEM\CurrentControlSet\Services\MSSQL$<anything>
HKEY_LOCAL_MACHINE\SYSTEM\CurrentControlSet\Services\SQLAgent$<anything>
```

If you have lost permission to any of the registry keys, log on as administrator and take ownership of them starting at the highest relevant level. Use regedt32 and check the box to take ownership of all subkeys as well.

After doing the uninstall it is recommended to reboot to remove the NT service details from memory.

Reference

v1.04 2000.06.13

Applies to SQL Server versions:	All
FAQ category:	Installation and Upgrades
Related FAQ articles:	n/a
Related Microsoft Knowledge Base articles:	n/a
Other related information:	n/a
Author:	Neil Pike

uninstallsp

Q: How can I un-install a SQL Server Service Pack and go back to the original version?

A: Check the readme.txt that came with the service pack. Some come with uninstall instructions —in which case follow them.

If there are no instructions, just replace the updated .EXEs and .DLLs with the previous ones. This won't back out any of the SQL script changes that would have been run as part of the service pack, but I don't know of any issues that require these being backed out.

Reference

v1.03 2000.06.05	
Applies to SQL Server versions:	All
FAQ category:	Installation and Upgrades
Related FAQ articles:	n/a
Related Microsoft Knowledge Base article:	Q216421 "INF: How to Downgrade From SQL Server 6.5 Service Pack 5 or 5a"
Other related information:	n/a
Author:	Neil Pike

versionchanges

Q: What are the changes or differences between version X and version Y of SQL Server?

A: Changes in functionality are typically documented in incremental steps from the previous release. The following sources are available:

- What's New section in the Books Online
- Q152032 Changes to SQL Server 6.5 That Affect 6.0 Apps
- Q133177 Changes to SQL Server 6.0 That May Affect 4.2x Apps

There is no particular Knowledge Base article for SQL 6.5 to SQL 7.0, or SQL 7.0 to SQL 2000 but there is extensive guidance in Books Online. There is also a FAQ article called "SQL7differences."

There are also occasionally changes introduced in service packs. These changes are documented in the readme.txt for the service pack, which is cumulative. So SP4's readme contains all changes from SP1, 2 and 3 as well.

Reference

v1.02 2000.06.01

Applies to SQL Server versions:	All
FAQ category:	Installation and Upgrades
Related FAQ article:	"Should I upgrade to SQL 7.0? Why or why not? What are the known bugs? What other differences are there between 6.5 and 7.0?" (sql7differences, see page 304)
Related Microsoft Knowledge Base articles:	Q152032 "Changes to SQL Server 6.5 That Affect 6.0 Apps" and Q133177 "Changes to SQL Server 6.0 That May Affect 4.2x Apps"
Other related information:	n/a
Author:	Neil Pike

win2000

Q: Does SQL Server run under Windows 2000?

A: SQL 7.0 and higher work fine under Windows 2000. For SQL 6.5 you need to upgrade to SP5a otherwise the DUMP and LOAD DATABASE commands will fail.

Reference

v1.01 2000.06.01

Applies to SQL Server versions:	All
FAQ category:	Installation and Upgrades
Related FAQ articles:	n/a
Related Microsoft Knowledge Base articles:	n/a
Other related information:	n/a
Author:	Neil Pike

y2k

Q: Is Microsoft SQL Server Y2K compliant? What known issues are there?

A: It is now 2000, so you should know by now!

That depends on what you mean by "compliant." If you mean the base SQL kernel functionality works as you would expect, then yes, as long as you are using "proper" datetime formats then all versions of SQL Server perform correctly—if you are holding dates in char/numeric format, then it totally depends on how you are processing them. It is not an Microsoft SQL Server issue.

SQL Server does date-windowing for two-digit dates. If you specify only the last two digits of the year, values less than 50 are interpreted as 20yy, and values greater than or equal to 50 are interpreted as 19yy. For example, if you specify 3, the result is 2003. If you specify 82, the result is 1982. You must type the century when the day is omitted or when you need a century other than the default. (In SQL 7.0/2000 you can modify the cut-off date for the windowing function).

However, if you mean the whole of the Microsoft SQL Server product set including all the GUI tools, then there are a few non-showstopper problems that have been found. These are all documented at `http://www.microsoft.com/y2k` along with Microsoft's stance and technical information on Y2K issues for all its products. The SQL 6.5 Y2K fix titles are also provided at the bottom of this article.

These problems have been found, fixed and tested in SQL 6.5 and are in Service Pack 5a.

SQL 7.0 and SQL 2000 are Y2K compliant.

SQL 1.x, 4.x and 6.0 are *not* being tested or certified by Microsoft. They are unlikely to have any other problems than those found in the 6.5 product though, so if you can live with those (and most people can), then they should be OK. I know of no Y2K issues that companies have found with their existing 4.x and 6.x systems that can be attributed to SQL Server.

You can check MS's Web site for any more Y2K info on them, but all it says is that the products are legacy and have not been tested or certified.

Vendor's certification should only be one part of Y2K testing anyway—the most important part is that *you* test your clients, servers, apps, databases and networks in your production environment.

SQL 6.5 Y2K BUG NUMBERS AND TITLES

17458	Year 2000 Problem with Expiredate
17937	Y2000, ExpireDate is not set correctly when year of 2000 used in DUMP DATABASE
17947	RETAINDAYS: expired dump media can not be overwritten if current year is >= 2000
17948	Dump db with RETAINDAYS during Y2000-9, EXPIREDATE will be set to NULL
17997	Y2000: dump device dumped with expiredate set to >=2000 can be override with init
17661	Task Manager UI: one time task date\time spin box doesn't pick up 2/29/2000
18153	Web Assistant: Cannot use Year as 00 on Scheduling
18170	Invalid Y2K dates are accepted with no error by sp_addtask
18180	Invalid Y2K dates are accepted with no error by sp_purgehistory and sp_updatealert

Reference

v1.08 2000.06.02

Applies to SQL Server versions:	All
FAQ categories:	Installation and Upgrades, Troubleshooting
Related FAQ article:	"Can I amend the "window" that SQL Server applies for two-digit dates for Y2K?" (y2kwindow, see page 459)
Related Microsoft Knowledge Base articles:	n/a
Other related information:	n/a
Author:	Neil Pike

Miscellaneous

This section covers everything that does not neatly fit into any of the other categories.

alphasupport

Q: As a user of Digital/Compaq Alpha technology, how does Microsoft's dropping support affect my use of SQL Server?

A: Three ways:

- Support for all currently released and supported SQL products and service packs continues and will not be affected.
- New service-packs for 6.5 and 7.0 will continue to be produced for the Alpha for the time being (previous versions of SQL Server are not under active support anyway).
- No future new versions of SQL Server will be released on Alpha. For example, SQL 2000 will not appear for the Alpha chip.

Reference

v1.04 2000.03.26

Applies to SQL Server versions:	4.x, 6.x, 7.0
FAQ category:	Miscellaneous
Related FAQ articles:	n/a
Related Microsoft Knowledge Base articles:	n/a
Other related information:	n/a
Author:	Neil Pike

ansi92

Q: Where can I get the ANSI92 SQL information?

A: This information is only available from ANSI. They charge for the information—they have to have some form of income stream after all.

More information can be obtained from their Web site at `http://www.ansi.org`. Or try: `http://www.cssinfo.com/`.

You also can get an overview of FIPS at `http://www.itl.nist.gov/fipspubs/fip127-2.htm`.

Reference

v1.01 2000.03.28	
Applies to SQL Server versions:	All
FAQ category:	Miscellaneous
Related FAQ articles:	n/a
Related Microsoft Knowledge Base articles:	n/a
Other related information:	n/a
Author:	Neil Pike

conferences

Q: What conferences covering SQL Server are coming up?

A: The following organizations either run conferences or have event information on their Web sites:

- SQL PASS (Professional Association for SQL Server): `http://www.sqlpass.org`
- SQL Connections: `http://www.sqlconnections.com` or `www.sqldevcon.com`
- SQL 2 the Max: `http://conferences.devx.com` and `www.sql2themax.com`
- For general Microsoft conference info try `http://events.microsoft.com/isapi/events/default.asp`

Reference

v1.03 2000.04.24	
Applies to SQL Server versions:	All
FAQ category:	Miscellaneous
Related FAQ articles:	n/a
Related Microsoft Knowledge Base articles:	n/a
Other related information:	n/a
Author:	Neil Pike

dbcccommands

Q: What are all the DBCC commands for SQL Server?

A: All the documented ones are in Books Online, or in publicly accessible Knowledge Base articles. The rest are undocumented because they are either irrelevant to people outside Microsoft or their use is dangerous and is to be discouraged.

The undocumented DBCC commands vary from release to release. However, as people always want to know, here is a predominantly Sybase-based list that will mostly work with SQL 6.5 and below—however there are no guarantees. Feel free to use any of these against a test system, but don't expect any help if you use any of them that are not documented officially elsewhere. With many undocumented DBCC commands, the DBCC command TRACEON must be used in order to get information: DBCC TRACEON(3604) must be used for information to be returned to a front-end's result area, and DBCC TRACEON(3605) must be used for the information to be written to the error log.

DBCC Commands or Options Not Documented by Microsoft

```
ALLOCDUMP( database_id, page_number )

BHASH( { PRINT_BUFS | NO_PRINT }, bucket_limit )

BUFFER( [ database_id ][, object_id ][, number_of_buffers ],
PRINTOPT = { 0 | 1 | 2 }, buffer_type )

BYTES( start_address, length )

DBINFO( [ database_name ] )

DBTABLE( database_id )

DELETE_ROW( database_id, page_number, DELETE_BY_ROW = { 1 | 0 }, row_number )

DELETEINSTANCE (perfmon_object, perfmon_counter | "%")

DES( [ database_id ][, object_id ] )

DROPCLEANBUFFERS

errorlog

extentcheck( database_id, object_id, index_id, SORT = {1|0} )
```

EXTENTCHAIN(*database_id*, *object_id*, *index_id*, SORT = {1|0},display(1,0))

EXTENTDUMP(*database_id*, *page_number*)

EXTENTZAP(*database_id*, *object_id*, *index_id*, SORT = {1|0})

FREEPROCCACHE

findnotfullextents(*database_id*, *object_id*, *index_id*, SORT = { 1 | 0 })

IND(*database_id*, *object_id*, *PRINTOPT* = { 0 | 1 | 2 })

INDEXALLOC(*table_name*|*table_id*, *index_id*, [FULL | OPTIMIZED | FAST],
[FIX | NOFIX])

LOCATEINDEXPGS(*database_id*, *object_id*, *page_number*, *index_id*, *level*)

lock

LockObjectSchema(*table_name*)

LOG([*database_id*][, OBJID=*object_id*] [,PAGE=*page_number*] [,ROW=*row_id*]
[,NRECORDS=*number*] [,TYPE={-1..36}], PRINTOPT={0|1})—see logview FAQ

NETMEMSHOW(OPTION = {1 | 2 | 3})

netmemusage

newalloc(*database_name*, OPTION = { 1 | 2 | 3 })

PGLINKAGE(*database_id*, *start*, *number*, PRINTOPT={0|1|2}, *target*, ORDER={1|0})

pktmemshow(option = *spid*)

procbuf(*database_id*, *object_id*, nbufs=*number*, printopt = { 0 | 1 })

prtipage (*database_id*, *object_id*, *index_id*, *page_number*)

pss(*suid*, *spid*, printopt = { 1 | 0 })—see storedproccurrentline FAQ

rebuildextents(*database_id*, *object_id*, *index_id*)—see rebuildextents FAQ

renamecolumn(*owner_and_object_name*,*unqualoldname*, *newname*)

resource

setinstance (*perfmon_object*, *perfmon_counter*, *instance_name*, *new_value*)

show_bucket(*database_id*, *page_number*, *lookup_type*)

tab(*database_id*, *object_id*, printopt = { 0 | 1 | 2 })

tablealloc(*table_name*|*table_id*, [full | optimized | fast],[fix | nofix])

UNDO(*database_id, page_number, row_number*)

upgradedb (database_name)

Other Undocumented DBCC Commands Described in Microsoft Knowledge Base

BUFCOUNT(N_CHAINS=*number_of_chains*)

FIX_AL(*database_name*)

GAMINIT [(*database_id*)]

PGLINKAGE(*database_id, start, number, print_option, target, order*)

PAGE({*database_id*|*database_name*}, *page_number_number* [,PRINTOPT={0|1|2}] [,CACHE={0|1}] [,LOGICAL={1|0}])

stackdump

Documented SQL 6.5 DBCC Commands

CHECKALLOC [(*database_name* [, NOINDEX])]

CHECKCATALOG [(*database_name*)]

CHECKTABLE (*table_name* [, NOINDEX | *index_id*])

CHECKDB [(*database_name* [, NOINDEX])]

CHECKIDENT [(*table_name*)]

DBREPAIR (*database_name*, DROPDB [, NOINIT])

dllname (FREE)

INPUTBUFFER (*spid*)

MEMUSAGE

NEWALLOC [(*database_name* [, NOINDEX])]

OPENTRAN ({*database_name*} | {*database_id*}) [WITH TABLERESULTS]

OUTPUTBUFFER (*spid*)

PERFMON

PINTABLE (*database_id, table_id*)

SHOW_STATISTICS (*table_name*, *index_name*)

SHOWCONTIG (*table_id*, [*index_id*])

SHRINKDB (*database_name* [, *new_size* [, 'MASTEROVERRIDE']])

SQLPERF ({IOSTATS | LRUSTATS | NETSTATS | RASTATS [, CLEAR]} {THREADS} | {LOGSPACE})

TEXTALL [({*database_name* | *database_id*}[, FULL | FAST])]

TEXTALLOC [({*table_name* | *table_id*}[, FULL | FAST])]

TRACEOFF (*trace#* [, *trace#...*])

TRACEON (*trace#* [, *trace#...*])

TRACESTATUS (*trace#* [, *trace#...*])

UNPINTABLE (*database_id*, *table_id*)

UPDATEUSAGE ({0 | *database_name*} [, *table_name* [, *index_id*]])

USEROPTIONS

Documented SQL 7.0 DBCC Commands, as Returned by DBCC HELP(?)

CATALOGCHECK [(*database_name*)]

CHECKALLOC [(*database_name*[, NOINDEX | REPAIR])]

CHECKCATALOG [(*database_name*)]

CHECKDB [(*database_name*[, NOINDEX | REPAIR])]

CHECKFILEGROUP [([{'*filegroup_name*' | *filegroup_id*}] [, NOINDEX])]

CHECKIDENT (*table_name*[, { NORESEED | {RESEED [, *new_reseed_value*] } }])

CHECKTABLE (*table_name*[, {NOINDEX | *index_id* | REPAIR}])

DBREINDEX (*table_name* [, *index_name* [, *fillfactor*]])

DBREPAIR (*database_name*, DROPDB [, NOINIT])

DLL_NAME (FREE)

HELP ('DBCC_command' | '?')

INPUTBUFFER (*spid*)

MEMUSAGE ['BUFFER']

NEWALLOC—please use CHECKALLOC instead

OPENTRAN [({*database_name*| *database_id*})] [WITH TABLERESULTS]

OUTPUTBUFFER (*spid*)

perfmon

pintable (*database_id*, *table_id*)

proccache

row_lock (*database_id*, *tableid*, *set*)–Not Needed

SHOW_STATISTICS (*table_name*, *target_name*)

SHOWCONTIG (*table_id [*, *index_id*])

SHRINKDATABASE ({*database_id* | *database_name*}, [*freespace_percentage*[,{NOTRUNCATE | TRUNCATEONLY}]])

SHRINKDB is no longer supported. Please use SHRINKDATABASE instead

SHRINKFILE ({*file_id* | '*filename*'}, [*compress_size* [, {NOTRUNCATE | TRUNCATEONLY | EMPTYFILE}]])

SQLPERF (LOGSPACE)

TEXTALL [({*database_name*|*database_id*}[, 'FULL' | FAST])]

TEXTALLOC ({*table_name*|*table_id*}[, 'FULL' | FAST])

TRACEOFF (*trace#* [, *trace#*...])

TRACEON (*trace#* [, *trace#*...])

TRACESTATUS (*trace#* [, *trace#*...])

UNPINTABLE (*database_id*, *table_id*)

UPDATEUSAGE ({*database_name*| 0} [, *table_name* [, *index_id*]]) [WITH COUNT_ROWS]

useroptions

Reference

v1.03 2000.05.15	
Applies to SQL Server versions:	All
FAQ category:	Miscellaneous
Related FAQ articles:	"How can I view the SQL Server log? Can I recover individual transactions or data from it?" (logview, see page 173 for DBCC LOG); "I'm getting an error 1117 or 2543 in SQL Server. Can I rebuild the extents somehow?" (rebuildextents, see page 525 for DBCC REBUILDEXTENTS); and "How can I see what line a stored procedure is on?" (storedproc-currentline, see page 201 for DBCC PSS)
Related Microsoft Knowledge Base articles:	search on "DBCC command name"
Other related information:	search `http://support.sybase.com/` for technical documents on DBCC in earlier releases of SQL Server
Author:	Neil Pike

eastererggs

Q: Are there any "easter eggs" in SQL Server?

A: Yes.

To view this in SQL 6.5 Enterprise Manager:

1. Using the Enterprise Manager, create a New Server Group called starfighter.

2. Register a Server called IS COOL (note there is a space there) under this new server group. Click "register anyway" as it won't connect.

3. Highlight "IS COOL" and click the About box to see the development team.

To view this in SQL 6.5 ISQL/W:

1. Connect to a server.

2. Choose Help About.

3. Hit <F1>. You will now see the ISQL/W development team.

Reference

v1.02 2000.04.22

Applies to SQL Server version:	6.5
FAQ category:	Miscellaneous
Related FAQ articles:	n/a
Related Microsoft Knowledge Base articles:	n/a
Other related information:	n/a
Author:	Neil Pike

enterpriseeditionfaster-thanstandard

Q: Does SQL Server Enterprise Edition perform better than Standard Edition?

A: Not with SQL 6.5 and 7.0 if exactly the same hardware and setup are used. But the Enterprise Edition supports more than four processors, more than 2GB memory and partitioning of OLAP cubes. So it allows you to throw more hardware at the problem.

With each release of SQL Server, Microsoft is differentiating the Enterprise Edition more. So it is possible that there will be more performance differences in the future.

Reference

v1.01 2000.05.25

Applies to SQL Server versions:	All
FAQ category:	Miscellaneous
Related FAQ articles:	n/a
Related Microsoft Knowledge Base articles:	n/a
Other related information:	n/a
Author:	Neil Pike

faq

Q: Where is the SQL Server FAQ? Or other useful SQL information?

A: Contrary to appearance this isn't strictly speaking a FAQ article—just something I have done to save some time answering common questions on the newsgroups. There isn't one all-encompassing FAQ as there is for some non-Microsoft newsgroups. See the "sqlbooks" FAQ article for lists of several places for good information.

This "FAQ" is held at various locations. The most up-to-date version is always on the Compuserve site and is held as a single zip file. The various other copies of it are maintained by the owner of each site and have their own formats and search engines. Note: there is no copyright or restriction whatsoever on other people using or publishing the FAQ as long as it is not for commercial gain. If you want to use the whole FAQ or any part of it, just let me know (neilpike@compuserve.com) and I will add you to the mailing list for FAQ updates.

Here are several sources of information:

- `http://forumsb.compuserve.com/gvforums/UK/default.asp?SRV=MSDevApps` (library 7 (SQL Public): faqrtf.zip. Anyone can download this—you don't have to be a CIS member.)
- `http://www.ntfaq.com/sql.html`
- `http://www.sqlserverfaq.com`
- `http://www.mssqlserver.com/faq`
- `http://www.swynk.com/faq/sql/sqlserverfaq.asp`
- `http://www.manyquestions.com`

The Microsoft " official" FAQ is at `http://support.microsoft.com/support/sql/content/faq/default.asp`.

Plenty more SQL articles and bug reports can be found by searching the Microsoft Knowledge Base at `http://www.microsoft.com/support`. An off-line copy of the Knowledge Base as well as hundreds of articles, white papers, resource kits, and service packs can be found on the Technet CD. If you don't subscribe to Technet, do so *now* as it is the single most important source of knowledge for support staff responsible for Microsoft technologies.

Reference

v1.12 2000.06.21	
Applies to SQL Server versions:	All
FAQ category:	Miscellaneous
Related FAQ article:	"What are some good SQL Server books and other reference sources?" (sqlbooks, see page 355)
Related Microsoft Knowledge Base articles:	n/a
Other related information:	n/a
Author:	Neil Pike

jukebox

Q: Can I use a Worm/MO/CD-ROM jukebox with SQL Server? I'd like to archive older transactions into a set of read-only databases there.

A: Yes and no.

- SQL can only access "disks," so first the jukebox must be made to look just like a disk or set of disks, complete with drive letters. There are a variety of products available to do this from Ascend, Kofax, OTG and Ixos to name a few (I've mainly used DiskXtender from `http://www.otgsoftware.com`).

- SQL needs immediate access to the data, but jukeboxes and related software typically don't offer this—they normally cache files to a real disk first. This all takes time—seconds to minutes or more for large files. Having SQL's i/o engine backed up waiting for i/o from a very slow device (compared to disks) is a very bad idea.

I would recommend that instead of WORM/jukeboxes you just buy another large RAID unit with the largest disks you can find and create databases on this RAID unit and then mark them as read-only with SQL Server.

Reference

v1.01 2000.05.07

Applies to SQL Server versions:	All
FAQ category:	Miscellaneous
Related FAQ articles:	n/a
Related Microsoft Knowledge Base articles:	n/a
Other related information:	n/a
Author:	Neil Pike

msmqinstall

Q: Why do I get the message "Unable to resize master database" when installing a Microsoft Messaging Queue (MSMQ) controller?

A: Installations of MSQM that need SQL Server (PEC, PSC, BSC) will talk directly to the SQL Server via Named Pipes. The setup routine requires your default Network Library to be set to Named Pipes for the duration of the installation, otherwise it will fail with this message.

Use the Client Network Utility to change this.

Reference

v1.00 2000.05.27

Applies to SQL Server versions:	6.5, 7.0
FAQ category:	Miscellaneous
Related FAQ articles:	n/a
Related Microsoft Knowledge Base articles:	n/a
Other related information:	n/a
Author:	Darren Green

MVP

Q: What is a "SQL Server MVP" and how do I become one?

A: An MVP is a Microsoft Valued Professional. These are people recognized by Microsoft as providing a "lot" of help on their Internet newsgroups for fellow users. You can't pass any exam or pay to become one. There are MVPs who cover most of the Microsoft product and development range—SQL Server is just one of many areas. MVP status is renewed yearly (or not, as the case may be).

MVPs are not paid by Microsoft, and are, by and large, not Microsoft groupies or yes-men/women. They do get some "freebies," but if you worked these out, their cash value at an hourly rate would be a few pennies per hour.

MVPs can report bugs and problems directly to Microsoft for you, but it is only feasible to do so if the problem is reproducible.

The SQL Server MVPs (as of 2000.09.06) are (I hope I haven't forgotten anyone):

Itzik Ben-Gan

Kalen Delaney

Trevor Dwyer

Russel Fields

Darren Green

Fernando Guerrero

Roy Harvey

Mike Hotek

Gianluca Hotz

Tibor Karaszi

Umachandar Jayachandran

Greg Mable

B.P. Margolin

Brian Moran

Bob Pfeiff

Neil Pike

Steve Robinson

Tony Rogerson

Wayne Snyder

Ron Talmage

To become an MVP you need to be "noticed" as being a regular, accurate, and knowledgeable contributor to the newsgroups and forums over an extended period of time. There is no fixed number of postings or length of time. You can then be nominated to Microsoft (usually by one of the existing MVPs).

Reference

v1.11 2000.09.06	
Applies to SQL Server versions:	All
FAQ category:	Miscellaneous
Related FAQ articles:	n/a
Related Microsoft Knowledge Base articles:	n/a
Other related information:	`http://support.microsoft.com/support/mvp/`
Author:	Neil Pike

MYSQL

Q: SQL Server only runs under NT. What cheap or free database runs under Linux?

A: There are two well known DBMSs that run on Linux, both of which are covered by a public license:

- MySQL: `http://www.mysql.com`

- Interbase: `http://www.interbase.com`

Reference

v1.02 2000.06.04

Applies to SQL Server versions:	All
FAQ category:	Miscellaneous
Related FAQ articles:	n/a
Related Microsoft Knowledge Base articles:	n/a
Other related information:	n/a
Author:	Neil Pike

oraclevssql

Q: Why is SQL Server better or worse than Oracle?

A: This is as much a "religious" debate as a technical one. Both products are good (as are others such as DB/2, Informix and Sybase). My advice would be to stick with whatever you have the technical skills and experience with, and don't change for the sake of it. SQL Server, Oracle, and DB/2 will all be around for a long time—and most of the other DBMSs should be too.

But for those who have to have a pro and con list, here is one to get you started (though no doubt some or all all of the points would be contested). It assumes SQL 2000 and Oracle 8.

Pros of SQL Server

- On the *same* hardware running NT, SQL Server has better TPC-C numbers. (`http://www.tpc.org`). It also has a higher number overall using a distributed set of servers running SQL 2000 (it is beaten by an IBM DB/2 distributed system). Oracle has the highest TPC-C number for a single server—but only on non-NT platforms—and the cost per TPC-C is higher.

- The mobile or client version of the product is exactly the same as the server one (with Oracle it isn't).

- SQL Server is generally accepted as easier to install, use, and manage.

- SQL Server is cheaper to buy than Oracle for most configurations (though this is such a small part of lifetime support costs it really shouldn't be a consideration).

- Extra facilities are "in the box" for no extra cost. For example, OLAP, English Query, and DTS.

Pros of Oracle

- Scales higher than SQL Server on a single server—whether your system needs to scale that high is a question you need to ask yourself (if you need ultimate performance you should be looking at DB/2 on a cluster of IBM 10-way mainframes). SQL 2000 should be fine for 5TB of data and 2500 users (I have heard of people using SQL Server with over 10TB of data). (These are conservative figures and have more to do with NT's scalability than SQL's).

- Clusters better than SQL.

- More powerful 3GL language than SQL: PL-SQL vs. T-SQL.

- Runs on non-NT platforms such as Unix or MVS.

- It's been around longer.

- More fine-tuning to the configuration can be done via start-up parameters.

Reference

v1.05 2000.09.07

Applies to SQL Server versions:	All
FAQ category:	Miscellaneous
Related FAQ articles:	n/a
Related Microsoft Knowledge Base articles:	n/a
Other related information:	n/a
Author:	Neil Pike

sqlbooks

Q: What are some good SQL Server books and other reference sources?

A: SQL Books Online is a good source, as is TechNet, with hundreds of techie articles and whitepapers on SQL as well as the Knowledge Base. The SQL 7.0 Books Online can be downloaded at `http://support.microsoft.com/download/support/mslfiles/sqlbol.exe`.

- An un-official "FAQ" is maintained at the following sites:

  `http://forumsb.compuserve.com/gvforums/UK/default.asp?SRV=MSDevApps`
  (download sqlfaq.zip from library 7 (SQL Public))

  `http://www.sqlserverfaq.com`

  `http://www.ntfaq.com/sql.html`

  `http://www.mssqlserver.com/faq`

  `http://www.swynk.com/faq/sql/sqlserverfaq.asp`

  The most up-to-date copy (apart from the one on my hard drive) is the one in the Compuserve library. You don't need to be a Compuserve member to download it. The other sites all take the info and put it into their own format.

- Online Microsoft resources:

  `http://www.microsoft.com/sql/`

  `http://www.microsoft.com/technet/sql/`

  `http://msdn.microsoft.com/sqlserver/`

- Other online resources:

  SQL Server newsgroups: `microsoft.public.sqlserver.*` and `comp.dcom.databases.ms-sqlserver`

  `GO MSDEVAPP` on Compuserve for SQL forums

  `http://www.sqlserverfaq.com` (copy of SQL FAQ, code samples, other material) `http://www.mssqlserver.com` (copy of SQL FAQ, reviews, lots of other resources)

`http://www.sqlwire.com` (SQL News)

`http://www.insidesqlserver.com` (updates to Kalen Delaney's *Inside SQL Server 7.0* book, Q&A, and lots of other information)

`http://www.ntfaq.com/sql.htm` (copy of SQL FAQ)

`http://www.swynk.com` (SQL Server mailing list and other resources)

`http://www.dbmaint.com` (code samples)

`http://www.umachandar.com/resources.htm`

`http://www.impetus-sql.co.uk/`

`http://www.betav.com/` (Bill Vaughn's Web site)

- Magazines:

  SQL Server Magazine (`http://www.sqlmag.com`)

  SQL Server Professional, Pinnacle Publishing (`http://www.pinpub.com`)

  NT Magazine has monthly articles on SQL plus the odd one-off article.

- Books: There are few good ones, but this doesn't mean anything not listed isn't good! Many of these go through various revisions, so make sure you're getting the latest and greatest version.

  Microsoft SQL Server 6.5/7.0 Programming Unleashed. Sams/various. Good for programming and T-SQL.

  Microsoft SQL Server 6.5/7.0 Unleashed. Sams/various. Good for DBAs, administration, performance, and general issues.

  SQL for Smarties. Morgan Kaufmann/Joe Celko. Advanced SQL programming techniques, tricks, and tips. Not SQL Server-specific but highly recommended.

  Hitchhikers Guide to VB and SQL Server. MSPress/Bill Vaughn. ISBN: 1572318481. If you're coding VB to access SQL and you're not sure whether or how to use DB-Library, ODBC, ADO, RDO, OLE-DB, RDS, RDO or DMO (I think that's all of them) then this is the bible.

BackOffice Resource Kit Part II. MSPress. Good material on SQL 6.5 connectivity and some internals, plus some nice utilities and white papers.

BackOffice 4.5 Resource Kit. MSPress. Same as *BackOffice Resource Kit Part II* but for SQL 7.0.

Teach Yourself Microsoft SQL Server 7.0 in 21 Days. Sams / Richard Waymire. ISBN: 0-672-31290-5. A good overall guide to SQL Server 7.0.

Inside Microsoft SQL Server 6.5. MSPress / Ron Soukup. SQL Server internals, how it works, why, the history. Plenty of good undocumented information.

Inside Microsoft SQL Server 7.0. MSPress / Kalen Delaney. ISBN: 0735605173. The bible for SQL 7.0 internals.

SQL Server 7 Database Administration. Prima Press / Ron Talmage. Probably the best SQL 7.0 administrator / DBA book.

The Guru's Guide to Transact-SQL. Ken Henderson. ISBN: 0-201-61576-2. Great SQL 7.0 / Transact-SQL book.

Microsoft OLAP Solutions. Microsoft Press / George Spofford and Erik Thomsen. ISBN: 0471332585. The definitive Microsoft OLAP book.

Database Modelling and Design. Morgan Kaufmann / Toby Teory.

Transact-SQL Programming. O'Reilly / Kline, Gould and Zanevsky. What the title says—specific to SQL Server 6.5 / Sybase 4.x. Nothing on later Sybase / SQL Server additions or changes to syntax.

Unlocking OLAP with SQL Server 7 and Excel 2000. Wayne Freeze. ISBN: 0764545876.

Microsoft SQL Server 7 OLAP Developer's Guide. Bill Amo. ISBN: 0764546430.

OLAP Solutions, Building Multidimensional Information Systems with CDROM. Erik Thomsen. ISBN: 0471149314.

OLAP Services Fundamentals, Online Analytical Processing Technology for Microsoft SQL Server with CDROM. OLAP Train. ISBN: 0735609047.

Microsoft OLAP Unleashed with CDROM. Tim Peterson, Bob Pfeiff, Jim Pinkelman. ISBN: 07672316714.

Anything by Ralph Kimball will be good for data warehousing.

Reference

v1.24 2000.06.11	
Applies to SQL Server versions:	All
FAQ category:	Miscellaneous
Related FAQ articles:	n/a
Related Microsoft Knowledge Base articles:	n/a
Other related information:	n/a
Author:	Neil Pike

sqlvsothers

Q: Why is SQL Server slower than Access, FoxPro, and DBase?

A: There are two reasons:

- The mentioned products are great for “small” numbers of users and “small” databases. They carry very little overhead and rely on the client for record and file locking. This is great for one or a few number of users, or when data is read-only, but when many users access the system the overhead of doing locking by file offset with SMB packets is enormous. The application will usually grind to a halt, connections will be lost and the database may be corrupted.

- SQL Server is a true client/server app and so scales far better, but the overhead of doing all of the locking at the server end is far higher in some cases.

- (Note that “small” is a relative term—this could be a hundred users and a 1GB database—which is large to many people.

- SQL Server logs all writes to a transaction log before it writes to actual data pages. It also (with 6.5 and below) has to update indices when records in the main table are changed due to page splits. This overhead is great for consistency and reliability, but not for raw performance. This logging cannot be turned off.

Reference

v1.01 2000.05.09	
Applies to SQL Server versions:	All
FAQ category:	Miscellaneous
Related FAQ articles:	n/a
Related Microsoft Knowledge Base articles:	n/a
Other related information:	n/a
Author:	Neil Pike

support65

Q: How much longer will Microsoft support SQL 6.5?

A: As a rule of thumb, Microsoft usually provides active support for at least the current and previous version of a product (service packs don't count). "Active" means fixing the code and issuing service packs and hot-fixes.

After that Microsoft continues to provide support for as long as they feel the customer base warrants it. This is weighed against the fact that Microsoft support doesn't make the company any money and they want to encourage users to upgrade (because that does make them money). For 6.5 I would expect this to be a fairly long period given the installed base of 6.5. During this time the likelihood of service packs substantially decreases but for major problems or major customers you will at least get hot-fixes written.

Once this period is over, Microsoft ends its "active" support. The source code is still available to the PSS support people for debugging, but no more fixes will be written. Microsoft will still take a support call and help out with a problem—be it performance, corruption, or other problems. They will help you fix the problem yourself or provide workarounds, but they will not fix the 6.5 code base. If a bug is found they will test it against the latest version of SQL Server and fix it in that if necessary, but your only option to get the fix would be to upgrade.

The other thing to note is that normal staff turn over, promotions and moves means that the Microsoft SQL support group's experience and knowledge will naturally migrate to the newer and current versions. Staying current with SQL versions and service packs is the best way to ensure the highest quality of support.

Microsoft has not been writing fixes for SQL 6.0 since 1998. Active support for SQL 4.21a concluded even earlier.

Additionally, here is an official Microsoft statement from May 2000:

"As many of you have seen, Microsoft continues to drive new product innovation by extending and reengineering the SQL Server database product. We believe these new product capabilities are properly suited for the needs of the ever-changing database community. We also realize, however, that there are strong needs to maintain legacy systems indefinitely while new technology rollouts take place. In the past 6 years, Microsoft has released four major versions of SQL Server.

The purpose of this note is to explain what you should expect from the official Product Support Services group if you were to call in on these versions. This holds for all worldwide releases.

- v4.21: We have officially begun the obsolescence of support for this product. Customers with Premier contracts should soon receive a letter explaining that phone support will end around the end of (CY) 2000. No additional maintenance work, either hotfix (patch) work or service packs, are considered at this time.

- v6.0: We will continue to take service requests on v6.0 indefinitely. We will watch the call volumes for this product, and as these volumes become negligible, we will begin the obsolescence process. There is no current timetable for this to occur. No additional maintenance work, either hotfix work or service packs, are considered at this time.

- v6.5: We will continue to take service requests on v6.5 indefinitely. There are no plans to discontinue support for v6.5, and it remains a reportable percentage of our call volumes. Official hotfix support for v6.5 will end when SQL Server 2000 ships, although we will extend hotfix support for v6.5 to the end of 2000 for Premier customers with mission-critical destabilizing issues. There will not be any more service pack releases for v6.5, although plans are being made to publicly post a recent v6.5 maintenance build for customer download. (It will contain many documented post-Service Pack 5 (SP5) fixes.)

- v7.0: We continue to take service requests on v7.0 and will continue providing traditional maintenance work, both in the form of hotfixes and service packs.

When in maintenance mode, hotfixes are generally considered for the current product and one prior version ('N-1'). We strive to release service packs every six months."

Reference

v1.06 2000.05.25	
Applies to SQL Server version:	6.5
FAQ category:	Miscellaneous
Related FAQ articles:	n/a
Related Microsoft Knowledge Base articles:	n/a
Other related information:	`http://www.microsoft.com/support/supportnet/suppobsolescence.htm`
Author:	Neil Pike

testdata

Q: What third-party tools are available to generate test data for SQL Server?

A: The following is by no means an exhaustive list, but here are some vendors and Web sites to check out for tools that could be used:

- `http://www.rational.com`
- `http://www.compuware.com`
- `http://www.datajunction.com`
- `http://www.testbase.com`

Microsoft has a couple of utilities in the SQL portion of the Back Office Resource Kit. FILLTABL.EXE is a very simple tool and dbgen is a bit more complex.

Reference

v1.04 2000.06.13	
Applies to SQL Server versions:	All
FAQ category:	Miscellaneous
Related FAQ articles:	n/a
Related Microsoft Knowledge Base articles:	n/a
Other related information:n/a	
Author:	Neil Pike

traceflag208

Q: What does DBCC TRACEON(208) mean in SQL Server? I see it in SQL's errorlogs, but I'm not issuing it.

A: This trace flag is set by some applications as they rely on SQL 6.5's quoted identifier behavior for object names. For differences introduced with 6.5 to this behavior look at the "What's New" section in the 6.5 Books Online.

You can turn off these messages if you wish by setting trace flag 2505.

Reference

v1.02 2000.05.27	
Applies to SQL Server versions:	6.5, 7.0
FAQ category:	Miscellaneous
Related FAQ articles:	n/a
Related Microsoft Knowledge Base article:	Q243352 "INF: 'DBCC TRACEON (208)' Messages in the Error Log When Using MSQuery"
Other related information:	n/a
Author:	Neil Pike

wishlist

Q: How can I get something added to the SQL Server wish list?

A: E-mail `sqlwish@microsoft.com`. All e-mails to this alias are looked at by SQL development and support. You are unlikely to get any reply or acknowledgement, but all feedback gathered this way is used to select features that go into new SQL Server versions.

Reference

v1.02 2000.04.24	
Applies to SQL Server versions:	All
FAQ category:	Miscellaneous
Related FAQ articles:	n/a
Related Microsoft Knowledge Base articles:	n/a
Other related information:	n/a
Author:	Neil Pike

OLAP

This section covers the setup and use of the OLAP functions in SQL Server.

AnalyzeOLAPQueryLog

Q: How can I find out who's been querying my OLAP server?

A: To find out who queries the OLAP Server, you can look into the Query Log (usually used for Usage Based Optimization). The late Mike Yocca wrote a utility for analyzing the query log which you can download from `http://beta.content.communities.msn.com/isapi/fetch.dll?action=get_message&ID_Community=MicrosoftOLAPServicesUsersCommunity&ID_Message=164`.

You'll have to join the community to download the file.

Reference

v1.00 2000.06.16	
Applies to SQL Server versions:	7.0, 2000
FAQ category:	OLAP
Related FAQ articles:	n/a
Related Microsoft Knowledge Base articles:	n/a
Other related information:	`http://beta.content.communities.msn.com/`
Author:	Karen Watterson

CantSeeCalcMember

Q: I can make a calculated member on my Local cube file, but I can't see it in the Excel Pivot Table. Why?

A: The Excel Pivot Table is only capable of showing calculated members on the Measures dimension. If you have created a calculated member on another dimension, it won't show up in Excel.

Reference

v1.00 2000.06.16	
Applies to SQL Server versions:	7.0, 2000
FAQ category:	OLAP
Related FAQ article:	"How can I create a local cube file that can be used standalone without being connected to the OLAP/Analysis Services engine?" (CreateOLAPLocalCube, see page 368)
Related Microsoft Knowledge Base articles:	n/a
Other related information:	Russell Whitney's February 2000 *SQL Server Magazine* column, `http://beta.communities.msn.com/MicrosoftOLAPServicesUsers-Community/homepage`
Author:	Karen Watterson

CreateOLAPLocalCube

Q: How can I create a local cube file that can be used standalone without being connected to the OLAP/Analysis Services engine?

A: Once you've created a Pivot Table cube in Excel 2000, you'll need to access Excel's PivotTable menu and select Client/Server settings. When you select "Create local data file," Excel will launch the Create Cube File Wizard. You'll probably want to use the File Save as Web Page option and check the "Add Interactivity" checkbox.

By the way, although local cube files can theoretically contain more than one cube, Excel's wizard only lets you create single-cube cube files. Third-party OLAP clients may allow you to save more complex cube files, and you can also create them programmatically.

Reference

v1.00 2000.06.16	
Applies to SQL Server versions:	7.0, 2000
FAQ category:	OLAP
Related FAQ article:	"I can make a calculated member on my Local cube file, but I can't see it in the Excel Pivot Table. Why?" (CantSeeCalcMember, see page 367)
Related Microsoft Knowledge Base articles:	n/a
Other related information:	Russell Whitney's February 2000 *SQL Server Magazine* column
Author:	Karen Watterson

MDXNotation

Q: I have a question about the MDX grammar. Why do some functions use the point/period (.) notation, for example: `[1999].CHILDREN`? It seems to me that `CHILDREN` is a function that returns children members. Why not use a `CHILDREN( [1999] )` notation?

A: As OLAP/Analysis Services team member Mosah Pasumansky explains, "There were long arguments about these issues when the MDX spec was drafted. But to make the answer short, the MDX functions were mostly targeted at the business analyst audience rather than the DBA audience. Also, for people familiar with VB, the notion of object.method is the most natural thing."

Reference

v1.00 2000.06.16	
Applies to SQL Server versions:	7.0, 2000
FAQ category:	OLAP
Related FAQ articles:	n/a
Related Microsoft Knowledge Base articles:	n/a
Other related information:	n/a
Author:	Karen Watterson

OLAPAggregations

Q: How much should I aggregate?

A: Here's what Amir Netz, OLAP/Analysis Services' chief architect, says:

"In most cases, the performance difference between 100 percent and 50 percent is negligible. Do yourself a favor and never use 100 percent aggregations. It is just a waste of lots of time and lots of disk space. So how much should you use?

Amir's Aggregations Golden Rule (that works 90 percent of the time):

In most cubes, never start with more then 30 percent optimization or more then 1000 aggregations. You'll see to your surprise that the system is already extremely fast. In many cases, you'll just be content with the performance and that's all there is to it.

Still, I do recommend using the usage-based optimization. It costs you almost nothing to do it and you may improve the system efficiency dramatically. What you have to do is let the system run with actual users for a couple of weeks. Then, activate the usage based optimization wizard and select all of the queries (don't filter at this point) and optimize for 96 percent optimization gain. You see that you can get to the 96 percent with the fraction of the cost it used to take you to get to 30 percent! This is because all of the aggregates that were never used by users are now not considered as part of the 100 percent.

In some rare cases, the rules will not work. In these cases, the cubes are extremely complex (14–20 dimensions) and getting to 30 percent is going to be very tough. I recommend that you try to build 3000 aggregations at most for these cubes before applying the usage-based optimization."

Reference

v1.00 2000.06.16

Applies to SQL Server versions:	7.0, 2000
FAQ category:	OLAP
Related FAQ articles:	n/a
Related Microsoft Knowledge Base articles:	n/a
Other related information:	`http://beta.content.communities.msn.com/`
Authors:	Amir Netz, Karen Watterson

olapbackup

Q: How can I move or back up my OLAP databases?

A: For SQL Server 7.0 there is an Archive and Restore Databases Add-in contained within the OLAP Manager Add-in Kit 1 (`http://www.microsoft.com/sql/70/gen/OLAPaddin.htm`). This provides a GUI interface within the OLAP Manager as well as msmdarch.exe, which can be scheduled. The OLAP Manager Add-in Kit, including the Archive and Restore Databases Add-in, has been integrated into SQL Server 2000.

Reference

v1.00 2000.03.19

Applies to SQL Server versions:	7.0, 2000
FAQ category:	OLAP
Related FAQ articles:	n/a
Related Microsoft Knowledge Base articles:	n/a
Other related information:	n/a
Author:	Darren Green

olapconnectionwizardipaddress

Q: Is it possible to put an IP address into the OLAP Connection Wizard?

A: Prior to SQL 7.0 OLAP Services SP2, this would give you an error and you had to use the server name. This was fixed in SP2.

Reference

v1.00 2000.06.13

Applies to SQL Server versions:	All
FAQ categories:	OLAP, Troubleshooting
Related FAQ articles:	n/a
Related Microsoft Knowledge Base articles:	n/a
Other related information:	n/a
Author:	Neil Pike

olapdsoscript

Q: Why can I not access the full Decision Support Objects (DSO) object model from VBScript?

A: This is because VBScript only supports the data type Variant. To access certain levels of the DSO object model you must use defined types, also known as *strong typing*. To overcome this issue you can write a DLL to perform the required operation and use this object from within VBScript. An example of this is my DSOCtrl.dll, which I wrote to allow cube processing from VBScript including ASP, and also for use via the OLE Automation stored procedures within a wrapper stored procedure.

Reference

v1.00 2000.03.18	
Applies to SQL Server versions:	7.0, 2000
FAQ category:	OLAP
Related FAQ articles:	n/a
Related Microsoft Knowledge Base articles:	n/a
Other related information:	`http://www.swynk.com/friends/green/dsoctrloverview.asp`
Author:	Darren Green

OLAPManager

Q: I installed the OLAP client software but I still can't run OLAP Manager on my Win9x system. Why not?

A: OLAP Manager doesn't run on Win9x systems (this is a DSO limitation).

Reference

v1.00 2000.06.16	
Applies to SQL Server versions:	7.0, 2000
FAQ category:	OLAP
Related FAQ article:	n/a
Related Microsoft Knowledge Base articles:	n/a
Other related information:	n/a
Author:	Karen Watterson

olapproc

Q: How can I automate OLAP cube and dimension processing?

A: For SQL Server 7.0 an OLAP Services Processing task for DTS is available from Microsoft (`http://www.microsoft.com/sql/70/gen/OLAPaddin.htm`). For SQL Server 2000 the task is installed along with the OLAP Manager. This task supports all processing methods including incremental updates.

Some EXE and DLL components are available from the Microsoft OLAP Services Users Community site.

Any of these methods may be scheduled from SQL Server Agent.

You could also build your own utility using the Decision Support Objects (DSO) object model. Some useful samples are available on the Microsoft OLAP Services Users Community site and the SQL Server Magazine site.

Reference

v1.01 2000.03.26	
Applies to SQL Server versions:	7.0, 2000
FAQ category:	OLAP
Related FAQ articles:	"Why can I not access the full Decision Support Objects (DSO) object model from VBScript?" (olapdsoscript, see page 372)
Related Microsoft Knowledge Base articles:	n/a
Other related information:	`http://www.microsoft.com/sql/70/gen/OLAPaddin.htm`, `http://communities.msn.com/MicrosoftOLAPServicesUsers-Community/homepage`, and `http://www.sqlmag.com/Articles/Content/8030_01.html`
Author:	Darren Green

OLAPviaTCP

Q: Is it possible to get the Excel 2000 Pivot Table service connecting over the Internet (via a dialup ISP) to a SQL Server 7.0 OLAP Services cube that resides behind a firewall?

A: Yes, but it takes some doing (SQL Server 2000's Analysis Services, by contrast, supports HTTP access).

If you're using OLAP Services, you need to keep in mind the TCP ports it uses since many firewalls are set to disable access to these ports by default. Clearly, if you want the PivotTable Service on the client to be able to access the OLAP Services server directly, you need to make sure the firewall allows it. The two TCP ports used by OLAP Services 7.0 are 2393 and 2394. Microsoft has reserved UDP ports 2393 and 2394 as well, although they're apparently not used in OLAP Services 7.0

Reference

v1.00 2000.06.16	
Applies to SQL Server version:	7.0
FAQ category:	OLAP
Related FAQ articles:	n/a
Related Microsoft Knowledge Base articles:	n/a
Other related information:	n/a
Author:	Karen Watterson

StrToMembervsMembers

Q: What's the difference between StrToMember() and Members()?

A: StrToMember can accept a string that's an MDX expression. It will parse the string and execute the expression. This expression will return a member.

Members() can accept only a valid member name. No MDX expressions are allowed.

Reference

v1.00 2000.06.16	
Applies to SQL Server versions:	7.0, 2000
FAQ category:	OLAP
Related FAQ articles:	n/a
Related Microsoft Knowledge Base articles:	n/a
Other related information:	n/a
Author:	Karen Watterson

Security

This section covers all aspects of security, including clients, network, physical storage, and encryption.

audit

Q: How do I audit what has been updated in a SQL Server?

A: The transaction log that SQL Server writes is not really useful for this purpose (see the "logview" FAQ entry for more information).

There are really two options:

- SQL Trace/Profiler. SQL Server has built-in tracing facilities that can be used for an audit trail if required. You can set up a trace to run automatically and to write output to a SQL table and/or flat file.

- Triggers. With this option you write insert/update/delete triggers on every table to audit all the access you want to audit (there is no such thing as a read trigger).

If the effort of writing hundreds of triggers isn't appealing, you can get one of these third-party products that automates this for you:

- `http://www.redmatrix.com`

- `http://www.cai.com/products/platinum` and search for "Erwin"

- `http://www.rlpsoftware.com`

Reference

v1.04 2000.07.02

Applies to SQL Server versions:	All
FAQ categories:	Security, Database Administration
Related FAQ article:	"How can I view the SQL Server log? Can I recover individual transactions or data from it?" (logview, see page 173)
Related Microsoft Knowledge Base articles:	n/a
Other related information:	n/a
Author:	Neil Pike

encrypt

Q: How do I encrypt fields in SQL Server? What about whole objects or the whole database?

A: Taking the fields first—there is no supported, documented way of doing this, and because you can't write user-defined functions yet, then your choices are:

- Write your own extended stored-procedure (XP) to do it. However this can't be applied as a function, so it is messy—you need to call the XP per column and then issue an update with the value it returns. A freeware example of this is available from `http://www.vtc.ru/~andrey/xp_crypt`.

- Do it in the application, back at the VB or C level. This is what most people do and it is the recommended method. Some pointers to other articles and examples follow:

  - `http://ruban.dp.ua/capi/wincrypt.zip`
  - `http://msdn.microsoft.com/library/periodic/period97/crypto.htm`
  - `http://msdn.microsoft.com/library/default.asp?URL=/library/psdk/crypto/portalapi_3351.htm`
  - `http://msdn.microsoft.com/library/default.asp?URL=/library/psdk/crypto/usingcrypto_84dv.htm`

- You can use the ODBC Encrypt function with SQL 7 and above, but I don't think you can decrypt it; for example, insert into x values ({Encrypt N'Hello'}).

- There are undocumented pwdencrypt() and pwdcompare() functions—they are for Microsoft internal use and their function is likely to change or break in the future. People who ignored advice and used them in 6.x applications have found that the passwords generated do not work in SQL 7.0.

  As many people now know about these functions, they are mentioned here for completeness, but if you use these functions you will not receive support from Microsoft and will be completely on your own when you get problems with a new service pack or version.

- SQL 2000 will implement user-defined functions. As long as you can write your own encrypt/decrypt function completely in T-SQL then this will be an option.

  Note that any field you use a function on you won't be able to index effectively as indices are ignored when a function is applied to a key in a where clause.

On to whole objects. SQL has a built-in function to encrypt stored procedures—however, the algorithms for 6.5 and 7.0 have been broken and so decryption is now possible if you know how to do it. There is no encryption facility for tables or data.

Finally, the whole database. There is no SQL-wide encryption function that would prevent users from hex-editing your devices and gleaning data from them. It is possible to use NT file-system level encryption because SQL won't know it is there. However, you have to put a password to "unlock" the files somewhere if you want to automate the process of starting SQL after NT reboots. Windows 2000 comes with file-level encryption with the new EFS (encrypted file system), which can be used with SQL Server.

You need to ask yourself if you need encryption—unless the persons you are worried about have physical or NT network access to the SQL devices, the only way to them is via a SQL logon that can be secured.

If the reason you want to prevent access is that the raw data or schema is being hosted by a third-party or customer and you want to protect your intellectual property rights, then currently all you can do is:

1. Make all access to data via stored-procedures. Put all logic you want to hide in these.

2. Give users access to these sp's, but *not* to any underlying tables or views.

3. Then delete the syscomments entries for the sp's—this leaves the compiled version in sysprocedures.

If you have to give someone sa rights to maintain the database they will still be able to get to the schema or data, but at least they won't be able to see the stored procedure code.

Reference

v1.13 2000.06.12	
Applies to SQL Server versions:	All
FAQ category:	Security
Related FAQ articles:	n/a
Related Microsoft Knowledge Base articles:	n/a
Other related information:	n/a
Author:	Neil Pike

firewall

Q: How do I connect to SQL Server through a firewall?

A: You have to open up the ports that SQL Server uses. If you've done this and it still doesn't work, look at the firewall logs to see what packets it is dropping or do a network trace either side of the firewall to see what packets are not getting through. (You may want to disable/allow all through the firewall during testing to see what extra packets are allowed through.)

Which ports to open depends on the Net-Lib you are using:

- For TCP-IP Sockets the default port for SQL Server is 1433.
- For Multiprotocol (rpc) the ports are normally variable, but you can fix them. See Q164667 in the Microsoft Knowledge Base for details.
- For Named Pipes over IP, 137, 138 and 139 are used. Because these are the same ones used for file/print, it is not recommended you allow these through the firewall.

Reference

v1.00 1998.10.29	
Applies to SQL Server versions:	All
FAQ categories:	Security, Connectivity
Related FAQ articles:	n/a
Related Microsoft Knowledge Base article:	Q164667 "INF: Replication Setup Over a Firewall"
Other related information:	"Filter Settings for Windows NT Services" in MSDN
Author:	Neil Pike

passwordsonnetworkinclear

Q: Are SQL Server userids and passwords passed in clear on the network?

A: If you use the Multiprotocol Net-Lib with encryption, SQL standard security userids and passwords are encrypted along with the data.

When using an NT userid/trusted connection, passwords are not passed at all — the sids are used as in all NT credential checks.

If you are using SQL 7.0 client drivers talking to a 7.0 server, the SQL standard security userid/password is encrypted regardless of the Net-Lib.

In any other case, the SQL standard security userid/password is sent in clear.

Reference

v1.01 2000.01.20	
Applies to SQL Server versions:	All
FAQ category:	Security
Related FAQ article:	"How does a client talk to SQL Server? What is a Net-Lib? What network protocols are used? What Net-Libs support NT authentication or encryption?" (netlibinfo, see page 125)
Related Microsoft Knowledge Base articles:	n/a
Other related information:	n/a
Author:	Neil Pikes

Server Administration and Tools

This section covers server-wide topics and the use of SQL Server tools, the setup and running of SQL Server with Microsoft Cluster Server (MSCS), the full-text indexing facility built in to SQL Server, and the built-in replication facilities of SQL Server.

1cpuusedsql65

Q: Why does only one CPU get used with my SQL 6.5 system for an extremely complex or long running query?

A: This is because under SQL 6.5 only a single CPU can be used for a query. The only time another CPU is used is if read-ahead is being done and this can then use another CPU.

With 7.0 and above, all CPUs can potentially be used for a single query if that query can be parallelized.

Reference

v1.03 2000.03.20	
Applies to SQL Server version:	6.5
FAQ category:	Server Administration and Tools
Related FAQ articles:	n/a
Related Microsoft Knowledge Base articles:	n/a
Other related information:	Microsoft White Paper "SQL Server 6.5: I/O Performance Tuning Quick Reference," "Parallel Query Processing" in Books Online 7.0
Author:	Neil Pike

256charsinqa

Q: Why do I only get 256 characters back in a column in Query Analyzer? I thought SQL Server supported chars up to 8,000 bytes now.

A: The 256 limitation is a Query Analyzer option. You can change it or use OSQL.EXE, which won't show this limitation.

Go to Query/Current Connection Options/Advanced, and change "maximum characters per column" to whatever maximum you desire.

Reference

v1.02 2000.06.06	
Applies to SQL Server versions:	7.0, 2000
FAQ category:	Server Administration and Tools
Related FAQ articles:	n/a
Related Microsoft Knowledge Base articles:	n/a
Other related information:	n/a
Author:	Neil Pike

addlanguage

Q: How can I add a language to SQL Server so that it knows about my localized date format?

A: This is easily done with sp_addlanguage. For details and examples see <sql>\install\instlang.sql, which has code in for many languages and nearly all European ones.

Once a new language is installed, you just need to make that the default for the SQL logins that will use it.

Reference

v1.01 2000.03.25	
Applies to SQL Server versions:	6.x
FAQ category:	Server Administration and Tools
Related FAQ articles:	n/a
Related Microsoft Knowledge Base articles:	n/a
Other related information:	n/a
Author:	Neil Pike

Server Administration and Tools

agentautostart

Q: How can I make sure the SQL Server Agent auto-starts when I start SQL Server?

A: As long as the service is set to "auto" it will start when the server starts, but if SQL and the Agent are shut down manually then the Agent won't auto-start when SQL does. You can run the following procedure or enable it as a startup stored procedure to overcome this. (This will only work with Windows NT/2000, because Win9x does not support services.)

```
CREATE PROC AUTOAGENT
AS
EXEC xp_cmdshell 'NET START SQLSERVERAGENT'
go
EXEC sp_procoption AUTOAGENT, STARTUP, TRUE
```

Reference

v1.02 2000.03.26

Applies to SQL Server version:	7.0
FAQ category:	Server Administration and Tools
Related FAQ articles:	n/a
Related Microsoft Knowledge Base articles:	n/a
Other related information:	n/a
Author:	Neil Pike

allowmachines

Q: How can I restrict access to my SQL Server so that it only allows certain machines to connect?

A: SQL Server has no built-in tools or facilities to do this. It also does not have the facility to run a stored procedure on a connection that could be written or used to do this. Therefore, you have the following choices:

- Put the SQL Server behind a firewall and use that to restrict access. This is the most secure and functional way to do what you want.

- Write your own ODS Gateway and point the clients at that instead of the SQL Server—the ODS Gateway will then do the checking. However, there is nothing stopping clients from figuring out the correct SQL client-config entries to point straight at the SQL Server, bypassing your gateway, so the security on this is limited. There are examples of ODS code in the SQL Programmers Toolkit available for free download from the Microsoft Web site.

- Write a constantly running or scheduled stored procedure that checks the relevant column in sysprocesses (net_address), and then issues a KILL command for any processes that should not be running. The net_address column is a layer-2 mac address, and so is much less useful than an IP address. This method allows people to connect and possibly make changes before they are spotted and killed.

Reference

v1.02 2000.03.26	
Applies to SQL Server versions:	All
FAQ categories:	Server Administration and Tools, Connectivity
Related FAQ articles:	n/a
Related Microsoft Knowledge Base articles:	n/a
Other related information:	n/a
Author:	Neil Pike

allowprograms

Q: How can I restrict access to my SQL Server so that it only allows certain programs to connect? (I don't want my clients using Access to hack data directly.)

A: SQL Server 6.5 and below have no built-in tools or facilities to do this, nor does it allow a stored procedure to be run on a client connection that could be used to do this. Of course, if all your data is protected correctly with SQL/Integrated security and all auditing and business rules are held with constraints or triggers, you won't need to worry because it doesn't matter what tool people use to connect. However, in a real-world application, these prerequisites are unlikely to be met.

SQL Server 7.0 has the idea of application *roles*, as well as user roles. If you have SQL 7.0, use application roles.

If you are still on 6.5 or below, you can try one of the following methods—but none of them are ideal

- Write your own ODS Gateway and point the clients at that instead of the SQL Server—the ODS Gateway will then do the checking. However, there is nothing stopping clients from figuring out the correct SQL client-config entries to point straight at the SQL Server. There are examples of ODS code in the SQL Programmers Toolkit available for free download from the Microsoft Web site.

- Write a constantly running or scheduled stored procedure that checks the relevant column in sysprocesses (program_name), and then issues a KILL command for any processes that should not be running. This method allows people to connect and possibly make changes before they are spotted and killed.

- Change servers to use standard security. When the apps connect they request a trusted connection and get dumped into a new database—the only one their trusted account can connect to. This database contains a table holding a lookup between the user's NT account and an alternative login name, password (encrypted), and perhaps server and database names to use. The only runnable object is a stored procedure that returns the user's rows from this table. The front-end calls the stored procedure, decrypts the password and reconnects to the server. One downside to this sort of approach is that the user's "real" name and password could potentially be cracked with an ODBC trace (several versions of the ODBC SDK tools allowed passwords to be displayed) or network sniffer.

- Another option is to place a CHECK constraint on the sensitive tables, which validates the application name. Try something like:

```
CHECK (APP_NAME() = 'Name of your VB app')
```

Reference

v1.02 2000.03.26

Applies to SQL Server versions:	All
FAQ categories:	Server Administration and Tools, Application Design and Programming
Related FAQ articles:	n/a
Related Microsoft Knowledge Base articles:	n/a
Other related information:	n/a
Author:	Neil Pike

automatescript

Q: How can I automate the scripting or transfer of a database or objects in SQL Server?

A: You can do this using the SQL-DMO objects that SQL supports. These can be called via the SQL OLE interface. There is a help file for the SQL DMO objects included with SQL Server (see following references) and there is an icon for it in your SQL Server 6.5 group.

For an example of using the SQL OLE interface, see Q152801 in the Microsoft Knowledge Base. Alternatively you can code your own VB app to call the DMO routines yourself.

For SQL 7.0 you could also use the SCPTXFR.EXE utility found in the UPGRADE directory to script objects. You can schedule this using SQLAgent or run from a stored procedure. Do a `SCPTXFR /?` to see the parameters, which are self-explanatory (if it isn't on your hard drive, look in the upgrade directory on the CD).

Reference

v1.04 2000.03.28

Applies to SQL Server versions:	All
FAQ category:	Server Administration and Tools
Related FAQ articles:	n/a
Related Microsoft Knowledge Base articles:	Q152801 "INF: Examples of Sp_OA Procedure Use and SQLOLE.Transfer Object," Q220163 describes SCPTXFR.EXE
Other related information:	sqlole.hlp in 6.x, sqldmo.hlp in 7.0
Author: Neil Pike	

boostsmp

Q: Should I set Boost Priority to 1 or SMP to -1 on SQL Server?

A: No (unless the following doesn't bother you).

Although these can offer a small performance improvement in TPCC environments (which is why Microsoft put them in the product), you run the risk of the SQL process hogging too much CPU time at the expense of NT, networking and drivers. If this happens, your other SQL connections will hang or disconnect as NT won't be able to service the network packets needed to keep the sessions running.

If you do have an environment where all SQL code is known in advance, there are no ad-hoc queries, and no heavy queries, then you may get a small improvement by turning them on. But the risks aren't worth the gains in 99 percent of situations.

Reference

v1.02 2000.04.01	
Applies to SQL Server versions:	4.x, 6.x, 7.0
FAQ category:	Server Administration and Tools
Related FAQ articles:	n/a
Related Microsoft Knowledge Base article:	Q166967 "INF: Proper SQL Server Configuration Settings"
Other related information:	n/a
Author:	Neil Pike

browserlistofsqlservers

Q: Where does the list of SQL servers in registration/dialog boxes come from? What reasons are there for not getting a list?

A: When SQL Server starts up it announces itself on the network. The list of workstations and servers is held in a browser list that is normally maintained by the domain controllers.

A client needing a list of resources—in this case, SQL servers—issues NetServerEnum commands to get the list back. This is provided by whichever server running as a browser master has the information. For more details on browsing see the NT resource kits.

You can include this functionality in your own applications by using SQL-DMO with the ListAvailableSQLServers method of the Application object, the DB-Lib C function dbserverenum, or the SQLBrowseConnect ODBC API.

Some restrictions:

- The client-side Win32 Named Pipe Net-Library (DBNMPNTW.DLL) does not support server enumeration on Windows 9x-based computers. This means you won't see a list from a Win9x client.

- There is no support for server enumeration with the Multiprotocol Net-Library. Any server just running Multiprotocol will not be visible.

Reference

v1.02 2000.04.01

Applies to SQL Server versions:	All
FAQ category:	Server Administration and Tools
Related FAQ article:	"How can I list all available SQL servers in my application?" (listsqlservers, see page 417)
Related Microsoft Knowledge Base articles:	n/a
Other related information:	"The Windows NT Browser Service" in Windows NT Server Resource Kit;" "ListAvailableSQLServers," "dbserverenum," and "SQLBrowseConnect" in Books Online
Author:	Neil Pike

changedefaultlocationforfiles

Q: How can I change the default location for database files that SQL creates?

A: Change or add the following values in the registry:

```
KEY: HKEY_LOCAL_MACHINE\Software\Microsoft\MSSQLServer\MSSQLServer
VALUE: DefaultData
VALUE: DefaultLog
```

Just put in a directory name (no trailing backslash) for these. You have to restart SQL Server for the change to take effect.

This works only for databases that you create with the CREATE DATABASE statement, not for databases created from Enterprise Manager.

Reference

v1.01 2000.04.05

Applies to SQL Server version:	7.0
FAQ category:	Server Administration and Tools
Related FAQ articles:	n/a
Related Microsoft Knowledge Base articles:	n/a
Other related information:	n/a
Authors:	Neil Pike, Kalen Delaney

changeservername

Q: How do I change the name of SQL Server?

A: If you change the NT name of a server and want to change SQL Server 6.5 or below to match it, do the following:

```
sp_dropserver "<oldname>"
go
sp_addserver "<newname>", local
```

You have to stop and restart SQL Server for the change to take effect. The SQL Server Programmers Toolkit recommends doing this with SQL Server started in minimal configuration mode (sqlservr –f from the command prompt). In addition, if you use the IPX/SPX Net-Lib for SQL Server connectivity, you must also run the SQL Setup, choose the option to change the network support, and fix the server name there too.

If you change the NT name, SQL 7.0 will warn you that your installation is corrupt and will insist you re-run setup. Setup will ask if you want to "upgrade," but all it does is detect the name conflict, resolve it, and then finish. You still have to run sp_dropserver and sp_addserver to get the new name in the error log and in @@servername.

Reference

v1.06 2000.04.15	
Applies to SQL Server versions:	All
FAQ category:	Server Administration and Tools
Related FAQ article:	"How can I check the name of the SQL Server I am on?" (computername, see page 399)
Related Microsoft Knowledge Base articles:	n/a
Other related information:	"How to change to the current server name in the 6.*x* master database (ISQL/w)" in SQL Server Programmers Toolkit and Books Online 7
Author:	Neil Pike

checkversionofsqlserverfrom-batchfile

Q: How can I check the version of SQL Server from a batch file?

A: One way would be to check the @@version returned from an ISQL query. The following example assumes connecting to the local machine with a trusted connection. It uses the ISQL/OSQL feature of setting the DOS return code for severity values of 11 or higher (the documentation says 10, but I've found it needs to be 11 to work consistently). The example assumes you are running the batch file on the local server and uses -E to request a trusted connection. See Books Online for other options.

```
@ECHO OFF
ISQL -E -b -Q"if charindex('6.00',@@version) > 0 raiserror(' ',11,127)" > nul
IF ERRORLEVEL 1 SET SQLV=6.0
IF ERRORLEVEL 1 goto foundver
ISQL -E -b -Q"if charindex('6.50',@@version) > 0 raiserror(' ',11,127)" > nul
IF ERRORLEVEL 1 SET SQLV=6.5
IF ERRORLEVEL 1 goto foundver
ISQL -E -b -Q"if charindex('7.00',@@version) > 0 raiserror(' ',11,127)" > nul
IF ERRORLEVEL 1 SET SQLV=7.0
IF ERRORLEVEL 1 goto foundver
REM For later versions, add similar section for version number as in @@version

@ECHO.
@ECHO Not found SQL version
@ECHO.
PAUSE
GOTO END

:foundver
@ECHO SQL Server %SQLV% found
PAUSE

:END
```

Reference

v1.01 2000.04.09

Applies to SQL Server versions:	All
FAQ categories:	Server Administration and Tools, Application Design and Programming
Related FAQ articles:	n/a
Related Microsoft Knowledge Base articles:	n/a
Other related information:	"isql utility" in Books Online
Author:	Neil Pike

clearprocedurecache

Q: How can I clear SQL Server's procedure cache?

A: With SQL 6.5 and below you can't. You have to stop and start SQL Server.

For SQL 7.0, use DBCC FREEPROCCACHE.

Reference

v1.01 2000.05.25

Applies to SQL Server versions:	All
FAQ categories:	Server Administration and Tools
Related FAQ articles:	n/a
Related Microsoft Knowledge base articles:	n/a
Other related information:	n/a
Author:	Neil Pike

clusterlicensing

Q: How many SQL Server licenses do I need for an active/active cluster? What about active/passive?

A: Active servers require a license, but since the release of SQL 2000 licensing, the passive node no longer requires a license.

Reference

v1.01 2000.10.29

Applies to SQL Server versions:	All
FAQ category:	Server Administration and Tools
Related FAQ articles:	n/a
Related Microsoft Knowledge Base articles:	n/a
Other related information:	`http://www.microsoft.com/sql/productinfo/licensing.htm`
Author:	Neil Pike

comparedatabases

Q: How can I compare two SQL Server databases?

A: This is not something that the Microsoft-supplied tools do out of the box, however plenty of resources are available:

- Microsoft supplies some tools in the SQL Server part of the Back Office Resource Kit (BORK) 4.5.
- The entityrelationship tool Erwin has facilities to do this: `http://www.cai.com/erwin`.
- A piece of freeware called SQLCompare can be used: `http://www.red-gate.com`.

Reference

v1.00 2000.06.13

Applies to SQL Server versions:	All
FAQ category:	Server Administration and Tools
Related FAQ articles:	n/a
Related Microsoft Knowledge Base articles:	n/a
Other related information:	n/a
Author:	Neil Pike

computername

Q: How can I check the name of the SQL Server I am on?

A: A `SELECT @@SERVERNAME` will tell you, but in a cluster you will get the same name back on both machines. If you want the physical server name, use one of the following two methods:

- xp_getnetname
- Run the following:

```
  declare @computername char (16)

exec master..xp_regread
'HKEY_LOCAL_MACHINE','SYSTEM\CurrentControlSet\Control\ComputerName\ActiveCom-
puterName'
,'ComputerName',@ComputerName OUTPUT

select @Computername
```

Reference

v1.01 2000.04.15

Applies to SQL Server versions:	All
FAQ category:	Server Administration and Tools
Related FAQ article:	"How do I change the name of SQL Server?" (changeservername, see page 395)
Related Microsoft Knowledge Base articles:	n/a
Other related information:	n/a
Author:	Neil Pike

dbccdes

Q: How can I see how many objects are actually open in SQL Server?

A: In SQL Server 6.5 and 7.0 you can use the DBCC DES command. This will list the descriptor data structure entries, one per open object.

```
dbcc traceon(3604)
go
dbcc des
go
```

To make it easy to count the objects, notice that in the output there are 10 lines printed for each open object. By scrolling to the end you can see how many lines there are in total and calculate the number of objects.

Reference

v1.01 2000.04.21

Applies to SQL Server versions:	6.5, 7.0
FAQ category:	Server Administration and Tools
Related FAQ articles:	n/a
Related Microsoft Knowledge Base articles:	n/a
Other related information:	See "Error 603" in Books Online 6 and "open objects Option" in Books Online 7
Author:	Neil Pike

defrag

Q: Can I do an NT defragmentation on a SQL Server .DAT device or file? Will it cause any problems or do any good?

A: Yes, you can, as long as you stop SQL first—NT needs exclusive access to a file in order to defragment it. As long as there are no bugs in the defragmentation program and the system doesn't crash in the middle of a defragmentation, there shouldn't be any problems. To be safe, first take a backup of the server with SQL Server stopped.

Will it help? Usually not much as SQL devices don't tend to change in size once they are created, so unless a disk was badly fragmented when the device was created so that NT could not allocate contiguous space for it all, then it won't be fragmented. It does nothing for SQL fragmentation of data or index pages—it only defragments the actual device.

If you create your SQL devices on a freshly formatted drive then you won't get any fragmentation.

Reference

v1.02 2000.04.21	
Applies to SQL Server versions:	All
FAQ category:	Server Administration and Tools
Related FAQ articles:	n/a
Related Microsoft Knowledge Base articles:	n/a
Other related information:	n/a
Author:	Neil Pike

diagram2000

Q: Why can't I see my diagrams on a SQL 7.0 Server when using SQL 2000 Enterprise Manager?

A: This is because SQL 2000 has an extra column in dtproperties which Enterprise Manager now expects. To fix this problem, run the following code for all databases with diagrams on the SQL 7.0 Server:

```
ALTER TABLE dtproperties ADD uvalue nvarchar(255) NULL
GO
UPDATE dtproperties SET uvalue = CONVERT(nvarchar(255), value)
GO
```

This will not affect the ability of SQL 7.0 Enterprise Manager to view diagrams on either server version.

Reference

v1.00 2000.05.27	
Applies to SQL Server versions:	7.0, 2000
FAQ categories:	Server Administration and Tools, Troubleshooting
Related FAQ articles:	n/a
Related Microsoft Knowledge Base articles:	n/a
Other related information:	See "Backward Compatibility Issues for SQL Server 2000" in SQL 2000 Books Online
Author:	Darren Green

errorlogfill

Q: My SQL Server error log is filling up with entries. How can I switch or truncate it?

A: With SQL 6.5 and below there is no way to truncate the error log or switch it either, short of stopping and starting the MSSQLSERVER service.

If the error log is filling up your disk then your choices are:

- Fix the applications that are causing the errors.
- NTFS compress the log directory to reduce the physical space it takes up.
- Move the error log to another directory and use the -e startup option to point the error logs to the new place.

With SQL 7.0 and above you can cycle the errorlogs with sp_cycle_errorlog.

Reference

v1.01 1999.02.15	
Applies to SQL Server versions:	All
FAQ category:	Server Administration and Tools
Related FAQ articles:	n/a
Related Microsoft Knowledge Base articles:	n/a
Other related information:	n/a
Author:	Neil Pike

errorlognumbers

Q: My SQL Server error log has switched several times and I've lost the evidence of a crash problem. How can I increase the number of error logs to prevent this?

A: With SQL 6.5 and below there is no way to increase the number. With SQL 7 you can do this by adjusting the following registry entry:

```
HKEY_LOCAL_MACHINE\SOFTWARE\Microsoft\MSSQLServer\MSSQLServer\
DWORD NumErrorLogs = <xx>
```

Alternatively, you can add a startup stored procedure to SQL 6.x or 7.x that copies out and renames the previous error log every time SQL restarts.

In SQL 7.0 you could also consider implementing xp_trace_setqueryhistory to provide a black box recorder facility of SQL Server events just before a crash.

Reference

v1.01 2000.04.22

Applies to SQL Server versions:	All
FAQ category:	Server Administration and Tools
Related FAQ articles:	n/a
Related Microsoft Knowledge Base article:	Q196909 "INF: How to Increase the Number of SQL Server Error Logs"
Other related information:	n/a
Author:	Neil Pike

estimatetablesize

Q: How can I estimate the size a table will be in SQL 7.0?

A: Try the following stored procedure from B.P. Margolin. Pass it the object id of the table and the number of rows you anticipate it will grow to, and it will estimate the number of data pages you will need. Data pages are 8KB in size.

```
drop procedure dbo.sp_EstTableSizeData
go

create procedure dbo.sp_EstTableSizeData
 @ObjId int, @Num_Rows int, @DataPages int OUTPUT
as
--<-- Addition #1: Computed columns do not consume physical space

set nocount on

declare @Num_Cols as smallint, @Num_Variable_Cols as smallint
declare @Fixed_Data_Size as int, @Max_Var_Size as int
declare @Null_Bitmap as smallint, @Variable_Data_Size as int
declare @Row_Size as int, @Rows_Per_Page as int
declare @Free_Rows_Per_Page as int

-- Pull together information about the columns, the size of the columns and
-- whether the column is fixed or variable
select@Num_Cols = count(*),
       @Fixed_Data_Size = sum(sc.length * (1 - st.variable)),
       @Num_Variable_Cols = sum(cast(st.variable as smallint)),
       @Max_Var_Size = sum(sc.length * st.variable)

from   sysobjects as so

join   syscolumns as sc
  on   so.id = sc.id

join   systypes as st
  on   sc.xtype = st.xtype

where  so.id = @ObjId
and    ObjectProperty (so.id, 'IsUserTable') = 1
and    ColumnProperty (so.id, sc.name, 'IsComputed')  = 0  --<-- Addition #1

set @Null_Bitmap = case when @Fixed_Data_Size = 0 then 0 else (2 + (( @Num_Cols
+ 7) / 8 ) ) end
set @Variable_Data_Size = case
                             when @Num_Variable_Cols = 0
                                  then 0
                               else 2 + (@Num_Variable_Cols + @Num_Variable_Cols) +
                                           @Max_Var_Size
                            end
```

```
set @Row_Size = @Fixed_Data_Size + @Variable_Data_Size + @Null_Bitmap + 4
set @Rows_Per_Page = 8096 / (@Row_Size + 2)

-- If there is a clustered index on the table, get the Fill Factor used

declare @Fill_Factor as int
select@Fill_Factor =    case
                          when IndexProperty (@ObjId, name, 'IndexFillFactor')
IS NULL
                              then 100
                         when IndexProperty (@ObjId, name, 'IndexFillFactor') = 0
                              then 100
                          else IndexProperty (@ObjId, name, 'IndexFillFactor')
                        end
from    sysindexes
where   id = @ObjId
and     IndexProperty(@ObjId, name, 'IsClustered') = 1
set @Fill_Factor = Coalesce (@Fill_Factor, 100)

set @Free_Rows_Per_Page = 8096 * ((100 - @Fill_Factor) / 100.0) / @Row_Size

set @DataPages = ceiling (1.0 * @Num_Rows / (@Rows_Per_Page -
@Free_Rows_Per_Page) )

RETURN(0)
```

Reference

v1.00 2000.06.13	
Applies to SQL Server version:	7.0
FAQ category:	Server Administration and Tools
Related FAQ articles:	n/a
Related Microsoft Knowledge Base articles:	n/a
Other related information:	n/a
Authors:	B.P. Margolin, Neil Pike

fastbcplog

Q: Why does my transaction log fill up when I use fast BCP, select into or the transfer tool? I thought this didn't log anything.

A: Fast BCP and select into do not log record updates. However, they *do* log extent allocations. They need to do this so that if the process is terminated unexpectedly (for example, if the power goes out) SQL can recover the space.

Therefore with large BCPs and select intos—when many extents need allocating—the log can still fill, in which case, it needs to be made larger.

Reference

v1.03 2000.04.24	
Applies to SQL Server versions:	All
FAQ category:Server Administration and Tools	
Related FAQ articles:	n/a
Related Microsoft Knowledge Base articles:	n/a
Other related information:	n/a
Author:	Neil Pike

filesystemmirroring

Q: Can I use disk-level mirroring software with SQL Server to provide a backup system?

A: In theory you can, and vendors like Vinca, Octopus, and Double Take all claim to work with SQL Server. However, when I and others have tested some of these products by powering down systems and yanking out network cables rather than doing planned fail-overs, we have sometimes seen database corruption.

If you want to use one of these products then test it properly in your environment—power the primary server down and pull out the network cables when there is a heavy update load occuring and make sure that the backup server recovers SQL Server correctly. Run DBCCs to make double sure.

Reference

v1.00 2000.03.03

Applies to SQL Server versions:	All
FAQ category:	Server Administration and Tools
Related FAQ articles:	n/a
Related Microsoft Knowledge Base articles:	n/a
Other related information:	n/a
Author:	Neil Pike

freeproccache

Q: How can I clear SQL Server's procedure cache?

A: With SQL 6.5 and below the only way is to restart SQL Server.

With SQL 7.0 there is an undocumented and unsupported command you can use: DBCC FREEPROCCACHE.

Reference

v1.00 1999.11.01

Applies to SQL Server versions:	All
FAQ category:	Server Administration and Tools
Related FAQ articles:	n/a
Related Microsoft Knowledge Base articles:	n/a
Other related information:	n/a
Author:	Neil Pike

gaminit

Q: When would I use DBCC GAMINIT in SQL Server?

A: This command only applies to SQL 6.5 and below. It can sometimes be useful when you have a very large and fragmented table, though typically, you will see performance degrade over time.

SQL by default tries to fit new rows (inserted via INSERT or BCP) into existing extents that are not full. The information on which extents are full is kept in the GAM structure (global allocation map) which is populated dynamically in memory and is cleared every time SQL is started.

It is sometimes useful to pre-populate this table fully. This can be done via `dbcc gaminit(database_id)` which can be put in a startup stored procedure.

Alternatively (or as well as) you could set trace flag 1140. This makes SQL put all new rows that won't fit in the current extent into a new extent rather than searching for old ones. This can lead to wasted space though. See Q174085 for more information.

Reorganizing indices with a sufficient fill factor when possible will also alleviate the situation.

Reference

v1.02 2000.05.02

Applies to SQL Server versions:	4.x, 6.x
FAQ category:	Server Administration and Tools
Related FAQ articles:	n/a
Related Microsoft Knowledge Base articles:	Q150748 "INF: Use of DBCC GAMINIT," Q174085 "INF: Enhancement to Trace Flag 1140"
Other related information:	n/a
Author:	Neil Pike

harddrivenotappear

Q: Why don't some of my drives appear in SQL Server?

A: SQL Server only directly addresses fixed disks, therefore, if you have a removable drive this probably won't appear. Also it may not see newly created disks until you have restarted NT—even though Explorer sees the new disks with no problem. So if you have created new disks in Disk Administrator, restart NT if you can't see them in SQL Server.

However, you should be able to create dumps or devices on any sort of NT addressable drive as long as you use the standard T-SQL DISK INIT... or CREATE DATABASE... (SQL 7.0) commands rather than the GUI.

If you still can't see the drives then check for the following:

1. Can you see the drives from `xp_cmdshell 'dir <x>:'`? If not, there may be a permissions issue—check which NT account the MSSQLSERVER service is running under.
2. Check the output from xp_fixeddrives.

Reference

v1.01 1999.02.28

Applies to SQL Server versions:	All
FAQ category:	Server Administration and Tools
Related FAQ articles:	n/a
Related Microsoft Knowledge Base articles:	n/a
Other related information:	n/a
Author:	Neil Pike

hardwaremoreorfasterprocessors

Q: With SQL Server, should I get more processors or faster processors?

A: It depends. Have both if you can.

With SQL 6.5 and below, a single query will only use a single processor, whereas in SQL 7.0 it will parellize queries if it thinks that will make it run faster.

Usually the processor isn't the bottleneck on SQL systems—it is usually the disk subsystem. But as a rule of thumb if you have few users or processes, go for faster processors, and if you have lots of users, go for more processors.

Reference

v1.00 1999.01.07

Applies to SQL Server versions:	All
FAQ category:	Server Administration and Tools
Related FAQ articles:	n/a
Related Microsoft Knowledge Base articles:	n/a
Other related information:	n/a
Author:	Neil Pike

hardwarespecremotely

Q: How can I remotely get the hardware spec of a SQL Server?

A: xp_msver will give you information on the processor and memory. If this is not enough, winmsd will show details of all hardware and its configuration from an NT viewpoint. See Q232848 for details of how to run it.

With SQL 7 there is a new utility that will run both of the above, and more, automatically. It is called sqldiag:

```
sqldiag -U<login> -P<password> -O<output filename>
```

In addition, some hardware and third-party manufacturers provide remote diagnostic and inventory software that will survey and report on anything you could possibly want to know about the hardware. This usually requires special services to be running on the server itself.

Reference

v1.01 2000.05.02

Applies to SQL Server versions:	All
FAQ category:	Server Administration and Tools
Related FAQ articles:	n/a
Related Microsoft Knowledge Base article:	Q232848 "How to Create a WinMSD Report"
Other related information:	n/a
Author:	Neil Pike

identifypseudotables

Q: How can I tell if a table is a "real" table or one that just exists in memory?

A: Check for ones with dpages set to 0 in sysindexes—if they have no data pages then they can't exist on disk.

```
SELECT * from
sysobjects o, sysindexes I
where
i.id = o.id
and
    o.type in ('S','U')
and
    i.dpages = 0
```

Reference

v1.00 2000.06.13

Applies to SQL Server versions:	All
FAQ categories:	Server Administration and Tools, Trouble-shooting
Related FAQ articles:	n/a
Related Microsoft Knowledge Base articles:	n/a
Other related information:	n/a
Author:	Neil Pike

instcatversion

Q: How can I tell what version of system stored procedures is installed on SQL Server?

A: Issue the following command:

```
select * from master..spt_server_info where attribute_id = 500
```

The system stored procedures are installed by running INSTCAT.SQL, which comes with SQL Server and MDAC releases. When you install MDAC on a SQL server, it doesn't actually run instcat.sql—you need to run it yourself with ISQL/OSQL/ISQLW if you want the new stored procedures installed.

If you look inside instcat.sql you will see the following or similar:

```
NOTE:  you MUST change the last row inserted into spt_server_info to be version
number of this file. the convention is j.nn.bbb, where j is the major version
number ('7' now), nn is the minor version number ('00' now), and bbb is the build
number.
insert into spt_server_info
    values (500, 'SYS_SPROC_VERSION', '7.00.bbb')
```

This comment is not directed at you, the DBA or sysadmin. It is directed at the Microsoft developers who update and maintain the file. They have to remember to update the SQL code in instcat.sql to mark the version on the SQL Server when it is run.

Reference

v1.01 2000.05.02

Applies to SQL Server versions:	All
FAQ category:	Server Administration and Tools
Related FAQ articles:	n/a
Related Microsoft Knowledge Base articles:	n/a
Other related information:	Search for "Catalog Stored Procedures" in Books Online
Author:	Neil Pike

isqlbatchreturncodenot10

Q: With SQL 6.5 and the ISQL /b option, a DOS error level code is supposed to be set when errors with a severity of 10 or greater are returned. This doesn't work for me with a severity of 10, but it does for 11 and higher. What is wrong?

A: This is a known "feature"—the actual severity needs to be 11 or higher. The following code demonstrates it:

```
@ECHO OFF
isql /b /Q "RAISERROR('severity 10',10,1)" -E
@IF not errorlevel 1 goto zero10
@echo errorlevel is 1 or greater
goto end10
:zero10
@echo errorlevel is 0
:end10
isql /b /Q "RAISERROR('severity 11',11,1)" -E
@IF not errorlevel 1 goto zero11
@echo errorlevel is 1 or greater
goto end11
:zero11
@echo errorlevel is 0
:end11
@echo finished
```

Reference

v1.01 2000.06.12

Applies to SQL Server versions:	6.5, 7.0, 2000
FAQ categories:	Server Administration and Tools, Application Design and Programming
Related FAQ article:	"How can I get ISQL.EXE to return a DOS error level for me to test?" (isqldoserrorlevels, see page 54)
Related Microsoft Knowledge Base articles:	n/a
Other related information:	n/a
Authors:	Neil Pike, Paul Munkenbeck

isqlincludefiles

Q: How can I run one script from another?

A: A couple of ways:

- Use the :r command in an ISQL script.

  For example, O1.SQL contains:

```
PRINT 'This is a common routine'
Go
```

  In O2.SQL put the commands:

```
PRINT 'About to run the common routine'
:r O1.SQL
PRINT 'Common routine should have run'
```

- Use xp_cmdshell from a script to kick off another script with ISQL:

```
xp_cmdshell 'ISQL -E -iO2.SQL'
```

Reference

v1.00 2000.06.13	
Applies to SQL Server versions:	All
FAQ categories:	Server Administration and Tools, Troubleshooting
Related FAQ articles:	n/a
Related Microsoft Knowledge Base articles:	n/a
Other related information:	n/a
Author:	Neil Pike

kill

Q: How can I stop a SQL Server process? What if it won't die?

A: Do a `sp_who` and identify the spid in question. Then do a `KILL <spidno>`.

This will mark the spid as "dead." Note that it may take a while for the process to end because it has to roll back all the updates that it has been doing. Because of the extra disk contention and thrashing this causes on the log, it is not unusual for the rollback to take several times longer than for the updates to finish. So if you killed it after an hour of updates, don't be too surprised if it is still rolling back four hours later.

Also, kill only marks the process as dead—the process itself needs to check for this, and if it is stuck in a loop as the result of a bug then it won't terminate. Also certain processes like DUMP and DBCC commands have significant code paths where the kill command is not checked for and so these can take some time to terminate.

Also, if the process is in an extended stored procedure, or is waiting for network traffic or a remote stored procedure, it will not check whether it has been terminated until these actions have been completed.

See Q171224 for more information, including details on the waittype that can tell you what a process is waiting for.

If the process won't die for one of the above reasons, your only choice is to stop the sqlservr.exe process itself and restart.

Reference

v1.03 2000.05.07

Applies to SQL Server versions:	All
FAQ category:	Server Administration and Tools
Related FAQ articles:	n/a
Related Microsoft Knowledge Base article:	Q171224 "INF: Understanding How the Transact-SQL KILL Command Works"
Other related information:	n/a
Author:	Neil Pike

licensing

Q: How do I know whether SQL Server is in per-seat or per-server mode? How can I change it? How can I add licenses? How does licensing work?

A: The answer to all these questions is the same:

1. Click Start.
2. Click Settings.
3. Click Control Panel.
4. Double-click the Licensing Manager applet.

All the information and changes are here.

For details on Microsoft's licensing policies, see:

- `http://www.microsoft.com/SQL/productinfo/licensesummary.htm`
- `http://www.microsoft.com/SQL/productinfo/pricing.htm`

Reference

v1.02 2000.01.08

Applies to SQL Server versions:	All
FAQ category:	Server Administration and Tools
Related FAQ articles:	n/a
Related Microsoft Knowledge Base articles:	n/a
Other related information:	n/a
Author:	Neil Pike

listsqlservers

Q: How can I list all available SQL servers in my application?

A: Two methods:

- The ISQL and OSQL commands have a -L option to list servers. This can then be run from xp_cmdshell. Note that they treat the local server differently.

```
Exec master..xp_cmdshell 'ISQL -L'
Exec master..xp_cmdshell 'OSQL -L'
```

- Use SQL-DMO. The method/API is ListAvailableSQLServers. This returns a NameList object enumerating network-visible SQL servers.

Details on DMO are provided in Books Online and a separate help file. These are installed as part of any SQL Server install.

A detailed example follows.

To enumerate all network-visible SQL servers using SQL-DMO objects, create a new standard EXE project, and add a reference to sqldmo.rll. This file can be found in \Binn\Resources\1033\sqldmo.rll under the SqlServer70 directory.

Now add this code and declaration in your form's code:

```
Private Function GetAllSqlServerCollection(colSqlServers As Collection) _
  As Boolean
    Dim intIndex As Integer
    Dim oApplication As SQLDMO.Application
    Dim oNameList As SQLDMO.NameList

    Set oApplication = New Application
    With oApplication
        Set oNameList = .ListAvailableSQLServers
        With oNameList
            For intIndex = 1 To .Count
                colSqlServers.Add (oNameList.Item(intIndex))
            Next
        End With
    End With
    Set oApplication = Nothing
    GetAllSqlServerCollection = True
End Function
```

This code quickly fetches a list of SQL servers and can be put inside a combo box's dropdown event to always get a refreshed list of SQL servers on your form.

Only SQL servers that are running on NT, in the same domain, and configured with the Named Pipes Net-Lib are listed using these methods. There is no way to list all SQL servers unless you are running SQL 2000 on a native-mode Windows 2000 environment. In this case all SQL servers will be registered with Active Directory and can be found via this.

Reference

v1.04 2000.05.25	
Applies to SQL Server versions:	All
FAQ categories:	Server Administration and Tools, Connectivity
Related FAQ article:	"Where does the list of SQL servers come from in registration/dialog boxes? What reasons are there for not getting a list?" (browserlistof-sqlservers, see page 393)
Related Microsoft Knowledge Base article:	Q142734
Other related information:	n/a
Author:	Neil Pike

masterlocation

Q: Where is the pointer to the master database stored in SQL Server? How can I move the master database?

A: It is one of the startup options for SQL Server. The default values for a particular server can be managed through Enterprise Manager and are kept under the following registry key:

```
HKEY_LOCAL_MACHINE\SOFTWARE\Microsoft\MSSQLServer\MSSQLServer\Parameters
```

The startup parameters are held in separate values named SQLArg0, SQLArg1, and so forth. The location of master is usually in SQLARg0 and is indicated by the –d parameter, for example, "-dD:\MSSQL\DATA\MASTER.DAT". Depending on the version of SQL Server, you may see other parameters relating to master. There may be a value that specifies the location of the master log file (-l), or a master mirror device (-r). See Books Online for details.

If SQL Server is running, you can change the value through Enterprise Manager. To move master just change the value, shut down SQL Server, move the device using Explorer / Move, and restart.

Reference

v1.01 2000.05.12	
Applies to SQL Server versions:	All
FAQ category:	Server Administration and Tools
Related FAQ article:	"How can I move a SQL Server device from one disk to another, or rename it?" (movedevice, see page 420)
Related Microsoft Knowledge Base articles:	n/a
Other related information:	"Startup Options" in Books Online
Author:	Neil Pike

maxmergerowsize

Q: Why am I limited to 6000 bytes per row when using merge replication?

A: SQL Server 7.0 allows you to create a table with 8060 bytes. Merge replication creates a conflict table in the published database. Each row in the conflict table stores the contents of a row from the published table plus some extra columns to manage conflict resolution. The 6000-byte limit is enforced to ensure the row size of the conflict table falls within the 8060 limit. The extra columns are:

COLUMN NAME	DATATYPE	SIZE (BYTES)
rowguid	uniqueidentifier	16
origin_datasource	nvarchar(255)	510
conflict_type	int	4
reason_code	int	4
reason_text	nvarchar(720)	1440
pubid	uniqueidentifier	16

These extra columns add 1990 bytes to the replicated table row length when creating the conflict table (8060 – 1990 = 6070). The remaining 70 bytes are reserved for the null bitmap and the data row header.

Reference

v1.03 2000.09.07	
Applies to SQL Server version:	7.0
FAQ categories:	Server Administration and Tools, Replication
Related FAQ articles:	n/a
Related Microsoft Knowledge Base articles:	n/a
Other related information:	"Estimating the Size of a Table" in Books Online 7
Authors:	Mike Hotek, Neil Pike

movedevice

Q: How can I move a SQL Server device from one disk to another, or rename it?

A: For SQL 7.0 user databases you can use:

```
sp_detach_db ...
<move devices physically>
sp_attach_db ...
```

For details on the attach and detach stored procedure parameters, see Books Online.

For SQL 7.0 tempdb only, use the special FILENAME parameter as follows:

```
ALTER DATABASE tempdb
MODIFY FILE (NAME=tempdev, FILENAME='new_file_name')

ALTER DATABASE tempdb
MODIFY FILE (NAME=templog, FILENAME='new_file_name')
```

SQL Server then needs to be restarted for this to take effect

For SQL 6.5 and below there are two ways:

- Use device mirroring. Mirror the device to the "new" location and then break the mirror and delete the old device. This method does not need SQL downtime and can be done via the gui or via T-SQL.

- Books Online for SQL 6.5 documents a stored procedure called sp_movedevice. Cut and paste this stored procedure into a query analyzer/ISQLW window and run it to create it. (It doesn't get installed automatically). Then run sp_movedevice with the required parameters to make the system table changes. Next, stop SQL Server. Then move the device using the MOVE command, Explorer, or File Manager. Finally, restart SQL Server. This method requires down time, but it is faster because using OS-level commands is faster than SQL mirroring.

  All that sp_movedevice does is update the phyname in the sysdevices table.

  Note that the method just described works for all *user* databases. If you want to move master this way, then note that the phyname parameter in sysdevices is only for documentation—you might as well change it anyway to keep things in line. The actual method SQL uses for locating the master device is by looking in the registry:

```
HKEY_LOCAL_MACHINE\SOFTWARE\Microsoft\MSSQLServer\MSSQLServer\Parameters\
```

  The location of master is usually in SQLARg0 and is indicated by the –d parameter, for example: -dD:\MSSQL\DATA\MASTER.DAT.

  If SQL Server is running, you can change the value through Enterprise Manager. To move master just change the value, shut down SQL Server, move the device using Explorer/Move, and restart.

Reference

v1.05 2000.05.15

Applies to SQL Server versions:	All
FAQ category:	Server Administration and Tools
Related FAQ article:	"Where is the pointer to the master database stored in SQL Server? How can I move the master database?" (masterlocation, see page 418)
Related Microsoft Knowledge Base articles:	Q187824 " INF: How to Move Tempdb to a Different Device," Q181602 "INF: How to Move a Device to Another Location," and Q224071 "INF: Moving SQL Server 7.0 Databases to a New Location"
Other related information:	n/a
Author:	Neil Pike

msdetools

Q: What tools can I use to administer MSDE and SSDE?

A: The only tool delivered with MSDE (SQL 7.0) and SSDE (SQL Server Database Engine [SQL 2000]) is OSQL.EXE.

You can use Access 2000 project tools to work with MSDE and SSDE as well. You also can use the Visual Database Tools that come with Visual Studio.

To use the "full" SQL Server tool set you will need to pay for a SQL Server Client Access License. You can then install SQL Enterprise Manager to work with MSDE and SSDE.

Reference

v1.02 2000.05.25

Applies to SQL Server versions:	7.0, 2000
FAQ category:	Server Administration and Tools
Related FAQ articles:	n/a
Related Microsoft Knowledge Base articles:	n/a
Other related information:	n/a
Author:	Neil Pike

negativedevice

Q: Why do my device sizes appear as negative values in SQL Enterprise Manager? It won't let me make any changes because of this.

A: This is caused by a known bug in Enterprise Manager when there is more than 2GB of free space on a disk. It was fixed in 6.5 SP3 and above. If you are running SQL Enterprise Manager from a client, you will need to apply SP3 to that as well.

Reference

v1.00 1999.09.30	
Applies to SQL Server version:	6.5
FAQ category:	Server Administration and Tools
Related FAQ articles:	n/a
Related Microsoft Knowledge Base articles:	n/a
Other related information:	n/a
Author:	Neil Pike

perfcountersnotappearoncluster

Q: Why can't I see the SQL performance counters on the second node in my cluster? I can see the NT counters with no problem.

A: This is a bug that won't be fixed until SQL 2000.

Reference

v1.01 2000.04.09	
Applies to SQL Server version:	7.0
FAQ categories:	Server Administration and Tools, Clustering, Troubleshooting
Related FAQ articles:	n/a
Related Microsoft Knowledge Base articles:	Q228804 "BUG: Perfmon Counters Missing for Active/Passive Cluster Setup"
Other related information:	n/a
Author:	Neil Pike

processmailsql7

Q: Why does sp_processmail fail with an error, “Supplied datatype for set_user is not allowed, expecting 'varchar'” on SQL 7.0?

A: This is a known problem. You have to rewrite sp_processmail (courtesy of Wayne Snyder).

The problem is actually with xp_sendmail which returns an error “(@set_user datatype is incorrect)”.

Microsoft changed the @set_user and @dbuse params in sp_processmail to sysname and did *not* go back and change xp_sendmail.

The temporary fix is to change sp_processmail as follows:

```
CREATE PROCEDURE sp_processmail
@subject varchar(255)=NULL,
@filetype varchar(3)='txt',
@separator varchar(3)='tab',
@set_user varchar(30)='guest',        --Change this back from sysname to varchar
@dbuse varchar(30)='master'           --Change this back from sysname to varchar
AS
-- New Version as per KB: Q239074

........./* rest of procedure */
```

Reference

v1.03 2000.04.13	
Applies to SQL Server version:	7.0
FAQ categories:	Server Administration and Tools, Trouble-shooting
Related FAQ article:	“How do I install SQL Mail? I’ve got problems installing it on SQL Server.” (sqlmail, see page 438)
Related Microsoft Knowledge Base article:	Q239074 “BUG: Sp_processmail Returns Datatype Error Message”
Other related information:	n/a
Author:	Neil Pike

querytimeout

Q: How do I configure the client query time-out for SQL Server?

A: If you are using a utility, this is normally under File / Options or Tools / Options from the menu. Set it to the value you require. 0 means infinite (no) timeout.

For example:

- The Enterprise Manager timeout is set in TOOLS / OPTIONS / Connection / Query Timeout.
- The Query Analyzer timeout is set in QUERY / Current Connect Options / Query Timeout

If you want to do it in C or VB code, this depends on the data access method. Look in Books Online for more details, but with raw ODBC you would use:

```
Retcode = SQLSetConnectAttr(m_hdbc, SQL_ATTR_CONNECTION_TIMEOUT,
(SQLPOINTER)dwSeconds, SQL_IS_UINTEGER);
```

Reference

v1.01 2000.01.04

Applies to SQL Server versions:	All
FAQ category:	Server Administration and Tools
Related FAQ articles:	n/a
Related Microsoft Knowledge Base articles:	n/a
Other related information:	n/a
Author:	Neil Pike

redlightningboltem

Q: What does the red lightning bolt next to a server in SQL Enterprise Manager mean?

A: It just means that you have a connection to that SQL Server. Nothing to worry about.

Reference

v1.00 1999.12.09

Applies to SQL Server versions:	All
FAQ category:	Server Administration and Tools
Related FAQ articles:	n/a
Related Microsoft Knowledge Base articles:	n/a
Other related information:	n/a
Author:	Neil Pike

registry

Q: What registry entries does SQL Server use?

A: The registry keys that SQL Server uses are listed in the "uninstall" entry.

Reference

v1.02 2000.04.15

Applies to SQL Server versions:	All
FAQ category:	Server Administration and Tools
Related FAQ article:	"How can I completely uninstall SQL Server?" (uninstall, see page 330)
Related Microsoft Knowledge Base articles:	n/a
Other related information:	n/a
Author:	Neil Pike

remotetape

Q: Can SQL Server back up to a tape unit on another server?

A: No. SQL doesn't support remote tapes. It can only enumerate and use devices that are local as far as NT is concerned (if an NT-level driver were able to make a remote tape look locally attached, SQL Server would be able to use it).

You can always dump the SQL database to disk locally (or to a network share—see FAQ article "networkbackup" for details) and then back that up to tape.

Some third-party backup tools that work with SQL Server agents offer this sort of functionality because they get the data from SQL Server via a standard named-pipe or VDI interface and then use their own drivers to write the backup. For example:

- BEI Ultrabac: `http://www.ultrabac.com`
- CAI Arcserve: `http://www.cai.com/arcserveit/`
- Legato: `http://www.legato.com`
- Veritas Backup Exec: `http://www.veritas.com`
- Tivoli ADSM: `http://www.tivoli.com`

Reference

v1.02 2000.04.15

Applies to SQL Server versions:	All
FAQ category:	Server Administration and Tools
Related FAQ article:	"Why can't I backup or restore my SQL Server databases to a share on another server?" (networkbackup, see page 178)
Related Microsoft Knowledge Base articles:	n/a
Other related information:	n/a
Author:	Neil Pike

replicationdifferentsortorder

Q: Can I use SQL Replication between machines of different sort orders, character sets or code pages?

A: Yes, you can replicate, but any data containing values unique to a code page or character set are going to be "corrupted" because they will have different values on different machines. As long as your data only uses the lowest 128 ASCII characters, you should be fine.

Reference

v1.01 2000.04.16	
Applies to SQL Server versions:	All
FAQ categories:	Server Administration and Tools, Replication
Related FAQ articles:	n/a
Related Microsoft Knowledge Base articles:	n/a
Other related information:	"Replicating Between Different Versions of SQL Server" in SQL Server Books Online
Author:	Neil Pike

sapassword

Q: I've forgotten the sa password for SQL Server. What can I do?

A: The easiest way around this is to logon to the actual SQL Server NT machine as administrator. Then connect to SQL Server using any of the tools and specify "." as the server name and ask for a trusted connection. As long as the Administrators group hasn't been explicitly removed from having sa rights, you should connect and be able to reset the password.

If you're in mixed mode and you know the NT userid of someone with sa rights, get their password reset and logon/connect as them.

Otherwise you can try to find the machine of a DBA who already has the server registered to SQL Enterprise Manager with sa and use that copy of SQL Enterprise Manager to connect.

If all these fail, you'll have to rebuild master and DISK REINIT (6.x) or sp_attach_db (7.x) all the user databases.

Reference

v1.02 2000.04.16	
Applies to SQL Server versions:	All
FAQ categories:	Server Administration and Tools, Troubleshooting
Related FAQ articles:	n/a
Related Microsoft Knowledge Base articles:	n/a
Other related information:	n/a
Author:	Neil Pike

schedulers

Q: What can I do if the SQL Agent or Executive scheduler doesn't support the features I need – such as multiple file dependencies or holidays?

A: The SQL Server Agent that comes with SQL 7.0 and above is vastly superior to the SQL Executive that came with 6.5, but it still doesn't have all the features of an enterprise-level scheduler.

Your choices are:

- Write your own code in batch files, rexx, Perl or VBScript to enhance the functionality of SQL Agent.
- Use a third-party NT scheduler with more features:
  - OpalisRobot: `http://www.opalisrobot.com`
  - Argent Job Scheduler or Argent Batch Facility (the JSO product is discontinued): `http://www.argentsoftware.com`
  - sys*ADMIRAL: `http://www.tidalsoft.com`
  - Job Management Partner 1 (JP1): `http://www.hitachi.com`
  - Tivoli Maestro: `http://www.tivoli.com`
  - (No order of preference or features is implied in this list.)

Reference

v1.02 2000.04.16	
Applies to SQL Server versions: All	
FAQ category:	Server Administration and Tools
Related FAQ articles:	n/a
Related Microsoft Knowledge Base articles:	n/a
Other related information:	n/a
Author:	Neil Pike

sectorsize

Q: Why do I get the error "Cannot use file <logfile> because it was originally formatted with sector size <xxx> and is now on a device with sector size <yyy>" when I move SQL Server's log file?

A: This only occurs with SQL 7.x, not 6.x. For performance and consistency, the log writes are aligned on physical sector boundaries. At least 95 percent of disks will have the same physical sector size, but if you try to move between different vendor RAID systems, or utilize some form of NAS device, you may see this problem.

The only workaround is to re-create the log file on the new device and backup and restore the database.

Reference

v1.00 1999.11.30	
Applies to SQL Server version:	7.0
FAQ categories:	Server Administration and Tools, Troubleshooting
Related FAQ articles:	n/a
Related Microsoft Knowledge Base articles:	n/a
Other related information:	n/a
Author:	Neil Pike

servicerunning

Q: How can I tell if a service is running from SQL?

A: Use one of the following methods:

- Write your own extended stored procedure to call the NT service API's.
- Write your own COM object to call the NT service APIs. Access the object via OLE automation stored procedures (sp_Oxxx).
- Capture and test the NET START output via xp_cmdshell. The following example tests for SQL Agent:

```
CREATE TABLE #List(Description  Char(255))

INSERT INTO #List
  EXEC master..xp_cmdshell 'NET START'

IF EXISTS (SELECT * FROM #List WHERE Description LIKE '%SQLServerAgent%')
    PRINT 'SQLServerAgent Running'
ELSE
    PRINT 'SQLServerAgent Stopped'
```

Reference

v1.02 2000.04.21

Applies to SQL Server versions:	All
FAQ category:	Server Administration and Tools
Related FAQ articles:	n/a
Related Microsoft Knowledge Base articles:	n/a
Other related information:	n/a
Author:	Neil Pike

smtp

Q: How can I use e-mail with SQL Server without using an MS-Mail or Exchange server? I'd like to use my standard SMTP or POP3 services.

A: A variety of methods:

- Use xp_cmdshell to run an SMTP sendmail program.
- Use an extended stored procedure with built-in SMTP functionality: `http://www.spudsoft.demon.co.uk/code/index.html`.
- Configure SQL Mail to use your normal SMTP or POP3 server.

For SQL Server and SQL Executive/SQL Server Agent to interact with SQL Mail, the SQL Server Service (MSSQLServer) and the SQL Executive (SQLExecutive) or SQL Server Agent (SQLServerAgent) service must be running under the same NT domain account.

This account must be a member of the local Administrators group and have the "Log on as a service" right. Verify this in User Manager, and that the services are running under this domain account. For more details on this refer to the following Books Online topics:

- SQL 6.5: "Assigning a Service Account to SQL Server or SQL Executive"
- SQL 7.0: "Creating SQL Server Services User Accounts"

You will need a messaging client such as Windows NT Messaging or Microsoft Outlook to be installed on the SQL Server as well.

To create and configure the mail profile you will need to log on interactively as your "service" account user.

Open the Mail applet in Control Panel and follow these steps to create your profile:

1. Click Add to begin creating a Windows Messaging Profile.
2. Uncheck the box next to Microsoft Mail (unless there is an Exchange Server available).
3. Make sure Internet Mail is checked, and click Next.

4. You will be asked for the method to connect to the mail server. Check Network, and click Next.

5. You will be asked to specify the mail server name or IP address. Enter either one, and click Next.

6. You will be asked to choose the mode for transferring messages. Check Automatic, and click Next.

7. You will be asked for the e-mail address. Enter it in the Email Address field.

8. Enter a suitably descriptive name in the Full Name field, and click Next.

9. You will be asked for the mailbox name. Enter a mailbox name in the mailbox name field, e.g., userid (this is the mail server login name).

10. Enter the password for the mailbox name in the password field (this is the mail server login name's password), and click Next.

11. You will be asked for a location for your personal address book. Use the default or move it as appropriate, and click Next.

12. You will be asked for a location for your personal folder file. Use the default or move it as appropriate, and click Next.

13. You should receive the message that setup is "Done!" Click Finish.

You will now need to configure SQL Mail to use your new profile. For SQL 6.5 you will need to run SQL Setup as described in the "Setting Up a SQLMail Client" topic in Books Online (see the section "To Set Up SQLMail"). For SQL 7.0 or 2000 this can be done from Enterprise Manager, via the properties sheet of the SQL Mail node. For both methods, ensure you select the profile created above, and I recommend you set the SQL Mail to auto-start.

Start SQL Enterprise Manager, and ensure SQL Mail is running. You can then test it from Query Analyzer (ISQL/W):

```
EXEC master.dbo.xp_sendmail 'myname@myaddress.com',@message='This is a test
message.'
```

You should receive a *Mail Sent* message in the results pane upon execution.

Reference

v1.02 2000.06.05	
Applies to SQL Server versions:	All
FAQ category:	Server Administration and Tools
Related FAQ articles:	"How do I install SQL Mail? I've got problems installing it on SQL Server." (sqlmail, see page 438), "Mail messages are stuck in my Outbox with SQL Mail. They don't get sent until I log in as the user locally and open the mail client manually. What can I do?" (sqlmailstuckinoutbox, see page 442)
Related Microsoft Knowledge Base articles:	n/a
Other related information:	`http://www.microsoft.com/technet/SQL/Tips/70mail.asp`
Author:	Neil Pike

sortorder

Q: How do I change the sort order or character set for a SQL Server database?

A: This is an installation option, and you have to reinstall to change it. You will have to:

1. Back up your data and objects using BCP or Transfer Manager. Do *not* use DUMP or BACKUP database.
2. Reinstall SQL Server with the correct sort order or character set.
3. Reload the data and objects.

The best way to do this is to install SQL Server on another server with the correct sort order and then transfer all the objects across.

Reference

v1.02 2000.04.22	
Applies to SQL Server versions:	All
FAQ category:	Server Administration and Tools
Related FAQ articles:	n/a
Related Microsoft Knowledge Base articles:	n/a
Other related information:	n/a
Author:	Neil Pike

sp_cursor

Q: When I do a SQL Server trace I see lots of sp_cursoropen and sp_cursorfetch commands being sent that I am not generating. What are they?

A: You are using ODBC ,OLE-DB or a higher-level method based on these. These procedures are used to provide cursor functionality. They should not be directly called by your own T-SQL.

Reference

v1.00 1999.01.19

Applies to SQL Server versions:	All
FAQ category:	Server Administration and Tools
Related FAQ articles:	n/a
Related Microsoft Knowledge Base articles:	n/a
Other related information:	n/a
Author:	Neil Pike

sp_sdidebug

Q: What does sp_sdidebug do?

A: It is a SQL Server-side component of Visual Studio Transact-SQL stored procedure debugger. It is an extended stored procedure and can be called only from a Visual Studio client. The only reason you may come across it is to grant permissions for developers to use it. See Q179023.

Reference

v1.01 2000.05.15

Applies to SQL Server versions:	6.5, 7.0
FAQ category:	Server Administration and Tools
Related FAQ article:	"How do I configure SQL Server to debug stored procedures?" (debugsp, see page 24)
Related Microsoft Knowledge Base article:	Q179023 "FIX: T-SQL Debugger Hangs When User Has No Execute Permission"
Other related information:	n/a
Author:	Neil Pike

sql7columnlevelpermissions

Q: What happened to the GUI for column-level permissions in SQL Server 7?

A: The GUI was left out (not the functionality), but is back in SQL Server 2000.

You can still use the standard T-SQL commands GRANT, REVOKE and DENY as documented in SQL Server Books Online.

Reference

v1.02 2000.04.28

Applies to SQL Server version:	7.0
FAQ category:	Server Administration and Tools
Related FAQ articles:	n/a
Related Microsoft Knowledge Base articles:	n/a
Other related information:	n/a
Author:	Neil Pike

sql7emremove65group

Q: Why do I get a 6.5 group in my SQL 7.0 MMC list of servers? How can I remove it?

A: This is there so you can manage your 6.5 servers and in case you switch back to a co-resident copy of 6.5. If you have no more 6.5 servers and want to delete the entry, delete the following registry key:

```
HKEY_CURRENT_USER\Software\Microsoft\MSSQLServer\SQLEW\Registered Servers\SQL 6.5
```

Reference

v1.00 1999.01.29

Applies to SQL Server version:	7.0
FAQ category:	Server Administration and Tools
Related FAQ articles:	n/a
Related Microsoft Knowledge Base articles:	n/a
Other related information:	n/a
Author:	Neil Pike

sql7hiddendbs

Q: Why can't I see master and msdb in SQL 7.0/2000 Enterprise Manager? Also I can't see the system tables in user databases.

A: The reason for this is that by default system objects are not viewable.

To fix this, right-click the server name in Enterprise Manager and select "Edit SQL Server Registration Properties." Check the box to "Show system databases and objects."

Reference

v1.01 2000.04.28	
Applies to SQL Server versions:	7.0, 2000
FAQ category:	Server Administration and Tools
Related FAQ articles:	n/a
Related Microsoft Knowledge Base articles:	n/a
Other related information:	n/a
Author:	Neil Pike

sqlhdtst

Q: What is SQLHDTST.EXE for SQL Server and where do I get it?

A: SQLHDTST.EXE is on your TechNet CD and can also be downloaded from `http://support.microsoft.com/download/support/mslfiles/SQLHDTST.EXE`.

This utility simulates SQL Server 4.x / 6.x type-I/O and stresses your disk and network connections. It should be run over an extended period (maybe a weekend) and will highlight any nasty intermittent hardware errors that may be causing corruptions, SQL hangs or crashes.

If it reports any errors, you have faulty hardware—such as CPU, memory, disks or SCSI controllers. If you can't track down the problem using hardware vendor tools, I would recommend swapping out the entire unit.

For SQL Server 7.0 use the SQL70IOStress Utility available from `http://www.microsoft.com/downloads/search.asp`.

Reference

v1.01 2000.04.30	
Applies to SQL Server versions:	All
FAQ category:	Server Administration and Tools
Related FAQ articles:	n/a
Related Microsoft Knowledge Base articles:	Q178444 "INF: SQL Server Utility Files Available," Q231619 " INF: SQL70IOStress Utility to Stress Disk Subsystem"
Other related information:	n/a
Author:	Neil Pike

sqlmail

Q: How do I install SQL Mail? I've got problems installing it on SQL Server.

A: First read the sections in Books Online.

Failing that, try the following Microsoft Knowledge Base (`http://support.microsoft.com`) articles:

- Q118501 "INF: Troubleshooting SQLMail with Post Offices"

- Q153159 "INF: Troubleshooting SQLMail with Microsoft Exchange Server"

For other problems you can do a search for "SQLMAIL" on the Knowledge Base and you'll find other more specific articles.

There is also a good TechNet acticle "How to Use SQL Mail in MS SQL Server 7.0 with MS Outlook and MS Exchange Server" (`http://www.microsoft.com/technet/SQL/Tips/70mail.asp`).

Reference

v1.02 2000.06.05	
Applies to SQL Server versions:	All
FAQ categories:	Server Administration and Tools, Troubleshooting
Related FAQ articles:	"How can I use e-mail with SQL Server without using an MS-Mail or Exchange server? I'd like to use my standard SMTP or POP3 services." (smtp, see page 432), "Mail messages are stuck in my Outbox with SQL Mail. They don't get sent until I log in as the user locally and open the mail client manually. What can I do?" (sqlmailstuckinoutbox, see page 442)
Related Microsoft Knowledge Base articles:	Q118501 "INF: Troubleshooting SQLMail with Post Offices," Q153159 "INF: Troubleshooting SQLMail with Microsoft Exchange Server"
Other related information:	n/a
Author:	Neil Pike

sqlmailhang

Q: SQL Mail keeps hanging—meaning I have to restart SQL Server to clear it. How can I resolve this?

A: This is a MAPI problem, not a SQL one, but having SQL Server acting as a MAPI client makes it nearly impossible to track down and fix. SQL 6.5 SP5a has a fix in to reduce these problems. I have seen at least one report of SQL 7.0 having the same problem—so it doesn't look like this handles it a whole lot better.

You can try a different mail client and see if the MAPI DLLs that install work better—some people have found that Outlook 98 works well, while others report that only very early versions of Exchange client work OK. Whatever the case, it is likely that bugs exist in all versions of the MAPI client and are exposed on fast or SMP machines due to race conditions—thus causing hangs.

The recommended workaround would be to not use SQL Mail at all. You can use a SENDMAIL.EXE command—either the one in the Exchange resource kit for MAPI, or an SMTP one for an Internet gateway. This can then be called in two ways:

- If you want mail to go synchronously, call SENDMAIL via xp_cmdshell. This then won't return control to your SQL task until the mail has been sent.

- If asynchronous sending of mail is OK, or you are worried about the mail process hanging individual threads, write out the mail message information to a flat file. Then have a looping batch process outside of SQL looking for e-mails and sending them when it sees the file. This process could update SQL tables to say they are sent if that is needed.

I prefer the second approach.

Reference

v1.03 2000.04.30

Applies to SQL Server versions:	All
FAQ category:	Server Administration and Tools
Related FAQ articles:	n/a
Related Microsoft Knowledge Base articles:	n/a
Other related information:	n/a
Author:	Neil Pike

sqlmailisitstarted

Q: How do I tell if SQL Mail is started or not?

A: Before SQL 2000 the only way was to issue another xp_startmail command and check for the message that it was already started. You also could issue an xp_sendmail and trap the error.

With SQL 2000 there is an extended stored procedure called xp_issqlmailstarted that can be used instead.

Reference

v1.00 2000.06.13

Applies to SQL Server versions:	All
FAQ categories:	Server Administration and Tools, Troubleshooting
Related FAQ articles:	n/a
Related Microsoft Knowledge Base articles:	n/a
Other related information:	n/a
Author:	Neil Pike

sqlmaillotusnotes

Q: How can I use Lotus Notes for SQL Mail?

A: You have two options for Notes and SQLMail interoperability—without using SMTP, but we'll assume you want to go to Notes directly.

- Use the standard Lotus Notes client on the server.

- Use Microsoft Outlook and install the Notes service.

For the first option:

1. Create a mapping between the MSSQLServer and SQLServerAgent NT accounts and a Notes mailbox.

2. Log on to the SQL Server as the MSSQLServer account (you cannot use LocalSystem).

3. Install the Notes MAPI service.

4. Install the Notes client. Make sure you install Notes MAPI first, or it *will not work*!

5. Install the latest MAPI DLLs (MAPI32.DLL and MAPI.DLL in <NT>\SYSTEM32).

6. Launch the Notes client and configure your mailbox.

7. Take note of the Notes MAPI profile name. It should be the same as your user, but you never know.

8. REBOOT the server. This is weird, but you have to do it.

9. Log in as same account you used in step 2.

10. Launch SQL Enterprise Manager.

11. Configure SQLMail or SQLAgentmail as appropriate.

12. Log off.

For the second option, the steps are the same except step 3 is not needed and the MAPI DLLs (step 5) will already be there.

Reference

v1.01 2000.01.06	
Applies to SQL Server versions:	All
FAQ category:	Server Administration and Tools
Related FAQ articles:	n/a
Related Microsoft Knowledge Base articles:	n/a
Other related information:	n/a
Authors:	Ted Malone, Neil Pike

sqlmailstuckinoutbox

Q: Mail messages are stuck in my Outbox with SQL Mail. They don't get sent until I log in as the user locally and open the mail client manually. What can I do?

A: This is a MAPI problem, specifically with the Mapi32.dll file, not a SQL Server issue. Mapi32.dll, which comes with NT 4.0 as part of basic "Windows Messaging," does not work properly when called from a service.

Versions of Mapi32.dll that people have reported to work are:

- 4.0.835.1381 (NT Service Pack 3)
- 1.0.2518.0 (Outlook 97/98)
- 5.5.1960.0 (MS Exchange client)
- 1.0.2536.0 (Outlook 2000)

The simplest solution is to either install an Outlook client or apply NT Service Pack 3.

Another cause of the problem can be having offline folders enabled on the mail client. Make sure this isn't the case.

Unfortunately there are several versions of Mapi32.dll for which the file properties will report as 4.0 when viewed from Windows Explorer, including the original NT version, which does not work. The correct Service Pack 3 version has a size of 717,072 bytes. The original version 4.0 (4.0.835.1374) has a size of 635,152 bytes. To get the full version of the DLL, use the Getvers.exe as described in Microsoft Knowledge Base article Q167597 "GetVers.exe Specifies Component FileVersion & #Version." For more information on DLL versions and where they come from, use the Microsoft DLL Help database (`http://support.microsoft.com/servicedesks/msdn/`).

Reference

v1.05 2000.06.05	
Applies to SQL Server versions:	All
FAQ categories:	Server Administration and Tools, Troubleshooting
Related FAQ article:	"How do I install SQL Mail? I've got problems installing it on SQL Server." (sqlmail, see page 438)
Related Microsoft Knowledge Base articles:	Q167597 "GetVers.exe Specifies Component FileVersion & #Version," Q236782 "Mapi32.dll File Is Not Included in Service Pack 4 or Later"
Other related information:	n/a
Author:	Neil Pike

sqlstress

Q: What tools are available to stress or benchmark test SQL Server?

A: A couple of tools are available from the Microsoft Download Center (`http://www.microsoft.com/downloads/`):

- SQL Server 6.0/6.5 File System Stress Utility (Sqlhdtst.exe). See Q135582 "SQL Server Utility Files Available."
- SQL Server 7.0 Stress Utility for Stress Disk Subsystem. See Q231619 "INF: SQL70IOStress Utility to Stress Disk Subsystem."

There are some additional useful tools available from Microsoft:

- TPC-B Benchmark Kit: `ftp://ftp.microsoft.com/bussys/sql/unsup-ed/benchmark-kit/`
- Web Application Stress Tool: `http://webtool.rte.microsoft.com/`
- SQL Load Simulator (SQLLS.EXE) available as part of the Microsoft BackOffice Server 4.5 Resource Kit

Some third-party programs are also available:

- Mercury: `http://www.merc-int.com`

- Blue Curve: `http://www.bluecurve.com`
- Rational: `http://www.rational.com`
- Benchmark Factory: `http://www.benchmarkfactory.com`

Reference

v1.06 2000.06.15	
Applies to SQL Server versions:	All
FAQ category:	Server Administration and Tools
Related FAQ articles:	n/a
Related Microsoft Knowledge Base articles:	Q135582 "SQL Server Utility Files Available," Q231619 "INF: SQL70IOStress Utility to Stress Disk Subsystem"
Other related information:	n/a
Author:	Neil Pike

sqlversionwithoutloggingon

Q: How can I check whether SQL 6.5, SQL 7.0 or SQL 2000 is installed without trying to connect to SQL Server?

A: The easiest way is to check the server for the relevant registry entries.

For SQL 6.5 or SQL7.0 you can check:

```
HKEY_LOCAL_MACHINE\SOFTWARE\Microsoft\MSSQLServer\MSSQLServer\CurrentVersion
```

However, in the case of a clustered server it may not be there. In this case you could check:

```
HKEY_LOCAL_MACHINE\SYSTEM\CurrentControlSet\Services\MSSQLServer\
Performance\Library
```

The value of this will either be sqlctr60.dll, sqlctr70.dll or sqlctr80.dll. This location will always be there for a default instance. For a named (SQL 2000) instance called FRED, replace MSSQLServer with MSSQL$FRED.

For SQL 2000 only you can also check:

```
HKEY_LOCAL_MACHINE\SOFTWARE\Microsoft\Microsoft SQL Server\InstalledInstances
```

which will list the instances on the machine.

Reference

v1.03 2000.06.06

Applies to SQL Server versions:	All
FAQ category:	Server Administration and Tools
Related FAQ articles:	n/a
Related Microsoft Knowledge Base articles:	n/a
Other related information:	n/a
Author:	Neil Pike

startsqlfromcommandlinehang

Q: Why does SQL Server "hang" when I start it from the command line?

A: There is rarely a reason to start SQL Server from the command line. The usual reason for this is to start it in single-user mode for a master database recovery—in which case you would run `sqlservr.exe -m`.

What you will see when SQL starts are the same messages that appear in the SQL error log when it runs as a service, but it does not actually put out any messages when it has finished initializing. Once the databases are recovered it will appear to "hang," but at this point it has merely finished initializing.

To stop SQL Server use <ctrl>-C as if you were breaking out of a batch file. It will then prompt you as to whether you really want to shut it down or not.

Reference

v1.00 2000.06.13

Applies to SQL Server versions:	All
FAQ category:	Server Administration and Tools
Related FAQ articles:	n/a
Related Microsoft Knowledge Base articles:	n/a
Other related information:	n/a
Author:	Neil Pike

stopstartcommandline

Q: How can I stop and start SQL Server from the command line? I want to back it up with NT Backup.

A: Use NET STOP MSSQLSERVER and NET START MSSQLSERVER.

However, you should really look at using SQL's own backup and restore commands rather than shutting down SQL Server.

Reference

v1.00 1999.02.25

Applies to SQL Server versions:	All
FAQ category:	Server Administration and Tools
Related FAQ articles:	n/a
Related Microsoft Knowledge Base articles:	n/a
Other related information:	n/a
Author:	Neil Pike

stopstartsqlclient

Q: Why can't I stop or start SQL from SQL Enterprise Manager?

A: There are several reasons for this:

- You are running SQL Enterprise Manager on a Windows 9x client. Windows 9x does not support Windows NT service control API's. Therefore you cannot start, stop or inquire on the status of the SQL Server service.
- SQL Server has been configured with a name different from that of the underlying NT Server.
- The NT userid you are logged on as does not have NT administrator privileges on the SQL Server machine you are pointed at.

Reference

v1.00 1999.01.12

Applies to SQL Server versions:	6.x, 7.0, 2000
FAQ category:	Server Administration and Tools
Related FAQ articles:	n/a
Related Microsoft Knowledge Base articles:	n/a
Other related information:	n/a
Author:	Neil Pike

suppressheaders

Q: How can I suppress the column headings that always come out in ISQL output on SQL Server?

A: Use the -h switch to turn them off (value of –1). For example:

```
isql -E -S -Q"select getdate()" -h-1
```

Reference

v1.00 1999.02.02

Applies to SQL Server versions:	All
FAQ category:	Server Administration and Tools
Related FAQ articles:	n/a
Related Microsoft Knowledge Base articles:	n/a
Other related information:	n/a
Author:	Neil Pike

systemdatabasescanbedeleted

Q: Which SQL Server databases can I safely delete?

A: Obviously, any user databases you have created yourself.

pubs and Northwind (SQL 7.0 and above) are really just there as examples, but there have been reports of service packs failing to install when these are deleted, so be aware of this before deleting them.

master, tempdb, and model should never be deleted.

msdb, found in SQL 6.0 and above, can be deleted if you don't ever want to run any scheduled jobs or keep backup history, but I strongly advise against deleting it. For SQL 7.0 and above, it is more important as it is holds the local DTS packages and the repository/Meta Data services tables.

Reference

v1.01 2000.06.06	
Applies to SQL Server versions:	All
FAQ category:	Server Administration and Tools
Related FAQ articles:	n/a
Related Microsoft Knowledge Base articles:	n/a
Other related information:	n/a
Author:	Neil Pike

tapecompat

Q: I can't use a tape drive with SQL Server, but it works OK with NT Backup. Why?

A: SQL 6.5 and below have compatibility problems with certain tape drives—usually because the tape driver advertises a block size that is too big for SQL to handle. With SQL 7.0 this problem goes away because SQL uses the NT Backup code and format and so any tape drive that works with NT backup *should* work with SQL 7.0 and above.

However, SQL Server will only work with drivers that support the TAPE_DRIVE_REVERSE_POSITION SCSI command. It uses this to skip back a filemark when handling end-of-media or malformed-media errors. NT Backup doesn't necessarily use this, so it is possible for a driver or drive that doesn't support this to work with NT Backup, but not with SQL Server. This is the case with some QIC-style (IDE-attached) tape units. In this case you will need to find a driver that supports this command, or get a different tape unit.

You can diagnose the problem on SQL 6.5 and earlier using a tapetest.exe tool. These are available from Microsoft PSS and have also been uploaded to `http://www.swynk.com/sql` in their library area. They are GUI-based and their usage is obvious.

It sometimes helps to try upgrading the firmware on your tape unit. But usually it is the driver that needs changing.

Check the vendor's Web site (`http://www.quantum.com`) which has updated DLT drivers.

Try applying the latest NT Service Pack (many drivers come with these). Specifically there is a bug with SQL 6.5 SP5a where it needs a driver from NT 4.0 SP4 or above for 4mm dat drives to work properly (otherwise it gets an error 87).

If you have licenses for a third-party backup utility that dumps in Microsoft standard format, try a driver from here instead of the NT-supplied one. I find that BEI Ultrabac drivers work well with SQL Server (`http://www.ultrabac.com`). Earlier versions of Arcada, Seagate, Veritas, and Backup Exec didn't, but newer ones do.

The last one leads to another workaround: If you use a third-party backup tool and it has an SQL agent, the tape unit will definitely work because SQL is writing to the named-pipes or VDI interface, and it is the third-party backup software and drivers that do the physical writing to the tape device.

Reference

v1.04 1999.12.30

Applies to SQL Server versions:	All
FAQ categories:	Server Administration and Tools, Troubleshooting
Related FAQ articles:	n/a
Related Microsoft Knowledge Base articles:	n/a
Other related information:	n/a
Author:	Neil Pike

tapeloader

Q: Does SQL Server support tape loaders?

A: SQL doesn't have tape loader support, so it will only use the first tape in a device.

You can use tape loaders with SQL Server by buying one of the third-party backup tools that work with SQL Server agents. These do dumps from SQL Server via named pipes (6.5) or VDI (7.0 and above) and then utilize their own drivers for device support.

Examples include:

- BEI Ultrabac: `http://www.ultrabac.com`
- CAI Arcserve: `http://www.cai.com/arcserveit/`
- Legato: `http://www.legato.com`
- Veritas Backup Exec: `http://www.veritas.com`
- Tivoli ADSM: `http://www.tivoli.com`

Reference

v1.01 2000.05.14

Applies to SQL Server versions:	All
FAQ category:	Server Administration and Tools
Related FAQ articles:	n/a
Related Microsoft Knowledge Base articles:	n/a
Other related information:	n/a
Author:	Neil Pike

tempdbinramrecommended

Q: Should I use tempdb in RAM?

A: The short answer is no. In almost all cases you are better off just letting SQL have the extra memory for caching.

Support for tempdb in RAM has been removed in SQL 7.0.

As an alternative, there is nothing stopping you from using an NT-level RAM drive—several exist—and putting tempdb on that.

Reference

v1.01 2000.05.14

Applies to SQL Server versions:	4.x, 6.x
FAQ category:	Server Administration and Tools
Related FAQ articles:	n/a
Related Microsoft Knowledge Base article:	Q115050 "INF: When to Use Tempdb in RAM"
Other related information:	n/a
Author:	Neil Pike

tempdbinramsql7

Q: Does SQL 7.0 or 2000 support tempdb in RAM?

A: No, this support has been removed since SQL 6.5.

There is nothing stopping you from using an NT-level RAM drive—several exist—and putting tempdb on that. However, in almost all cases you are better off just letting SQL have the extra memory for caching.

Reference

v1.01 2000.05.14

Applies to SQL Server versions:	7.0, 2000
FAQ category:	Server Administration and Tools
Related FAQ articles:	n/a
Related Microsoft Knowledge Base articles:	n/a
Other related information:	n/a
Author:	Neil Pike

textindexing80004005

Q: Why do I get the error "An unknown full-text failure (80004005) occurred in function EnumCatalogs on full-text catalog" when I try to enable text indexing?

A: The NT account that the MSSQLSERVER service runs under needs administrator privileges on the server in order to access to the registry to create full-text catalogs. Make the account a member of the local Administrators group and it should work fine.

Reference

v1.00 1999.05.26	
Applies to SQL Server version:	7.0
FAQ categories:	Server Administration and Tools, Full Text Indexing, Troubleshooting
Related FAQ articles:	n/a
Related Microsoft Knowledge Base articles:	n/a
Other related information:	n/a
Author:	Neil Pike

traceflagy

Q: What does -y<xxxx> mean as a SQL Server startup option?

A: It is set as a debug option, typically at the request of PSS support to track down certain errors—for example, 604 or 3307. When SQL gets an error specified in the -y options, it takes a snap dump of memory at the time—much like when it intercepts a GPF problem. This can be used to see how SQL Server got into the problem area.

Reference

v1.00 1999.02.25	
Applies to SQL Server versions:	All
FAQ category:	Server Administration and Tools
Related FAQ articles:	n/a
Related Microsoft Knowledge Base articles:	n/a
Other related information:	n/a
Author:	Neil Pike

transferdiagrams

Q: How can I transfer database diagrams?

A: Database diagrams are stored in the dtproperties table, with each diagram being made up of several related rows. The primary row has a property of DtgSchemaOBJECT. The component rows can be identified as having the primary row's id value in their objectid column.

When the two databases are exactly the same, and the destination does not have contain any diagrams, use the following statement:

```
SET IDENTITY_INSERT DestinationDB..dtproperties ON

INSERT DestinationDB..dtproperties
SELECT id, objectid, property, value, lvalue, version
FROM SourceDB..dtproperties T1
WHERE EXISTS(SELECT * FROM SourceDB..dtproperties T2 WHERE T2.property = 'Dtg-
SchemaOBJECT' AND T1.objectid = T2.id)

SET IDENTITY_Insert DestinationDB..dtproperties OFF
```

For SQL 2000, amend the preceding SELECT statement to include the new uvalue column.

To transfer between servers use DTS and the DataPump task, with the preceding SELECT statement as your source, and the dtproperties table as your destination. Remember to set the Enable Identity Insert property of the DataPump to maintain integrity of the data.

For databases that have existing diagrams, you will have to transform the data to ensure you do not try to insert duplicate id values as this is an IDENTITY column, as well as maintaining consistency of the objectid values as outlined previously.

A slightly different bit of SQL code designed for copying the diagrams to another server follows:

```
-- View to simplify diagrams import & export.
-- This can be created in the model database so that it will
-- present in all newly created databases.
CREATE VIEW dbDiagrams
AS
SELECT id, objectid, property, value, lvalue, version
FROM dtproperties d1
WHERE EXISTS(SELECT * FROM dtproperties d2
                              WHERE d2.property = 'DtgSchemaOBJECT' AND
                                             d1.objectid = d2.id)
go
```

In order to move database diagrams from one server to another, the data from dtproperties needs to be copied over. This will work only if the database is identical. The data can be exported using a DataDrivenQueryTask in DTS, BCP, or using a linked server setup. The following code sample can used to move diagrams using linked servers. Create the dbDiagrams view in the databases on both servers.

```
-- [SourceServer] is the name of the linked server &
-- [SourceDb] is the name of the database.
-- Insert only rows with conflicting identity values first.
INSERT dtproperties
SELECT dg2.newobjectid, dg1.property, dg1.value, dg1.lvalue, dg1.version
FROM [SourceServer].[SourceDb].dbo.dbDiagrams dg1 JOIN
(
SELECT d1.objectid, (SELECT MAX(id) FROM dtproperties d3) +
   (SELECT COUNT(*) FROM dbDiagrams d4
    WHERE d4.objectid <= d2.id And
    d4.property = 'DtgSchemaOBJECT') AS newobjectid
FROM [SourceServer].[SourceDb].dbo.dbDiagrams d1 JOIN dbDiagrams d2
ON d1.objectid = d2.id
WHERE d1.property = 'DtgSchemaOBJECT' And d2.property = 'DtgSchemaOBJECT'
) AS dg2
ON dg1.objectid = dg2.objectid
```

```
-- Insert the rest now using explicit identity values.
SET IDENTITY_INSERT dtproperties ON
INSERT dtproperties ( id, objectid, property, value, lvalue, version)
SELECT id, objectid, property, value, lvalue, version
FROM [SourceServer].[SourceDb].dbo.dbDiagrams d1
WHERE NOT EXISTS(SELECT * FROM dbDiagrams d2
                 WHERE d2.property = 'DtgSchemaOBJECT' AND
                       d1.objectid = d2.id)
SET IDENTITY_INSERT dtproperties OFF
```

Reference

v2.00 2000.06.13

Applies to SQL Server versions:	7.0, 2000
FAQ category:	Server Administration and Tools
Related FAQ articles:	"Why can't I see my diagrams on a SQL 7.0 Server when using SQL 2000 Enterprise Manager?" (diagram2000, see page 401)
Related Microsoft Knowledge Base articles:	n/a
Other related information:	n/a
Authors:	Neil Pike, Darren Green, Umachandar Jayachandran

transferoptionssql

Q: How do I transfer data between SQL Server databases or across servers?

A: There are a variety of methods:

- The fastest method for whole databases is to use the DUMP DATABASE and LOAD DATABASE commands. You need to make sure that the databases are the same size and made up of the same segment fragments in the same order. If you do an `sp_help_revdatabase` on both, this will allow you to check the required DDL for this. You can DUMP and LOAD from a local tape device and transport the tape if you do not have a network connection. (With SQL 7.0/2000 the commands are BACKUP DATABASE and RESTORE DATABASE.)

- If you only want tables and data you can use the SQL BCP.EXE tool. This is a command-line program and is fully documented in the Books Online. It works on one table at a time and allows you to create a flat file on disk.

- For stored procedures and views there is an old command-line based tool called DEFNCOPY.EXE that works like BCP. It isn't used much these days unless you still have SQL Server on OS/2—though it still works on NT at least up until 6.5.

- SQL Enterprise Manager comes with a built-in GUI transfer function. This allows transfer of all objects between two databases or servers but requires a network connection between the two.

- The transfer tool supplied with SQL Enterprise Manager is exposed via the DMO interface and can be called using the SQLOLE calls from T-SQL or your own VB program for automation purposes. See the Knowledge Base article Q152801 "INF: Examples of Sp_OA Procedure Use and SQLOLE.Transfer Object" for an example of how to do this.

- For SQL 7.0 and above the obvious choice is to use Data Transformation Services. You can transfer objects and data by simply using the Import/Export Wizard to build a package based on the DataPump/Transform Data task. The TransferObjects task can be used to move all objects as well as tables, and supports the transfer of keys, indexes and pemissions as well as just data. In SQL 2000 there is also the Transfer Database task, which greatly simplifies the task of transferring an entire database.

- Third-party DBMS management tools no doubt offer similar or better transfer or scripting tools.

Reference

v1.04 2000.05.27

Applies to SQL Server versions:	All
FAQ category:	Server Administration and Tools
Related FAQ article:	"I need to move SQL Server to a new NT server. What are my options?" (movesqltonewserver, see page 271)
Related Microsoft Knowledge Base article:	Q152801 "INF: Examples of Sp_OA Procedure Use and SQLOLE.Transfer Object"
Other related information:	n/a
Author:	Neil Pike

unixbcp

Q: Why can't I BCP a Unix file into SQL Server? I get "UNEXPECTED EOF" messages.

A: This is because Unix files use just a linefeed (LF, 0x0A) as a record terminator. NT uses a carriage return plus linefeed (CR+LF, 0x0D0A). The BCP \N character resolves to CR+LF.

You have to reformat the file using a tool like AWK/SED/PERL to convert the 0x0D character to 0x0D0A.

Reference

v1.00 1998.11.27	
Applies to SQL Server versions:	All
FAQ categories:	Server Administration and Tools, Trouble-shooting
Related FAQ articles:	n/a
Related Microsoft Knowledge Base articles:	n/a
Other related information:	n/a
Author:	Neil Pike

win95sqlem

Q: What can't I do with SQL Enterprise Manager under Windows 9x?

A: Windows 9x does not support Windows NT service control APIs. Therefore, you cannot start, stop or inquire on the status of the SQL Server service.

Everything else should work, but many people have reported Windows 9x crashes when running SQL utilities. This is due to bugs in the network stack or drivers being used. Upgrading to the latest fixes for Windows 9x may help with this.

While this refers to SQL Server Enterprise Manager, it is worth noting that OLAP Manager (Analysis Services) cannot be installed Windows 9x clients.

Reference

v1.01 2000.06.02	
Applies to SQL Server versions:	6.5, 7.0, 2000
FAQ category:	Server Administration and Tools
Related FAQ articles:	n/a
Related Microsoft Knowledge Base articles:	n/a
Other related information:	n/a
Author:	Neil Pike

xcopynowork

Q: Why can't I do an XCOPY via xp_cmdshell or a scheduled job?

A: Because XCOPY requires input handles, which these environments do not supply. As an alternative you can use the ROBOCOPY program which is shipped with the NT Resource Kit and is a superset of XCOPY.

Reference

v1.02 2000.04.28	
Applies to SQL Server versions:	All
FAQ categories:	Server Administration and Tools, Trouble-shooting
Related FAQ articles:	n/a
Related Microsoft Knowledge Base article:	Q152134 "PRB: XP_CMDSHELL Does Not Work with XCOPY"
Other related information:	n/a
Author:	Neil Pike

y2kwindow

Q: Can I amend the "window" that SQL Server applies for two-digit dates for Y2K?

A: With SQL 6.5 the answer is no. The date is fixed at 1950. "01-01-01" will be parsed as 2001, and "01-01-49" will be parsed as 1949.

With SQL 7.0 this can be changed:

```
sp_configure 'two digit year cutoff', 2070
go
reconfigure
go
```

This forces SQL Server 7.0 to interpret any two-digit year as occurring between 1971 and 2070. This means that 12/30/70 is interpreted as 12/30/2070 and 1/3/71 is interpreted as 1/3/1971.

This two-digit year cutoff value can be any year that occurs between 1753 and 9999; it can also be set using the Enterprise Manager interface. Right-click the SQL Server name and then click Properties. Set this value at the bottom of the Server Settings tab.

You can also use traceflag 8816 to log all implicit conversions that occur to the errorlog:

```
i.e. "1998-12-22 18:36:51.23 spid7 2-digit year 47 converted to 2047."
```

Reference

v1.01 2000.06.02

Applies to SQL Server versions:	6.5, 7.0, 2000
FAQ category:	Server Administration and Tools
Related FAQ articles:	n/a
Related Microsoft Knowledge Base articles:	n/a
Other related information:	n/a
Author:	Neil Pike

Troubleshooting

This section covers all aspects of troubleshooting such as database corruption, recovery, error message analysis and resolution, queries returning wrong results, and other miscellaneous bugs.

#deleted

Q: I'm getting "#deleted" entries in result sets from ODBC since installing SQL 7.0. What is going on?

A: There are two possibilities:

- It could be a bug that only occurs with ODBC driver 3.70.0623 and a DSN configured with the "Perform translation for character data option," where the SQL Server database has been configured to override the default code pages and Sort Order (see Q236825 listed below). Upgrade to 3.70.0690, which comes with SQL 7.0 SP1 and/or MDAC 2.1 SP2.
- Under certain conditions the Jet engine cannot find a record that has just been updated (see Q128809 listed below).

Troubleshooting

Reference

v1.04 2000.03.20

Applies to SQL Server version:	7.0
FAQ categories:	Troubleshooting, Connectivity
Related FAQ articles:	n/a
Related Microsoft Knowledge Base articles:	Q128809 "ACC: '#Deleted' Errors with Linked ODBC Tables," Q236825 "PRB: #deleted Seen When SQL Server 7.0 Tables Containing Numeric and Text Fields Are Opened"
Other related information:	n/a
Author:	Neil Pike

1112

Q: I'm getting a 1112 error on SQL Server. What's going on?

A: This message will only occur with SQL 4.x and is fixed in all subsequent versions. The only permanent fix is to upgrade to SQL 6.0 or above.

The error occurs if SQL has crashed during the allocation of an extent—this sometimes leaves a "being allocated" bit set in the extent. When SQL needs that extent to expand a table, you get the error because SQL thinks the bit should never be set and some form of corruption has occurred.

Because SQL always allocates extents in the same order, once you get the error you will continue to get it unless you drop some objects and free up extents nearer the start of the database that it can allocate. This delays the time until the next 1112.

To "fix" the error you can get and run a file called 1112.EXE from Microsoft PSS or 1112.ZIP from `ftp.microsoft.com/bussys/sql/transfer`–you will need to contact Microsoft PSS for the password. This contains details of what to do to run it—note the database needs to be in single-user mode at the time. All it does is traverse the extent map and reset any bits that show as "being allocated."

Note this fix only fixes that particular occurrence of the problem. The problem will come back, so move to a supported version of SQL that has a permanent fix for this problem.

Reference

v1.03 2000.09.16

Applies to SQL Server version:	4.x
FAQ category:	Troubleshooting
Related FAQ articles:	n/a
Related Microsoft Knowledge Base articles:	n/a
Other related information:	n/a
Author:	Neil Pike

1203

Q: I'm getting a 1203 error message on SQL Server. What's going on?

A: This error is caused by an internal memory structure problem with SQL Server.

It could be a database corruption—running a `dbcc checkdb/newalloc` is always a good idea.

But usually it is a bug with the SQL Server code (Microsoft's, not yours). Many 1203 errors have been fixed with SQL service packs—make sure you are on the latest one. You can get a list of known 1203 errors and fixes from `http://support.microsoft.com` searching on "kbbug" and "1203."

Reference

v1.02 2000.09.16

Applies to SQL Server version:	All
FAQ category:	Troubleshooting
Related FAQ article:	"What are some good SQL Server books and other reference sources?" (sqlbooks, see page 355)
Related Microsoft Knowledge Base articles:	Search on: "sql" and "1203"
Other related information:	Try newsgroups and discussion groups.
Author:	Neil Pike

1314

Q: I am getting a 1314 error when I run xp_cmdshell commands. Why?

A: The full error message is

```
Msg 50001, Level 1, State 50001
xpsql.c: Error 1314 from LogonUser on line xxx
```

The usual reason for this error is that the NT user account concerned (either the account that the MSSQLSERVER service is running under or SQLCMDExec) is not an administrative account on the NT server concerned. If it is not, either make it one or grant it the "Replace a process level token" user right via the NT User Manager applet.

Reference

v1.01 2000.03.25

Applies to SQL Server version:	6.5
FAQ category:	Troubleshooting
Related FAQ articles:	n/a
Related Microsoft Knowledge Base article:	Q171291 "PRB: Non SA CmdExec Task or Xp_cmdshell May Cause Error 1314"
Other related information:	n/a
Author:	Neil Pike

1501

Q: I'm getting a "sort failed 1501" message on SQL Server. What's going on?

A: This is usually caused by a timeout when creating an index—if you see "state 12" after the 1501, it definitely is. This hard-coded timeout was increasedwith SQL 6.5 SP3 and is rarely seen now (though it still sometimes occurs). It is normally caused by a slow or congested disk subsystem—either get some faster disks and controllers or make sure that no other processes are contending on the same disks at the time of the query that causes the error.

If the above doesn't help, you can try increasing the "sort pages" parameter in sp_configure. This may keep more of the sort in memory and reduce the iterations it goes through and thus prevent the error.

Other than that, all you can do is contact Microsoft PSS with the error message, including the state number, and let them delve through the code to see what piece of code the state message you're getting is in (the state codes are unique).

Reference

v1.01 2000.03.09

Applies to SQL Server version:	6.x
FAQ category:	Troubleshooting
Related FAQ articles:	n/a
Related Microsoft Knowledge Base articles:	n/a
Other related information:	n/a
Author:	Neil Pike

1608

Q: I am getting an error 1608 on SQL Server. What can I do?

A: The full error text is: "A network error was encountered while sending results to the front end. Check the SQL server error log for more information."

The usual cause of this error is that a client has been turned off, GPF'd, or the client program has stopped listening on the connection the results are coming back on.

A network trace (performed with Microsoft Network Monitor) is needed at the client and server end to verify this.

Reference

v1.02 2000.03.20

Applies to SQL Server versions:	All
FAQ category:	Troubleshooting
Related FAQ articles:	n/a
Related Microsoft Knowledge Base article:	See references in Q135684 "INFO: Frequently Asked Questions About Microsoft SQL Server"
Other related information:	Search Books Online 6.x on "1608"
Author:	Neil Pike

2503

Q: I am getting an error "Msg 2503, Level 16, State 1 Table Corrupt" on my SQL Server. What can I do?

A: The full error message is "Msg 2503, Level 16, State 1 Table Corrupt: Page linkage is not consistent; check the following pages: current page#=xxx; page# pointing to this page=yyyy; previous page#=zzzz."

Make sure that your error is a "real" 2503 by running the DBCC in single-user mode because it can be spuriously reported if updates are occurring at the time as the DBCC.

At this point if you have a good backup and will not lose any data, now is the time to use it. If you don't have a good backup, look at your backup procedures! To try to resolve the problem read on:

Use DBCC PAGE (documented in Books Online) to determine whether the page is a data or index page. If it is an index page, you are in luck and you may be able to drop and re-create the index.

If it is not an index page or this does not work, you will need to transfer all the data and objects into a new database. For the problem tables this may not work because the page chain is broken, so you will probably need to manually select out data in ranges based on keys above and below the broken point.

Once you have transferred all the objects across, drop the old database and rename the new one.

If you don't want to transfer all the data across, you can just transfer the broken table. When this is done, rename the broken table by directly updating its name in sysobjects. Then create a new table with the old name. Make sure no other errors are in the database before doing this. Also, make sure you re-create any views or stored procedures that reference the table so that they start pointing to the new one.

If the above is not possible because of the size of the database or for other reasons, your only alternative is to pay for Microsoft PSS support. They may be able to patch the pointers in the tables or pages directly for you. However, this sort of fix is not guaranteed and is done (if at all) on a best-effort basis totally at your risk.

Reference

v1.01 2000.03.11

Applies to SQL Server versions:	4.x, 6.x
FAQ category:	Troubleshooting
Related FAQ articles:	n/a
Related Microsoft Knowledge Base articles:	n/a
Other related information:	"2503" and "Associating a Page with an Object" in Books Online 6.x
Author:	Neil Pike

2521

Q: I am getting an error 2521 on my SQL Server. What can I do?

A: The full error is "Msg 2521, Level 16, State 1, Server <xxx>, Table Corrupt: Page is linked but not allocated; check the following pages and table: alloc page#=xxx extent id=6676856 logical page#=6676856 object id in extent=8 (object name = syslogs) index id in extent=0."

Make sure that the error is a "real" 2521 by running the DBCC in single-user mode because it can be spuriously reported if updates are occurring at the time of the DBCC. Make sure there are no other errors in the DBCC either. Note that 6.5 service pack 5a greatly reduces the probability of getting spurious 2521 errors while users are updating the database.

At this point if you have a good backup and will not lose any data, now is the time to use it. If you don't have a good backup, look at your backup procedures! However, note that pages with a 2521 condition are missed during a database dump, so make sure you go back to a good backup. To try to resolve the problem read on:

Use DBCC PAGE (documented in Books Online) to determine whether the page is a data or index page. If it is an index page, you are in luck and you may be able to drop and re-create the index.

If it is not an index page or this does not work, you will need to transfer all the data and objects into a new database. It must be a different database because otherwise the pages your table is using that aren't allocated may be allocated for the new table and cause more problems. If the transfer fails, manually select out data in ranges based on keys above and below the broken point.

Then drop the old table, re-create it and transfer the data back in.

If the above is not possible because of the size of the database or for other reasons, your only alternative is to pay for Microsoft PSS support. They may be able to patch the pointers in the tables or pages directly for you. However, this sort of fix is not guaranteed and is done (if at all) on a best-effort basis totally at your risk.

Reference

v1.01 2000.03.11

Applies to SQL Server versions:	4.x, 6.x
FAQ category:	Troubleshooting
Related FAQ articles:	n/a
Related Microsoft Knowledge Base article:	Q132448 "INF: Using DBCC FIX_AL"
Other related information:	"2521" and "Associating a Page with an Object" in Books Online 6.x
Author:	Neil Pike

17122

Q: Why am I getting an error "17122: InitdatWarning: Could not set working size to <xxx>K"?

A: The reason for this error is that you are trying to set a working size for a non-fixed memory configuration.

Either turn the "set working set size" advanced sp_configure option to 0 (the default), or set "min server memory" and "max server memory" to the same value.

Reference

v1.00 2000.06.13	
Applies to SQL Server versions:	7.0, 2000
FAQ category:	Troubleshooting
Related FAQ articles:	n/a
Related Microsoft Knowledge Base articles:	n/a
Other related information:	n/a
Author:	Neil Pike

17832

Q: I am getting an error 17832 on SQL Server. What can I do?

A: Error 17832, "Unable to read login packet(s)," occurs if a client never successfully completes an attempt to connect because of some usually intermittent failure. If your users are not complaining of problems, ignore it. Otherwise check out Q169521 for some possible reasons for the error. It also could be a configuration or firmware problem on your switches or bridges.

Reference

v1.02 2000.03.20	
Applies to SQL Server versions:	All
FAQ categories:	Troubleshooting, Connectivity
Related FAQ articles:	n/a
Related Microsoft Knowledge Base article:	Q169521 "INF: How to Troubleshoot SQL Server Communication Error 17832"
Other related information:	n/a
Author:	Neil Pike

28000

Q: After applying SP5a/MDAC2.1 to our servers we get the following problem with replication: "28000[Microsoft][ODBC SQL Server Driver][SQL Server] Login failed." Why?

A: This is because MDAC has updated DLL's in <nt>\system32 but not in <sql>\binn (see Knowledge Base article Q216848). Compare the version numbers between the two and replace any older DLL's in BINN with the newer ones from the NT directory:

```
DBNMPNTW.DLL
DBMSRPCN.DLL
DBMSSOCN.DLL
DBMSSPXN.DLL
DBMSVINN.DLL
DBMSADSN.DLL
DBMSSHRN.DLL
```


Reference

v1.01 2000.03.20

Applies to SQL Server version:	6.5
FAQ category:	Troubleshooting, Installation and Upgrades
Related FAQ articles:	n/a
Related Microsoft Knowledge Base article:	Q216848 "BUG: MDAC: SQL Server Driver May Return Error 'Login Failed'"
Other related information:	n/a
Author:	Neil Pike

4409sp5

Q: I am getting an error 4409 selecting on a view ever since I applied SP5 or SP5a to SQL 6.5. What's wrong?

A: This is a bug introduced with SP5. You should contact Microsoft PSS for a hot-fix — build 422 and greater contain this fix. Therefore SP6 will contain the fix if and when it is released.

Reference

v1.05 2000.05.25

Applies to SQL Server version:	6.5
FAQ category:	Troubleshooting
Related FAQ articles:	n/a
Related Microsoft Knowledge Base articles:	Q219413 "FIX: Select on a View May Generate Error 4409,", Q218834 "BUG: Select with ANSI Joins Against View with Union Operator and ANSI Joins Fails with Error 4409"
Other related information:	n/a
Author:	Neil Pike

5302

Q: Why is my application locking up in SQL Server? If I check the locks, I am seeing syscolumns being blocked.

A: This is due to a documented change in SQL 6.5 because tables created by using SELECT INTO hold to the ACID (atomicity, consistency, isolation, durability) transaction properties. This also means that system resources, such as pages, extents, and locks, are held for the duration of the SELECT INTO statement. With larger system objects, this leads to the condition where many internal tasks can be blocked by other users performing SELECT INTO statements.

For example, on high-activity servers, many users running the SQL Enterprise Manager tool to monitor system processes can block on each other, which leads to a condition where the SEM application appears to stop responding. (This happens on tempdb, which is the biggest problem with this new feature for most users.)

You can revert to the old 6.0 and below behavior where these locks are not held by applying at least SQL 6.5 ServicePack 1 and then setting traceflag 5302 on startup.

It is recommended that you amend your application to not use SELECT INTO, or if you do, create the table using `SELECT ... INTO .... WHERE 1=0` to create the table and then use standard inserts to populate the table.

(This problem does not occur in SQL 7.0 and above, because row-level locks are taken and so system table pages aren't unnecessarily blocked.)

Reference

v1.02 2000.03.20

Applies to SQL Server version:	6.5
FAQ category:	Troubleshooting
Related FAQ articles:	n/a
Related Microsoft Knowledge Base article:	Q153441 "FIX: SELECT INTO Locking Behavior"
Other related information:	n/a
Author:	Neil Pike

602

Q: Why do I get an error "Msg 602, Level 21, State 3. Could not find row in Sysindexes for dbid 'x', object 'yyyyyyyy', index 'z'." when running a SQL Server query?

A: It could be that a stored procedure is referencing a table that has been dropped. Recreating the stored procedure will show whether this is the case.

First of all, the problem could be a corruption exactly as the message says. Run a `dbcc checktable` against sysindexes on the database concerned. Also try a `dbcc checkcatalog`.

If these return clean, the problem is a SQL bug. There are lots of bugs and fixes for 602 errors. Look for reasons for this bug at `http://support.microsoft.com`—just search on "602" and "SQL" and "kbbug." If your problem does not match any of these reasons and you have already applied the latest service pack, either post a reproduction script for an MVP to report for you or call the problem in to Microsoft PSS yourself.

Reference

v1.02 2000.05.25

Applies to SQL Server version:	All
FAQ category:	Troubleshooting
Related FAQ articles:	n/a
Related Microsoft Knowledge Base articles:	Search on "602" and "SQL" and "kbbug."
Other related information:	Search Books Online 6.x on "602"
Author:	Neil Pike

603sp5

Q: I am getting an error 603 restoring a database ever since I applied SP5 to SQL 6.5 What's wrong?

A: This is a nasty bug that slipped through the cracks in SP5 testing and betas—the build for SP5 is 415. It is caused when someone runs `sp_sysbackuphistory`–the most common way to do this is just to go into the Backup/Restore GUI (you don't even have to do anything).

The fixed build is 416 and is known as SP5a. I would recommend all SQL users make sure they use this SP rather than SP5. Using build 416, it is possible to load "corrupt" dumps by setting trace flag 3282.

This build also contains a number of other hot-fixes that did not make SP5 but were in the base build that Microsoft applied this fix to.

If you are already on SP5 (415), the only files you need to update are sqlservr.exe (and .dbg) and opends60.dll (and .dbg).

Reference

v1.05 2000.03.20

Applies to SQL Server version:	6.5
FAQ category:	Troubleshooting
Related FAQ articles:	n/a
Related Microsoft Knowledge Base article:	Q215458 "FIX: LOAD DATABASE Fails with Error 603"
Other related information:	n/a
Author:	Neil Pike

603sql60

Q: I am getting an error 603 on database recovery in a SQL 6.0 system. What's wrong?

A: This happens only on SQL 6.0 SP3. There is no fix, but the workaround is:

1. Stop SQL Server.
2. Rename sqlservr.exe in <sql>\binn to sqlservr.sp3.
3. Copy the sqlservr.exe from your SQL 6.0 CD into <sql>\binn.
4. Restart SQL Server. It should now recover OK.
5. Stop SQL Server.
6. Rename <sql>\binn\sqlservr.exe to sqlservr.org for later use.
7. Rename <sql>\binn\sqlservr.sp3 to sqlservr.exe.
8. Restart SQL Server.

The database may still be marked as suspect—if so, then use the sp_resetstatus procedure (as per Books Online) to change the status back to normal.

Reference

v1.01 2000.03.20

Applies to SQL Server version:	6.0
FAQ category:	Troubleshooting
Related FAQ articles:	n/a
Related Microsoft Knowledge Base article:	Q157845 "BUG: Errors 603, 3313 and 3414 May Mark Database as Suspect"
Other related information:	n/a
Author:	Neil Pike

605

Q: I am getting an error 605 on SQL Server. What can I do?

A: This problem is caused by a cross-link in the page chains of two or more tables, causing them to point to each other's data. Make sure that the problem is a "real" 605 by running the DBCC in single-user mode, because this error can be spuriously reported if updates are occuring at the time of the DBCC. These spurious errors are also known as "transient" because they are not repeatable and do not indicate an actual corruption.

At this point if you have a good backup and will not lose any data, now is the time to use it. If you don't have a good backup, look at your backup procedures! To try to resolve the problem read on:

First, if you haven't already done a full `DBCC checkdb/newalloc`, then do one. You need to ascertain how much corruption exists. You may have one 605 or hundreds—there may also be other corruptions. Make sure you have a backup at this point, just in case attempts to fix things make things worse.

Use `DBCC PAGE` (documented in Books Online) to determine whether the page is a data or index page.

If it is an index page, you are in luck and you may be able to drop and recreate the index.

If it is not an index page or this does not work, you will need to transfer all the data and objects into a new database. For the problem tables this may not work because the page chain is broken, so you will probably need to manually select out data in ranges based on keys above and below the broken points.

Once you have transferred all the objects across, drop the old database and rename the new one.

If you don't want to transfer all the data across, you can just transfer the broken tables. When this is done, rename the broken tables by directly updating their name in sysobjects. Then create new tables with the old names. Make sure no other errors are in the database first. Make sure you also recreate any views or stored procedures that reference the tables so that they start pointing to the new ones.

If the above is not possible because of the size of the database or other reasons, your only alternative is to pay for Microsoft PSS support. They may be able to patch the pointers in the tables or pages directly for you. However, this sort of fix is not guaranteed and is done (if at all) on a best-effort basis totally at your risk.

Reference

v1.03 2000.05.25	
Applies to SQL Server versions:	All
FAQ category:	Troubleshooting
Related FAQ articles:	n/a
Related Microsoft Knowledge Base articles:	n/a
Other related information:	Search Books Online for "605"
Author:	Neil Pike

610and925

Q: Why do I get an error "610 - Maximum number of databases that may be accessed by a transaction is <x>. This number has been exceeded by this query." when running a SQL Server query?

A: There is also a very similar error 925.

Assuming the query doesn't really access more than <x> databases, this is a SQL bug caused by a complex query that has confused the SQL parser/optimizer.

It could also be that you're using more than 15 temporary tables—this message isn't very meaningful in this case. Do a `showplan` and see whether this might be the case.

Look for any known reasons for this bug at `http://support.microsoft.com`–just search on "610" (or "925") and "SQL" and "kbbug." If your problem does not match any of these reasons and you have already applied the latest service pack, either post a reproduction script for an MVP to report for you or call the problem in to Microsoft PSS yourself.

Reference

v1.02 2000.03.21	
Applies to SQL Server versions:	All
FAQ category:	Troubleshooting
Related FAQ articles:	n/a
Related Microsoft Knowledge Base article:	Q225490 "BUG: Error 610 When a Query Generates More than 15 Worktables"
Other related information:	n/a
Author:	Neil Pike

702

Q: Why do I get an error "Error: 702, Severity: 20, State: 1" running a SQL Server query?

A: The full message continues: "Memory request for 2928 bytes exceeds the size of single page of 2044 bytes." This error only affects SQL 6.5 and below.

This is a SQL bug and cannot be fixed other than by rewriting the query in a different way—there is no way to expand SQL's page size.

Some reasons for this bug are already documented in `http://support.microsoft.com`–just search on "702" and "sql server." If your problem does not match any of these reasons and you have already applied the latest service pack, either post a reproduction script for an MVP to report for you or call the problem in to Microsoft PSS yourself.

Reference

v1.02 2000.03.21	
Applies to SQL Server versions:	4.x, 6.x
FAQ category:	Troubleshooting
Related FAQ articles:	n/a
Related Microsoft Knowledge Base articles:	Search on "702" and "sql server"
Other related information:	n/a
Author:	Neil Pike

80004005

Q: I'm getting an error "80004005" message connecting to SQL Server. What's going on?

A: This is an ODBC/ADO error message and is a generic one—all it tells you is that an error has occurred. After the error number is a description giving specific information on what is going on. To debug this message, look at Q183060 in the Microsoft Knowledge Base.

Reference

v1.03 2000.03.21	
Applies to SQL Server versions:	All
FAQ category:	Troubleshooting
Related FAQ article:	Q183060 "INFO: Troubleshooting Guide for 80004005 & Other Error Messages"
Related Microsoft Knowledge Base article:	n/a
Other related information:	n/a
Author:	Neil Pike

8623

Q: Why do I get this error under SQL 7.0 when the query worked OK under 6.5? "Msg 8623, Internal Query Processor Error: The query processor could not produce a query plan."

A: One reason for this error is that it is a bug that happens with some complex queries on single-processor machines. The problem does not occur on multiple-processor machines. It has been reported as a bug to Microsoft and is fixed in SP2.

Reference

v1.01 2000.03.21	
Applies to SQL Server version:	7.0
FAQ category:	Troubleshooting
Related FAQ articles:	n/a
Related Microsoft Knowledge Base articles:	Search on "8623" and "sql server"
Other related information:	n/a
Author:	Neil Pike

accessdenied

Q: I'm getting an "access denied," "CreateFile" or "1326" message when connecting to SQL Server. What should I do?

A: The message may be one of the following:

```
Msg No 10004 Severity 9  State 0
Unable to connect: SQL Server is unavailable or does not exist.  Access denied

Microsoft OLE DB Provider for ODBC Drivers error '80004005'
[Microsoft][ODBC SQL Server Driver][dbnmpntw]ConnectionOpen(CreateFile()).

MSG 10004, Severity 9.( sqlserver not available).  OS 1326
```

This is not a SQL Server issue, it is an NT issue. If you are using a Net-Lib that requires NT authentication—for example, Named Pipes or Multiprotocol with 6.5 or below or any Net-Lib with 7.0—then you *must* be able to authenticate to the copy of NT running SQL Server.

You can test whether you can do this by doing a `NET VIEW \\servername` from a command prompt on the client. If you get an access denied message, or get prompted for a password, then you aren't being authenticated.

If this happens, you need to set up a trust between the domains. Or, you could use a Net-Lib that does not need authentication —for example, TCP-IP Sockets.

If you can't have a trust (and really this *is* the best method) then you can override your NT account details by doing a `net use \\<server>\ipc$ /user:<serverdomain>\<userid> <password>` with an account that is in the domain. But this is a manual process and prone to fail when the password changes.

Note that the above override technique will not work with Win9x clients because these do not support the passing of credentials in this manner.

Reference

v1.03 2000.05.25	
Applies to SQL Server versions:	All
FAQ categories:	Troubleshooting, Security, Connectivity
Related FAQ articles:	n/a
Related Microsoft Knowledge Base articles:	Q175671 "PRB: 80004005 ConnectionOpen (CreateFile()) Error Accessing SQL," Q183060 "INFO: Troubleshooting Guide for 80004005 & Other Error Messages"
Other related information:	"Troubleshooting SQL Installation and Connection Problems" at `http://support.microsoft.com/support/tshoot/default.asp`
Author:	Neil Pike

accessviolation

Q: I am getting a message "dbprocess dead" or "language exec" from SQL Server. I am seeing an "Exception Access Violation" message in the SQL errorlog. I am getting an error "SqlDumpExceptionHandler: Process <x> generated fatal exception." I am getting *.DMP files in the <sql>\log directory. I am getting "symptom dump" messages. What is going on?

A: Basically SQL is internally GPFing or AVing (they are the same thing). You should see one or more of the above messages in the SQL errorlog.

There are only three reasons for this to happen (in order of ascending probability):

- A database corruption. You should rule this out by running DBCC checkdb, newalloc and checkcatalog commands.
- A hardware problem. Usually a faulty SIMM or DIMM memory chip. Run vendor-supplied diagnostic routines and/or sqlhdtst/sql7iostress utilities to check out the hardware. See Q231619 "INF: SQL70IO Stress Utility to Stress Disk Subsystem" and Q135582 "INF: SQL Server Utility Files Available."

- Bugs in the SQL Server code. (This is the most likely cause—a database corruption rarely cause GPFs, and hardware errors normally show up in other ways.) This is the Microsoft C code that makes up SQLSERVR.EXE and associated DLL's, *not* your T-SQL code. If you have SQL code that causes an AV, it is Microsoft's bug, not yours. There is nothing anyone outside of Microsoft support can do to help you.

Assuming the problem is not a database corruption or hardware fault, try the following diagnostic process:

1. Check the Microsoft Knowledge Base on TechNet (if you don't have TechNet, order it now!). Also check the on-line Web site at `http://support.microsoft.com`, which is more up to date than TechNet. Search on "kbbug*" and "AV" and "SQL Server" to find all documented AV bugs—note that AV's are a generic symptom of lots of bugs. Many articles contain workarounds but it is usually difficult to match up the stack traces listed to see if one of the workarounds is relevant to your problem.

2. Are you on the latest version of SQL Server and the latest service pack? Microsoft fixes a lot of AV errors in every service pack, so it is definitely worth getting current. If you're not on the latest service pack, that is the first thing Microsoft is going to ask you to do if you contact them anyway. If you can't apply it to the production system immediately, apply the latest SP on a test system and see if it fixes the problem.

3. Check the SQL errorlog and save all the messages—especially anything telling you what SQL was being executed at the time.

4. Check the \<sql>\LOG directory for SQLxxxx.DMP files that may have been created. These contain information on what SQL Server was doing at the time, such as module stack traces. Save these for Microsoft support as necessary. (Though there is a PRINTDMP.EXE utility supplied, the output of this is still of limited use without the SQL Server C source code, although you can sometimes see the SQL command being run and who was running it.)

5. Can you recreate the problem at will? If the SQL being run is not shown in the errorlog, find out what the user or developer was doing at the time. Use SQL Trace/Profiler to capture the actual SQL code being run if you can. If you can't recreate it, it's still worth reporting as long as you have the errorlogs and dump files.

6. If you can recreate the problem, see if you can create a reproduction script to show the problem. This needs to be capable of running on a brand new install of SQL Server on a new database. Therefore it needs to contain all

tables, user defined data types, triggers and views needed to show the problem. If it needs data, try to keep this to a minimum. (If the script or data is reasonably short, post to one of the newsgroups and one of the MVP's can report it to Microsoft for you). Alternatively, rewrite your query (if possible) to run against the pubs or Northwind (version 7 only) database as these are always installed with SQL Server and come complete with a variety of tables, foreign keys, indices and data.

7. Can you work around the problem by rewriting the SQL? Even with a reproduction script, Microsoft is unlikely to turn a fix around quickly—unless you are a multi-million dollar customer. Even then, you wouldn't just be applying one small fix. It would be a latest build with lots of other fixes too—it won't have been regression tested, so it could cause more problems than it fixed anyway.

8. If SQL Server terminates from the Access Violation and there is no dump file produced, a possible cause of the problem is the use of SQL Trace. There is a bug in this (fixed in 6.5 SP5 and above) that can terminate the SQL Server being monitored. Another cause of this problem is heavy deadlocking—also fixed in SP5a.

9. Report the problem to Microsoft PSS. *Please* do this even if you can work around it. Unless Microsoft gets these bug reports, they can't fix the bugs. See the "MSPSS" FAQ article for more details.

Microsoft will need you to supply:

- SQL Errorlogs
- NT event logs, if any NT errors were occuring at the time
- T-SQL code running at the time
- Details of hardware, version of NT, and service packs. WINMSD output is good for this.

With SQL 7.0 there is a new utility that will garner most of this information for you automatically. It is called sqldiag:

```
sqldiag -U login -P password [-O output_file]
```

Reference

v1.02 2000.03.25

Applies to SQL Server versions:	All
FAQ category:	Troubleshooting
Related FAQ articles:	"Why is a reproduction (repro) script used to report a SQL Server bug?" (reproscript, see page 530), "How can I report a SQL Server bug to Microsoft?" (bugreport, see page 495), "What is Microsoft Product Support Services and how do I contact them?" (MSPSS, see page 517)
Related Microsoft Knowledge Base articles:	See references in article.
Other related information:	n/a
Author:	Neil Pike

ansiwarnings

Q: Why do I get arithmetic overflows and "string truncated" errors with SQL 7.0? I didn't with 6.5.

A: Look up the SET ANSI_WARNINGS ON/OFF command and option in the Books Online. To meet ANSI standards the default for this is ON.

When it is ON, any numeric summarization function with a NULL will result in an error. Also, trying to fit 23 characters in a 20-byte field will produce the error.

Either fix the code concerned (the best option), or turn the warnings off.

Reference

v1.01 2000.03.28

Applies to SQL Server version:	7.0
FAQ categories:	Troubleshooting, Installation and Upgrades
Related FAQ article:	"Should I upgrade to SQL 7.0? Why or why not? What are the known bugs? What other differences are there between 6.5 and 7.0?" (sql7differences, see page 304)
Related Microsoft Knowledge Base articles:	n/a
Other related information:	n/a
Author:	Neil Pike

assertions

Q: Why do I get an error "SQL Server Assertion : File:<xxx.c> Line=yyy Failed Assertion='zzz'"?

A: An assertion is typically raised when a program gets to a bit of C code that it shouldn't be possible to enter, or has been entered with wrong parameters. An assertion is raised by the developer to let them know of this bug and to prevent the code running any further and thus cause unknown further problems.

With SQL 6.5, assertions are typically only raised with the debug (checked) version of sqlservr.exe. In the normal supplied version the debug code is removed for performance. Checked versions are normally provided by Microsoft PSS specifically to help a customer track down bugs.

With SQL 7.0 it is possible to get these errors from the normal compiled executables.

In any event, if you get one of these errors then you need to raise it as a paid fault call with Microsoft PSS via your normal support channel.

Reference

v1.02 2000.01.31

Applies to SQL Server version:	All
FAQ category:	Troubleshooting
Related FAQ articles:	n/a
Related Microsoft Knowledge Base articles:	n/a
Other related information:	n/a
Author:	Neil Pike

autodial

Q: When I use some of the SQL Server GUI tools, I get the "dial-up" remote network prompt. How can I disable this?

A: In Windows NT:

1. In Control Panel ⌀ Services, choose Remote Access Autodial Manager.

2. Click Startup and choose Disable.

In Windows 9x:

1. In Dial-Up Networking, click the Connections menu, and then click Settings.

2. Click "Don't prompt" to use Dial-Up Networking.

You may also get problems with Internet Explorer causing the dial-up (usually with SQL 7.0). In this case (for any operating system):

1. In Control Panel, double-click Internet, and then click the Connection tab.

2. In the Connection box, select Connect to the Internet using a local area network.

3. Set a local page to be the IE default page so it doesn't try to open `http://www.microsoft.com` (or another page) automatically.

The last problem only occurs with IE versions less than 5.0.

Reference

v1.05 2000.04.24

Applies to SQL Server versions:	All
FAQ category:	Troubleshooting
Related FAQ articles:	n/a
Related Microsoft Knowledge Base articles:	n/a
Other related information:	n/a
Author:	Neil Pike

backuplognotruncatefails

Q: If I lose my primary data file (MDF) in SQL 7.0, I can't back up the log to recover to a point in time. Why not?

A: A small oversight on Microsoft's part—which is fixed in SQL Server 2000.

Under 6.5 you would do:

```
DUMP TRANSACTION dbname TO dump_device WITH NO_TRUNCATE
```

Under SQL 7.0 this gets you an error:

```
Server: Msg 3446, Level 16, State 1
    Primary file not available for database <xx>
```

This is because the metadata that tells SQL where the files are for the database are in the primary file—in SQL 6.5 this information was held in system tables in master.

A workaround for this is:

1. Use only *one* file in the primary file group (the primary file), and place this file on the same drive (mirrored) as your log files. This gives it the same protection as the log.

2. Add another file group, with one or more files for data—obviously this goes on different disks from the log. Mark this second file group as the default (Alter database).

3. Then, when your data file is lost, backup NO_TRUNCATE will work because the primary file with the metadata (but no user data) is still available.

Reference

v1.01 2000.03.28	
Applies to SQL Server version:	7.0
FAQ categories:	Troubleshooting, Database Administration
Related FAQ articles:	n/a
Related Microsoft Knowledge Base article:	Q218739 "PRB: BACKUP with NO_TRUNCATE Not Possible with Missing Primary Data File"
Other related information:	n/a
Author:	Neil Pike

badtoken

Q: I'm getting a "bad token" error message from SQL Server. What causes this?

A: The full errors for this problem are "Bad token from SQL Server" and "Datastream processing out of sync."

There are lots of things that could cause this problem because it is a generic message that can occur when the TDS code in SQL Server generates invalid packets.

Some articles addressing this are listed in the following Reference section, but always check the Microsoft Knowledge Base for the most up-to-date information.

Few of these errors still exist in SQL 7.0 and higher.

Reference

v1.01 2000.05.25	
Applies to SQL Server versions:	All
FAQ categories:	Troubleshooting, Connectivity
Related FAQ article:	"Where can I get details on the layout of the TDS protocol that SQL Server uses to talk to clients?" (tds, see page 138)
Related Microsoft Knowledge Base articles:	Q199105 "BUG: ROUND Function with NULL Length Returns TDS Error"; Q73215 "PRB: Reasons for Error 10008: Bad Token from SQL Server"; Q152128 "BUG: Multiple TDS Packets Cause 'Bad Token' Error for DBLIB"; Q112700 "BUG: sp_sqlexec with Two Selects Causes Bad Token Error"; Q164215 "FIX: Bad Token or AV If Sp_cursoropen After Dropping Index"; Q138746 "FIX: Cursor w/ Union May Cause Errors if Not First in Batch"; Q147674 "BUG: Cursor Open 533 Error on UNION if MAX or MIN in Subquery"; Q152024 "BUG: DB-Lib Client Apps Access Violation in Ntwdblib.dll"; Q152063 "BUG: DB-Lib Unable to Handle Burst of TDS Packets Under TCP/IP"; Q136390 "BUG: RPC w/ Execute That Changes Database Causes Error 7222"; Q138013 "FIX: DBCC SQLPERF(THREADS) Fails w/ AV on 6.0 SP 1"; Q187857 "FIX: RPC Returns Error 7222 When Re-executed After Canceled RPC"
Other related information:	n/a
Author:	Neil Pike

bcpeof

Q: Why do I get an "UNEXPECTED EOF" message in BCP?

A: Basically because the file layout does not match the one you've specified to BCP. If you are running BCP with interactive responses, try using a BCP format file instead. If you are using a format file, check it carefully by referring to "Using the bcp Format File" in Books Online.

If you have a file where all the fields and records are supposedly a fixed length, make sure there are no different sized records such as header and trailer records.

If you have a native 6.5 format file, make sure you specify the -6 option on the 7.0 version of BCP.

Otherwise, use a hex-editor to open the file and check the layout. Look especially for missing carriage-returns and line-feeds—UNIX files use just a linefeed (LF, 0x0A) as a record terminator. NT used a carriage return plus linefeed (CR+LF, 0x0D0A).

There are also some known bugs with BCP that may cause this—search the Knowledge Base on "Unexpected EOF" and "BCP."

Reference

v1.03 2000.03.30	
Applies to SQL Server versions:	All
FAQ categories:	Troubleshooting, Server Administration and Tools
Related FAQ articles:	n/a
Related Microsoft Knowledge Base articles:	Q238455 "BUG: BCP IN with 4GB or Larger File Fails with Unexpected EOF," Q113728 "BUG: bcp_exec May Cause Unexpected EOF Message"
Other related information:	n/a
Author:	Neil Pike

bcpxpcmdshell

Q: I am having problems with SQL Server running BCP from xp_cmdshell—why does it not run or see the files I want it to?

A: First, make sure you have the rights to run xp_cmdshell—do an `xp_cmdshell 'dir'` and be sure you get a resultset of filenames back.

The MSSQLSERVER service is running under a separate set of NT credentials. It doesn't matter who *you* are logged on as (after all SQL runs quite happily when no one is logged on to the console). Therefore your logon account and any mapped drives are irrelevant. It is SQL Server running the program (BCP), not you.

If you're logged on as "sa" or are still running SQL 4.x, then xp_cmdshell runs with the NT account that the MSSQLSERVER service is configured to run under.

The default set of NT credentials used by MSSQLSERVER is the Localsystem account. You can check what userid MSSQLSERVER is running under by looking at Control Panel ⌀ Services, highlighting MSSQLSERVER and choosing the Start-up option. If no username is present, you are using the localsystem account—this account has no access to shares on the network, because it isn't an authenticated network account.

If you're not logged on as "sa," the credentials that apply depend on how you got permission to run xp_cmdshell:

- With 6.5 and below, if you were granted execute permission on xp_cmdshell, it runs in the security context of the MSSQLSERVER service.

- If you got permission through security option "Use SQLExecutiveCmdExec Account for Non SAs," the credentials are those of the SQLExecutiveCmdExec account.

- With SQL 7.0, users who are not members of the sysadmin group always run xp_cmdshell under the SQLAgentCmdExec account.

- These accounts, SQLExecutiveCmdExec for SQL 6.x and SQLAgentCmdExec for SQL 7.0, are only in the local user group by default.

So, if you want BCP running under xp_cmdshell to access a network resource, you have two choices:

- Change the account the MSSQLSERVER service runs under to a user account with the relevant network rights.

- Amend the following registry value on the TARGET server and add the sharename you want to access—the share does not then authenticate who is coming in and so a localsystem account will work. The server service on the target server must be restarted before the change takes effect. Note that this effectively removes security on that share, so you need to be careful about what is in the share.

```
HKEY_LOCAL_MACHINE\SYSTEM\CurrentControlSet\Services\LanmanServer\
Parameters\NullSessionShares
```

Whichever method you use, you *must* use a UNC name to reference the resources required and not a drive letter:

```
xp_cmdshell 'bcp servername..tablename out \\server01\share\bcp.fil
.............'
```

Reference

v1.02 2000.03.30	
Applies to SQL Server versions:	All
FAQ categories:	Troubleshooting, Application Design and Programming
Related FAQ articles:	n/a
Related Microsoft Knowledge Base article:	Q124184 "Service Running as System Account Fails Accessing Network"
Other related information:	"xp_cmdshell" in Books Online 7
Author:	Neil Pike

bluescreen

Q: I am getting a blue screen, completely hung machine, or server restart on my SQL Server or client. What might be the cause?

A: All the above can *only* be caused by:

- A hardware problem: Dodgy memory SIMMS, an overheating processor, or a cracked motherboard, for example
- Part of NT running in kernel mode: SCSI drivers, network drivers, or video drivers

The vast majority of the SQL Server code runs in user mode, just like any normal program. Therefore it is no more capable of causing a blue screen than something like Word is. It can only "cause" the problem in as much as it stresses the hardware/memory/PCI bus/disk subsystem and exposes a bug in an NT driver. Drivers must typically lock all their memory so that it doesn't get swapped to the pagefile – SQL Server may "cause" un-locked driver pages to be swapped out because of its memory needs. When the driver goes to access the page, boom, blue screen!

The small minority of the code that runs in kernel mode is the SQLPERxx.DLL module (xx = 60 or 70). Because of the way the NT performance monitor works, this code works under the winlogon process rather than sqlserver.exe, and is in kernel mode. To see if this is an issue, rename the sqlperxx.dll and restart SQL. It won't find the DLL and therefore won't load it – SQL performance counters will be disabled.

If you are getting one of these problems, it needs to be investigated like any other NT blue screen problem. Check the driver or program in control at the time, use DUMPEXAM.EXE to look at the dump, apply a newer service pack, upgrade all system drivers, and contact Microsoft PSS for WINNT support if needed.

You also may wish to download and run SQLHDTST (for 6.5) or SQL70IOSTRESS (for 7.0). These stress the hardware in the same way as SQL Server and could be used to show hardware, compatibility or driver problems.

Reference

v1.06 2000.04.01	
Applies to SQL Server versions:	All
FAQ categories:	Troubleshooting
Related FAQ article:	"I am getting a message "dbprocess dead" or "language exec" from SQL Server. I am seeing an "Exception Access Violation" message in the SQL errorlog. I am getting an error "SqlDumpExceptionHandler: Process <x> generated fatal exception." I am getting *.DMP files in the <sql>\log directory. I am getting "symptom dump" messages. What is going on?" (accessviolation, see page 481)
Related Microsoft Knowledge Base articles:	Q170576 "How to Determine When SQL Server Causes a Windows NT Blue Screen" (also in Books Online 7), Q192463 "Gathering Blue Screen Information After Memory Dump"
Other related information:	n/a
Author:	Neil Pike

bobwrite

Q: What does the SQL Server error message "sort: bob write not complete after xx seconds." mean?

A: Bob is the Big Output Buffer. It is used for writing out intermediate tables created during a sort. Because it is doing heavy sequential writes it can stress the disk subsystem.

As long as SQL Server carries on, and no other errors are being reported, there is usually nothing to worry about. The error merely shows that the disk subsystem is unable to keep up with the level of i/o that SQL Server is asking it to handle. SQL just waits and retries these requests.

If the timeout is already high, or the error occurs frequently, then you need to look at the disk subsystem for misconfiguration or bad cabling.

To increase the amount of time that SQL waits before issuing this message and retrying, amend the "resource timeout" parameter via sp_configure.

You *may* need to decrease your max async i/o or max lazywrite i/o if these errors are continuous, invest in a faster disk subsystem, or spread your devices across more of your existing spindles.

Also make sure that non-SQL processes are not causing disk contention.

Reference

v1.01 2000.09.12

Applies to SQL Server version:	All
FAQ category:	Troubleshooting
Related FAQ articles:	n/a
Related Microsoft Knowledge Base articles:	n/a
Other related information:	n/a
Author:	Neil Pike

bufdiscard

Q: What does "bufdiscard: WARNING, page xx (dbid n, bp 0xzzzzzzzz) has stat0x10080(), skipping" mean?

A: This exact message can safely be ignored. It just says that the SQL lazy writer has found a page in an inappropriate state. This can happen, typically on SMP machines. It doesn't indicate there is a problem.

The message is suppressed in later versions of SQL Server.

Other similar-looking messages may indicate a problem, so check the text carefully.

Reference

v1.01 2000.05.25

Applies to SQL Server versions:	4.x, 6.x
FAQ category:	Troubleshooting
Related FAQ articles:	n/a
Related Microsoft Knowledge Base articles:	n/a
Other related information:	n/a
Author:	Neil Pike

bufwait

Q: What do the "bufwait," "writelog" and "buffer latch" errors in SQL Server mean?

A: The following errors can occur:

```
writelog: timeout, dbid <x>, ..........
bufwait: timeout, BUF_IO .....
Time out occurred while waiting for buffer latch type 2, bp 0x11cfc580, page
(0:0), stat 0x405, object ID 7:1:0, waittime 500.  Continuing to wait.
```

As long as SQL Server carries on, and no other errors are being reported, there is usually nothing to worry about. These errors are merely showing that the disk subsystem is unable to keep up with the level of i/o that SQL Server is asking it to handle. SQL just waits and retries these requests. (The message *may* indicate that the disk subsystem is experiencing problems—check the NT event log for SCSI errors and any hardware monitoring tools you have.)

To increase the amount of time that SQL waits before issuing this message and retrying, amend the "resource timeout" parameter via sp_configure. Note that with SQL 6.5 SP4 and above, the timeout is always a minimum of 60 seconds regardless of any lower setting in sp_configure.

You *may* need to decrease your max async i/o (SQL 7.0 and below) or max lazy-write i/o (SQL 6.5 and below) if these errors are continuous, invest in a faster disk subsystem or spread your devices across more of your existing spindles.

If SQL does not automatically carry on, either a memory corruption has occurred with the internal SQL data structures or a hardware error is preventing SQL from getting a response.

Reference

v1.04 2000.05.25

Applies to SQL Server versions:	4.x, 6.x, 7.0, 2000
FAQ category:	Troubleshooting
Related FAQ articles:	n/a
Related Microsoft Knowledge Base article:	Q167711 "INF: Understanding Bufwait and Writelog Timeout Messages"
Other related information:	n/a
Author:	Neil Pike

bugreport

Q: How can I report a SQL Server bug to Microsoft?

A: There are several ways, but the *only* way you can be sure of an engineer looking at it and providing you with a workaround or fix is to report it to Microsoft's PSS (Product Support Services) team. These are people who support all MS's products, write fixes, take the calls and sort out workarounds. They work 24 x 7 x 365. You can call them by phone (in the U.S.: 1-800-936-3500).

For details of your nearest PSS support center and other information try:

- `http://support.microsoft.com/support/supportnet/default.asp`
- `http://www.microsoft.com/support/customer/itpro.htm`

To report a problem on the Web:

- `http://www.microsoft.com/technet/support/incident.asp`
- `http://support.microsoft.com/support/webresponse.asp`

All incidents are chargeable either to your credit card or an existing account. The charge *will* be reimbursed if the problem turns out to be a Microsoft bug, or a feature that hasn't been publicly documented. The person answering the phone cannot know it's a bug, so they have to take your credit card information before passing you on to a technician. When the call is closed the technician decides whether to mark the call as "free," in which case you get a refund automatically. (Microsoft follows the same procedure for reports made on the Web.)

If you don't want to pay for a call, there are "free" e-mail and Web response methods that you can use by e-mailing `ntbugs@microsoft.com`. However, this method merely gets the bugs filed somewhere—it does not currently guarantee that anyone will even look at them, let alone do something about them. You will almost certainly get no feedback so there is no way of knowing what has happened to your bug report.

Can't I report it to a Microsoft newsgroup? Yes, but Microsoft employees do not officially monitor these forums. It is possible that they will notice a bug report, they may even look into it—it's not even unheard of them to contact the person with the problem. However these are all the exception rather than the rule. The newsgroups are there for peer-to-peer support and are not an official bug reporting channel.

If you can provide a reproduction script on the newsgroups, one of the MVP's (we are *not* Microsoft employees!) can pass this to PSS for you. It has a much greater chance of being looked at that way, but again, is not a guarantee. If you do post a repro script, there is a good chance that someone will be able to find you a workaround.

Whatever method you use, in order for Microsoft to resolve a bug they need to recreate it on their systems. The best way to do this is to provide them with a repro script. This needs to show the problem when run on a brand-new install of SQL Server on a new database. Therefore it has to contain all tables, user defined data types, triggers and views needed to show the problem. If it needs data, try to keep this to a minimum.

Reference

v1.04 2000.04.02	
Applies to SQL Server versions:	All
FAQ category:	Troubleshooting
Related FAQ articles:	"Why is a reproduction (repro) script used to report a SQL Server bug?" (reproscript, see page 530), "What is a 'SQL Server MVP' and how do I become one?" (MVP, see page 351)
Related Microsoft Knowledge Base articles:	n/a
Other related information:	n/a
Author:	Neil Pike

couldnotproducequeryplan

Q: A query produces this error in SQL 7.0: "Internal Query Processor Error: The query processor could not produce a query plan." What can I do?

A: This means that the query processor or optimizer is "confused." With SQL 6.5 these sorts of queries would typically produce access violations that could potentially affect the whole of SQL Server. In SQL 7.0 the problem is handled a bit better—with this error being produced.

However, it is still really a bug, and you should report it to Microsoft as a bug.

Sometimes queries will work on SMP systems but not on single-processor systems. This is because query parallelization is available on SMP boxes.

In order for Microsoft to resolve a bug, they need to recreate it on their systems. The best way to do this is to provide them with a repro script—this needs to show the problem when run on a brand-new install of SQL Server on a new database. Therefore it has to contain all tables, user defined data types, triggers and views needed to show the problem. If it needs data, try to keep this to a minimum.

If the script and data are reasonably short, post to one of the newsgroups and one of the MVP's can report it to Microsoft for you. (See FAQ entries "bugreport" and "reproscript" for more information.)

Reference

v1.02 2000.04.15	
Applies to SQL Server version:	7.0
FAQ category:	Troubleshooting
Related FAQ articles:	"How can I report a SQL Server bug to Microsoft?" (bugreport, see page 495), "Why is a reproduction (repro) script used to report a SQL Server bug?" (reproscript, see page 530)
Related Microsoft Knowledge Base article:	Search on "Internal Query Processor Error" for workarounds to specific causes of this error.
Other related information:	n/a
Author:	Neil Pike

currentactivity

Q: I'm not seeing anything in the current activity screen in SQL Enterprise Manager. What's gone wrong?

A: This is usually caused by the "select into/bulkcopy" database attribute for tempdb being unchecked.

Set the option on again using SQL Enterprise Manager or sp_dboption and that should fix it.

Reference

v1.01 2000.04.16	
Applies to SQL Server versions:	All
FAQ categories:	Troubleshooting, Server Administration and Tools
Related FAQ articles:	n/a
Related Microsoft Knowledge Base articles:	Q149695 "PRB: Current Activity in SEM May Not Be Displayed," Q161522 "BUG: Current Activity Blank in Enterprise Manager 6.5" for a related bug in 6.5 service pack 1.
Other related information:	n/a
Author:	Neil Pike

cxpacket

Q: What does a wait type of CXPacket or Exchange mean?

A: You will get this only with versions of SQL that support parallel queries—SQL 7.0 and later. It means that one thread of the query is waiting for a message packet from another, and the one it is waiting for is either blocked by a traditional cause or has hit some sort of parallelism bug.

CXPacket means SQL is waiting for a data packet—e.g., the results of an internal query is being passed. Exchange means that it is waiting for a control packet—i.e., waiting for a child or sibling process to tell you that it is finished.

If the query doesn't complete, make sure the latest service pack is applied because there are several parallel query fixes in each one. If it still doesn't fix it, you have run into an unfixed bug and will need to contact Microsoft PSS and file a bug report. You should be able to work around the problem by adding (MAXDOP=1) as a query hint, which will prevent the query being parallelized.

Reference

v1.03 2000.04.16	
Applies to SQL Server version:	7.0
FAQ category:	Troubleshooting
Related FAQ article:	"How can I report a SQL Server bug to Microsoft?" (bugreport, see page 495)
Related Microsoft Knowledge Base article:	Q244455 " INF: Definition of Sysprocesses Waittype and Lastwaittype Fields for SQL Server 7.0"
Other related information:	n/a
Author:	Neil Pike

dataserversemaphore

Q: Why do I get the message "WARNING: Process being freed while holding Dataserver semaphore" in SQL Server?

A: This is a fairly common error. Try the following:

1. Check for previous errors—this is often not the actual error that occurred but is a symptom of a previous error that has caused SQL Server to get confused. It then ends up trying to exit a routine without having cleared up all the resources that it owns. You should look up the previous error in Technet or the Microsoft Knowledge Base.

2. It can be a symptom of not having enough resources. Increase the number of open objects, locks and open databases. This may help.

3. Apply the latest service pack—this or the underlying error may well have been fixed already.

4. If none of the above apply, and your problem does not match any known, documented issue, you will have to call Microsoft PSS and open a paid fault call. If you can reproduce the problem with a script run against a new, clean database, Microsoft will have a much better chance of identifying a fix.

Reference

v1.01 2000.04.16	
Applies to SQL Server version:	6.x
FAQ category:	Troubleshooting
Related FAQ articles:	"How can I report a SQL Server bug to Microsoft?" (bugreport, see page 495), "Why is a reproduction (repro) script used to report a SQL Server bug?" (reproscript, see page 530)
Related Microsoft Knowledge Base articles:	n/a
Other related information:	n/a
Author:	Neil Pike

datewrong

Q: Why do I get the wrong date in SQL Server when I use `select getdate()`?

A: The usual reason for this is an old bug that caused the date in SQL Server to wrap around after a month or so of continuous running. The date was taken from NT at SQL Server startup, held in an internal variable and updated regularly as SQL Server was running. This internal variable was defined too small for the job.

The bug was fixed in one of the 6.5 service packs—probably SP2. Apply the latest service pack and it should be fixed.

Later versions of SQL Server regularly poll the operating system for the time and so cannot suffer in the same way.

Reference

v1.02 2000.09.12	
Applies to SQL Server versions:	4.x, 6.x
FAQ category:	Troubleshooting
Related FAQ articles:	n/a
Related Microsoft Knowledge Base articles:	n/a
Other related information:	n/a
Author:	Neil Pike

diskreinit

Q: How can I recover a SQL Server database when all I have left is the original .DAT devices or files?

A: For SQL 7.0 use the sp_attach_db stored procedure, documented in Books Online.

For SQL 6.5 and below use the DISK REINIT and DISK REFIT commands. These are also documented in Books Online.

An alternative for SQL 6.5 is the following procedure:

1. Stop SQL Server.
2. Backup or copy the original .dat files on the target server, if any.
3. Start SQL Server.
4. Drop any databases and devices you want to recover, and delete the associated physical files.
5. Create new devices and databases the right size, with the right names and in the right order.
6. Stop SQL Server.
7. Copy the original .dat files over the newly recreated ones.
8. Start SQL Server.

Reference

v1.03 2000.04.21	
Applies to SQL Server versions:	All
FAQ categories:	Troubleshooting, Database Administration
Related FAQ articles:	n/a
Related Microsoft Knowledge Base articles:	n/a
Other related information:	n/a
Author:	Neil Pike

dllhost

Q: What is the dllhost.exe process on my machine that seems to use a lot of CPU?

A: DLLHOST.EXE is used to execute any COM DLL outside the SQL Server address space.

This may be used for a linked-server/OLE-DB-type connection to another machine or if you are invoking a COM object out-of-process using the sp_OAcreate stored procedures.

Reference

v1.02 2000.04.21

Applies to SQL Server versions:	6.5, 7.0
FAQ categories:	Troubleshooting, Server Administration and Tools
Related FAQ articles:	n/a
Related Microsoft Knowledge Base article:	Q198891 "INF: Enabling DLL-based COM Object Execution Outside SQL Server"
Other related information:	n/a
Author:	Neil Pike

dmologinslow

Q: Why does my DMO program connect to SQL Server incredibly slowly?

A: The usual reason for this is that you are running NT authentication and have a large number of logins defined on the server.

This bug was fixed in SP2 for SQL 7.0.

Reference

v1.00 2000.06.13

Applies to SQL Server version:	7.0
FAQ category:	Troubleshooting
Related FAQ articles:	n/a
Related Microsoft Knowledge Base articles:	n/a
Other related information:	n/a
Author:	Neil Pike

domains

Q: I've just changed the NT domain for my SQL Server or clients. Why can't I connect to the server any more?

A: This isn't a SQL issue, it's an NT one. If you are using a Net-Lib that requires NT authentication—for example, with 6.5 and below, Named Pipes or Multiprotocol—then you *must* be able to authenticate to the copy of NT running SQL Server. With 7.0 all Net-Libs require NT authentication.

For possible solutions, see the FAQ article "accessdenied."

Reference

v1.03 2000.04.22	
Applies to SQL Server versions:	All
FAQ categories:	Troubleshooting, Connectivity, Security
Related FAQ article:	"I'm getting an 'access denied,' 'CreateFile,' or '1326' message when connecting to SQL Server. What should I do?" (accessdenied, see page 480)
Related Microsoft Knowledge Base articles:	Q175671 "PRB: 80004005 ConnectionOpen (CreateFile()) Error Accessing SQL," Q183060 "INFO: Troubleshooting Guide for 80004005 & Other Error Messages"
Other related information:	"Troubleshooting SQL Installation and Connection Problems" at `http://support.microsoft.com/support/tshoot/default.asp`
Author:	Neil Pike

droptable

Q: Why can't I drop a SQL Server table?

A: Here are two possible reasons why a table can't be dropped:

- Its status is in an invalid condition. Change the status field in sysobjects for the table to 67, and then DROP it.

- The table has suffered errors such as 605 or 2521, indicating the page or extent chain is invalid. If this is the case, there is nothing you can do. Rename the table directly in sysobjects, or, preferably, transfer all the good objects and data to a new database and drop the old one.

Reference

v1.01 2000.04.22	
Applies to SQL Server versions:	All
FAQ categories:	Troubleshooting, Database Administration
Related FAQ articles:	n/a
Related Microsoft Knowledge Base articles:	n/a
Other related information:	See "Ghost Tables" by Kalen Delaney in *SQL Server Professional,* December 1997, `http://www.pinpub.pro`
Author:	Neil Pike

dtcerr

Q: What does the error message "Failed to obtain TransactionDispenserInterface: XACT_E_TMNOTAVAILABLE" mean in SQL Server? Should I be worried?

A: This error message is put in the SQL errorlog at startup if the MSDTC service isn't running or configured. Unless you are using DTC, this is perfectly normal.

More details on DTC can be found in the SQL Server Books Online.

Reference

v1.00 1998.11.19	
Applies to SQL Server versions:	6.x, 7.0
FAQ category:	Troubleshooting
Related FAQ articles:	n/a
Related Microsoft Knowledge Base articles:	n/a
Other related information:	n/a
Author:	Neil Pike

fixindex

Q: How can I fix a corruption in a system table?

A: If the problem can be fixed with an index recreate, there is a system stored procedure to do this.

```
sp_fixindex database_name,system_table_name,index_id
```

For example:

```
sp_fixindex pubs,sysusers,2
```

It is not possible to rebuild the clustered index on sysindexes or sysobjects.

If this fix does not work then the only choice is to create a new database and use the transfer tools in SQL Enterprise Manager to copy the good data and objects across.

Reference

v1.01 2000.04.24

Applies to SQL Server versions:	All
FAQ category:	Troubleshooting
Related FAQ articles	n/a
Related Microsoft Knowledge Base article:	Q106122 "INF: Use of sp_fixindex"
Other related information:	n/a
Author:	Neil Pike

getoverlappedresult

Q: I am getting a message "GetOverLappedResult()" from a SQL Server query. What is going on?

A: Two things may be happening:

- SQL Server is internally GPFing or AVing (they are the same thing). You should see messages to this effect in the SQL error log.

• There is a Net-Lib bug with overlapped or fragmented packets.

For either problem you can try applying the latest service pack to the server.

For Net-Lib bugs you will need to apply the service pack to the client as well. Also the version of ADO or ODBC can help cause the problem as well, so try upgrading. The latest versions of these drivers can be obtained at `http://www.microsoft.com/data`.

If you're getting access violation messages, see the FAQ entry on access violations.

If you are getting a problem with TDS packet fragmentation (TDS is SQL's application-level protocol), try a different Net-Lib—for example, TCP-IP instead of Named Pipes or vice versa. If you still have a problem, you'll need to call Microsoft PSS. See the FAQ entries "MSPSS" and "reproscript" for more details.

Reference

v1.02 2000.06.05	
Applies to SQL Server versions:	All
FAQ category:	Troubleshooting
Related FAQ articles:	"I am getting a message "dbprocess dead" or "language exec" from SQL Server. I am seeing an "Exception Access Violation" message in the SQL errorlog. I am getting an error "SqlDumpExceptionHandler: Process <x> generated fatal exception." I am getting *.DMP files in the <sql>\log directory. I am getting "symptom dump" messages. What is going on?" (accessviolation, see page 481), "What is Microsoft Product Support Services and how do I contact them?" (MSPSS, see page 517), Why is a reproduction (repro) script used to report a SQL Server bug? (reproscript, see page 530)
Related Microsoft Knowledge Base articles:	n/a
Other related information:	n/a
Author:	Neil Pike

indextuningwizarderror60

Q: I am trying to load a trace file into the SQL 7.0 Profiler/Index Tuning Wizard, but all I get is "Error analyzing workload (60)." What does this mean?

A: This means that it failed to find or load the file. Check that the filename is correct and you have permissions to read the file. There is also a bug in builds 623 (RTM) and earlier—the filename cannot have spaces in it.

Reference

v1.00 1999.01.19

Applies to SQL Server version:	7.0
FAQ categories:	Troubleshooting, Server Administration and Tools
Related FAQ articles:	n/a
Related Microsoft Knowledge Base articles:	n/a
Other related information:	n/a
Author:	Neil Pike

intellimousecrash

Q: Why does ISQL/W GPF when I move the mouse pointer with an Intellimouse?

A: This happens because of a bug in the Intellimouse drivers. Try applying the latest version of the drivers. If that still fails, you'll need to use ordinary mouse drivers.

Reference

v1.00 1999.10.12

Applies to SQL Server versions:	All
FAQ category:	Troubleshooting
Related FAQ articles:	n/a
Related Microsoft Knowledge Base articles:	n/a
Other related information:	n/a
Author:	Neil Pike

lazywriterwarn

Q: What does the SQL Server error message “Lazywriter: WARNING, couldn’t find slot, 8/8, scanned 8” mean?

A: Basically SQL Server is trying to write out “dirty” data to disk via the lazy writer thread that the CHECKPOINT process kicks off. It has been unable to find a free slot—which is basically a memory buffer. The number of slots is set via the sp_configure “max lazywrite io” parameter and dictates the number of concurrent i/o’s that this process is allowed to have.

The reason why it couldn’t find a slot is either of the following:

- There has been an internal corruption that is stopping the lazy writer process from working properly. This is rare, but there was a known bug in SP3, fixed in SP4, that could cause this. If this were happening then you would see other errors or AV’s before this particular error appeared.

- The normal reason is just that the disk subsystem is too busy to process the i/o requests. In this case, look for non-SQL tasks that may be causing contention on the same disks—such as NT backups, file transfers or paging. Look for contending SQL processes on the same disks—table scans or log file writes. You may need to move SQL devices to prevent contention. Alternatively you may have the overall level of i/o’s that SQL is making too high—you may need to reduce the number of “max async io’s” that sp_configure allows.

In any event the message is not usually a problem—SQL will wait until it can continue with the lazy write i/o’s for as long as necessary. You could try increasing the “max lazywrite io” parameter, but normally this doesn’t help with this particular problem.

(Under SQL 7.0 and above lazywrite io is dynamically tuned, so this error should never appear.)

Reference

v1.02 2000.05.07	
Applies to SQL Server version:	6.x
FAQ category:	Troubleshooting
Related FAQ article:	"What do the 'bufwait,' 'writelog,' and 'buffer latch' errors in SQL Server mean?" (bufwait, see page 494)
Related Microsoft Knowledge Base articles:	n/a
Other related information:	n/a
Author:	Neil Pike

loadtableschemamismatch

Q: Why do I get the SQL Server error "Msg 8412—Schemas differ" when doing a LOAD TABLE even though I have defined the table identically?

A: The most common reason for this is when the exact error is "Msg 8412, Level 16, State 3"—with the state of 3 being the giveaway. This problem occurs if both of the following conditions are true:

- The table has a nullable char or varchar column and was created under one ANSI_PADDING setting.
- The table was dumped, dropped, and re-created from a script, but with adifferent ANSI_PADDING option set.

This is usually caused by using a different tool to create the table for the load from that used to create the table that was dumped. Different tools have different defaults for the ANSI_PADDING setting. (ANSI_PADDING causes varchar and varbinary values to be padded with spaces or nulls. See Books Online.)

Reference

v1.01 2000.05.12	
Applies to SQL Server version:	6.5
FAQ category:	Troubleshooting
Related FAQ articles:	n/a
Related Microsoft Knowledge Base article:	Q170639 "BUG: Load Table May Fail If Created with Different ANSI_PADDING"
Other related information:	"SET Statement (6.5)" in Books Online 6
Author:	Neil Pike

loginfailed

Q: I am getting a SQL Server error message "login failed," even though I am sure I am using the right login.

A: This is a pretty common occurrence. The "login failed" message is unfortunately a generic message that should really say "unable to make connection" because it often isn't a logon validation problem. Try the following:

1. Remember it is the SQL Server login and password that SQL is expecting, *not* an NT one. The default SQL login and password is "sa" and no password. However, if your server and network libraries are set up to accept a "trusted" connection, your administrator may have set up your SQL Server login name to be the same as your NT login, but the passwords may be different. Assuming you have logged into your NT domain, try leaving the password blank to establish a trusted connection.

2. It could be a "network" connection problem. If you're registering a local server with SQL Enterprise Manager, register it as "." without the quotes. Try connecting using an appropriate tool locally on the server without specifying the server name—this forces a local named-pipe connection.

3. It could be that SQL is out of connections or client licenses. If you cannot check the SQL error log from Enterprise Manager, look directly in <sql>\log\errorlog file for messages indicating this. Check if SQL has been started in single-user mode using the start-up parameter /m. You can determine this from Enterprise Manager or by checking the following registry key:

```
HKEY_LOCAL_MACHINE\SOFTWARE\Microsoft\MSSQLServer\MSSQLServer\Parameters
```

Here you will find SQLArg0, SQLArg1......–type parameters—the single-user one is "/m".

4. Finally, if you're sure that the login is correct (and remember SQL can be case-sensitive) then try disabling any virus-checking software because this may be interfering.

For other more obscure reasons, check the Knowledge Base searching for "login failed."

Reference

v1.01 2000.05.12

Applies to SQL Server versions:	All
FAQ category:	Troubleshooting
Related FAQ articles:	n/a
Related Microsoft Knowledge Base article:	Search on "login failed"
Other related information:	n/a
Author:	Neil Pike

logonfailedservice

Q: How can I resolve the error "An error 1069—(The service did not start due to a logon failure)" for SQL Server?

A: SQL Server is just like any other NT service in that it can be defined to run using the credentials of an NT user account. It can also run under localsystem account, but if you are getting this error then you must have defined a user account.

Go to Control Panel/Services. Choose the mssqlserver service (or SQLExecutive/SQLAgent if they are failing) and then choose Startup. Note which NT account is being used. Make sure that the password is correct and check with the NT user manager that the account has not been deleted or expired. It also needs to be a member of the local Administrators group.

If the account details seem OK, check that it has the "logon as a service" user right (again with user manager).

If this doesn't resolve the issue, try logging on locally to the NT box with the same NT account and see what errors you get.

Reference

v1.01 2000.05.12	
Applies to SQL Server versions:	All
FAQ category:	Troubleshooting
Related FAQ articles:	n/a
Related Microsoft Knowledge Base articles:	n/a
Other related information:	n/a
Author:	Neil Pike

memoryleak

Q: Does SQL Server have memory leaks? How can I tell? Why is SQL Server using so much memory? What do I do about virtual memory errors?

A: Generally speaking, SQL Server doesn't have much of a problem with memory leaks and it is almost always other programs or drivers that cause the problem. For specifics on known SQL Server bugs causing memory leaks, see the end of the article. It's always a good idea to apply the latest service pack if you haven't already—MS fixes these bugs as soon as they find them.

Remember that SQL Server will grab memory for its data cache up to the amount you have specified via **sp_configure**. This is in 2KB pages (for SQL 6.5) and in 1MB chunks for SQL 7.0 and above. This amount does not include any amount for tempdb in RAM (6.5 and below only—SQL 7.0 and above don't support tempdb in RAM) or for the SQL kernel and some other internal memory structures. It would not be unusual for the SQL kernel and other memory structures to use an extra 10–20MB of RAM. In addition, it requires o/s buffers and memory for things like BULK INSERT and OLE/COM. These don't come out of the memory that SQL allocates for data cache.

Therefore if you configured SQL Server to use a maximum of 50MB RAM, don't worry until the memory allocated to sqlservr.exe goes over, say, 70MB.

With SQL 7.0 the default is to dynamically allocate memory—though you can set an upper limit if you wish. SQL Server 7.0 will keep grabbing memory, up to the set limit (default no limit), until NT tells it that other processes need the memory. On a dedicated machine this won't happen, so it is not unusual for SQL 7.0 to seem to keep grabbing more and more memory.

Also, introduced in SQL 7.0 SP2 was the –g startup switch, which specified an amount of memory that SQL Server will leave available for memory allocations within the SQL Server process, but outside the SQL Server memory pool. The memory pool is the area used by SQL Server for loading items such as extended stored procedure .dll files, the OLE DB providers referenced by distributed queries and OLE Automation objects referenced in Transact-SQL statements.

After reading the preceding explanations, if you still think you have a memory leak, run Performance Monitor and select the processes object. Choose all running processes (make sure everything you normally run is going at the time) and for these choose the paged pool, non-paged pool and virtual bytes objects. Put these on a chart or log with a long interval period. Monitor these objects over time to see what always increases. If SQL Server (sqlservr.exe) continues increasing above the maximum memory (+20MB) it should have allocated, it may be responsible for a memory leak. You could also check for handles and threads always increasing as these could also potentially be leaking—and running out of these is just as bad as running out of memory.

You can also get these parameters from Task Manager—go into the process view, choose View Columns and add the relevant columns.

If no processes in Task Manager or Performance Monitor show a memory leak, but the overall memory is still going up, the leak must be down at the kernel level. To trace this, use the poolmon.exe program. Instructions are in Microsoft Technet and the Microsoft Knowledge Base—just search for "poolmon."

Known Memory Leak Issues

- If you are running the Novell network client v4.5 or above on the server, you may experience a memory leak. Go back to version 4.11 to resolve it (I don't know whether this is an Microsoft bug or a Novell one).
- SQL 7.0 RTM had a couple of leaks that were resolved in SP1.
- If you do thousands of BULK INSERTs, you will notice a fairly significant memory leak with SQL 7.0 RTM and SP1. This will be fixed in 7.0 SP2 (or contact Microsoft PSS for a post-SP1 hot-fix).
- SQL 6.5. If you utilize performance counters and connect using the local computer name, a leak may occur in WinLogon.exe. (NT Performance Monitor doesn't cause the problem). See Q249343 for more information. The problem is scheduled to be fixed in 6.5 SP6.
- If you use xp_sendmail with the @query and @attached_results option, this leaks memory, on both SQL 6.5 up to SP5a and SQL 7.0 up to SP2. See Q245803 (SQL 7.0) and Q250493 (SQL 6.5) for more infromation. For 6.5 the problem is scheduled to be fixed in SP6.

Reference

v1.07 2000.05.15	
Applies to SQL Server versions:	All
FAQ category:	Troubleshooting
Related FAQ articleS:	n/a
Related Microsoft Knowledge Base articles:	Search on "sql server" and "memory leak"
Other related information:	"Monitoring Memory Usage" in Books Online 7
Author:	Neil Pike

memoryoverallocatednostart

Q: I've overallocated memory for SQL Server and now it won't start. What can I do?

A: To recover from this:

1. Stop all applications and services that log into SQL Server, such as SQL Executive and SQL Enterprise Manager.

2. From a command prompt on the server, go to the <sql>\binn directory and type **sqlservr -c -f**—this will start SQL in single-user mode with a minimum config.

3. Ignore the text messages in this window, but wait for them to finish appearing (this shouldn't take more than 10-20 seconds).

4. SQL Server is now started. Note that because of the startup options used, SQL Server will appear in Enterprise Manager with a red traffic light as if it had not started.

5. Go to another window and start ISQL/W and connect locally with the sa userid.

6. In ISQL/W, issue the following commands (remember the memory value is in 2K pages not Mb):

```
sp_configure memory, <new memory value>
go
reconfigure
go
```

7. Now go back to the window SQL is running in and type **shutdown** and enter.

8. SQL Server should shut down. If it doesn't, press <ctrl-c> to shut it down.

9. Now you should be able to start SQL normally and connect.

Reference

v1.01 2000.05.15

Applies to SQL Server version:	6.x
FAQ category:	Troubleshooting
Related FAQ articles:	n/a
Related Microsoft Knowledge Base article:	Q173090 "INF: Changing Configuration Values When SQL Server Won't Start"
Other related information:	n/a
Author:	Neil Pike

mmcfilenotfound

Q: When attempting to start Enterprise Manager I get this error message: "The selected file could not be found." How can I fix this?

A: In fact, the missing file is <sqldir>\binn\SQL Server Enterprise Manager.MSC, which is the settings file for Microsoft Management Console. This file appears to get damaged occasionally and it causes this message. I have noticed it happening on the rare occasions when Query Analyzer has crashed.

You can reinstate the settings file by running MMC.EXE from <winnt>\system32 and selecting the option to add a snap-in. Once reinstated, save the settings and give it the name of the missing file.

Reference

v1.00 2000.05.15

Applies to SQL Server version:	7.0
FAQ category:	Troubleshooting
Related FAQ articles:	n/a
Related Microsoft Knowledge Base articles:	n/a
Other related information:	n/a
Author:	Paul Munkenbeck

mmcsnapin

Q: Why do I get an error message when I try to run SQL 7.0 EM: "MMC—Snap-in failed to initialize"?

A: It could be that one or more DLLs have not been registered. Try:

- regsvr32 <sqldir>\BINN\dtsui.dll
- regsvr32 <sqldir>\BINN\sqldmo.dll
- regsvr32 <sqldir>\BINN\sqlns.dll
- regsvr32 <sqldir>\BINN\sqllex.dll

Reference

v1.04 1999.03.19	
Applies to SQL Server versions:	7.0, 2000
FAQ category:	Troubleshooting
Related FAQ articles:	n/a
Related Microsoft Knowledge Base articles:	n/a
Other related information:	n/a
Author:	Neil Pike

modelfull

Q: I have filled the model database's log and now SQL won't start with a 1105 error. What can I do?

A: This is because tempdb gets created with model's attributes at SQL startup. To overcome this:

1. Start SQL Server with the -T3607 or -T3608 trace flag. See Books Online for how to do this.
2. Login to SQL Server as sa with ISQL or ISQLW.

3. Do a `DUMP TRANSACTION model WITH NO_LOG`.

4. Stop SQL Server.

5. Remove the trace flag.

You should now be able to restart SQL again.

If this does not work, try starting SQL Server in minimum configuration using the –c –f startup options (see FAQ "memoryoverallocatednostart"), and then issuing the dump transaction from an ISQL connection.

Reference

v1.01 2000.05.15	
Applies to SQL Server version:	6.x
FAQ category:	Troubleshooting
Related FAQ article:	"I've overallocated memory for SQL Server and now it won't start. What can I do?" (memoryoverallocatednostart, see page 514)
Related Microsoft Knowledge Base articles:	n/a
Other related information:	"Error 1105" in Books Online 6
Author:	Neil Pike

MSPSS

Q: What is Microsoft Product Support Services and how do I contact them?

A: These are people who support all of Microsoft's products, write fixes, take the calls and sort out workarounds. They work 24 × 7 × 365. You can call them by phone (in the U.S.: 1-800-936-3500).

For details of your nearest PSS support center and other information try:

- `http://support.microsoft.com/support/supportnet/default.asp`
- `http://www.microsoft.com/support/customer/itpro.htm`

To report a problem on the Web:

- `http://support.microsoft.com/support/webresponse.asp`

All incidents are chargeable either to your credit card or an existing account. The charge *will* be reimbursed if the problem turns out to be a Microsoft bug or a feature that hasn't been publicly documented. The person answering the phone cannot know it's a bug, so they have to take your credit card information before passing you on to a technician. The only way to not have to give your credit card information is to quote a Knowledge Base article number that contains a hot-fix that you need. In this case, and this case only, you will be transferred to an engineer without having to hand over your credit card details.

When the call is closed the technician decides whether to mark the call as "free," in which case you get a refund automatically. (Microsoft follows the same procedure for problems reported via the Web.)

Reference

v1.04 2000.09.12

Applies to SQL Server versions:	All
FAQ category:	Troubleshooting
Related FAQ articles:	n/a
Related Microsoft Knowledge Base articles:	n/a
Other related information:	n/a
Author:	Neil Pike

notenoughserverstorage

Q: Why do I get an error message "Not enough server storage is available to process this request"?

A: This is caused by a mismatched set of NT networking layer files. It is usually caused by installing new network protocols from the original NT media onto a machine that has had an NT service pack applied previously. Reinstalling the latest or installed NT service pack will fix the problem.

Reference

v1.01 2000.04.08	
Applies to SQL Server versions:	All
FAQ category:	Troubleshooting
Related FAQ articles:	n/a
Related Microsoft Knowledge Base articles:	n/a
Other related information:	n/a
Author:	Neil Pike

ODBCCMPT

Q: Why do I get an error connecting to a working SQL 7.0 datasource with MSQUERY, Access or other programs?

A: This is probably because the application concerned does not like the very latest version of ODBC. MSQUERY 8.0e should work.

To solve the problem use ODBCCMPT.EXE to set the ODBC compatibility level on a per application/exe basis. Full details of this utility are in the SQL 7.0 Books Online.

Reference

v1.00 1999.03.03	
Applies to SQL Server version:	7.0
FAQ categories:	Troubleshooting, Connectivity
Related FAQ articles:	n/a
Related Microsoft Knowledge Base articles:	n/a
Other related information:	n/a
Author:	Neil Pike

odbclog

Q: Why do I have a large file called SQL.LOG that I can't delete?

A: This is the default name for the ODBC trace file—it defaults to the root of the C drive but can be moved or renamed.

Go to Control Panel/ODBC (called Data Access Components on W2K/SQL2000 or the latest MDAC's). Check the tracing option here and turn it off. You should then be able to delete the file.

Reference

v1.01 2000.04.08

Applies to SQL Server versions:	All
FAQ category:	Troubleshooting
Related FAQ articles:	n/a
Related Microsoft Knowledge Base articles:	n/a
Other related information:	n/a
Author:	Neil Pike

only10userscanconnect

Q: I am getting an error saying only 10 users can connect. I have more licenses than this. What is going on?

A: Reasons this can happen:

- You are running an MSDN copy of SQL Server. For SQL 7.0 a SELECT @@VERSION will show you using the Developer edition. You need to remove it and re-install a retail version. See the FAQ entry "evalupgrade" for details.
- You are running SQL Server on NT Workstation. This has a 10-user incoming limit. You need to upgrade this to the Server version.

- You have installed SQL on an MSDN copy of NT Server—the MSDN copy of NT Server has a 10-user limit that SQL inherits. Tools are available at `http://www.ntfaq.com` and `http://www.sysinternals.com` that tell you what sort of copy of NT you have. You need to uninstall and reinstall NT. See the FAQ entry "reinstallnt" to learn how to make this less painful.

Reference

v1.01 2000.04.08	
Applies to SQL Server versions:	All
FAQ categories:	Troubleshooting, Connectivity
Related FAQ articles:	n/a
Related Microsoft Knowledge Base articles:	n/a
Other related information:	n/a
Author:	Neil Pike

pagefaults

Q: Why do I see page faults per second above 0 when I have a dedicated SQL Server machine?

A: This is because "page faults" are *not* the same as paging to disk. A page fault occurs every time SQL accesses a page in memory that is outside it's "working set." Due to the way that the SQL performance monitor counters work in SQL 6.5 and earlier, this area of memory is held outside of the SQL working set, so access and updates to these counters actually *cause* page faults.

However, most page faults are to areas that are still held in memory and so do not result in expensive or slow reads or writes to the pagefile on disk. There is some CPU overhead caused by the NT Virtual Memory Manager (VMM) becoming involved and context switches, but these don't affect performance unless you are getting hundreds or thousands of page faults per second.

The counter you should monitor is pages per second, which is the actual i/o caused to the pagefile, and is what you should be worried about.

For more information on performance and monitoring issues there is no better reference than the NT Server Resource Kit, which has a volume dedicated to these topics.

Reference

v1.02 2000.04.09	
Applies to SQL Server versions:	All
FAQ category:	Troubleshooting
Related FAQ articles:	n/a
Related Microsoft Knowledge Base article:	Q168778 "BUG: Page Fault Statement in Admin Companion Is Incorrect"
Other related information:	n/a
Author:	Neil Pike

performancecounters

Q: I can't see the SQL performance counters in Performance Monitor. What could be wrong?

A: It could be a variety of things.

1. Sometimes rebuilding the registry for 6.5 and below fixes the problem. From the <sql>\binn directory run the following, making sure the case is correct:

   ```
   setup /t RegistryRebuild = On
   ```

   The setup routine will now run and ask you all the normal questions. Answer these as if you were performing the install again (use the same paths) and it will update all the registry entries and icons. It will leave the databases alone.

2. For SQL 7.0 try unloading and reloading the counters:

   ```
   unlodctr.exe MSSQLServer
   lodctr.exe <sql>\BINN\sqlctr.ini
   ```

3. For 6.5 machines running on NT 4.0 it could be a permissions problem. To work around this problem, use Regedit.exe to grant READ access to the following key of the target machine:

   ```
   HKEY_LOCAL_MACHINE\SOFTWARE\Microsoft\MSSQLServer\MSSQLServer
   ```

   Grant this to those wanting SQL counter access. As when granting any NT access permission, you can grant based on an individual user or a group.

4. For SQL 6.5 and below the probe password is not null.

5. SQL Server is listening on an alternate pipe, not \\.\pipe\sql\query.

Reference

v1.01 2000.04.09	
Applies to SQL Server versions:	All
FAQ category:	Troubleshooting
Related FAQ article:	"Why can't I see the SQL performance counters on the second node in my cluster? I can see the NT counters with no problem." (perfcountersnotappearoncluster, see page 423)
Related Microsoft Knowledge Base article:	Q137899 "BUG: SQL Counters Not Available Under Integrated Security"
Other related information:	n/a
Author:	Neil Pike

printdmp

Q: What are the *.DMP files that appear in the SQL Server log directory? I've tried printing them with PRINTDMP.EXE but it doesn't work.

A: These are a sign that SQL Server has had a "handled access violation"—a GPF.

The dump files contain information on what SQL Server was doing at the time, such as module stack traces. Though a PRINTDMP.EXE utility is supplied, the output of this is of no use to anyone unless they have the SQL Server C source code—which no-one outside the Microsoft development and support teams does.

Save the dumps away, together with error log info, what SQL was running at the time and contact Microsoft PSS for support in resolving the problem. See the "MSPSS" FAQ entry for more information on Microsoft PSS. (Before calling make sure that the problem still occurs when you are running the latest service pack and that DBCC health checks on the database report no problems.)

Reference

v1.03 2000.04.13	
Applies to SQL Server versions:	All
FAQ category:	Troubleshooting
Related FAQ article:	"What is Microsoft Product Support Services and how do I contact them?" (MSPSS, see page 517)
Related Microsoft Knowledge Base article:	n/a
Other related information:	n/a
Author:	Neil Pike

queryslowersqlagent

Q: When I run a query under SQL Executive or SQL Agent it is much slower than when run via Query Analyzer. Why?

A: Put a `SET NOCOUNT ON` at the start of the query or stored procedure. This will stop most of the handshaking going on between SQL Server and SQL Agent or Executive. This handshaking can significantly slow down a query that is being executed by a background task.

Reference

v1.01 2000.04.13	
Applies to SQL Server versions:	All
FAQ category:	Troubleshooting
Related FAQ articles:	n/a
Related Microsoft Knowledge Base articles:	n/a
Other related information:	n/a
Author:	Neil Pike

raidsetrestoreerror

Q: Why am I getting an error "The RAID set for database <xxx> is missing member number <x>. Backup or restore operation terminating abnormally"?

A: If you've used the Enterprise Manager GUI to back up the database, you have probably accidentally selected more than one backup device in the destination list in the backup screen.

What SQL Server will then do is stripe the backup to all devices. Therefore you need to select the same set of backup devices for the restore to work.

Reference

v1.02 2000.09.12

Applies to SQL Server versions:	All
FAQ category:	Troubleshooting
Related FAQ articles:	n/a
Related Microsoft Knowledge Base articles:	n/a
Other related information:	n/a
Author:	Neil Pike

rebuildextents

Q: I'm getting an error 1117 or 2543 in SQL Server. Can I rebuild the extents somehow?

A: It is recommended that you select or BCP out all the relevant data and then recreate the objects concerned. Alternatively you could just rename the object and leave it in the database with a dummy name—you won't be able to drop the object. If you choose this option, ensure you drop and recreate all views and stored procedures that reference the damaged object otherwise they will continue to use it.

However, if you want to attempt a rebuild of the extents, make a backup first, and then try using the following undocumented DBCC command:

```
DBCC REBUILDEXTENTS (@db_id, @object_id, @index_id)
```

The parameters are:

• @db_id: Id of the database.

• @object_id: Id of the object to be rebuild.

• @index_id—Id of the index to be rebuild

You have to put the database into single-user/read-only mode first as follows:

```
dbcc traceon(3604)
go
use master
go
sp_dboption <dbname>,'read only',true
go
use <dbname>
go
checkpoint
go
dbcc rebuildextents(<dbid>,<objid>,<indid>)
go
use master
go
sp_dboption <dbname>,'read only',false
go
```

Reference

v1.04 2000.05.15	
Applies to SQL Server versions:	4.x, 6.x
FAQ category:	Troubleshooting
Related FAQ articles:	n/a
Related Microsoft Knowledge Base articles:	n/a
Other related information:	"Error 1117" and "Error 2543" in Books Online 6
Author:	Neil Pike

rebuildlog

Q: I have a corrupt log file. Can I rebuild it?

A: Yes you can, but any uncommitted transactions will be lost. This command is unsupported and undocumented so should be used with caution. It works on SQL 6.5.

```
dbcc rebuildlog (@dbname, 1, 0)
```

Reference

v1.01 2000.04.15	
Applies to SQL Server version:	6.5
FAQ category:	Troubleshooting
Related FAQ articles:	n/a
Related Microsoft Knowledge Base articles:	n/a
Other related information:	n/a
Author:	Neil Pike

recoverdatabadpage

Q: How can I recover data from a SQL table that is corrupt with a bad page or pointer?

A: Assuming only one page is bad, the situation isn't too serious. If there are lots of bad pages, this process must be amended to do random selects above the low key to find the next good page each time.

1. Do a `SELECT key FROM table`, and note the last key value (low key) returned when it fails.

2. Do a `SELECT key FROM table ORDER BY key DESC`, and note the last key (high key) again.

3. Create a "dummy" table with the same structure

4. Insert rows into the "dummy" table with key values less than or equal to the low key.

5. Insert rows into the "dummy" table with key values greater than or equal to the high key.

Reference

v1.00 1999.06.04	
Applies to SQL Server versions:	All
FAQ category:	Troubleshooting
Related FAQ articles:	n/a
Related Microsoft Knowledge Base articles:	n/a
Other related information:	n/a
Author:	Neil Pike

recovering

Q: My SQL Server database is showing as "recovering." Why and what can I do?

A: Every time SQL Server starts up it recovers all databases so that all transactions are either committed or rolled back. This recovery process normally only takes a few seconds or minutes, but if the server was terminated in the middle of a long running update, the recovery can take at least as long as the update had taken so far—sometimes longer due to the extra contention on the log device. When writing the original updates to the log, these are all written sequentially to the end. When recovery occurs, SQL has to scan through the log looking for these updates as well as committing new updates that might be occurring on other databases.

Give it plenty of time to recover, but at the same time check the current and previous errorlog files and NT errorlogs for any indications of what has happened. If you've hit a hardware problem or SQL bug, there *will* be errors there to give an indication of what happened.

Check the physical disk activity lights on the server, and also check the sysprocesses activity to see if the recovery task is using CPU and or disk I/O. Only on very rare occasions will SQL Server not recover the database correctly.

In addition, to check on recovery progress you could set trace flag 3412. This writes an entry to the errorlog when each transaction is rolled forward or back.

If a database will not recover and you do *not* have a backup, you can use the following trace flags to bypass recovery. If you use these, the database and data may not be in a consistent state, but if you have no other choice, use them and then immediately transfer out all the objects you require using BCP or transfer tools.

- 3607: Skips automatic recovery for all databases.

- 3608: Skips automatic recovery for all databases except the master database.

If the database is still unavailable—marked as suspect—then issue the following command to put the database into emergency mode (you'll need to allow updates first). You can then go into the database (no need to restart SQL) and extract out the data.

```
UPDATE master..sysdatabases SET status=-32768 WHERE name='<dbname>'
```

If all else fails, or you are unsure what to do, don't hesitate to place a call with Microsoft Product Support Services (PSS). They are there 24 × 7 × 365 to deal with problems like this and the charge is nominal compared to the loss of your data! (See details on Microsoft PSS in the "MSPSS" FAQ article.)

Troubleshooting

Reference

v1.04 2000.04.15	
Applies to SQL Server versions:	All
FAQ category:	Troubleshooting
Related FAQ articles:	MSPSS
Related Microsoft Knowledge Base articles:	n/a
Other related information:	"Trace Flags" in SQL Server Books Online
Author:	Neil Pike

remapsp

Q: Why do I get an error "Bad pointer 0xABCDEF encountered while remapping stored procedure" in SQL Server?

A: This is a bug in SQL Server. Chances are you are using a temporary table with an identity column. You can re-write the stored procedure or apply the latest SQL service pack (this was fixed in Service Pack 2).

Reference

v1.01 2000.04.15	
Applies to SQL Server version:	6.x
FAQ category:	Troubleshooting
Related FAQ articles:	n/a
Related Microsoft Knowledge Base articles:	Q167353 " BUG: Stored Procedure with Multiple Cursors May Cause Error 2805," Q158401 "FIX: Selecting From Views with Nested Select Causes Errors," Q160732 " FIX: SQL Server 6.5 Service Pack 2 Fixlist"
Other related information:	n/a
Author:	Neil Pike

reproscript

Q: Why is a reproduction (repro) script used to report a SQL Server bug?

A: In order for Microsoft to resolve a bug they need to re-create it on their systems. The best way to do this is for the customer to provide them with a repro script. They don't have access to your database, so the script needs to be able to show the problem when run on a brand-new install of SQL Server on a new database.

Therefore it needs to contain all tables, user defined data types, triggers, views, and any other objects needed to show the problem. If it needs data, keep this to a minimum—use `INSERT INTO <tbl> VALUES (.....)`-type statements if possible. If not a small amount of zipped BCP data is OK.

Alternatively, rewrite your query, if possible, to run against the pubs or Northwind (SQL 7.0 and above only) databases as these are always installed with SQL Server and come complete with a variety of tables, foreign keys, indices and data.

If the script and data are reasonably short, post to one of the newsgroups and one of the MVPs can report the problem to Microsoft for you.

If it isn't short or a repro script is not practical due to the amount of information or data needed, you will need to report a bug toMicrosoft PSS directly. (See the "MSPSS" FAQ article for details.)

A sample repro script follows:

```
--
-- Bug Title : Access violation
--

--
-- Versions affected : SQL 6.5
--

--
-- Fixed in : SQL 7.0
--

--
-- Microsoft incident / bug number : unknown/16767
--

--
-- Bug Description.
--
print
'
As title
'

--
-- Actual Repro script below here
--

use tempdb
go

CREATE TABLE table1
(
id int
)
GO

CREATE TABLE table2
(
id int
)
GO
```

```
CREATE TABLE table3
(
id int
)
GO

CREATE VIEW view1 AS
SELECT id
FROM table1
UNION ALL
SELECT id
FROM table2
GO

SELECT view1.id
FROM view1, table3
WHERE view1.id *= table3.id
GO
```

Reference

v1.05 2000.04.16

Applies to SQL Server versions:	All
FAQ category:	Troubleshooting
Related FAQ articles:	"How can I report a SQL Server bug to Microsoft?" (bugreport, see page 495), "What is Microsoft Product Support Services and how do I contact them?" (MSPSS, see page 517)
Related Microsoft Knowledge Base articles:	n/a
Other related information:	n/a
Author:	Neil Pike

selectinto

Q: I have a query that seems to lock other users out of the system, especially with tempdb. What is going on?

A: In situations like this the usual problem is with locks. Check with sp_lock or sp_lock2 what the offending query is doing.

One common cause was introduced in SQL 6.5 when Microsoft decided to allow table creation in transactions by making it an ATOMIC transaction. A side effect of this is that when a SELECT INTO is done, it locks out system tables in the database concerned and prevents other users from accessing them. With a long-running SELECT INTO, this can cause real problems.

Microsoft recognized this, and as long as you have at least Service Pack 1 applied, you can set the trace flag 5302 to remove this behavior. See Microsoft Knowledge Base article Q153441, "FIX: SELECT INTO Locking Behavior," and FAQ article 5302 for more information.

SQL 7.0 has row-level locking and so does not block on system tables like this.

Reference

v1.02 2000.04.16	
Applies to SQL Server versions:	4.x, 6.x
FAQ category:	Troubleshooting
Related FAQ article:	"Why is my application locking up in SQL Server? If I check the locks, I am seeing syscolumns being blocked." (5302, see page 472)
Related Microsoft Knowledge Base article:	Q153441 "FIX: SELECT INTO Locking Behavior"
Other related information:	n/a
Author:	Neil Pike

sometimesslow

Q: Why does my SQL Server code sometimes respond slower than normal when I haven't changed anything?

A: This could be for a variety of reasons:

- Are you passing the same parameters through the code each time? SQL could be choosing a different access path for different values in an index. Showplan would tell you what is going on here.
- Could be that another process has filled the data cache with pages from other tables, meaning you need to do a lot more physical i/o. The show i/o stats will help diagnose this.

- You could be contending with the checkpoint process—this flushes all dirty pages to disk and creates quite a lot of i/o contention especially on versions prior to SQL 7.0. You could increase the "recovery interval" parameter in sp_configure to get less (and bigger) checkpoints, or reduce it to get more frequent (and smaller) ones.

- You could be contending with another user SQL process for disk i/o or being blocked on allocation of locks. Check sysprocesses and syslocks for the locks and blocking issues. Check NT Performance Monitor disk statistics for disk contention.

- Another non-SQL process could be running—such as NT backup, virus check or disk compression.

- If the process is an update one, it could be that this particular run of the process needs more page and extent splits than normal. Extent splits especially can take some time.

- Does the process do any SELECT INTOs? If so, you may be falling foul of system table locking in SQL 6.5. Set traceflag 5302 if this is the case (you need at least SP1 on 6.5 to apply this).

- Unless you are sending raw/pass-through SQL via DB-Library or ODBC direct, monitor the process to see what SQL is actually being passed. ODBC and all higher level access methods all make use of stored procedures and cursors, even for the simplest SQL query. It may be a side-effect of some system-generated SQL that is causing you the problems.

Reference

v1.02 2000.04.22

Applies to SQL Server versions:	All
FAQ category:	Troubleshooting
Related FAQ article:	"Why is my application locking up in SQL Server? If I check the locks, I am seeing syscolumns being blocked." (5302, see page 472)
Related Microsoft Knowledge Base articles:	n/a
Other related information:	n/a
Author:	Neil Pike

spid-1blocking

Q: Why am I being blocked by spid -1? I am not able to kill it and have to restart SQL Server to get around it.

A: This is a bug found on stressed SQL 6.5 systems with SP4 or 5a installed. Contact Microsoft PSS for hotfix build 466 or above to resolve this problem. The fix will also be in SP6 (when released).

Reference

v1.03 2000.04.22	
Applies to SQL Server version:	6.5
FAQ category:	Troubleshooting
Related FAQ article:	"What are SQL Server hot fixes and where can I get them?" (hotfixes, see page 252)
Related Microsoft Knowledge Base article:	n/a
Other related information:	n/a
Author:	Neil Pike

spinloop

Q: I have a SQL Server process that shows as being in SPINLOOP. What does this mean?

A: The process concerned is accessing an area of memory that SQL Server needs to protect against multiple access — typically on SMP servers. To this end it locks that area of memory (via a spin lock) so that any other access to it gets paused. In concept it is very similar to row/page locking in a database, but is used for internal memory areas within a program. There is plenty of documentation in the Win32 SDK/MSDN about spin locks and their usage.

If the SPINLOOP process does not give up control, it is very likely that SQL Server will become unresponsive. It is unlikely that you will be able to KILL a process in this state and you will probably have to kill SQL Server itself (use the KILL command from the NT Resource Kit).

If you are suffering a lot of degradation due to spinloops, you will need to raise a paid fault call with Microsoft PSS to resolve it.

Reference

v1.00 1999.02.16	
Applies to SQL Server versions:	All
FAQ category:	Troubleshooting
Related FAQ article:	"What is Microsoft Product Support Services and how do I contact them?" (MSPSS, see page 517)
Related Microsoft Knowledge Base articles:	n/a
Other related information:	n/a
Author:	Neil Pike

sql7databasesappearinlist

Q: Under SQL 6.5 a user of ISQL/W or other tools could only see the databases they had permissions for in the dropdown boxes. Under 7.0 and 2000 they can see all the databases even if they don't have permission to go into them. Why?

A: This is because when developing SQL 7.0, the code necessary to evaluate the user's permissions was deemed too expensive. However, this is a legitimate security concern and Microsoft is thinking about changing this back to the old behavior.

Reference

v1.01 2000.04.28	
Applies to SQL Server versions:	7.0, 2000
FAQ category:	Troubleshooting
Related FAQ articles:	n/a
Related Microsoft Knowledge Base article:	n/a
Other related information:	n/a
Author:	Neil Pike

sql7odbc2vbdb300

Q: Why does my ODBC v2 application not work with SQL 7.0? Why do I get a GPF in VBDB300.DLL?

A: This is probably because the data types returned by sp_datatype_info to the application are not understood. Microsoft has not yet provided an official fix because of concerns for compatibility with other applications (I've not seen any, but they are cautious). In lieu of an official fix, I have supplied below the necessary modification to the stored procedure concerned.

Note that changing Microsoft-supplied stored procedures is not recommended or supported and if something goes wrong with the new stored procedure you are completely on your own. It is supplied as is, with no warranty!

It is based on the SQL 7.0 SP1 version, so apply SP1 before making this change. It has not been fixed in SP2, so you will need to retrofit these changes into the SP2 version as well.

Look for ** to see where the changes are:

```
--
-- Script to update Microsoft supplied version of sp_datatype_info to work prop-
erly with
-- ODBC v2 applications and to fix a GPF it causes in vbdb300.dll
--
-- Note the SP modified here is the one from SP1 for SQL 7.
-- Changes made are :-
--
-- 1.  Do not return any types below -7.  These are nchar, ntext etc. that are
--     SQL 7 only and not understood by ODBC2 applications
--
-- 2.  For varchar/char do not return 8000 as the length, return 255
--
--

USE master
go

DROP PROC sp_datatype_info
go
```

```
SET QUOTED_IDENTIFIER ON
go

--
-- Object will be created with MSShipped flag
--
EXEC sp_MS_upd_sysobj_category 1
go

/*  Procedure for 7.0 server */
CREATE PROC sp_datatype_info
    (@data_type int = 0, @ODBCVer tinyint = 2)
AS
    DECLARE @mintype int
    DECLARE @maxtype int

    IF @ODBCVer <> 3
        select @ODBCVer = 2
    IF @data_type = 0
    BEGIN
        SELECT @mintype = -32768
        SELECT @maxtype = 32767
        -- ** Change started **
        -- For ODBC version 2 apps don't let them see new types
        IF @ODBCVer = 2
        BEGIN
            SELECT @mintype = -7
        END
        -- ** Change ended **
    END
    ELSE
    BEGIN
        SELECT @mintype = @data_type
        SELECT @maxtype = @data_type
    END

    SELECT
        CONVERT(sysname,CASE
            WHEN t.xusertype > 255 THEN t.name
            ELSE d.TYPE_NAME
        END) TYPE_NAME,
        d.DATA_TYPE,
        CONVERT(int,case
           WHEN d.DATA_TYPE in (6,7) THEN d.data_precision          /* FLOAT/REAL
```

```
*/
            WHEN type_name(d.ss_dtype) IN ('numeric','decimal') and
                t.xusertype <= 255 THEN @@max_precision /* DECIMAL/NUMERIC */
            -- ** Change Started **
            -- Reduce max length returned for char/varchar for ODBC 2 apps
            WHEN @ODBCVer = 2 AND OdbcPrec(t.xtype, t.length, t.xprec) = 8000
THEN 255
            -- ** Change ended **
            ELSE OdbcPrec(t.xtype, t.length, t.xprec)
        END) "PRECISION",
        d.LITERAL_PREFIX,
        d.LITERAL_SUFFIX,
        e.CREATE_PARAMS,
        CONVERT(smallint,case
            WHEN d.AUTO_INCREMENT = 1 THEN 0 /* IDENTITY*/
            ELSE TypeProperty (t.name, 'AllowsNull')
        END) NULLABLE,
        d.CASE_SENSITIVE,
        d.SEARCHABLE,
        d.UNSIGNED_ATTRIBUTE,
        d.MONEY,
        d.AUTO_INCREMENT,
        CONVERT(sysname,case
            WHEN t.xusertype > 255 THEN t.name
            ELSE d.LOCAL_TYPE_NAME
        end) LOCAL_TYPE_NAME,
        CONVERT(smallint,case
            WHEN type_name(d.ss_dtype) IN ('numeric','decimal') AND t.xusertype
> 255 THEN TypeProperty (t.name, 'Scale')
            ELSE d.numeric_scale
        END) MINIMUM_SCALE,
        CONVERT(smallint,case
            WHEN type_name(d.ss_dtype) IN ('numeric','decimal') AND
d.AUTO_INCREMENT = 0 AND t.xusertype <= 255 THEN @@max_precision /* DECIMAL/
NUMERIC */
            WHEN type_name(d.ss_dtype) IN ('numeric','decimal') AND
d.AUTO_INCREMENT = 1 then 0 /* DECIMAL/NUMERIC IDENTITY*/
            ELSE TypeProperty (t.name, 'Scale')
        END) MAXIMUM_SCALE,
        d.SQL_DATA_TYPE,
        d.SQL_DATETIME_SUB,
        NUM_PREC_RADIX = convert(int,d.RADIX),
        INTERVAL_PRECISION = convert(smallint,NULL),
        USERTYPE = t.usertype
```

Troubleshooting

```
    FROM master.dbo.spt_datatype_info d
        INNER JOIN systypes t on d.ss_dtype = t.xtype
        LEFT OUTER JOIN master.dbo.spt_datatype_info_ext e on
            t.xusertype = e.user_type
            and isnull(d.AUTO_INCREMENT,0) = e.AUTO_INCREMENT
    WHERE
        d.DATA_TYPE between @mintype and @maxtype
        AND (d.ODBCVer is null or d.ODBCVer = @ODBCVer)
        AND (t.xusertype <= 255 or
            isnull(d.AUTO_INCREMENT,0) = 0)
    ORDER BY 2, 12, 11,
    CASE
        WHEN t.usertype=18 then 255
        ELSE t.usertype
    END
GO

GRANT EXEC ON sp_datatype_info TO public
GO


--
-- Turn off MSShipped flag for any other SP's (not that we're creating any)
--
EXEC sp_MS_upd_sysobj_category 2
GO


--
-- Allow updates and hack sysobjects directly.  Make sure sp is marked as with
-- quoted identifiers and MSShipped
--
EXEC sp_configure 'allow updates', 1
RECONFIGURE WITH OVERRIDE
GO

UPDATE sysobjects SET status = 0x80000009 WHERE name = 'sp_datatype_info'
GO

EXEC sp_configure 'allow updates', 0
RECONFIGURE WITH OVERRIDE
go
```

Reference

v1.01 1999.06.12

Applies to SQL Server version:	7.0
FAQ category:	Troubleshooting
Related FAQ articles:	n/a
Related Microsoft Knowledge Base articles:	n/a
Other related information:	n/a
Author:	Neil Pike, Alasdair Cunningham-Smith

sql7runoutoflocks

Q: Why do I get a "SQL Server has run out of locks" error message with SQL 7.0? I thought it dynamically allocated them.

A: First check that you haven't given locks a fixed number rather than letting it automatically expand (the default)—check sp_configure.

If dynamic allocation is set, then this works—it allocates them as long as there is *enough memory* to allocate them from. The error should really say that SQL has no more memory to allocate the locks from.

If you have artificially limited the amount of memory SQL Server has allocated, then consider resetting it the default (unlimited maximum) and let it handle it itself. If it is already automatic, you will need to reduce the memory requirements of the queries or workload concerned or add more memory to the server.

Reference

v1.03 2000.09.12

Applies to SQL Server version:	7.0
FAQ category:	Troubleshooting
Related FAQ articles:	n/a
Related Microsoft Knowledge Base articles:	n/a
Other related information:	"Locks Option" in Books Online 7
Author:	Neil Pike

sql7win2krc1mmc

Q: Why do I get weird messages using SQL 7.0's MMC on Windows 2000 RC1?

A: This is caused by bugs in the version of IE5 shipped with RC1. They are fixed in the RC2 and above builds, so as long as you're running the RTM version of Windows 2000, you should be fine.

Reference

v1.02 2000.02.28

Applies to SQL Server version:	All
FAQ category:	Troubleshooting
Related FAQ articles:	n/a
Related Microsoft Knowledge Base articles:	n/a
Other related information:	n/a
Author:	Neil Pike

sqlexecutiveversion

Q: When SQL Executive starts, I get an event id 109 in the event log with the error message "This version of SQLExecutive requires SQL Server version 6.5 or later." Why does this happen?

A: Usually this is because the NT account that the SQL Executive service is running under does not have permissions to read the HKEY_LOCAL_MACHINE\SOFTWARE\MICROSOFT\MSSQLSERVER registry key.

Reference

v1.02 2000.05.15

Applies to SQL Server version:	6.5
FAQ category:	Troubleshooting
Related FAQ articles:	n/a
Related Microsoft Knowledge Base article:	Q158585 "PRB: SQL Executive Service Fails to Start"
Other related information:	n/a
Author:	Neil Pike

sqlimage

Q: What is sqlimage.dll?

A: It is the DLL used by SQL 7.0 to write away memory areas to a dump file during a handled exception violation (GPF). See the FAQ article "accessviolation" for more information.

Reference

v1.01 2000.04.30

Applies to SQL Server version:	7.0
FAQ category:	Troubleshooting
Related FAQ article:	"I am getting a message "dbprocess dead" or "language exec" from SQL Server. I am seeing an "Exception Access Violation" message in the SQL errorlog. I am getting an error " SqlDumpExceptionHandler: Process <x> generated fatal exception." I am getting *.DMP files in the <sql>\log directory. I am getting "symptom dump" messages. What is going on?" (accessviolation, see page 481)
Related Microsoft Knowledge Base articles:	n/a
Other related information:	n/a
Author:	Neil Pike

sqlolereg

Q: I can't run SQL Server Enterprise Manager. I'm getting this error: "SQLOLE OLE object could not be registered. Class not registered (80040154)." What's wrong?

A: This is a problem with the class not being registered in the registry properly. Use the regsvr32 utility to re-register it:

```
regsvr32 <sql>\binn\sqlole65.dll
```

Replace <sql> with the full drive and directory that SQL is installed into.

Reference

v1.01 1998.11.02	
Applies to SQL Server version:	6.5
FAQ categories:	Troubleshooting, Server Administration and Tools
Related FAQ articles:	n/a
Related Microsoft Knowledge Base articles:	n/a
Other related information:	n/a
Author:	Neil Pike

sqlserverhang

Q: SQL Server hangs and becomes unresponsive. What can I do?

A: This is not an easy question, but here's a checklist that you can run through. It assumes that NT itself responds—if it doesn't, SQL Server isn't the problem, and you should see the FAQ entry "bluescreen" for more information on this condition.

- When it locks up, can you connect at all to SQL Server? Try connecting locally on the server using `ISQL.EXE - ISQL -Usa -P<pwd>` and see if it connects. This doesn't run any stored procedures when it connects, so any blocking going on (say, in tempdb) won't affect it.

- If you can connect, what does a SELECT * FROM sysprocesses or sp_lock show? Look for blocked spids or unusual wait types.

- If you can't connect to SQL Server, are you able to make a network drive connection to the NT server itself? Are you able to PING its IP address?

- Are there any errors in the SQL errorlog?

- Are there any errors in the NT system or application event logs?

- Do you have `SMP=-1` and/or `priority boost=1` set in sp_configure? If you do, then SQL queries can monopolize your system at the expense of NT or network drivers. This can cause spasmodic lock-ups. Set SMP and Priority Boost to 0 (the default).

- What do Task Manager and Performance Monitor show SQL Server doing? Is it using 100 percent CPU?

If you can't get to the bottom of the problem, you need to call Microsoft PSS (see the FAQ entry "MSPSS" for more information) and give them details of the problem and the results of the above tests.

In the meantime, if you need to stop and start SQL Server quickly, use the following (because normal service shutdown commands probably won't work, but try them first anyway).

You can kill SQL Server with KILL sqlservr.exe. The KILL command is in the NT Resource Kit. It can then be started with NET START MSSQLSERVER. *Only* do this if SQL Server does not respond to a normal shutdown or NET STOP MSSQLSERVER command. This will at least stop you from having to reboot NT.

Reference

v1.04 2000.05.09	
Applies to SQL Server versions:	All
FAQ category:	Troubleshooting
Related FAQ articles:	"I am getting a blue screen, completely hung machine, or server restart on my SQL Server or client. What might be the cause?" (bluescreen, see page 491), "What is Microsoft Product Support Services and how do I contact them?" (MSPSS, see page 517)
Related Microsoft Knowledge Base articles:	n/a
Other related information:	n/a
Author:	Neil Pike

storedproceduresloweundersql7

Q: Why is SQL Server 7.0 slower than 6.5 at running some of my stored procedures?

A: Chances are this is due to the use of temporary tables in the stored procedure.

In SQL 7.0, a stored procedure will be recompiled whenever a table is encountered that did not exist at the time the stored procedure was created. So, if you scatter the creation and use of temp tables throughout a stored procedure, the stored procedure will undergo multiple recompilations. However, if you place all your temporary table creates at the beginning before any other T-SQL, there will only need to be one recompilation when the first temp table is referenced. Make sure you create the relevant indices on the temp tables at the start as well. The reason for this is to get better optimization for the later queries in the SP.

With 6.5 and below, the optimizer didn't know what indices were available on the temp tables and so had to guess at the start of the stored procedure. These guesses would often lead to inappropriate access plans.

You can also try putting the "OPTION KEEP PLAN" hint on selects to reduce the recompilations.

For more info on the above see `http://msdn.microsoft.com/library/techart/sqlqa.htm`.

There is also a bug you may be running into (fixed in SP1). If the following conditions are true you may be getting excessive recompilations:

- Stored procedure is in master.
- Database being referenced is in 65 compatibility mode.
- CONCAT_NULL_YIELD_NULL is being set (usually because you are using ODBC).

Reference

v1.03 2000.05.14	
Applies to SQL Server version:	7.0
FAQ category:	Troubleshooting
Related FAQ article:	"Should I upgrade to SQL 7.0? Why or why not? What are the known bugs? What other differences are there between 6.5 and 7.0?" (sql7differences, see page 304)
Related Microsoft Knowledge Base article:	n/a
Other related information:	n/a
Author:	Neil Pike

suspect

Q: My SQL Server database has been marked "suspect." What can I do?

A: First, look in <sql>\LOG and look at all recent error logs. There will be an indication here as to why the database has been marked suspect. You need to fix whatever the problem is first (for example, a missing file, permissions problem or hardware error).

Then, when the problem has been fixed and you're either sure that the data is going to be OK, or you have no backup anyway, so you've nothing to lose, change the database status to normal and restart SQL Server. To change the database status, and to get more information on recovery, look up the sp_resetstatus stored procedure in the Books Online.

If you don't have access to sp_resetstatus information, the short version of this is:

```
UPDATE master..sysdatabases SET status = status^256 WHERE name = <dbname>
```

If the database still goes back into suspect mode, and you can't fix the original problem, and you have no recent backup, you can get information out of the database by putting it into emergency mode. If you do this, extract the data and objects out with BCP or Transfer Manager and then rebuild the database. Note that the data may be corrupt or transactionally inconsistent.

Issue the following command to put the database into emergency mode (you'll need to allow updates first):

```
UPDATE master..sysdatabases SET status=-32768 WHERE name='<dbname>'
```

In addition to these ideas, check out `http://support.microsoft.com/` for the Microsoft Knowledge Base, specifically Q165918 "INF: Bypass (Emergency) Mode and DUMP TRANSACTION WITH NO_LOG."

Reference

v1.06 2000.05.14

Applies to SQL Server versions:	All
FAQ category:	Troubleshooting
Related FAQ articles:	n/a
Related Microsoft Knowledge Base article:	Q165918 "INF: Bypass (Emergency) Mode and DUMP TRANSACTION WITH NO_LOG"
Other related information:	n/a
Author:	Neil Pike

tablecorrupt

Q: I have a corrupt SQL Server table that I can't drop. What can I do?

A: Run DBCC CHECKDB and DBCC NEWALLOC on the database in question and look up any other error messages that occur—then you can see the extent of the problem.

The reason SQL won't let you drop a table in this situation is because the allocation pages or extent chain appear to be damaged or cross-linked in some way. So SQL Server thinks that there is actually data from other tables in pages or extents belonging to the problem object. If it let you drop the table, it might remove data from another table by mistake.

Your choices are:

- Restore from a backup known to be good.
- Create a new database and copy all the data and objects out. You can use Transfer Manager, BCP or DTS for this. Then rename the databases round (or dump and re-load if you had to do this across a network connection).
- With a *very* large database with consequent loss of data, if you don't want to do the first two options, you can rename the table by directly updating sysobjects. Then create a new table and just leave the old one there. Note that this is dangerous as there may be more severe corruption problems that will still be there.
- Call Microsoft PSS and pay for a support call. They have utilities that allow page and link editing and they may try to "fix" the problem for you. However this is not 100 percent successful, they may cause more damage, and you have to sign a form accepting all responsibility (and absolving them of any) for any problems that occur.

Reference

v1.01 2000.05.14

Applies to SQL Server versions:	All
FAQ category:	Troubleshooting
Related FAQ articles:	n/a
Related Microsoft Knowledge Base articles:	n/a
Other related information:	n/a
Author:	Neil Pike

tdsprotocolerror

Q: I am getting a message "Protocol error in TDS Datastream" from a SQL Server query. What is going on?

A: Three things may be happening:

- SQL Server is internally GPFing or AVing (they are the same thing)—you should see messages to this effect in the SQL errorlog.
- You have a Net-Library bug with overlapped or fragmented packets.
- A complex query is generating incorrect TDS syntax in the packets

For all problems you can try applying the latest service pack to the server. You should also search the knowledgebase at `http://support.microsoft.com`.

For Net-Library bugs you will need to apply any service packs to the client as well. Also the version of ADO or ODBC can help cause the problem as well, so try upgrading your data access components. The latest versions of these drivers can be downloaded from `http://www.microsoft.com/data/` and are normally included with service packs.

If you're getting access violation messages, see the FAQ article "accessviolation."

If the problem is being caused by a complex query, try rewriting the query and break it up into smaller chunks. If this is not possible, see if the problem occurs when you run the query via ISQL/W instead of via the application.

If you are getting a problem with TDS packet fragmentation (TDS is SQL's application-level protocol), try a different Net-Library such as TCP/IP instead of Named Pipes or vice-versa. If you still experience problems, you'll need to call Microsoft PSS.

Even if a different Net-Library fixes the problem, please still report the problem to Microsoft PSS. Unless Microsoft gets these bug reports then they can't fix the problems. See the FAQ entry "MSPSS."

Reference

v1.01 2000.05.14

Applies to SQL Server versions:	All
FAQ categories:	Troubleshooting, Connectivity
Related FAQ articles:	"I am getting a message "dbprocess dead" or "language exec" from SQL Server. I am seeing an "Exception Access Violation" message in the SQL errorlog. I am getting an error "SqlDumpExceptionHandler: Process <x> generated fatal exception." I am getting *.DMP files in the <sql>\log directory. I am getting "symptom dump" messages. What is going on?" (accessviolation, see page 481), "What is Microsoft Product Support Services and how do I contact them?" (MSPSS, see page 517), "I am getting a message "GetOver-LappedResult()" from a SQL Server query. What is going on?" (getoverlappedresult, see page 505)
Related Microsoft Knowledge Base articles:	n/a
Other related information:	n/a
Author:	Neil Pike

tempdbfull

Q: Why has my tempdb in SQL Server filled up?

A: For SQL 7.0 and above, tempdb is created as an individual data file, with the Automatically Grow File option set on, and unrestricted file growth so this will not occur. If you have changed the default settings, you can manually expand the size or un-restrict file growth.

For SQL 6.5 and below, first make sure that you have actually expanded tempdb, as it defaults to 2MB on the master device only. Create one or more new devices for it and expand it onto these devices. Do *not* expand it on master.

How big is tempdb? Remember that for joins and sorts, SQL Server may need a significant amount of space depending on the size of the input tables. If you're doing an order by or a group by, SQL is probably using a temp table as an intermediate step. If you're doing a cartesian join, you're going to need a *lot* of space.

You can execute the query `SELECT type, name FROM tempdb..sysobjects` to see what is in tempdb. This should give you clues as to what is generating the objects in question and why they are not being deleted.

A prime cause of this is ODBC, which has the option per DSN of generating temporary stored procedures for all the queries per user connection. Most of the time you are better off disabling this option, which you can do via the ODBC applet in the Control Panel.

Reference

v1.03 2000.05.14

Applies to SQL Server versions:	All
FAQ category:	Troubleshooting
Related FAQ articles:	n/a
Related Microsoft Knowledge Base article:	Q187824 "INF: How to Move Tempdb to a Different Device"
Other related information:	n/a
Author:	Neil Pike

tempdbinramnostart

Q: I've put tempdb in RAM and now I can't restart my SQL Server.

A: This is because the memory allocated by SQL Server does *not* include tempdb in RAM. There must be enough memory for SQL, tempdb *and* NT, otherwise SQL will fail to start. To recover from this:

1. Stop SQL Server and SQL Executive. Also make sure SQL Enterprise Manager isn't running.
2. Go to the <sql>\binn directory and type **sqlservr -c -f**—this will start SQL in single-user mode with a minimum configuration.
3. Ignore the text messages in this window—but wait for them to finish appearing (this shouldn't take more than 10-20 seconds).
4. SQL Server is now started.
5. Go to another window and start ISQL/W and connect locally with the sa userid.

6. In ISQL/W issue the following commands:

```
sp_configure tempdb, 0
go
reconfigure
go
```

7. Now go back to the window SQL is running in and type **shutdown** and enter.

8. SQL Server should shut down. If it doesn't, press <Ctrl-C> to shut it down.

9. Now you should be able to start SQL normally and connect. You will need to resize tempdb as it will have gone back to the original 2MB in master.

If you get an error 615 running the sp_configure command, drop the tempdb device first (`sp_dropdevice tempdb`) and start again.

Reference

v1.02 2000.05.14

Applies to SQL Server versions:	4.x, 6.x
FAQ category:	Troubleshooting
Related FAQ articles:	n/a
Related Microsoft Knowledge Base articles:	n/a
Other related information:	n/a
Author:	Neil Pike

tempdbsingleuser

Q: I've accidentally set my SQL Server tempdb to single-user mode. I can't connect to put it back in multi-user mode. What can I do?

A: Don't connect using SQL Enterprise Manager, because it requires tempdb and makes multiple connections to SQL Server. Make sure that SQL Executive isn't running. Connect with ISQL/W and make the change to tempdb with sp_dboption.

Reference

v1.00 1999.02.01	
Applies to SQL Server versions:	All
FAQ category:	Troubleshooting
Related FAQ articles:	n/a
Related Microsoft Knowledge Base articles:	n/a
Other related information:	n/a
Author:	Neil Pike

topsql7notwork

Q: Why does the new TOP command in SQL 7.0 not work? I get a syntax error. The same thing happens with ALTER TABLE and other SQL 7.0-only commands.

A: The usual reason for this is that the command only works on SQL 7.0-mode databases. If you have migrated an existing 6.5 database, it is probably still set to 6.5 compatibility mode. Use sp_dbcmptlevel to check and set it to SQL 7.0 mode.

SQL Server 2000 retains these behavioral differences, although it introduces a new compatibility level of 80. The difference between 70 and 80 is minor compared to versions prior to SQL 7.0.

Reference

v1.02 2000.05.27	
Applies to SQL Server versions:	7.0, 2000
FAQ category:	Troubleshooting
Related FAQ articles:	n/a
Related Microsoft Knowledge Base articles:	n/a
Other related information:	See "sp_dbcmptlevel" in Books Online
Author:	Neil Pike

transfermanagerdeletesource

Q: I'm doing a transfer using the SQL Enterprise Manager transfer tool, and not only is it not transferring the objects, it is dropping them from the source. What is going on?

A: This is a known bug with SQL 6.x (fixed in 7.0) that is caused when the server you are connecting to has a period in the name. Typically this is because you are referring to it by TCP/IP address.

SQL sees the period and does a local named-pipe connect—which it should do if the name consists of just a period, but not when it *contains* a period—this means that SQL connects to the local machine as the target. Because most people have checked the "drop objects first"" box, it proceeds to drop all the objects concerned from what it thinks is the target machine—which is unfortunately the local (source) machine.

To prevent this problem, do not refer to your SQL servers by IP address. Do either of the following:

- Put an entry for the name/address in your NT HOSTS file: `<NT>\SYSTEM32\DRIVERS\ETC\HOSTS.`
- Use SQL Client Configuration Utility to define a named connection for the Server in question. In the Advanced Properties put the server's IP address as well as the Net-Library DLL needed to connect.

Then just use the server "name"' instead of the IP address in the Transfer To and From fields.

Reference

v1.01 2000.05.27

Applies to SQL Server version:	6.x
FAQ categories:	Troubleshooting, Server Administration and Tools
Related FAQ articles:	n/a
Related Microsoft Knowledge Base articles:	n/a
Other related information:	n/a
Author:	Neil Pike

versionswitchnotworking

Q: Why could the SQL version switch utility not work?

A: Normally this is a problem with registry permissions. Check that you have full permission on the following registry keys:

```
HKLM\Software\Microsoft\MSSQLServ65
HKLM\Software\Microsoft\MSSQLServ70
HKLM\Software\Microsoft\MSSQLServer
```

Take control of the keys with regedt32.exe if necessary. Make sure the account you are logged on as (presumably an admin account) has full permissions.

Reference

v1.00 1999.12.08	
Applies to SQL Server version:	7.0
FAQ category:	Troubleshooting
Related FAQ articles:	n/a
Related Microsoft Knowledge Base articles:	n/a
Other related information:	n/a
Author:	Neil Pike

win9xsqltoolsunstable

Q: Why am I getting GPFs and hangs running SQL tools under Windows 9x? I don't get the same problems with Windows NT clients.

A: This has always been a problem with the SQL tools—it may be bugs in the SQL tools code, but then the same EXEs and DLLs work fine on NT. The most likely reason is the sheer amount of gdi, icon and graphics-type resources that they use is exposing some sort of Win9x limitation or bug.

You should try resetting mouse settings and pointers back to defaults, and also, if you're using an Intellimouse, loading the very latest drivers.

You could also try applying the latest service pack or edition to Win9x, but the best bet is to develop with NT clients.

Reference

v1.02 1999.12.13	
Applies to SQL Server versions:	All
FAQ category:	Troubleshooting
Related FAQ articles:	n/a
Related Microsoft Knowledge Base articles:	n/a
Other related information:	n/a
Author:	Neil Pike

xpcmdshellnetwork

Q: Why can't I get at a network file when I run a program with xp_cmdshell from SQL Server?

A: The reason is that the MSSQLServer service is running under a separate set of NT credentials. It doesn't matter who *you* are logged on as (after all SQL runs quite happily when no one is logged on to the console). Therefore your logon account and any mapped drives are irrelevant. It is SQL Server running the program (e.g., BCP), not you.

If you're logged on as "sa" or are still running SQL 4.x, xp_cmdshell runs with the NT account that the MSSQLServer service is configured to run under. The default set of NT credentials used by MSSQLServer is the LocalSystem (SYSTEM) account. You can check what NT account MSSQLServer is running under by looking at Control Panel/Services, highlighting MSSQLServer and choosing the Start-up option. If no username is present, you are using the LocalSystem account—this account has no access to shares on the network because it isn't an authenticated network account.

If you are not logged on as "sa" then another account may be used:

- With 6.5 and below it is used if the option (in SQL setup) "xp_cmdshell—simulates Client" is checked.
- With SQL 7.0 and above the other account is always used for non-sa users (if you are a member of the sysadmin role then you are effectively sa).

The NT account used or created is SQLExecutiveCmdExec for SQL 6.x and SQLAgentCmdExec for SQL 7.0. These accounts are only in the local user group by default.

So, if you want a program running under xp_cmdshell to access a network resource, your choices are:

- Change the account the MSSQLServer service runs under to a user account with the relevant network rights.
- For non-sa users give the "xxCmdExec" account the relevant permissions.
- To get LocalSystem to work — amend the following registry value on the *target* server and add the share name you want to access — the share does not then authenticate who is coming in and so a LocalSystem account will work. The server service on the target server must be re-started before the change takes effect. Note that this effectively removes security on that share, so you need to be careful about what is in the share.

```
HKEY_LOCAL_MACHINE\SYSTEM\CurrentControlSet\Services\LanmanServer\
Parameters\NullSessionShares
```

Whichever method you use, you *must* use a UNC name to reference the resources required and not a drive letter. For example:

```
xp_cmdshell 'dir \\server01\share'
```

Reference

v1.03 2000.06.01

Applies to SQL Server versions:	All
FAQ categories:	Troubleshooting, Connectivity
Related FAQ articles:	n/a
Related Microsoft Knowledge Base articles:	n/a
Other related information:	n/a
Author:	Neil Pike

Subject Index

C

E

F

G

H

I

J

K

L

M

N

O

S

T

U

V

W

Question Index

A

B

C

D

E

F

G

H

M

N

P

Q

R

S

U

V

W

X

Y

The Story Behind Apress

APRESS IS AN INNOVATIVE PUBLISHING COMPANY devoted to meeting the needs of existing and potential programming professionals. Simply put, the "A" in Apress stands for the "author's press™." Our unique author-centric approach to publishing grew from conversations between Dan Appleman and Gary Cornell, authors of best-selling, highly regarded computer books. They wanted to create a publishing company that emphasized quality above all—a company whose books would be considered the best in their market.

To accomplish this goal, they knew it was necessary to attract the very best authors—established authors whose work is already highly regarded, and new authors who have real-world practical experience that professional software developers want in the books they buy. Dan and Gary's vision of an author-centric press has already attracted many leading software professionals—just look at the list of Apress titles on the following pages.

Would You Like to Write for Apress?

APRESS IS RAPIDLY EXPANDING its publishing program. If you can write and refuse to compromise on the quality of your work, if you believe in doing more then rehashing existing documentation, and if you are looking for opportunities and rewards that go far beyond those offered by traditional publishing houses, we want to hear from you!

Consider these innovations that we offer every one of our authors:

- Top royalties with *no* hidden switch statements. For example, authors typically only receive half of their normal royalty rate on foreign sales. In contrast, Apress' royalty rate remains the same for both foreign and domestic sales.

- A mechanism for authors to obtain equity in Apress. Unlike the software industry, where stock options are essential to motivate and retain software professionals, the publishing industry has stuck to an outdated compensation model based on royalties alone. In the spirit of most software companies, Apress reserves a significant portion of its equity for authors.

- Serious treatment of the technical review process. Each Apress book has a technical reviewing team whose remuneration depends in part on the success of the book since they, too, receive a royalty.

Moreover, through a partnership with Springer-Verlag, one of the world's major publishing houses, Apress has significant venture capital behind it. Thus, Apress has the resources both to produce the highest quality books *and* to market them aggressively.

If you fit the model of the Apress author who can write a book that gives the "professional what he or she needs to know™," then please contact any one of our editorial directors, Gary Cornell (gary_cornell@apress.com), Dan Appleman (dan_appleman@apress.com), or Karen Watterson (karen_watterson@apress.com), for more information on how to become an Apress author.

Apress Titles

ISBN	LIST PRICE	AVAILABLE	AUTHOR	TITLE
1-893115-01-1	$39.95	Now	Appleman	Dan Appleman's Win32 API Puzzle Book and Tutorial for Visual Basic Programmers
1-893115-23-2	$29.95	Now	Appleman	How Computer Programming Works
1-893115-09-7	$24.95	Now	Baum	Dave Baum's Definitive Guide to LEGO MINDSTORMS
1-893115-84-4	$29.95	Now	Baum, Gasperi, Hempel, Villa	Extreme MINDSTORMS
1-893115-82-8	$59.95	Now	Ben-Gan/Moreau	Advanced Transact-SQL for SQL Server 2000
1-893115-14-3	$39.95	Winter 2000	Cornell/Jezak	Visual Basic Add-Ins and Wizards: Increasing Software Productivity
1-893115-85-2	$34.95	Winter 2000	Gilmore	A Programmer's Introduction to PHP 4.0
1-893115-17-8	$59.95	Now	Gross	A Programmer's Introduction to Windows DNA
1-893115-86-0	$34.95	Now	Gunnerson	A Programmer's Introduction to C#
1-893115-10-0	$34.95	Now	Holub	Taming Java Threads
1-893115-04-6	$34.95	Now	Hyman/Vaddadi	Mike and Phani's Essential C++ Techniques
1-893115-79-8	$49.95	Now	Kofler	Definitive Guide to Excel VBA
1-893115-75-5	$44.95	Now	Kurniawan	Internet Programming with VB
1-893115-19-4	$49.95	Now	Macdonald	Serious ADO: Universal Data Access with Visual Basic
1-893115-06-2	$39.95	Now	Marquis/Smith	A Visual Basic 6.0 Programmer's Toolkit
1-893115-22-4	$27.95	Now	McCarter	David McCarter's VB Tips and Techniques
1-893115-76-3	$49.95	Now	Morrison	C++ For VB Programmers
1-893115-80-1	$39.95	Now	Newmarch	A Programmer's Guide to Jini Technology
1-893115-81-X	$39.95	Now	Pike	SQL Server: Common Problems, Tested Solutions
1-893115-20-8	$34.95	Now	Rischpater	Wireless Web Development
1-893115-24-0	$49.95	Now	Sinclair	From Access to SQL Server
1-893115-16-X	$49.95	Now	Vaughn	ADO Examples and Best Practices

ISBN	LIST PRICE	AVAILABLE	AUTHOR	TITLE
1-893115-83-6	$44.95	Winter 2000	Wells	Code Centric: T-SQL Programming with Stored Procedures and Triggers
1-893115-05-4	$39.95	Winter 2000	Williamson	Writing Cross-Browser Dynamic HTML
1-893115-02-X	$49.95	Now	Zukowski	John Zukowski's Definitive Guide to Swing for Java 2
1-893115-78-X	$49.95	Now	Zukowski	Definitive Guide to Swing for Java 2, Second Edition